DEPTH ANALYSIS OF
THE NATAL CHART

*How the Birthchart Depicts Psychodynamics,
Psychopathology, and Integration of Parts Over Time*

Other books by Glenn Perry

An Introduction to AstroPsychology
A Synthesis of Modern Astrology & Depth Psychology

The Shadow in the Horoscope
Five Essays on Jung's Concept of the Shadow

Mapping the Landscape of the Soul
Inside Psychological Astrology

From Royalty to Revolution
The Sun Uranus Relationship

Stealing Fire from the Gods
New Directions in Astrological Research

Issues & Ethics
In the Profession of Astrology

From Ancient to Postmodern Astrology
An Evolution of Ideas, Techniques & Perspectives

Depth Analysis of
THE NATAL CHART

*How the Birthchart Depicts Psychodynamics,
Psychopathology, and Integration of Parts Over Time*

GLENN PERRY

Published by
The Academy of Astro △ Psychology
Melbourne-Viera, FL • www.aaperry.com

Copyright © 2021 by Glenn Perry

All rights reserved. No part of this book may be reproduced or transmitted in any form or by any electronic or mechanical means including information storage and retrieval systems without permission in writing from the publisher, except for the inclusion of brief quotations in review.

For permission requests, write to the publisher, addressed "Attention: Permissions," at the address below.
The Academy of Astro△Psychology
1421 Republic Pl., Melbourne, FL 32940
www.aaperry.com

Ordering Information: Quantity sales. Special discounts are available on quantity purchases by corporations, associations, and others. For details, contact the publisher at the address above.

ISBN 13: 978-1-7370966-2-7 (hardback)
ISBN 13: 978-1-7370966-0-3 (paperback)
ISBN 13: 978-1-7370966-1-0 (ebook)

*To my clients, who have always
been my best teachers.*

BRIEF CONTENTS

Preface	xvii
INTRODUCTION	1
PSYCHODYNAMICS OF ASTROLOGY	25
AN ASTROLOGICAL THEORY OF MOTIVATION	57
PLANETARY EMOTION & TARGET STATES	87
COGNITION IN ASTROLOGY	103
PSYCHOPATHOLOGY OF THE ZODIAC	153
ASTROLOGY AND THE ORIGINS OF SUFFERING	195
PLANETARY CONFLICT, DEFENSE AND INTEGRATION	237
COMPLEXES IN THE BIRTHCHART	289
PSYCHOPATHOLOGY AND CHARACTER	309
A ZODIACAL DEVELOPMENTAL MODEL	343
References	397

CONTENTS

Preface	xvii

Chapter One
INTRODUCTION — 1
- SOUL IS THE ESSENCE OF THE MATTER — 2
- THE ARCHETYPAL REALM IS PREPOTENT — 3
- ALL MEANING IS AN ANGLE — 5
- VALUE NEUTRAL AND EVIDENCE BASED — 8
- THE HOROSCOPE IS AN OPEN SYSTEM — 10
- CONTENT MIRRORS PROCESS — 13
- OUTER EXPERIENCES CONSTITUTE FEEDBACK — 14
- DEVELOPMENT TOWARD WHOLENESS — 18
- TELEOLOGY AND CONSCIOUS EVOLUTION — 22

Chapter Two
PSYCHODYNAMICS OF ASTROLOGY — 25
- CONVENTIONAL PSYCHODYNAMICS — 26
- ASTRO-PSYCHODYNAMICS — 26
- PSYCHIC ENERGY — 27
- UNIVERSAL CONSCIOUSNESS — 28
- HUMAN CONSCIOUSNESS — 31
- OPERATIONS OF CONSCIOUSNESS — 32
- CATHEXIS AND VALUE — 34
- DISPLACEMENT AND SUBLIMATION — 37
- DIFFERENTIATION AND COUNTERCATHEXIS — 41
- THE SUN AS CONSCIOUS WILL — 42
- DRIVING AND RESTRAINING FORCES IN ASTROLOGY — 45
- ENTROPY — 49
- NEGENTROPY — 51
- SUMMARY — 53

Chapter Three
AN ASTROLOGICAL THEORY OF MOTIVATION — 57
- A ZODIACAL SYSTEM OF MOTIVES — 57
- EXTRINSIC VS. INTRINSIC MOTIVATION — 58
- ARCHETYPAL IMAGES OF NEEDS — 59
- SIGNS AS ARCHETYPAL MOTIVES — 60
- ZODIAC AS STRUCTURE OF NEEDS — 62
- A DEVELOPMENTAL PERSPECTIVE — 65
- PRIORITIZING DEVELOPMENTAL TASKS — 67
- THE MASTER MOTIVE — 70
- THE PROCESS OF INDIVIDUATION — 70
- THE SELF — 71
- TELEOLOGICAL VERSUS EFFICIENT CAUSATION — 72
- SELF, MANDALA, AND ZODIAC — 76
- THE TRANSCENDENT FUNCTION — 79
- EMERGENT PROPERTIES — 80
- URANUS AS TRANSCENDENT FUNCTION — 82
- SUMMARY — 84

Chapter Four
PLANETARY EMOTION & TARGET STATES — 87
- CALIBRATION AND TARGET STATES — 91
- PLANETS AS PSYCHOLOGICAL STATES — 95
- PLANETARY BEHAVIORAL GOALS — 100
- SUMMARY — 102

Chapter Five
COGNITION IN ASTROLOGY — 103
- COGNITIVE ASTROLOGY — 103
- EARLY THEORIES OF COGNITION — 104
- CONSTRUCTIVISM — 105
- PERSONS AS EMBODIED THEORY — 107
- THE IMPORTANCE OF CHILDHOOD — 108
- EQUIFINALITY OR STRUCTURE DETERMINISM — 112
- CONTROL STRUCTURE OF THE PSYCHE — 115
- LEVEL I BASIC NEEDS — 116
- LEVEL II PROCESSES — 117

THE SELF IS HIERARCHICALLY ORGANIZED	118
LEVEL III – THE EXECUTIVE CONTROL CENTER	121
AN OVERVIEW OF THE SELF-SYSTEM	124
COALITIONAL, HETERARCHICAL CONTROL	126
ASPECTS AS COGNITIVE STRUCTURES	128
REPETITION COMPULSION	145
FILLING UP THE HOLLOW	148
SUMMARY & CONCLUSION	151

Chapter Six
PSYCHOPATHOLOGY OF THE ZODIAC — **153**

THE VALUE OF DIAGNOSIS	153
THE PURPOSE OF DIAGNOSIS	155
DEFINING PSYCHOPATHOLOGY	156
SYMPTOMS AND SIGNS	157
TWO DIAGNOSTIC APPROACHES	158
A MULTIAXIAL SYSTEM	160
MENTAL DISORDERS	161
PERSONALITY DISORDERS	162
ASTROLOGICAL CORRELATIONS	163
ADDITIONAL CONSIDERATIONS	166
STORY CONCEPT AS ALTERNATIVE METAPHOR	167
CENTRALITY OF BASIC NEEDS	171
PATHOLOGY OF DEVELOPMENTAL STAGES	171
ETIOLOGY OF DISORDERS: AN INTRODUCTION	172
ASTROLOGICAL CORRELATES	174
A PROVISIONAL MODEL	175
ARIES/MARS	176
TAURUS/VENUS	178
GEMINI/MERCURY	181
CANCER/MOON	182
LEO/SUN	183
VIRGO/MERCURY	184
LIBRA/VENUS	185
SCORPIO/PLUTO	186
SAGITTARIUS/JUPITER	187
CAPRICORN/SATURN	188

AQUARIUS/URANUS	189
PISCES/NEPTUNE	190
SUMMARY AND CONCLUSION	192

Chapter Seven
ASTROLOGY AND THE ORIGINS OF SUFFERING — 195

DIMENSIONS OF CAUSATION	196
TRANSPERSONAL ETIOLOGIES	197
THE PERENNIAL PHILOSOPHY	200
THE SIGNIFICANCE OF KARMA	202
INTEGRATING TRANSPERSONAL ETIOLOGIES	205
A HIERARCHY OF CAUSES	208
CONSCIOUSNESS AS CAUSAL REALITY	212
REINCARNATION AND GENETICS	215
PSYCHOSOCIAL THEORIES OF CAUSATION	218
SUMMARY & CONCLUSION	236

Chapter Eight
PLANETARY CONFLICT, DEFENSE AND INTEGRATION — 237

ETIOLOGY	238
INHERENT AND CONSEQUENTIAL FACTORS	240
NECESSARY AND SUFFICIENT CAUSES	244
INTRAPSYCHIC CONFLICT	245
SINS OF OMISSION & COMMISSION	248
CONFLICTING BELIEFS	250
INTRAPSYCHIC CONFLICT IN THE ZODIAC	251
DECONSTRUCTING THE CONFLICT	254
A BRIEF CASE HISTORY	255
DEFENSE MECHANISMS	258
ARCHETYPAL DEFENSE MECHANISMS	260
ASTROLOGICAL CORRELATES TO DEFENSES	262
A BLENDING OF ARCHETYPAL DEFENSES	273
INTEGRATING NEUROTIC CONFLICT	278
COMORBIDITY	280
STABILIZING SCHEMAS	283
DEVELOPMENTAL INTERFERENCES	284
SUMMARY AND CONCLUSION	287

Chapter Nine
COMPLEXES IN THE BIRTHCHART — 289
- LOCATING THE COMPLEX IN THE CHART — 291
- EVALUATING A COMPLEX — 295
- FRANK'S COMPLEX — 296
- COMPLEXES, KARMA, AND REINCARNATION — 301
- ATONEMENT AND FORGIVENESS — 303
- RECOVERY — 306
- SUMMARY AND CONCLUSION — 307

Chapter Ten
PSYCHOPATHOLOGY AND CHARACTER — 309
- LOSS OF AGENCY AND VOLITION — 311
- DISORDER AS CHARACTER BASED — 313
- THE TWIN TOWERS OF DETERMINISM — 317
- CHARACTER IS PRIMARY — 318
- UNDERLYING DYNAMICS & EXTERIOR STYLE — 321
- ASPECTS AND CHARACTER STYLES — 323
- A CONSTRUCTIVIST VIEW — 325
- RESTORING PERSONAL AGENCY — 325
- IS IT MEMORY OR IS IT CHARACTER? — 328
- SIGNIFICANCE OF ENVIRONMENT — 332
- JUNG'S RELIGIOUS WOUND — 333
- THE ACORN THEORY — 338
- SUMMARY — 340

Chapter Eleven
A ZODIACAL DEVELOPMENTAL MODEL — 343
- DEVELOPMENTAL STAGES & PSYCHOPATHOLOGY — 343
- ASTRO-PSYCHOLOGICAL EPIGENESIS — 345
- REVISITING ASTROLOGICAL STAGES — 347
- ZODIAC AS INTEGRATIVE MODEL — 350
- INTEGRATION AND DEVELOPMENT OF PLANETARY FUNCTIONS — 354
- HOLONOMIC DEVELOPMENT — 356
- PROPENSITIES & PATHOLOGIES OF CHILDHOOD — 358
- CHILDHOOD STYLES AND PSYCHOPATHOLOGY — 362
- THE INEVITABILITY OF DEVELOPMENTAL CONFLICT — 363

DEVELOPMENTAL FIXATION AT SIGN-STAGES	365
THE PSYCHOGENETIC FALLACY	368
THE FORCE OF CHARACTER	371
POST-CHILDHOOD EXPERIENCES	373
PATHOGENIC CHARACTER	374
TELEOLOGICAL CAUSATION	377
THE CASE OF MADONNA	381
THE SIGNIFICANCE OF TRANSITS & PROGRESSIONS	390
SUN LEO CONJUNCT PLUTO IN THE 12TH	391
SUMMARY	395

References   397

LIST OF FIGURES

Figure 1: Freud's T-Square — 36
Figure 2: Three Categories of Motivation — 61
Figure 3: Maslow's Hierarchy of Needs/Signs — 66
Figure 4: A Zodiacal Developmental Stage Model — 69
Figure 5: The Basic Mandala Image — 77
Figure 6: The Zodiac as a Mandala Image — 78
Figure 7: Planets as Emotions — 90
Figure 8: A Listing of Planetary States — 97
Figure 9: Top View of The Self-System — 116
Figure 10: The Capricorn-Saturn System — 119
Figure 11: The Saturn-Mercury System — 120
Figure 12: Side View of the Self-System — 125
Figure 13: Planetary Heterarchical Control — 127
Figure 14: Mental & Personality Disorders — 165
Figure 15: Signs, Stages, and Goals — 172
Figure 16: A Hierarchy of Causes — 209
Figure 17: Birthchart of Marilyn Monroe — 224
Figure 18: Hierarchical Structure of the Family System — 230
Figure 19: A Systemic Conflict — 231
Figure 20: Birthchart of Muhammed Ali — 234
Figure 21: Birthchart of Moon Pisces Woman — 256
Figure 22: A List of Archetypal Defenses — 262
Figure 23: Birthchart of Frank — 297
Figure 24: Birthchart of Carl Jung — 334
Figure 25: A Sign/House Developmental Stage Model — 348
Figure 26: Birthchart Madonna — 383

Preface

Over the centuries, a multitude of explanations have been proffered to account for the cause of human suffering—the wrath of the gods, possession by demonic entities, bad karma, attachment and aversion, a faulty environment, traumatic experiences, pathogenic beliefs, dysfunctional families, genetic abnormalities, faulty brain chemistry, the list goes on. In the field of psychology, the subject of psychopathology addresses the topic directly. Psychopathology literally means "study (logos) of the suffering (pathos) of soul (psyche)."

During graduate school and over the course of thirty years in private practice, my interest in the topic of psychopathology never waned. I am convinced, however, that psychopathology can only be understood in the context of a more encompassing view of the human psyche than currently prevails. A good argument can be made that conventional psychology has never adequately understood the root cause of human suffering, much less its purpose. Wedded to a medical model, psychology is forced to explain the pathos of the soul in terms that are consistent with scientific reductionism and materialism. This has led to endless, ad hoc theorizing and a stalemate between so-called nature and nurture explanations.

Nature theories purport that psyche can be reduced to the brain, which allegedly is "nothing but" a machine fueled by chemical interactions that derive from a pre-determined genetic template. Conversely, nurture theories argue that personality is a *tabula rasa*, a blank slate, waiting to be imprinted by the vicissitudes of random experience. While syntheses of nature/nurture theories are the current norm in contemporary psychology, these, too, have been unsatisfying. Both accounts help us to understand the human condition; yet, each is handcuffed by the mechanistic reasoning that lies at its heart. The upshot, as one expert describes it, is that "Psychiatry is the *only* medical specialty that, virtually by definition, treats disorders without clearly known causes or definitive cures."

A worldview operates like a filter that constrains the viewer from seeing anything that lies outside the parameters of that view. In the vernacular, if all you have is a hammer, everything looks like a nail. It follows that if all you have is a mechanistic worldview, everything looks like the effect of an externally originating, mechanistic cause. The presumption of linear causation in psychology is reflected in a variety of personality theories that attempt to explain the workings of the psyche in ways that, again, are consistent with an *a priori* determinism.

A major school of thought in this regard is psychodynamic theory. The very term *psychodynamics*—activity of soul—implies that psychic energy is marked by continuous motion and change. In graduate school, I was fascinated with accounts of how psychic energy was impacted by outer events, directed by autonomous internal processes, blocked, released, and redistributed throughout the psyche in myriad ways. However, psychodynamics became even more interesting in the context of astrology. For a horoscope could be regarded as the depiction of psychic energy in motion, a living, evolving process in continuous dynamic exchange with its environment—in short, an open system not determined solely by external, material causes.

There was nothing comparable to this in psychology. Lacking the benefit of a model with clear external referents (signs, planets, and aspects) for tracking the flow of psychic energy, psychodynamic theory had to invent hypothetical organs of the psyche that interacted in obscure, mechanistic ways. Conversely, the horoscope exposed the inner world of the soul, revealing its true complexity and the multifaceted workings of its various parts. As if seen through a powerful microscope that magnified what heretofore could only be imagined, the birthchart illumined the arcane world of psychodynamics.

Moreover, the horoscope disclosed how inner and outer worlds were connected in ways that went beyond the implicit determinism of conventional psychodynamic theory. Rather than being merely the effect of random, externally originating causes, the psyche manifests simultaneously in internal and external conditions. Environment mirrors the intrapsychic world from the first breath. This strongly suggests that psyche is reflected in, but not caused by, external events. Planetary processes also show up in physiology, physical appearance, and bodily health. This implies that a reductionistic, biochemical approach to the psyche is insufficient. For even biochemistry is in some mysterious way prefigured in the horoscope.

In my work with psychotherapy clients over the last three decades, I have continued to explore how standard psychiatric diagnoses and explanations could be enriched by a psychodynamic understanding of the birthchart. Although traditional astrology, too, has been mired in a deterministic outlook, the approach offered herein views psyche and matter as two faces of the same thing. I do not believe that consciousness is determined by planetary movements any more than it is caused by biochemistry or random events. To assume otherwise is to confuse correlations with causes. Accordingly, AstroPsychology tries to retain what is useful in psychology while situating its major ideas in a broader, more encompassing framework that regards the psyche as its own cause; that is, an eternal, self-producing, and self-transcending entity evolving through matter back to its own source.

Each chapter of the present work addresses a fundamental question that pertains to how astrology can clarify the structure, dynamics, and evolution of the psyche. Particular emphasis is placed on how to identify and address potential challenges in the birthchart. Proper use of the horoscope in diagnosis is explored, and colleagues are introduced to DSM diagnostic criteria. An explanation is offered for how astrological archetypes, when carried to dysfunctional, unbalanced extremes, can be correlated to various mental disorders.

A substantial portion of the text provides a model for understanding linkages between motivation, feeling, and behavior. Motivation is rooted in sign-drives that are experienced as distinct feeling states. Heightened activation of specific drives occurs during developmental stages that are implicit in the zodiac. Planetary placements by sign, house, and aspect provide information about how these stages will be experienced (events) and whether potential problems, or complexes, could result. Pathogenic beliefs resulting from developmental trauma are explained in terms of hard aspects, which symbolize both the origins of psychopathology and its possible consequences.

Special attention is given to hard aspects from outer planets and their relationship to intrapsychic conflict, defense, and symptom formation. Concepts of healing are also explored, especially as these relate to how suffering can be a catalyst to the actualization of inherent capacities. In examining the etiology of pathology, conventional theories of causation are compared with traditional ideas of fate, karma, and reincarnation. All of this is done from an astrological perspective.

Depth Analysis of the Natal Chart should appeal to anyone who aspires to utilize astrology as a counseling tool—a counseling tool that is intrinsically therapeutic. Its primary focus is on character and pathology as reflected in the birthchart, while also providing a theoretical model that challenges the underlying determinism that has plagued both astrology and psychology over the centuries. AstroPsychology refutes determinism in general by substantiating the primacy of consciousness as causal reality. And it repudiates astral determinism in particular by showing the centrality of free will in the unfoldment of consciousness. Numerous case histories illustrate the potential of astrology to facilitate the actualization of human potential.

Forty years of studying horoscopes has convinced me that the birthchart depicts psychic structure; yet the psyche is intrinsically dynamic and constantly evolving within the framework of that structure. Character is not fixed, but malleable, molded by choices freely made. Fate reflects the unfoldment of character while also acting as a spur to its further development.

In short, this book offers an astrological approach to psychopathology and healing. Borrowing from psychodynamic, Jungian, and general systems theories, the foundational ideas of AstroPsychology are thoroughly explained, including intrapsychic conflict, defense, psychopathology, cognitive structure, integration, indeterminism, synchronicity, evolutionary feedback, and a growth oriented, developmental perspective.

Glenn Perry
Haddam Neck, CT
March 4, 2021

Chapter One

INTRODUCTION

SOME FIRST PRINCIPLES OF ASTROPSYCHOLOGY

Not every concept in psychology has equal merit, but some are indispensable. This book incorporates ideas that are maximally relevant to an astrological understanding of psychodynamics, psychopathology, and psycho-spiritual development. Psychology is itself a combination of two words—psyche (soul) and logos (knowledge, or rational discourse). Psychology, therefore, means "knowledge of soul." The term AstroPsychology adds something extra: astro means star; thus, AstroPsychology can be taken to mean "knowledge of the soul via discourse with the stars". As psyche is inserted in the middle of astro-psych-ology, it suggests that soul is at the center of the study.

This is not a small matter, as not all of astrology is concerned with soul. Horary, electional, and mundane astrology have little if anything to do with the inner essence of the human being, which is what we generally mean by soul. Traditional astrology has something to say about temperament and behavior, but this is limited to the surface of the person. Very little was known about the complex, interior lives of human beings until the 20th century when it became the subject of intense study through depth psychology, courtesy of Freud, Jung, and a host of others who stood upon the shoulders of those two giants.

In the remainder of this chapter, I will outline what I regard as some first principles of AstroPsychology. This listing is by no means complete, but it does provide a general overview and gets us moving in the right direction. Each principle will be further elaborated and discussed in association with other concepts in the remaining chapters. So, let us begin.

SOUL IS THE ESSENCE OF THE MATTER

As stated, the main focus of AstroPsychology is psyche, which means *soul*. The psyche can be conceptualized as an open system—an assemblage of parts with relations between them. As an open system, soul is not limited to what occurs inside the person. Events are relevant, too, as anyone familiar with systems theory will attest. Before exploring this idea further, let us first turn our attention to what soul *is*.

Historically it has been notoriously difficult for philosophers to define the soul, for it is generally regarded as a nonphysical entity and thus cannot be seen, felt, or touched. Soul is the subjective dimension of being human, our interior realm, the within of a person. Its primary attribute is *awareness*. Extended further, soul is that complex of attributes experienced as thought, feeling, and will.

Precisely because soul is nonphysical, it is assumed to survive the death of the physical body and may reincarnate at some future time; thus, soul is thought to be immortal. In Hindu traditions, psyche evolves over the course of many lifetimes and is therefore the deepest and truest nature of a person—that which gives someone a distinctive character. Current research into reincarnation has provided impressive evidence in support of this assertion (Bache, 1994). Because the very nature of an open system is to evolve, soul has a dynamic quality. It is active and intentional; it learns, changes, and transforms into more complex states, and may even reincarnate into new bodies in order to do so. Just as a plant can only grow by sinking its roots deep into the loam, so the soul appears to grow and develop through its immersion in material reality.

The relationship between motivation, emotion, cognition, and behavior is the prime topic of psychodynamics ("movements of soul"). From an astrological perspective, this necessarily involves parts of psychic structure as symbolized by signs, planets, and their angular relations, all of which reflect how psychic energy is organized, distributed, and transformed over time.

Every individual soul is organized in accord with a specific structure of motives (zodiacal signs), psychological functions (planets), and angular relations between them (aspects). The flow of psychic energy within the chart depicts various transformations of consciousness as it shifts, settles, hides, reacts, and ricochets about the labyrinth of soul.

One might think that soul is synonymous with consciousness. However, consciousness is the more general term. Just as a Ford Thunderbird is a particular automobile, so one's soul is a particularization of consciousness. As the collective source out of which soul precipitates, consciousness can be defined as an evolutionary process of organized relations.

Consciousness is evolutionary because it has a tropism toward higher states of awareness, regardless of the vehicle through which it operates—matter, plant, animal, or human. It is a process because it constitutes a series of operations conducive toward an apparent end goal (wholeness/unity); and it entails organized relations because consciousness is constituted by the relations between its constituent parts.

If consciousness is an evolutionary process of organized relations, the concrete product of this process is different physical systems of lesser and greater complexity. By virtue of their complexity, living systems exhibit different forms and levels of awareness as evidenced, for example, in the consciousness of plants, animals, and humans. As the archetypal components of psyche-as-system become more intricately woven into a harmonious, collaborative, and complex tapestry of soul, there is a concomitant growth of awareness and freedom. This pattern of development, which evolves through matter by processing lived experience, is precisely what the horoscope symbolizes.

THE ARCHETYPAL REALM IS PREPOTENT

In virtually all metaphysical traditions, human consciousness derives from a Universal Consciousness that is the divine ground, source, and ultimate goal of all dynamic activity. Issuing forth from Universal Consciousness are certain formative principles that Plato called *Forms* or *Ideas*. Plato regarded Forms as the generative matrix for phenomena at lower levels of mind, body, and matter. In yet earlier traditions, these were the gods and goddesses of celestial pantheons. More recently, the Swiss psychoanalyst, C.G. Jung, simply called them *archetypes*.

Just as with soul, it is difficult to define an archetype, for archetypes are nonphysical, energetic patterns more like fields than concrete things. In developing his theory of archetypes, Jung noticed that certain motifs kept reoccurring in lives of his patients that matched up with myths, fairytales, and religious systems across cultures and centuries. He concluded that these repeating motifs were both psychological and cosmological. They seemed to be the basic organizing principles of reality itself while, at the same time, being structural elements of psyche that humans experience as motives, ideals, fantasies, affective states, and behavioral impulses.

AstroPsychology is rooted in an archetypal perspective. Everything is thought to derive from *archai*—living dynamisms akin to Ideas in the mind of a divine being. Like gods and goddesses of the heavenly realms, archetypes populate and structure the Universal Psyche in the pattern of which all lesser souls are made. In this view, the multiplicity of forms in the phenomenal world are merely combinations and precipitations of a more limited number of transcendent, abstract Forms that serve as their generative matrix on a higher plane—what perennial philosophers call "the subtle realm". As divine absolutes, archetypes order the natural world. Transcendent in that they constitute general types that supersede any particular concrete form, yet immanent within all concrete particulars, archetypes shape our bodies, instincts, feelings, thoughts, and behavior. If psyche is dynamic, it is archetypes that make it so, for they are the animating forces that dwell within.

Human beings are not, however, merely puppets at the end of archetypal chords to be manipulated by the will of a superordinate being. Rather, we embody the archetypes, giving them a particular inflection in accord with how they are uniquely combined and integrated at a psychological level. Just as our physical bodies are made up of combinations of atomic elements, so our souls are comprised of archetypal elements, all of which must be harnessed, actualized, and brought into proper balance for a person to be fully functional.

Because Jungians are generally not privy to the natural ordering framework of the zodiac, they tend to postulate a seemingly unlimited number of archetypes, as if there is an archetype for every type of human experience. Yet, astrology suggests there are twelve meta-types or primary categories. *Metatype* is a useful term for describing how astrological archetypes—signs of the zodiac—constitute groupings of Jungian archetypes. The archetype of Capricorn, for instance, can manifest as senex, father, control freak, scrooge, miser, authority, executive, or master, all of which are simply variations on a theme. In this context, the concept of metatype provides an organizing framework for classifying Jungian archetypes whose self-similarity might otherwise not be recognized. It could even be argued that many Jungian archetypes are not archetypes at all; rather, they are compounds or blends of certain core, primary archetypes symbolized by the twelve zodiacal signs—the metatypes.

Everything one experiences is a consequence of how these primary forms are combined, integrated, and expressed. Further, each of the twelve metatypes can be represented astrologically in four different ways: sign, planet, house, and aspect. The archetype of Scorpio, for instance, is linked to the planet Pluto, the 8th house, and the closing quincunx. Each of these factors expresses an archetypal kinship, a point we will return to shortly when discussing why all meaning in astrology derives from angles (numbers).

As Jung repeatedly stressed, a symbol of an archetype must be distinguished from the archetype as such. This distinction is critical to understanding how an astrological configuration—a planet in sign, house, and aspect—can manifest in a multiplicity of ways while still remaining consistent in meaning. Manifestations vary depending upon how the configuration is situated in the chart as a whole as well as its degree of integration. With regard to the latter—degree of integration—it cannot be overstated that expression of an archetypal configuration evolves in accord with the growth and development of the person.

ALL MEANING IS AN ANGLE

A little recognized and insufficiently understood truth is that astrology's most fundamental meanings derive from angles formed by planetary movements. As stated previously, there are four variations: planet, sign, house, and aspect. All but planets are angles, which are phase relationships of whole cycles. However, since cycles are formed by planetary movements, a planet is the primary variable that allows for all the others. Without planetary cycles there would be no phase relationships to measure.

Consider, for example, the meaning of the first 90 degrees of the 360-degree zodiac cycle. The tropical zodiac begins where the plane of the earth's equator intersects the plane of the ecliptic (the Sun's equator), a point we call 0° Aries, or the first day of spring.[1] Over the course of the next three months, the earth's orbital journey takes it to a point 90° from the vernal equinox, which is 0° Cancer, or the first day of summer. Thus, the phase relationship we call Cancer is actually a 90° angle measured from the vernal equinox.

Likewise, at any place and time on earth there is an eastern horizon where the plane of the earth's horizon intersects the sky. We call this point of intersection the Ascendant, or the beginning of the 1st house. If we extend our measurement from the Ascendant approximately 90 degrees east (below the horizon), we will arrive at the cusp of the 4th house. Accordingly, the area of

---

[1] Because the earth's axis is tilted an angle of 23° to the plane of the ecliptic, its equator will intersect the plane of the ecliptic in two locations. When the earth reaches one of these two points of intersection during its orbital journey about the Sun, it is either the first day of spring, or the first day of fall, both occasions occurring when days and nights of are equal length—hence, the equinoxes (equal nights).

geometric space-time we call the 4th house is actually a 90° angle measured from the eastern horizon.[2]

This situation repeats itself when considering the synodic cycle of two planets. The point where the two bodies come together (the conjunction) inaugurates the beginning of their cycle. When the faster moving of the two planets reaches a point 90° from the slower planet, we call that the opening square. Hence, the opening square is actually the first 90° phase in the synodic cycle between the two planets.

This is significant when we consider that the phase relationship of Cancer, the 4th house, and the opening square all have a similarity of meaning. Cancer, for example, has a caring but somewhat timid, inhibited quality; the 4th house is associated with family that provides a container to care for its members; and the opening square has an inhibiting, constraining quality that requires restraint and reflection. The kinship between these three variables could be explored further; however, suffice to say that the basis of rulerships in astrology is recognition that signs, houses, and aspects that derive from the same angle have a similarity of meaning. This extends to planets associated with those angles. The Moon, for instance, has been observed over millennia to have a quality and meaning associated with the sign Cancer, the 4th house, and the opening square.

The upshot is that astrological archetypes (metatypes) are geometric angles formed by division of a whole cycle by 12. The meaning is the phase/angle. And for every phase relationship, there is a planet that has a parallel meaning. Although astrologers are in the habit of referring to planets, signs, and even houses as archetypes, the unifying factor is actually the corresponding angle.

This principle can usefully be applied when interpreting planetary meanings in sign, house, or aspect. Since meanings in astrology are derived from angles, an expedient way of assessing quality of planetary position is by determining the intrinsic angular relationship that pertains to that position. Hence, in assessing planetary sign position, the operative question becomes: what is the intrinsic relationship (angle) between the sign the planet occupies and the sign it rules? If the Moon is in Capricorn, it is in a sign to which it is naturally opposed since Cancer (which the Moon rules) and Capricorn (the sign occupied) are opposed in the natural zodiac. It follows that the quality of Moon in Capricorn is oppositional. If the Moon is in Aries, the quality of fit is square-like, and so on.

---

[2] Different house systems may vary in the actual number of degrees from the Ascendant, but the general rule is that the 4th house begins approximately at right angle to the Ascendant.

Application of this simple rule provides a wealth of information about the compatibility of planetary sign positions. Again, if the Moon is in Aries, its capacity to listen, care and understand (lunar actions) is compromised by virtue of Aries' impatience, aggression, and tendency toward spontaneous action (shoot first, ask questions later). A good illustration of Moon Aries was the bellicose talk show host, Bill O'Reilly, who could barely get a question out before interrupting his guest's attempt to respond.

The same rule can be applied to planetary house position. The question then becomes: what is the essential relationship of the house the planet occupies to the house it rules? Consider that Mars is the natural ruler of the 1st house. If Mars is in the 6th, it is in a house to which it is essentially quincunx. Mars may have a problem in the 6th because its spontaneity and egocentricity is not well suited to 6th house requirements for service, efficiency, and sustained employment. It may have difficulty getting along with co-workers, clients, or customers, or staying with one job long enough to develop competence. Mars in the 5th, however, would be a trine-like position; thus, its spontaneity can be effectively utilized in an environment that requires play, performance, and creative self-expression.

Assessing intrinsic angular relationships can also be applied to aspect analysis. An aspect between two planets not only entails an actual angular relationship between the planets, but an essential one based on the angle between the signs the planets rule. For example, if Jupiter is squaring the Sun, the actual angle is 90°; however, the essential relationship is a trine, since Leo and Sagittarius (the signs ruled by Sun and Jupiter) are 120° apart. This means that the Sun-Jupiter dynamic is intrinsically compatible regardless of the actual aspect. However, the square—the actual angle—suggests the relationship might manifest as too much of a good thing, such as overconfidence and foolish optimism. Perhaps the person, like Napoleon (who had the square), brashly expresses intentions that are beyond his capacity to fulfill. Two hundred years ago when Napoleon overextended his French forces in an attempt to simultaneously defeat the British, Austrian, and Prussian armies at Waterloo, he was roundly defeated. Since that time, the expression "He met his Waterloo," has become synonymous with defeat as a consequence of overconfidence, overextending, and going too far.

The above examples serve to illustrate that while there are only twelve fundamental meanings (angles) in astrology, they can combine and interact in an almost infinite variety of ways. Whether interpreting a planetary sign position, house position, or aspect, the essential angle between the operative variables provides a means for assessing the quality of that position. This interpretive procedure can be applied to more complex configurations as well, such as assessing a planet in a sign, house, and in aspect to another planet—in other words, combining assessments to arrive at a more complex, thorough understanding of the configuration as a whole. Such assessments are not designed merely to judge whether a planet is in a good or bad state or a strong or weak position as typifies traditional astrology's obsession with planetary dignity; but rather to provide a means for understanding the complexity of factors involved in someone's actual behavior and experience vis-à-vis that planet.

VALUE NEUTRAL AND EVIDENCE BASED

All meanings in AstroPsychology are value neutral and based on factual data rather than presupposition. Value-neutrality and evidence-based practice go hand-in-hand because there is nothing in astrology that is inherently good or bad. The tendency in traditional astrology to make evaluative statements about virtually all astrological variables appears to derive from earlier periods in history when human beings thought in more limited, linear, dualistic terms, and perhaps had greater difficulty meeting the challenges that certain planets and planetary positions entailed. As a result, traditional astrology is riddled with evaluative jargon such as malefic and benefic planets, strong and weak houses, detriments and dignities, exaltations, falls, evil aspects, afflictions, and debilitations.

Implicit in such terminology is a deterministic mindset that ascribed experiential outcomes to planetary configurations rather than to the person's capacity to manage the energies of his or her horoscope. If benefic Venus was in detriment in the house of secret enemies and afflicted by an evil aspect from malefic Saturn, it was taken as a matter of relative certainty that the native's love life would be a *disaster*—literally 'against the stars'. In AstroPsychology, value judgments based on *a priori* assumptions about the relative merit (strong/weak, better/worse) of a planetary position are rejected on principle. Such archaic conventions not only are arbitrary, they fix the thinking of the practitioner in one particular way rather than allowing for the recognition that even the most challenging placement can potentially be turned to advantage.

As there was no concept of psychological growth or healing in early astrology, preoccupation with good and bad judgments pertained to what was good or bad for what we now call the *ego*—the need for self-esteem and the wish for control over preferred outcomes. Conversely, AstroPsychology is value-neutral in that it regards every astrological symbol—sign, planet, house, and aspect—as an integral part of the whole and capable of development toward higher levels of functionality over time. Every part of the chart is equally 'good' in the sense of constituting an indispensable function perfectly placed by sign, house, and aspect for that person's unique destiny.

This is not merely wishful thinking, for study of the charts of noteworthy people reveal that their accomplishments are frequently in areas symbolized precisely by their most difficult configurations. Planetary placements that appear challenging are thought to be necessary for the optimal growth and development of the person. Accordingly, interpretations are not focused on helping clients avoid difficulties via foreknowledge of predicted outcomes; rather, they are geared toward supporting clients in facing challenges with an enhanced awareness of their meaning, educative purpose and optimal expression.

Assessments of compatibility between two or more variables, such as Venus in Scorpio, can be made on the basis of their essential angular relationship as explained in the previous section. Such assessments assist the astrologer in understanding the actual nature of the relationship rather than simply making a judgment as to whether the position is good or bad. It should also be recognized that the functionality of a planetary placement is less a matter of essential angular relationship than degree of integration.

Evidence based astrology entails the conscientious use of current best evidence in making decisions about the care of clients. By best evidence, I mean relevant research from the field of astrology and related disciplines. This would include both formal studies as well as anecdotal accounts backed up by persuasive reasoning. At the current stage of our discipline, it would probably be fair to say that most astrologers' interpretations do not reflect the principles of evidence-based practice, but rather are based upon tradition, mandate, or blind faith. Part of the reason for this is the paucity of good research that is actually available to study.

A critical point in conducting sound research in astrology is determining which techniques and concepts *can* be researched—that is, whether a knowledge claim is falsifiable. Many ideas prevalent in traditional astrology, such as sect and exaltation, constitute arbitrary value judgments that not only are highly speculative but impossible to test. These speculative ideas sprang from the imagination, were subsequently passed on by traditional authorities, and accepted on faith since there was no possibility of acquiring data to either refute or confirm them.

Evidenced-based practice implies that the meaning of a configuration is derived solely from synthesis of parts that comprise that configuration, and subsequently tested via observation. With Jupiter in Cancer, for example, both planet and sign have a known quality based on empirical observation. These consensually based meanings are then blended according to the standard rules of chart synthesis. Such interpretations are descriptive rather than judgmental. I would not say, "Jupiter is exalted in Cancer and therefore is the best of all possible positions," for that is an arbitrary judgment of little or no informational value. Instead, I would say:

> When Jupiter is in Cancer, the function of hope, faith, and optimism may be expressed through Cancerian themes involving family and country. You may, for example, place great faith in family values, believing that the welfare of children trumps all other moral considerations.

This interpretation could be further elaborated by matching various Jupiterian states and actions with Cancerian domains and traits, taking into consideration that Jupiter in Cancer is a naturally quincunxial position and therefore could be problematic in some ways. Such an interpretation would contain no judgment as to whether it is a good or bad placement; rather, the focus is on what it might mean psychologically and behaviorally in the context of the chart as a whole. Such inferences can then be tested against available evidence – that is, the native's life story.

THE HOROSCOPE IS AN OPEN SYSTEM

Recall that soul is the primary focus of AstroPsychology. This should not be construed to mean that AstroPsychology is disinterested in external events. An open systems model of the psyche includes its relations with the environment. Environmental events are incorporated into a definition of the psyche itself. Systems theorists refer to this as *organizational closure* wherein a system is conceptualized with no reference to an absolute outside environment.

Let us consider what actually constitutes a system. In general systems theory (GST), a system can be defined as the ordered composition of elements into a unified whole—or, more precisely, as a set of units with relationships between them. Any complex of components in mutual interaction constitutes a system, whether a biological organism, a family, or a country. The essential premise underlying these definitions is that a system as a whole is qualitatively different, and behaves differently, from the sum of the system's individual elements. Thus, GST is an organismic, or holistic, view that depicts systems as living, self-regulating wholes not reducible to the mechanical interactions of their component parts.

It should be immediately apparent that the psyche is a system, which is precisely what the birthchart symbolizes. Before considering the significance of the psyche's relationship with its external environment, let us first outline the essential components of what we might call the self-system—the psyche as such. The first level of psyche is comprised of twelve fundamental drives, or sign-needs, which are linked to animating, archetypal powers rooted in Nature itself. These motivating dynamisms impel their planetary representatives to act in the service of need-fulfillment. Each planet signifies a set of interrelated functions; that is, specific types of action designed to satisfy the needs of the sign that planet rules. As ruler of Taurus, for example, Venus signifies the actions *to secure, attract, possess, own,* and *hold*, all of which are in the service of Taurean needs for security, safety, and comfort.

Planetary functions, however, are also in relationship with one another. These are aspects—angular relations between planetary bodies—that constitute a higher level of organization within the self-system. Depending upon the nature of the angle, the two planets engage in a type of relationship in which energy and information is exchanged in a process of reciprocal influence. Experientially, these relationships produce cognitive structures, or schemas, which are patterns of feeling, thinking, and behavior that pertain to the individual's convictions about the relative likelihood of fulfilling sign-needs. Taken as a whole, this entire process constitutes the psychodynamics of the birthchart.

By definition, needs signify drives that motivate the individual to engage with other systems—friends, partners, groups, institutions, and so on. Again, this implies the psyche is an open system, which means there is a constant exchange of inputs and outputs across system boundaries. To survive and thrive, the self-system must be in constant interaction with its environment, inputting substances, energy, and information, eliminating waste products, and producing outputs—creative works, achievements, services, and the like. Open systems are more like flowing process structures than static objects. This is what the horoscope symbolizes: a learning, evolving, open system. Maintenance of system order is achieved by converting inputs into a regular sequence of metabolic, emotional, and cognitive reactions that reproduce the system's structure.

Astrologically, houses are key factors in understanding types of environmental inputs, for they provide the situational contexts within which planetary processes operate. Each astrological variable—sign, planet, and aspect—signifies not only an intrapsychic factor, but also an external one. These factors will manifest in the context of their house environments as particular kinds of event patterns. In other words, both subjective and objective reality is symbolized by the same chart components. If Uranus in Sagittarius in the 7th squares Moon Virgo in the 4th, a woman may have a pattern of attracting erratic, emotionally distant men who justify their lack of commitment via radical theories of open marriage and communal families, which could be upsetting to her traditional values. It may appear this pattern is entirely circumstantial since it describes her partners (7th house); yet, this same configuration also symbolizes the subject's unconscious, psychological attitudes toward marriage and family, even if these unconscious tendencies are compensatory to her conscious values and projected onto the men she attracts.

The above example illustrates how a planetary aspect, which by definition involves two planets in signs and houses forming an angle to one another, is going to manifest simultaneously as a psychological and environmental condition. This is due to the non-local, psychoid nature of archetypes that enables them to manifest as both psyche and matter. Accordingly, the astrological chart can be interpreted as describing both the interior, psychological realm of the person, and the exterior physical realm that includes both the subject's body and his or her relations with others.

It is in this sense that an astrological chart can be conceptualized in terms of organizational closure. Person and environment are part of each other; the psyche is a determinant of its own milieu. It selects those features of the environment that are relevant to its structural and metabolic needs, and then couples with them. In this view, the psyche's relations with its environment are part of the psyche itself. There is no absolute separation between what is inside and what is outside the self-system.

This should not imply that the environment is irrelevant, but rather that no external condition directs the pattern of growth of the living being. In an open systems model, the psyche is not conceptualized as an effect of externally originating causes, which is the norm in conventional psychology. To the contrary, the self-determinism of open systems makes them relatively independent of outside forces since what is outside is also inside and vice versa. Psyche and environment are not merely interacting but interpenetrating. The true significance of external events is that they reflect and maintain the psyche's internal processes of self-organization as symbolized by the horoscope. And because a person's experiences tend to form a reoccurring, self-replicating pattern, they can have substantial diagnostic value.

CONTENT MIRRORS PROCESS

At the heart of AstroPsychology is the idea that content mirrors process. Content can be defined as the outcomes one experiences in various departments of life. These include formative childhood events, parental relationships, personal finances, education, health, work relations, marriage, sexuality, career, group associations, transient everyday encounters—in short, anything that can be directly experienced or observed by the individual. Process, on the other hand, entails all that occurs inside the psyche. Again, internal processes fall under the general heading of psychodynamics—specifically, the relationship between motivation, emotion, cognition, attitude, and behavior. All of this is process.

An individual's character is the emergent, summary product of psychodynamics and constitutes the boundary where content and process meet. By character, I mean the relative attainment by the person of the full actualization and integration of his various parts and capacities. Integrity is a measure of character; the stronger the character, the greater its integrity (and vice versa). Character is thought to evolve over time in accordance with a specific evolutionary imperative. Accordingly, character development is inextricably bound up with fate. Character produces events consistent with itself such that every outer experience is a metaphor of an inner condition. More importantly, certain key events—or event themes—provide a vehicle and a catalyst for facilitating the soul's evolutionary process. Fate, in this view, is the unfoldment of character; content mirrors process.

Jung theorized that the confluence of inner and outer events was due to a general acausal orderedness in nature that derived from the psychoid nature of archetypes. Again, an archetype is psychoid in the sense that it shapes both matter and mind, which means it can manifest simultaneously as both an inner attitude and a corresponding outer event. Jung (1960) termed this phenomena *synchronicity* and defined it as: "A coincidence in time of two or more causally unrelated events which have the same or similar meaning" (p. 441). Emphasis here should be placed on the word *meaning*. For unless one is able to discern equivalences between outer physical factors and inner psychic ones, their synchronistic import will be lost. In such cases, an entirely different meaning may be attributed to the event.

For example, a child born with Mars square Saturn may express a tendency to 'break the rules' on a regular basis. This inner attitude of defiance may be paralleled outwardly in the form of an egocentric, abusive father who resorts to excessive force in response to his son's disobedience. Synchronistically, the father's lack of control is meaningfully related to his son's noncompliance with the rules. However, a conventional psychological explanation for such a correspondence would be based on linear, deterministic, cause-effect reasoning—namely, that the son's attitude of defiance is an outgrowth of the father's use of excessive force. From this perspective, the objective meaning of the father's behavior is that his son is a victim of abuse and bears no responsibility for the treatment he receives. Moreover, the child's anger and defiance are merely the unfortunate effects of an externally originating cause embodied in the person of his abusive father.

Again, however, from a synchronistic perspective, the father's behavior has a more complex meaning. It may still be abusive, but it also mirrors the son's inborn psychological attitude. In the absence of the astrological chart, this might not be apparent; yet, that the child has Mars square Saturn confirms that the inner attitude and outer condition is a matched pair. Recognizing this parallel can shift one's perspective to a higher, more systemic understanding that punctuates the relationship in terms of circular causality. Moreover, it suggests that the father's violence may be necessitated by a destiny factor implicit in his son's birthchart. This gives the father's behavior an import that extends beyond its merely abusive nature. For the abuse may serve a formative, educative purpose that is essential for realization of his son's ultimate destiny. While this comes dangerously close to blaming the victim, I am not suggesting that his son deserves the abuse; only that it has a meaning that cannot be fully understood unless we perceive it circularly and in the context of the overall life pattern.

OUTER EXPERIENCES CONSTITUTE FEEDBACK

Content not only mirrors process; it constitutes feedback that can be utilized to assure one's further development. All open systems are learning systems that utilize feedback to regulate their internal processes and evolve toward more balanced, integrated states. Feedback can be defined as that effect of a system's output which is reintroduced to the system as information about the output. The importance of information is due to the purposive nature of systems that are self-regulating and goal-directed with respect to their environment.

Astrologically, this can be understood in terms of planetary functions striving to satisfy their motivating sign-needs. If, for example, the aforementioned boy with Mars square Saturn experiences negative consequences related to his inability (or unwillingness) to comply with the rules, he may utilize this information to make a self-corrective response. To achieve this, he would need to pay attention to feelings related to his Mars and Saturn functions. Mars says, "Go! Do want you want and do it now!" Saturn, however, counters this Martian imperative with, "Slow down; control yourself and manage your impulses. Anticipate the consequences of your actions and plan accordingly." The square further underscores the importance of containment and control. If he takes responsibility for the consequences of his actions, then he can utilize feedback in the service of learning and begin to develop greater Saturnian control over his Martian impulses.

This illustrates how system behavior (output) impacts the surrounding environment which, in turn, produces information that is synchronistically related to the internal functioning of the self-system. By processing this information, individuals are able to regulate their behavior in accord with their various purposes and goals. In other words, feedback is the return of information to form a closed control loop. The self-system will utilize information as feedback in order to adapt to environmental contingencies, solve problems, and evolve toward greater balance. Wiener (1954) explains:

> Feedback is a method of controlling a system by reinserting into it the results of its past performance….If, however, the information which proceeds backward from the performance is able to change the general method and pattern of performance, [then] we have a process which may be called learning. (p. 84)

There are two types of feedback: negative and positive. In negative feedback, information is used to decrease output deviation from a set norm or bias—hence the term "negative." Consider, for example, that Aries-Mars has a bias toward a target state of freedom and aliveness. At the same time, Capricorn-Saturn has a bias toward a goal-state of control. If a child with Mars square Saturn suffers a negative Saturnian experience—punishment—as a consequence of inadequate self-control, he may utilize this feedback to develop more control over his impulse to act without restraint. In effect, he must strengthen his Saturn to better regulate his Mars in order that it not deviate too markedly from Saturn's bias toward control. If he is able to bring these functions into proper balance, then he will enjoy both freedom and control to a realistic, appropriate degree.

Positive feedback, on the other hand, is information that amplifies output deviation from a set norm and is thus positive in relation to the already existing trend; that is, it reinforces a deviation-amplifying situation in a self-stimulating manner. In this instance, the Mars-Saturn boy may resent his father's abusive tactics and actually double-down in his defiance to see if he can defeat his father's attempts to control him. In so doing, however, he is avoiding awareness of his own need for self-control. Capricorn-Saturn feelings convey the need for restraint, discipline, and patience in recognition of limits and in the service of long-term goals. If he represses these Saturnian needs, they will be projected onto a suitable carrier—like his father. Still influenced by Mars but not in a way that can be consciously managed, his Saturn is inflamed and out-of-control; hence, it materializes outwardly as an oppressive, abusive authority figure. The more the father overreacts to his son's defiance, the more hostile the son becomes; the more hostile the son becomes, the more violent the father.

This escalating cycle of defiance and violence typifies a positive feedback loop. Note, however, that this deviation amplifying feedback cycle has both an internal and external form. Externally, it is observable in the father-son dynamic. Internally, the boy is deviating from a set norm that pertains to the target state of Saturn, which is not being attained because of his overvaluation of Martian impulses. This pulls the self-system further and further away from Saturnian control. It is precisely this escalating deviation from an internal standard of control that, tragically, evokes feedback from the environment that is increasingly extreme. In other words, the boy's behavior is not merely a reaction to his father; it is also helping to shape the father's response.

Ultimately, positive feedback tends to be subject to a more encompassing negative feedback cycle. The first law of systems is survival. Unchecked positive feedback leading to uncontrolled escalation will eventually destroy a system due to its failure to learn. Such "runaways" in one direction, such as an escalating reliance upon Martian combativeness, represent an effort to maximize one variable in an effort to counterbalance an environmental response that seems to have gone too far in the other direction.

Synchronistically, we can understand the extremity of the external response as reflecting the unbalanced internal state; that is, the lack of integration between the boy's Martian and Saturnian potentials. In effect, our Mars-Saturn situation is a power struggle that has resulted from the boy projecting his Saturn function onto his father. Although the father, too, is characterized by the same aspect (he is the external embodiment of the boy's Mars-Saturn), his response compensates the imbalance in his son by overemphasizing Saturn.

From a system's perspective, what is generally called a symptom is really a corrective response that has gone too far in one direction. It is a solution that has become a problem. The boy's attempt to resolve his Mars-Saturn conflict entails an overreliance upon his Mars at the expense of his Saturn—that is, at the expense of his capacity for self-control. Again, symptoms represent a tendency to maximize a particular experience or behavior; in this case, always being free (Mars) versus controlled (Saturn). As Keeney (1983) put it, "This view of symptomology suggests that any pattern of behavior that can be characterized as an effort toward maximizing or minimizing a variable is pathological" (p. 123).

Such efforts may result in what appears as an escalating runaway. Eventually, however, the person will encounter some external situation that can potentially curb the behavior. For example, the boy grows up and loses a series of jobs because of his unwillingness to respect authority and accept limits. This, in turn, may motivate him to get help and reform his ways. Accordingly, system runaway may ultimately lead to a change in system structure and behavior. Positive feedback can be seen as "a partial arc or sequence of a more encompassing negative feedback process," says Keeney (p. 72). By enlarging one's frame of reference, it is possible to see system runaway as a temporary variation subject to higher orders of control. Positive feedback eventually converts to negative feedback or deviation-countering information. Finally recognizing his self-destructiveness, our young man with Mars-square-Saturn may enter an anger management program that transforms his life. In other words, he learns by suffering the consequences of his own behavior.

Feedback loops exemplify the processes by which the self-system (psyche/horoscope) controls its growth and behavior via circular causality. This refers to the patterned relations between system components that are in a process of simultaneous, reciprocal influence. It also refers to the purposefulness of living systems that not only react to their environment, but also act upon it due to self-generated activity arising from their own goals.

In astrological terms, the psyche, as symbolized by the horoscope, constitutes a living system whose behavior impacts the environment which, in turn, reacts upon the psyche in a continuous interactive cycle. In accord with the concept of organizational closure, human behavior is both a cause of and a response to environmental conditions. Understanding circular causality and self-regulative feedback enables astrologers to explain how the psyche can maintain itself with respect to a desired state or change itself with respect to a target to be reached.

DEVELOPMENT TOWARD WHOLENESS

A central theme in AstroPsychology is that the deeper purpose of experience is to facilitate development toward an ideal state of personality differentiation and integration. As an open system, the internal processes of the psyche/birthchart perform three main functions: being, behaving, and becoming. *Being* simply means maintenance of internal structure and stability; *behaving* entails taking action to achieve self-regulation in the face of environmental disturbances; and *becoming* necessitates progressive transformation to higher levels of adaptation. It is this latter function that concerns us here.

In the previous section, I outlined how negative, stabilizing feedback processes are complemented by positive, de-stabilizing feedback loops that lead to the spontaneous emergence of new behavior. These processes operate in such a way that the psyche and its environment mutually and reciprocally evolve each other; that is, they co-evolve. The psychoid nature of archetypes gives us a clue as to how this occurs. As we have seen, every astrological configuration constitutes a dynamic pattern that expresses itself internally and externally; it symbolizes both behavior and the consequences of behavior (feedback).

Because archetypes are intelligent fields of formative causation, their outward manifestation constitutes feedback that can potentially inform the system and bring about a change of behavior. This entire process necessarily implicates what Jung called the *Self*—the totality of the psyche that includes its relations with the environment by virtue of symbolic correspondences. The Self is analogous to what in Hindu traditions is called *Atman,* the core divinity within, which is identical with *Brahman,* the soul and intelligence of the Universe. As an image of wholeness yet to be attained, the Self orchestrates events to compensate for what is unconscious, unintegrated, and unbalanced within the existent structure of the psyche. In so doing, the Self functions as an evolutionary field, a kind of transcendent, all-knowing consciousness immanent within personal experience that pulls development toward an ideal state of balance and wholeness.

The Jungian analyst, Edward Whitmont, referred to this as the destiny concept. Certain events seem to involve insertion into the present of information that derives from one's deepest, but as yet unknown identity—in other words, from the future. To achieve wholeness and realize the Self, the individual is required to experience a specific pattern of events designed to facilitate an evolutionary process unique to that person. "Thus destiny, or fate," says Whitmont (2007) "is the unfoldment of the Self-archetype in time and space." This need not imply an absolute determinism, for self-realization requires the cooperation and creative participation of the individual.

From a systems perspective, this same process is called *negentropy*, which means 'negative entropy'. Negentropy was Schrondinger's term for how a system prevents entropy (disorder leading to death) and, instead, builds itself into an increasingly ordered structure. By receiving energy and matter from the less organized (more entropic) outside world, and converting these inputs into its structure, living systems gradually evolve into more organized, complex, and differentiated organisms. However, living systems are not only open, adaptive, and learning; they are also self-transcendent, meaning capable of transforming themselves by actively importing matter-energy inputs and using these inputs to evolve beyond their current structure.

Astrologically, the process by which this occurs can be described in four stages. The first stage is when the individual is simply behaving normally in accord with existent attitudes, beliefs, and habits as reflected in his horoscope. Stage two begins when the person experiences something he or she is not psychologically equipped to handle. A man with Sun square Neptune, for example, experiences a humiliating defeat in response to an act of self-expression. This induces massive perturbations within the psyche that throws him into a state of despair and confusion. Stage two accelerates as he attempts to regain control by resorting to his usual solar habits, such as arrogant defensiveness and an exaggerated sense of entitlement, which only make things worse (positive feedback cycle).

Stage three commences when, realizing the futility of his actions, he collapses and regresses to an earlier, less mature level of functioning—a fork in the road, a choice point in his own developmental history when a decision was made that sealed his fate for the immediate future. Regression entails the lifting of a repression and the remembrance of an old injury to which current attitudes and habits constitute a defensive compensation. Perhaps as a child he was abandoned by his father, whose indifference to his son was both hurtful and devaluing. Unable to win his father's love, and unable at the time to process the feelings and meaning of this humiliating defeat of the will (Neptune square Sun), the loss was repressed, and its meaning replaced with an exaggerated sense of self-importance—in a word, ego-inflation—as befits Sun square Neptune.

Stage three continues as he opens to the earlier trauma and allows himself to fully experience its associated pain and meaning. The French call this *reculeur pour mieux sauter*, or "step back to leap" (Koestler, 1978). Regression seems to involve a loosening up, a letting go, an increase in malleability in order that some new understanding and integration may occur. From an evolutionary perspective, regressive inducing fluctuations allow the psyche to either adapt to the current experience by spontaneously reorganizing at a higher level of complexity, or become further entrenched in dysfunctional, defensive attitudes.

All of this is prelude to stage four, the bifurcation point for the self-system, another fork in the road in which there is an opportunity to rewrite the story and redo an old decision. If the person chooses to adapt, his Sun square Neptune will reorganize itself at a higher level of integration, conferring new, emergent properties of greater humility, compassion, and resiliency. He may begin to identify more fully with a God-concept, thus strengthening his spiritual capacity to allow himself to be guided by a higher power. All of this would constitute a fundamental redefinition of self, a transformation of the self-system.

Recall how our Sun square Neptune person initially compensated for his humiliating childhood experience by developing an exaggerated sense of importance and entitlement. Neptune, in other words, was repressed in favor of the Sun; yet, the Sun is still unconsciously influenced by Neptune, but in a manner that leads to narcissistic grandiosity, a transcendent, even magical identity that imagines itself capable of extraordinary feats of heroism. If Neptune symbolizes the reality of a higher power without limits—omniscient and omnipotent—the Sun can appropriate Neptune in the service of its own agenda. The ego becomes inflated, overreaching, and without boundaries. This eventually must be met by a compensatory environmental response designed to defeat and deflate an overblown sense of self-importance; hence, the inevitability of humiliating defeat that brings chaos and disillusionment in its wake.

Negentropy is the system's attempt to maintain its current order by processing inputs from the environment and converting them into its structure. However, as Jantsch (1980) pointed out, systems can also utilize feedback to transform themselves into more complex structures. This type of feedback operates in the service of *becoming*; not mere maintenance of being, but evolution of a more complex and resilient structure. Systems theorists refer to it as "evolutionary feedback" because it tends to create massive perturbations within the system that can result in a non-linear, discontinuous leap to a higher order. Also known as 'order through fluctuation' or 'order out of chaos', the larger whole—the Self—is impacted by an imbalance within the individual psyche and responds with a custom-made, corrective experience to jump start an evolutionary process that had been temporarily suspended by the original defensive compensation. In effect, evolutionary feedback is the system's equivalent to what is otherwise known as fate.

If one accepts this hypothesis, we must consider the possibility that the earlier, humiliating defeat of the will at the hands of an abandoning father was itself part of the Self's plan all along. While defenses are necessary to prevent the self-system from becoming completely overwhelmed, they merely delay fulfillment of a destiny presaged by the birthchart and orchestrated by the Self. This is reminiscent of the famous quip by world heavyweight champion Joe Louis when asked how he would defeat Billy Conn, a quicker, more elusive opponent. "He can run, but he can't hide," said Louis. Likewise, the individual can run from his destiny by avoiding and delaying the full experiencing of an event-pattern required by a planetary configuration, but he cannot hide from it. For in one form or another, the same event-pattern will be replicated in the future, providing yet another opportunity for doing the soul work necessary for full actualization of the aspect's potential.

From an astrological perspective, the life-pattern of the chart does not unfold in a linear, cause-effect, deterministic manner with one event leading inexorably to another. Rather, it unfolds holonomically with every segment of time from birth to death encapsulating the whole pattern.[3] Earlier experiences are not the cause of later experiences, for all experience is a manifestation of the same life-pattern. Conversely, when deterministic thinking is applied to questions of causation, the natural tendency is to presume that traumatic childhood experiences are the cause of later, adult psychopathology. This argument is so presumptive that it not only affects the way psychology is taught in the academic sphere at virtually every level, it is even applied in the courts with regard to the guilt or innocence of a criminal defendant. Lawyers effectively argue that defendants are not morally culpable for crimes they commit because they are mere victims of their childhoods.

The astrological concept of a holistic life-pattern leading to the fulfillment of a particular destiny invites us to re-evaluate certain common assumptions in the treatment of clients. Key events in a client's history that we habitually assume to be causes of his current psychopathology may simply be early, prototypical events of a more encompassing life-pattern. As Whitmont (2007) put it, "What must be experienced at the age of sixty-six could well

---

[3] Holonomy refers to a structural properly of systems in which the whole (system) is contained in the part—or, stated in the reverse, the part reflects the whole. This is evident both temporally and spatially. Temporally, living systems incorporate larger astronomical cycles and rhythms as internal cycles and periodicities; that is, biological clocks. The part reflects the whole; as above, so below.

necessitate and precipitate experiences at the age of three or four." Rather than seeing those events as the tragic precursors and generative matrix of a subsequent mental disorder that might, under more ideal circumstances, have been prevented, they may actually be important developmental landmarks essential for future psycho-spiritual advances. In effect, they constitute the first stage and provide the necessary impetus for actualizing a particular pattern of wholeness.

This idea is not without precedent in spiritual frameworks. Christian theology, for example, holds that God sacrificed his only begotten son in order that humankind could be saved. The suffering and crucifixion of Jesus at the hands of Pontius Pilot was for the sake of Man's ultimate redemption, a divine sacrifice in order that our sins could be forgiven. Allegedly, it served a larger purpose that opened the way for a new stage of human consciousness. Regardless of how one views this story, whether as myth or spiritual reality, its archetypal significance is the same: present suffering is in the service of the soul's future development. As Jung (1958) repeatedly emphasized, every psychic advance of man arises from the suffering of the soul. Neurosis is simply suffering yet to find its meaning.

TELEOLOGY AND CONSCIOUS EVOLUTION

The notion that something happens in order that a future goal can be realized is known as teleological causation. It was Aristotle (384-322 BC) who first formalized this idea in his notion of final causes. Aristotle distinguished "efficient" from "final" causes—the former being what moderns would consider a cause, and the latter being the end *(telos)* for which a thing exists. A final cause was that for the sake of which something occurs. The power of attraction, thought Aristotle, was a better model for causation than propulsion; things are lured more than they are driven. "Aristotle's universe," says Huston Smith (1982) "is like a pyramid of magnets."

> Those on each tier are attracted to the tier above while being empowered by that tier to attract the magnets below them. At the apex stands the only completely actual reality there is, the divine Prime and Unmoved Mover. (p. 153)

For Aristotle, the supreme final cause was reunion with the divine ground. Teleology, or goal-oriented behavior, is based on the idea that everything in the physical universe is a consequence of things superior to it.

Aristotelian teleology is consistent with general systems theory. In downward causation, a lower level subsystem must comply with the dictates of the higher level suprasystem of which it is a part. A molecule, for example, is guided to behave in a certain way by the more encompassing logic of the cell in which it resides. Likewise in Jungian psychology, every individual experience is thought to be orchestrated from a higher level—the Self—and occurs for the sake of bringing this more encompassing pattern to fruition. From this perspective, to evolve consciously entails choosing to cooperate with an evolutionary imperative that supersedes short-sighted wishes for an easy life.

This general attitude can apply to outcomes that flow from planetary aspects. For example, any experience that conforms to Sun square Neptune is conducive to an end that represents the full realization of that aspect's potential. Every Sun-Neptune experience is part of a larger pattern that pertains not only to the aspect but to the destiny pattern of the chart as a whole. Such experiences will occur in different ways for different people, depending how the aspect is situated by sign and house. But the point remains the same: every manifestation of Sun square Neptune is subordinate to the evolutionary pattern of the birthchart that pulls the person toward higher degrees of realization. Conscious evolution is simply the intention to cooperate with an evolutionary process that is built into the very fabric of the horoscope.

It may seem strange to consider that a child's abandonment by his father might actually be necessary for actualization of the child's potential. Yet, according to Hillman (1996), evidence for this is abundant in the lives of both famous and ordinary people. A case in point is the story of American President Barack Obama, who has Sun square Neptune. At two years old, Obama was abandoned in Hawaii by his idealistic father who went off to Harvard to study economics so that he could help his native country, Kenya, recover from the ravages of colonialism. After returning to Kenya upon graduation, Obama Sr. completely neglected his son except for a one-month visit to Hawaii when Obama was ten.

Neptune often correlates to loss, which in this case would impact Barack's self-esteem (Sun) and thus potentially confer humility and recognition of the self's limitations. Neptune also symbolizes a transcendent ideal and the wish to rescue others from a fallen state, as in his father's intention to help his native Kenyans. Although Obama never really knew his father, he eventually followed in his footsteps by going to Harvard to study law. Prior to attending Harvard, however, Obama spent three years in Chicago's South

Side as director of the Developing Communities Project, a church-based organization dedicated to helping the disadvantaged.

Obama's experience as a community organizer was difficult and heart-wrenching. Not only had many of the children he sought to help been abandoned by their own fathers, but the program as a whole was sorely neglected due to an entrenched apathy on the part of a self-serving political bureaucracy. In this we see an echo of the neglect and apathy that Obama suffered at the hands of his abandoning father. One might surmise that both experiences provided fodder for Obama's eventual decision to enter politics as a liberal Democrat dedicated to helping the poor, the underprivileged, and all who felt abandoned by the system. In so doing, he could become the father for others that he never had—virtually, the father (president) of his country.

While this is a vast oversimplification of a complex human being, it serves to illustrate how an early version of an astrological configuration (Sun square Neptune) has later reiterations that carry the process forward. In effect, the aspect evolves from humble beginnings—abandonment by his father—to more inspired expression as a father-figure devoted to those who feel abandoned. All this is detailed in Obama's (1995) autobiography.

It is in this sense that certain types of early events are not only purposive but appear to involve a future state somehow intervening to shape and guide experience in order that the future state can be concretely realized. Destiny beckons from the future, but also reaches backward into the present, grabs you by the scruff of the neck, and drags you forward along a certain trajectory though you may be howling in protest. An individual's capacity to surrender to such a process is evidence of what Jung called *amor fati*, meaning "Love of one's fate". To be entirely without such love, claimed Jung, is to be neurotic—suffering excessively and unnecessarily the slings and arrows of life's outrageous fortune.

Conversely, to see everything that happens as food for the soul, including and especially suffering, is to enter into a conscious collaboration with one's higher Self. It is to forge a co-creative, participatory relationship with the divine that requires not merely accepting what happens but discerning its meaning and aligning with its purpose so to actualize potentials it is calling forth. This is where astrology can be invaluable, for it provides a tool for deciphering the meaning of experience and a roadmap for pointing the way to higher ground.

Chapter Two

PSYCHODYNAMICS OF ASTROLOGY

This chapter introduces a psychodynamic formulation of astrology. Borrowing from psychoanalytic, Jungian, and General Systems models, we will explore how the chart symbolizes a complex information processing system made up of multiple, interacting control centers—planets—that determine thoughts, feelings, and behavior.

Sigmund Freud introduced the concept of psychodynamics in the early part of the 20th century. While his thinking constantly changed and evolved over the next fifty years, certain core ideas of psychodynamics persist to this day. Freud, Jung, and later theorists struggled to explain how the psyche functioned as a whole. What was the structure of the psyche and how did its various parts interact to produce behavior? Their task was difficult, for they had nothing to guide their explorations other than the patient's symptoms, confessions, and dreams. The psyche itself was a mystery, a black box that only hinted at its structure and contents. Still, the fruits of psychoanalytic psychology were tantalizing and offered an account of psychic life that gripped the public imagination. Terms like id, ego, and superego have become so much a part of our everyday language that we scarcely question whether they have any basis in reality.

Without a model that provided clear referents for psychological processes, Freud was like a medieval physician with no knowledge of human anatomy. Forced to explain the psyche without being able to actually see it, his formulations were the product of a brilliant, intuitive genius. Yet, they were necessarily limited, perhaps even clumsy and primitive in comparison to what can be glimpsed through an astrological lens. For astrology provides a model with clear external referents. Signs and planets symbolize the anatomy of the soul and give it a metaphorical concreteness that is immediately accessible. What is revealed is a psyche infinitely more complex and extensive than Freud imagined.

CONVENTIONAL PSYCHODYNAMICS

A good place to start our discussion of psychodynamics is with a definition of *psyche*. This Latin word essentially means "spirit" or "soul." It signifies a subtle entity that includes but transcends the physical body. Psyche is the personality as a whole and embraces all psychological processes, both conscious and unconscious. As a self-regulating system comprised of antipodal forces, the psyche is dynamic, meaning it is characterized by continuous change, activity, or progress.

Psychodynamics explains how the psyche is comprised of self-activating, goal-directed, and interacting forces that underlay all thoughts, feelings, and behavior. A psychodynamic formulation concerns itself with how the psyche develops and how hypothesized energies are distributed in the course of the psyche's various adaptational maneuvers. The relation between motivation, emotion, cognition, and behavior is the prime topic of psychodynamics.

According to Freud, the psyche was a tripartite structure made up of id, ego, and superego. The id represents the instinctual drives of sex and aggression, the ego the executive and inhibiting agency, and the superego the influence of socially mandated rules that have been internalized, what we commonly call *conscience*. All three structures were thought to be involved in any psychic phenomenon. Pressures from the id compel one to seek immediate satisfaction through a discharge of tension.

For example, if a person experiences an aggressive urge to harm a rival, the ego then judges the safety or danger of gratification and exerts restraining forces to frustrate, delay, or detour such discharge so that its ultimate expression is in keeping with the demands of reality and the superego. Opposition between id, ego, and superego gives rise to intrapsychic conflict. Resultant unconscious mental arbitration may emerge into conscious awareness as a neurotic symptom. For example, if aggression (id) is repressed due to superego restraints, it may be projected onto others so that the person feels afraid, imagines that others don't like him, and thus behaves in a defensive manner that creates the very condition he is imagining: hostility from others.

ASTRO-PSYCHODYNAMICS

By reformulating psychoanalytic concepts within an astrological framework, it is possible to retain some of the useful insights of psychoanalytic theory without, at the same time, including its more questionable assumptions.

Freud's theory of psychodynamics can serve as a take off point for astrological theory. The chart as a whole depicts the psyche. Rather than a limited, tripartite structure, however, astrology presents a more complex ten-planet, twelve-sign model that, nevertheless, can be understood in a manner consistent with psychodynamic theory.

Whereas the id signifies merely two drives—sex and aggression—the zodiac depicts twelve distinct drives, each related to the others in a discernable way by virtue of it's placement within the structure as a whole. Aries, for example, is square Capricorn in the natural zodiac, thus signifying that the drive for freedom is in conflict with the need for control. This is a fundamental human challenge. However, if the planetary representatives of Aries and Capricorn—Mars and Saturn—were actually square in someone's birthchart, this would highlight an intrapsychic conflict that is especially salient for that individual.

The astrological meaning of Mars square Saturn parallels Freud's depiction of the id's relationship to the superego: the instinct for aggression (Mars) is in conflict with the civilizing rules of society (Saturn). In fact, Freud actually had Mars square Saturn in his natal chart, so it is not surprising that his theory of psychodynamics emphasized this fundamental, human dilemma. Because it was an intrapsychic conflict for him, he assumed it must necessarily be a conflict for everyone. Within the astrological model, however, this is merely one of innumerable psychic conflicts that can be depicted.

PSYCHIC ENERGY

Since psychodynamics concerns itself with forces that produce activity within the psyche, *psychic energy* was postulated to be the carrier of all psychological activity. As a hypothetical, quantifiable energy analogous to electricity, psychic energy is a heuristic device; that is, it serves as a guide in the investigation and solution of problems that relate to psychological functioning. However, one must be careful not to reify the concept of psychic energy, for no one has actually seen or measured it. We presume it to exist simply because it is convenient and necessary for further theorizing. In fact, concepts like id, ego, and superego are all heuristic devices—hypothetical structures that have been invented to account for rough categories of observable behavior. As we will see, however, the astrological model provides a far more complete and detailed accounting of the structure and dynamics of the psyche.

The origins of the concept of psychic energy date back to the early days of psychology, which were wedded to a 17th century movement called "physicalism." According to this doctrine, all the phenomenon of life could be subsumed under the principles of classical physics. Scientists concluded that psychology, like any other study, must of necessity be a study of matter in motion. This mechanical conception of nature gave rise to the assertion that human consciousness was a by-product of external forces. Behavior was thought to be governed almost entirely by the nervous system, the function of which was to receive, conduct, and discharge electrical energy. Brain was simply an electrical switchboard for receiving and transmitting energy. Ultimately, the whole of psychic life could be reduced to physical processes.

Psychic energy was assumed to flow through the components of the psyche the way electricity flows through a computer. It activates our programming and enables us to process, store, and create information. Perhaps a laptop computer would be an even better metaphor, for the laptop is battery powered and completely self-sufficient. Analogously, psychic energy is presumed to be self-generating and limited to what occurs inside the human brain and body. Like most theorists of the 20th century, Freud's thinking was mechanistic; he thought psychic energy was rooted in matter—the primary reality.

Conversely, astrology is wedded to an organic paradigm that holds consciousness to be the primary stuff of the Universe. Within this view, consciousness is psychic energy, but consciousness is not limited to the inside of a person's brain. Rather, it extends indefinitely outwards to encompass all of life. Human consciousness is the precipitate of a larger, parent consciousness—God, Tao, or Brahman—that subsumes the individual. The brain and body are merely crystallizations of this consciousness onto a physical plane, like steam condensing into ice. Situated midway in the great hierarchy of Being, human consciousness subsumes its own parts, so that even the body's cells and atoms have a kind of primitive awareness. Within an organic paradigm, there is nothing that is not consciousness.

While psychic energy in the Freudian model is completely dependent upon its material substrate, and thus lives and dies within a physical realm, the astrological world-view suggests that psyche and cosmos are connected by virtue of a single consciousness that unites them. Universal Consciousness is both the alpha and omega of individual existence; it is the source of soul, while also being the end toward which soul strives to reunite by natural inclination.

UNIVERSAL CONSCIOUSNESS

Since consciousness is at the heart of our astrological model, it is important to define what I mean by this term. First, let me differentiate Universal Consciousness from human consciousness. Smith (1976) points out that all major religious traditions agree that Universal Consciousness is substantially incomprehensible and can be known only through its attributes, or by negative definition. That is, we can say what Universal Consciousness is not, but we can never say what it is. This is due to the claim that Universal Consciousness is a non-embodied intelligence from which all things are fashioned and which permeates all conditions of existence. In other words, Universal Consciousness cannot be objectified or differentiated since it constitutes the very nature of all that is.

In the wisdom traditions, or what is sometimes referred to as "the perennial philosophy," Consciousness is described as a kind of animated spirit infinitely diffused and therefore present as the very life in living things. Taoism refers to a timeless and dimensionless reality—the *Tao*—that moves in and through all things but whose shape or substance cannot be known. In Vedic texts, *Brahman* is the name of the absolute and eternal existence that is believed to be the source of the phenomenal universe. Neoplatonic philosophy refers to the ultimate, transcendent reality as the *One* and the *Good*—the One because it is the principle or essence of all things, and the Good because it is the supreme object of aspiration for all things.

Such descriptions of Universal Consciousness are characterized by an essentially organic worldview that perceives all phenomena in the universe as integral parts of an inseparable, harmonious, and conscious whole. Brahman, for instance, is both the All and the One, as both these terms imply unity. Vedantists believe that creation is not the child of Brahman, but is Brahman. Since, according to this view, there is nothing that is not consciousness, any truly scientific or objective description of the subject is impossible.

While it may not be possible to define Universal Consciousness in terms of specific content, it is possible to describe it in terms of process. By this, I mean that Consciousness can be thought of as a spontaneous ordering principle in Nature. It is that ineffable reality which brings order out of chaos and makes the world intelligible. In simpler terms, I would describe Consciousness as an evolutionary process of organized relations: "evolutionary" because as a movement in time it brings about increasing complexity; "process" because it is intrinsically dynamic, intentional, and conducing toward a definite end; and "organized relations" because unless relationships between entities—from subatomic particles to human beings—were organized in precisely the way that they are, there would be no Universe to know. This latter point is supported by the "Anthropic Cosmological Principle" of modern physics, which states that the conditions of the Universe appear to be specially contrived to facilitate the appearance of conscious intelligence as manifest in human beings (Barrow & Tipler, 1986).

Universal Consciousness can be further described through its attributes. For example, Wilber (1979) states, "the most striking feature of the perennial philosophy/psychology is that it presents being and consciousness as a hierarchy of dimensional levels" (p. 43). That is, the perennial wisdom holds that Universal Consciousness is **hierarchically structured**, consisting of at least five dimensional-levels—the ultimate, the subtle, the mental, the biological, and the physical. "It is important to understand," says Wilber, "that *all* major perennial traditions agree with that general hierarchy, and most of them right down to details" (p. 44). Universal Consciousness is both a **transcendent whole** in that the ultimate level transcends but includes all previous levels, and it is an **immanent presence** as the Ground or Being of all realms. In this sense, Universal Consciousness is both the cause of evolutionary processes while also comprising the essence of that which is being evolved. The purported immanence of a divine whole in all the parts of Nature is linked to another property of Universal Consciousness, that of **holographic organization**, meaning the whole is reflected in the part. In astrology, this principle is succinctly expressed by the Hermetic dictum, "as above, so below."

Universal Consciousness is thought to be **purposive**, or intentional, in that the various properties, processes, and manifestations of time seem to be serving some Divine purpose—specifically, evolution toward states of increasing unity. In this regard, Universal Consciousness is both **intelligent** and **creative**. Its intelligence is evidenced by the tendency of parts to find ways to conjoin together to produce more complex wholes at precisely those times in history when such couplings were necessary for evolution to continue. And the creativity of the whole is everywhere apparent in the free, indeterminate nature of evolutionary processes that conspire to bring about the infinite variety of natural forms.

The Neoplatonists distinguished the intelligent, creative, and purposive quality of the divine whole from that which was its essence. To the latter they gave the name *Psyche*, meaning the Soul of the Universe, which was both the dynamic behind manifestation and the common denominator of all that was manifested. To the intelligence that derived from this Soul, however, they gave the name *Nous*, meaning the Mind that ordered the Universe into intelligible wholes, microcosms within the macrocosm. In this sense, *Nous* is a derivative or property of *Psyche* and constitutes the subtle level of Consciousness.

To summarize, Universal Consciousness is the eternal, all-pervasive, primordial source from which all things, both seen and unseen, emerge, in which they are sustained, and to which they return. It is a hierarchically structured, holographically organized transcendent whole that is simultaneously immanent in all the parts and processes of Nature. As an evolutionary process of organized relations it evidences purpose, intelligence, and creativity in its operations. Terms such as Brahman, Tao, The Godhead, Spirit, The Absolute, the divine Ground, Psyche, and World Soul are but linguistic place-markers and, for our purposes, will be considered interchangeable. My intent in using these terms is not to contrast or compare their respective parent philosophies, but merely to call attention to the almost universal agreement as to the existence and essential nature of Universal Consciousness.

HUMAN CONSCIOUSNESS

From the perennial perspective, the easiest and simplest way to define human consciousness is to say that it is a subsystem of Universal Consciousness. As such, it would evidence the same properties as the source from which it is derived, though in a more limited sense. Chief among these properties is **awareness**, which constitutes a quality of human consciousness having to do with the capacity to direct one's attention, thoughts, and behavior—that is, *to choose*. In astrology, this is the primary function of the Sun. However, human consciousness also includes those aspects of the psyche that are generally termed unconscious (outside of awareness). Despite being unconscious, however, these dimensions evidence the same higher mental properties as conscious awareness; that is, the capacity to reason, make plans, and solve problems (Sampson & Weiss, 1986). An assumption here is that human consciousness evolves by attaining progressively greater degrees of awareness over time until, ultimately, it realizes its oneness with Universal Consciousness. In eastern traditions, it is presumed that this process unfolds slowly over a series of lifetimes.

Following the properties and attributes of Universal Consciousness, human consciousness is **wholistic** in that it is more than the sum of its parts no matter how these parts may be defined, whether as id, ego, and superego, or as archetypes, cognitive structures, basic needs, or simple neurons. Human consciousness could also be thought of as **hierarchically structured**, evidencing both spiritual (soul), mental (mind), biological (body), and physical (sub-cellular) attributes. Consciousness itself **transcends** its various manifestations on mental, biological, and physical levels, while also being **immanent** in the processes of all levels. The property of immanence is further related to the notion of **holographic organization**, an attribute of mind and brain put forth by Karl Pribram (1978). This principle states that the whole of consciousness is implicate in each and every part of the body-brain. In other words, the hermetic dictum "as above, so below" (the whole is in the part) applies to the human level, too. This is the basis for alleged mind-body interaction, psychosomatic illness, psychoneuroimmunology, and the fact that the entire genome is encoded in each and every cell of the body. In other words, the psyche as a whole is immanent and thus influential throughout every level and part of the body.

Human consciousness evidences mental properties, or *mind*. The human mind, both in its conscious and unconscious aspects, is purposive, or intentional, in that it can be described as serving some purpose—specifically, the integration of psychological processes into a more unified whole. Maslow (1968) termed this purposive tendency "the growth motive" or the universal human tendency toward self-actualization. **Intelligence** is another property of the human mind, as evidenced by the ability of human beings to learn from experience. Finally, human consciousness is **creative** in that it has the capacity to construct experiences and artifacts that mirror the psychic structure of their creator.

Our description of Universal Consciousness as an evolutionary process of organized relations applies equally well to human consciousness, or psyche. The psyche is an evolving process engaged in the organizing of various relations—whether between archetypes, cognitive structures, neurons, or subatomic particles—into increasingly complex wholes. This spontaneous ordering process is hierarchically structured, holographically organized, transcends and is immanent within bodily processes, and evidences intrinsic purpose, intelligence, and creativity in its operations.

There are a number of terms that I will be using interchangeably in reference to human consciousness. In later chapters the origins of these terms will be more fully explicated. Suffice to say here that *atman*, psyche, and *Self* are more or less synonymous. These terms will be appropriately differentiated from cognitive structure, ego, self, self-system, self-concept, and conscious awareness, all of which have their own meanings and are not synonymous with human consciousness *per se*.

OPERATIONS OF CONSCIOUSNESS

Although Freud was the first to abandon explaining behavior through neuro-physiological principles in favor of a pure psychology, his theories were directly derived from the German physiological mechanism that prevailed in the latter half of the 19th century. Psychodynamics was a simple scheme of cause and effect. The psyche was a conductor of energy, and energy itself was produced by an external, material cause; that is, an event stimulus. Health was attained by a relatively free flow of this energy. Sickness, conversely, resulted when energy was excessively blocked. His formula was simple mechanism: blocked instinctual urge equals psychic complex equals neurosis. The cure consisted, theoretically, of merely reversing the process: observe the neurotic symptom (blocked energy), remove the repression, and assist the individual to a more satisfactory expression of instinctual urges.

Freud's psychology held that consciousness, or ego, was largely the product of the never-ending struggle between instinctual drives (id) and the demands of society (super-ego). Conflict is mediated and resolved by the ego. In the process, energy is released and health is restored. As Freud put it, "where id was, there ego shall be."

Astrology can utilize Freud's model, albeit with slight modification. The psyche conducts energy between and among its various energy centers—symbolized by planets—much as Freud envisioned. Consciousness is differentiated into various dimensions, i.e., two polarities, four elements, three modalities, and twelve signs, all of which must find a way of blending and harmonizing. Yet, because consciousness extends beyond the boundaries of the individual, it interacts with external systems of consciousness—people and situations—in a way that magnetizes and draws to itself that which it needs for its further evolution.

If one kind of energy/consciousness is blocked or out of balance within the psyche, it tends to create a corresponding blockage with an external system. For example, if Mars is repressed, a woman may attract aggressive men who continually violate her rights until she learns to assert herself. Unlike conventional psychodynamic models, there is not a linear, cause-effect relationship between outer stimulus and inner response. Rather, the relationship is synchronistic, or circular; psyche is both the cause and effect of it's own operations.

The psyche, in effect, is a living system in continuous interaction with its environment. The concept of system derives from the Greek *systema*, meaning "a composite thing". A system can be most generally defined as the ordered composition of elements into a unified whole—or, even more precisely, as a set of units with relationships between them. In effect, a system is any complex of components in mutual interaction. Systems are purposive, hierarchically structured, self-regulating and self-transforming wholes not reducible to the mechanical interactions of their component parts.

For our purposes, the astrological chart is a system that details the functioning of the human body-mind in relation to its environment. It should always be kept in mind, however, that the environment itself is a part of the self-system. In systems theory, this is referred to as *organizational closure*, meaning that the structure of the psyche necessarily includes its relations with the environment. This implies that behavior is both a cause of and a response to environmental conditions.

Conventional psychodynamics implies that psychological wounding occurs randomly and bears no relevance to the individual except as an externally originating cause. In astrology, however, apparent random events, such as the conditions of childhood, are directly traceable to an innate, pre-inherited psychic disposition that is mirrored by external conditions from the first breath. Astrology implies that character is fate—or, put in the reverse, fate is soul spread out in time. The model suggests that every individual is fated to experience certain conditions as a consequence of karmic factors that were generated in past lives. These conditions are purposeful in that they provide the necessary stimulus for further evolution.

Regardless of how a problem's origins are conceptualized, as random or karmic, Freud's model of healing still has relevance for astrology. Once it is determined that a planetary process is dysfunctional—blocked or excessive in some way—the cure consists of bringing that function into proper balance with the rest of the psyche so that consciousness can flow freely. This may require greater awareness of exactly how and why a particular function is blocked.

For example, why does the person fear intimacy (Venus) and how is this fear affecting his thoughts, feelings, and behavior? If there was a significant childhood trauma that involved the Venus function, this would likely show up in the chart. Venus might be in the 12th house squaring Pluto, which would suggest a repression of the Venus function with corresponding negative memories. Awareness, catharsis, and support can bring about healing, thus enabling the individual to express his Venus urges in a more satisfactory way. Just as in Freud's model, consciousness is expanded through facilitating greater awareness and acceptance of previously blocked portions of the psyche.

CATHEXIS AND VALUE

Freud postulated two distinct kinds of energy: *sexual energy (libido)* and *aggressive energy*. These were related to the two fundamental drives—sex and aggression—that originated in the id. Psychic energy was depicted as something spread over the memory traces of ideas, somewhat as an electric charge is spread over the surface of a body. This investment of an idea or mental representation with psychic energy is termed a **cathexis;** an idea or image is *cathected* or "charged" with psychic energy. Essentially, cathexis means interest, attention, or emotional investment. The term implies that psychic energy is capable of increase, diminution, and discharge. As a metaphorical quantitative conception, it does not refer to any actual measurable force; rather, it represents the relative intensity of psychological activities.

In Jung's theory of analytical psychology, the concept of **value** is roughly analogous to Freud's concept of *cathexis*. Value refers to the amount of psychic energy invested in a particular element of personality. As a measure of intensity, it relates to how much power a particular idea or feeling may have as a motivating force in the psyche. Value can be thought of in terms of degree of cathexis, or the extent to which a force with potential to instigate behavior is "invested" with available psychic energy. The investment of energy in an action or relationship that will gratify an instinct is called an instinctual *object-choice* or *object-cathexis*. To the extent that psychic energy is invested, that object is valued. A person, for example, might be intensely motivated to achieve a promotion. The object of the goal—promotion—is strongly valued and thus highly cathected.

Again, we can see parallels to this in astrology. Rather than two primary drives, however, astrology postulates twelve drives (signs). Depending upon how the planets are arranged in the birthchart, consciousness tends to be spread throughout the system in a manner that is reflected, in part, by (1) which signs are tenanted by planets, and (2) by the angles between the planets themselves.

Soft aspects between planets connote a relatively smooth, unblocked flow of psychic energy, whereas hard aspects suggest where psychic energy may be restricted and condensed. Consider, for example, a T-square between Saturn, Mars, and Jupiter with Saturn as the focal planet in the 8th house. As the focal planet of a T-Square, we could say that Saturn is "cathected" to a significant degree; that is, charged with psychic energy. Since Saturn symbolizes the need for achievement, such a person might feel compelled to achieve distinction within an 8th house field of endeavor (sexuality).

Mars and Jupiter will contribute to the final outcome, each in its own way. Perhaps he might feel ambitious (Saturn) in pioneering (Mars) a new theory (Jupiter) about sexuality (8th house). A central tenet of his theory could be that psychological health is impaired by the inevitable conflict between aggressive impulses (Mars) and the civilizing restraints of society (Saturn).

This, of course, was precisely the conflict that Freud had to negotiate, for this T-Square dominated his natal chart (see Figure 1).

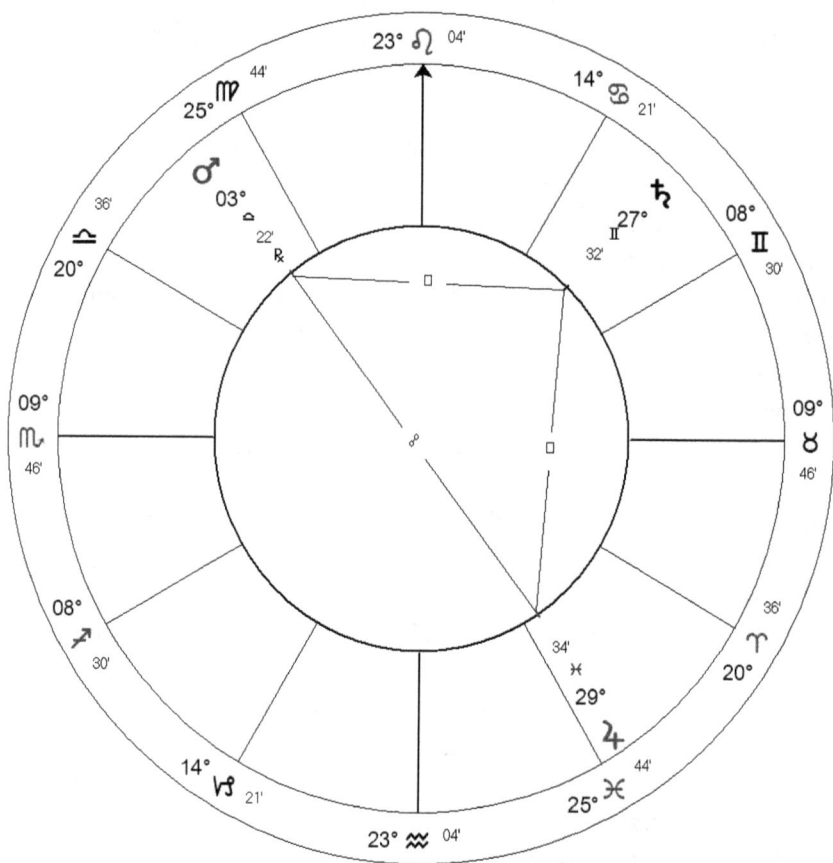

Figure 1: Freud's T-Square

In astrology each sign represents a specific drive and a distinct type of energy, which we experience as a feeling. Thus, drive, energy, and affect (feeling) are three faces of the same thing. Psychic energy is distributed by planetary sign placements the way water falls into separate cubes in an ice tray. In natal astrology, however, certain signs will be filled (cathected) with psychic energy more than others. As motives, signs are cathected to the extent that planets tenant them. The more planets in a sign, the greater the cathexis or value of that motive.

Aspects generate ideas. These ideas, or beliefs, are cathected by the nature of the energy associated with the signs and planets that comprise them. Freud, for example, experienced a mixture of Saturn, Mars, and Jupiterian energies all impinging upon his 8th house. With Saturn in Gemini, he felt driven to direct his curiosity (Gemini) toward a study of sexual dysfunction. In fact, he couldn't stop thinking and writing about sex (8th house) for his entire life.

That he wanted to be successful in this area was symbolized by Saturn in Gemini in the 8th house. The specific nature of his success was qualified by the theories (Jupiter) that he founded (Mars). Moreover, these theories were *about* the conflict symbolized by his T-Square. In short, his T-square symbolizes an emotionally charged idea and activity that synthesizes the various components involved.

Areas of a chart that are highly emphasized, either by sign, house, or aspect, are said to be *hypercathected*. A planet receiving many aspects can be said to be hypercathected because its behavior and achievements are going to be overdetermined by the planets that aspect it. Overdetermined means that more than one factor contributes to a phenomenon.

For example, Freud's Saturn in Gemini in the 8th was hypercathected in that it's ultimate expression—masterful knowledge of sex—was overdetermined due to the fact that it was the focal planet of a T-Square involving Mars and Jupiter. In other words, Freud's Saturnian achievements involved the participation of Mars and Jupiter and the particular nature of their interaction with Saturn.

Signs and houses can be hypercathected, too. Consider, for example, a stellium wherein one sign or house is occupied by several planets. If a person has a stellium in Scorpio in the 5th house, then several different planetary functions contribute to the development of a single common interest, such as sex (Scorpio) in a context of creative self-expression (5th house). Thus, an activity such as "sexual performance" takes on an overdetermined psychological organization that integrates the various functions involved. Larry Flynt, the founder of Hustler magazine, has Sun, Venus, and Mars all conjunct in Scorpio in the 5th house—an apt signature for his reputation as a purveyor of pornographic literature and strip shows.

DISPLACEMENT AND SUBLIMATION

Psychoanalytic theory postulates that psychic energy can be transformed, but not destroyed. If the energy connected to one object is removed, it will reappear elsewhere. When an external or internal barrier blocks the object choice of a drive, a new cathexis is formed. If that cathexis is blocked, the energy will shift to a new object, until eventually an outlet is found to release the pent-up tension. The substitution of one object for another is called

displacement. While the source and aim of the drive remain constant, the object may vary. For example, the source of a behavior may be a need for perfection (Capricorn), and the aim of the drive a feeling of a success—the target state. These remain invariant; yet, the object of the drive may take any number for forms. If a man strives for a promotion at work, yet is continually passed over, he may displace the energy into something else, such as becoming a triathelete.

Jung's concept of **equivalence** is similar to displacement. The principle of equivalence is borrowed from the first law of thermodynamics, or the conservation of energy. It states that if the amount of energy consigned to a given psychic element decreases or disappears, that amount of energy will reappear in another psychic element. Psychic energy cannot be lost; it is simply transferred from one interest to another.

A person with Saturn conjunct Mars in Scorpio in the 2nd, for example, might invest a considerable amount of energy acquiring and restoring antique cars. At some point, however, his interests might shift to "strategies of medieval warfare" and he sets about collecting weaponry and armor that was typical of that period. The interest he shows in this latter pursuit is equivalent to his passion for restoring antique cars.

Jung pointed out that in transferring energy from one structure to another, some characteristics of the first structure are transferred to the second structure. Thus, while the two hobbies may seem completely unrelated, the astute astrologer will recognize that both interests are a reflection of energies associated with Mars conjunct Saturn in Scorpio in the 2nd house. Saturn is associated with things that are old and traditional, such as antiques or relics from another historical period (old cars or suits of armor). Mars relates to instruments of aggression (weaponry), but also to objects that enable us *to move*—like cars (which can be instruments of aggression, too).

As a qualifier of Saturnian and Martian energies, Scorpio shows both *how* these planets will express themselves and *what* will be the object of their intentions. Regeneration is a Scorpionic activity, as in restoring antique cars back to their original Saturnian perfection. However, Scorpio can also be the object of Mars and Saturn's interest, as in "strategies of medieval warfare." War, of course, is Martian territory and medieval is Saturnian (old/traditional), while "strategies" relates to Scorpio's province of calculated moves designed to overpower and destroy an enemy. Thus interest in old (Saturn) warfare (Mars) strategies (Scorpio) represents an amalgamation of the archetypal principles involved. The 2nd house simply refers to resources or that which is secured. Whether our hypothetical hobbyist is collecting antique cars or medieval weaponry, both are possessions that contribute to his storehouse of wealth.

Jung asserts that as a general rule, psychic energy can be transferred from one structure to another only on the basis of equivalence. This means if a person has an intense attachment to a person, object, or activity, it can only be replaced by something of an equally intense value. Our two examples of Mars conjunct Saturn illustrate how loss of interest in one thing means a gain of interest in something else. Because astrology is a metaphorical language, it can readily show how one pursuit is analogous to another. Also, it shows how two or more activities may have similar "value" in a Jungian sense. How a person relates sexually can be a metaphor for how that person deals with joint finances, both of which relate to the 8th house. If Jupiter is in the 8th, the person may become overextended sexually (excessive desires leading to promiscuity) and/or financially (foolish investments due to overoptimistic forecasts). One activity is analogous to another.

In psychoanalytic theory, displacement generally refers to a defensive maneuver wherein the interest or intensity (value/cathexis) attached to one idea is shifted to another idea that is associatively related but more acceptable to the ego. The man who was passed over for promotion may want to kill his boss, but he settles for killing the competition (as a triathlete). While aggressive feelings toward authority figures can be channeled into a competitive sport, it can work the other way, too. If a person fails in a competition, he may displace his frustration by attacking someone he holds responsible. For example, a person might be upset with himself for not making the grade as a Special Forces soldier. Rather than seek an appropriate outlet for his frustration, he may displace his anger through an act of terrorism against the federal government. This was the case with Timothy McVeigh, who blew up a Federal Building in Oklahoma City after failing in his efforts to become a Green Beret.

Astrologically, displacement works in a similar manner. A given planetary aspect can manifest in a diverse number of ways and still be true to itself. A man with an unintegrated Mars-Neptune opposition might be unconscious of his own capacity for violence and, instead, identify with victims of violent crimes. McVeigh, who had this aspect, reportedly identified with Branch Davidian cult members who were tragically burned alive when federal agents attacked their building in Waco, Texas. This same aspect, however, quickly devolved into being the victimizer when McVeigh retaliated against the government. In both instances, the outcome can be interpreted as an expression of an unintegrated Mars-Neptune opposition. Energy is displaced from one form, his failure as a Green Beret and subsequent identification with the victims of Waco, to another form—victimizing innocent people when he blew up the federal building in Oklahoma City. In other words, his identification with Branch Davidian cult members provided him with a convenient rationale for venting displaced rage against the government. Presumably, it was more acceptable to McVeigh's ego to be the perpetrator than the victim.

Actually, McVeigh's case is a good example of how one can identify with either side of an aspect. If he identifies with Neptune, he experiences himself as the victim of Mars aggression. If he identifies with Mars, he experiences himself as a warrior battling an elusive and deceptive enemy. To the extent that the opposition is not integrated, he remains unaware of the contradictory beliefs and behaviors that characterize his actions.

At higher levels of integration, aspects tend to become more stable and balanced. A displacement that produces a higher cultural achievement is called **sublimation**. In such instances, psychic energy is displaced from more primitive, instinctive, and less differentiated processes to more enlightened, mindful, and differentiated ones. For example, a Mars-Neptune opposition could be expressed as a willingness to fight for those unable to fight for themselves; compassion (Neptune) is combined with activism (Mars). Human rights advocate, Eleanor Roosevelt, exemplified how this aspect can be elevated to a higher level of functionality. She once said, "Justice cannot be for one side alone, but must be for both."

Displacement suggests that the psyche is characterized by fixed rules and flexible strategies. What is fixed is the arrangement of zodiacal signs and the drives they symbolize. Also fixed is the arrangement of planets that constitute the structure of a horoscope. However, a person's strategies for meeting needs will vary depending upon (1) the availability of objects (people, opportunities) within the environment, and (2) the native's level of psychological maturity and integration.

The concept of displacement underscores that the archetypal energy of a planetary configuration can transform itself into a wide variety of expressions over the course of a lifetime. Whereas displacement refers to maneuvers to find more acceptable outlets for planetary energies, sublimation implies that a planetary configuration has the potential to evolve toward higher levels of functionality over time. Accordingly, the expression of an aspect will vary along a continuum of integration, with less stable, dysfunctional forms at one end, and more stable, balanced forms at the other.

DIFFERENTIATION AND COUNTERCATHEXIS

Some analysts postulate a quantum of neutral energy available to the psyche from birth. In the beginning of life, psychic energy and psychic structure are thought to be relatively undifferentiated. The various structures of the psyche—id, ego, and superego—are still undeveloped and so the infant operates on pure impulse. Accumulation of psychic energy provides a directional force striving for discharge, thus impelling or driving behavior. This tension-reduction model is central to a psychoanalytic theory of motivation. In less mature states, wherein the id dominates, energy is said to be mobile (unbound), meaning it tends to be expressed impulsively. In more differentiated, mature states, the cathected energy is bound, i.e., restrained from immediate discharge. In other words, a certain amount of psychic energy has to be expended to restrain the person from acting impulsively and irrationally. These restraining forces are known as *anticathexes* in contradistinction to the driving forces or *cathexes*.

Likewise in astrology, consciousness (psychic energy) is always expressing itself through the agency of the planets. The archetypal energy of each planet is relatively undifferentiated at birth; i.e., the infant has little capacity for distinguishing between one type of impulse and another. His Mars impels him one moment to engage in an adventurous crawl across the room, but before he gets there his Moon screams out for his mother.

At earlier stages of life, planetary processes operate impulsively like the id in Freudian psychology. In fact, each planet exhibits id-like properties to the extent that it remains undifferentiated, unconscious, and presses for immediate discharge. Even Saturn may operate impulsively, as when a child's early manifestations of conscience are relentlessly persecutory. If a three-year-old perceives himself as bad for disobeying a rule, he may experience himself as "all bad," as if he has no redeeming qualities whatsoever, never did have them, and never will have them. This type of all or nothing conscience is extreme precisely because it is unregulated. To differentiate a function means to bring it into awareness so that it can be regulated on a conscious level by the Sun. Each planet accumulates a charge of psychic energy until it becomes strong enough to make its will known to solar awareness, which then must decide whether and how to express that impulse. Astrology, in other words, can be described in terms of a tension-reduction model. Each planet represents a motivational drive and presses for discharge.

As stated, at earlier stages of life there is less ability to regulate the energy of the planets. If Venus is triggered (cathected), a young girl may have little awareness of how to socialize in a skilled manner. She might feel off balance and ill at ease when encountering new people. Her Venus energy is relatively mobile (unbound), meaning she socializes impulsively and awkwardly. As she matures, however, and her Venus function becomes increasingly differentiated, her ability to socialize is more skillfully regulated.

Psychoanalytic theory postulates that the ego, as the executive of the personality, is gradually able to gain control over the instinctual energy of the id, suppressing it when necessary, and directing it towards socially acceptable outlets. Over time, the child also internalizes the moral sanctions and prohibitions of its parents and thus develops a superego. The work performed by the superego is usually in direct opposition to the impulses of the id. Development of a conscience represents society's attempt to control and even inhibit expression of the sexual and aggressive drives.

Once the ego and superego are differentiated from the id, a complicated interplay of driving and restraining forces becomes possible. The id demands immediate gratification of whatever has been cathected, but the superego imposes moral restraints, a *countercathexis*, that inhibits impulsive behavior. Situated between the two like a referee in a prizefight, the ego must find a way to balance and harmonize these conflicting forces. If the id predominates, the person will tend to be impulsive and primitive in character. Conversely, if the superego is too strong, the personality becomes rigid, up tight, and dominated by moralistic considerations. The ego's job is to both forward and frustrate the aims of the instincts, while also keeping one's conscience from becoming too severe. While the first several decades of life are generally characterized by sudden and unpredictable shifts of energy between these three systems, eventually the distribution of energy in the psyche becomes more or less stabilized—a hallmark of adulthood.

In summary, psychodynamics consist of the interplay of the driving forces, cathexes, and the restraining forces, anticathexes. These two sets of forces are at the heart of all intrapsychic conflict. All tensions with the self, whether short-lived or prolonged, are due to the counteraction of a driving force by a restraining force. In subsequent sections, we will explore how these ideas can be applied to our astrological model of the psyche.

THE SUN AS CONSCIOUS WILL

Astrologically speaking, we can think of the Sun as performing some of the same functions as the ego in psychoanalytic theory. As the "decider subsystem" of the psyche (conscious awareness and will), the Sun is responsible for expressing or suppressing the various functions that the planets symbolize. In this respect, the Sun's task is more complicated than that of the ego, for the Sun has to regulate the expression of every planet, not just a hypothetical id and superego. Again, each planet has id-like qualities to the extent that it functions unconsciously, in which case it will operate in a more primitive, impulsive manner.[4]

It doesn't matter whether the Sun actually aspects a planet. That planet is still subject to solar influence. For example, a Jupiterian impulse to lecture a friend on the evils of abortion may be suppressed if the native judges that his opinion is likely to damage the friendship. The Sun has to decide, "should I or shouldn't I express my opinion (Jupiter)?" Although the Sun cannot stop Jupiter from formulating opinions (for that is the nature of Jupiter), it can decide whether *to express* those opinions. Likewise, the Sun can decide whether to express other planetary impulses as well. Like feudal lords in medieval Europe, each planet will seek to gain the King's favor. It is the King (Sun), however, that ultimately must decide who shall be recognized and to what extent.

Normally we think of the Sun as representing self-expression rather than self-suppression. As a yang planet, the Sun is naturally expressive and outgoing. How can we assume, therefore, that it also exerts a suppressive function? The answer lies in a proper understanding of *will* or intentionality. As the symbol of will, the Sun's job is to choose what to express. By definition, this also involves choosing what not to express. Jung (1971) writes, "consciousness, because of its directed function, exercises an inhibition (which Freud calls censorship) on all incompatible material, with the result that it sinks into the unconscious" (p. 274). Here, what Jung refers to as "consciousness" is that agency of the mind which is synonymous with conscious awareness and that exhibits a capacity to direct attention toward or away from a given phenomena. This is precisely what astrologers mean by the Sun, which symbolizes conscious awareness and conscious will.

Thus we can say that if a particular impulse is deemed unworthy of expression, the Sun suppresses it (does not attend to it). "The quality of directedness," says Jung, "makes for the inhibition or exclusion of all those psychic elements which appear to be, or really are, incompatible with it,

---

[4] While every planet may have id-like qualities to the extent that it remains unconscious and undifferentiated, Freud's depiction of the id as a primitive, seething cauldron of instinctual drives pressing for immediate discharge probably has more in common with Mars than any other concept. However, it is important not to reify the id, for it, again, is merely a heuristic concept. Moreover, it is a term largely in disuse among contemporary psychoanalytic theorists. In addition, Mars has additional meanings that do not relate to the id. This should remind us that there are no absolute correlations between psychoanalytic and astrological concepts of the psyche.

i.e., likely to bias the intended direction to suit their purpose and so lead to an undesired goal" (p. 275). If a person directs herself to lose weight, she will tend to inhibit an impulse to eat foods that contain a high percentage of fats because desire for those foods is incompatible with the direction the woman has chosen.

In other words, psychic material (an impulse, thought, feeling, desire, or memory) is deemed "incompatible" by an act of judgment based on the path that is chosen and desired. A person does this constantly throughout the day, directing attention toward that which is intended—foods leading to weight loss—and away from what is incompatible with that intention—foods leading to weight gain. Problems arise when particular kinds of normal impulses are chronically suppressed, a point we will return to in Chapter 5 when we take up the subject of shadows and complexes.

In short, self-expression implies that the Sun has directed attention toward something—that is, identifying with it and thus permitted its expression. Conversely, suppression means the Sun has directed attention away from something; the person disidentifies with that function and so blocks its expression.

The Sun not only determines what we express or suppress, it even determines what we choose to perceive. We know from studies in hypnosis that a subject can be induced to not see or experience certain things that are plain to everyone else. For example, if a woman's husband is having an affair and leaving copious clues all about, she may unconsciously choose to not see what is obvious to all her friends.

The Sun is also capable of suppressing an internal reality, and even changing it. When I was a young man living in Los Angeles, I remember seeing the famous hypnotherapist, Jack Schwartz, push a knitting needle through his arm without feeling any pain and without a drop of blood! Schwartz said he simply decided not to recognize the pain or the damage that the knitting needle could cause. Because he decided not to give it any reality, it had none for him. I submit this is an act of will. Specifically, it can be a decision to not perceive, recognize, or allow a natural instinct to express itself.

We can assume, at the very least, that Schwartz's sensual feeling (Venus) was shut off and his instinct for preservation (Mars) was suppressed. What was allowed to express itself was his willingness to be penetrated and violated (Pluto). The point is that Schwartz's Sun was involved in decisions to suppress and ignore certain aspects of his being because they were antithetical to what he intended to accomplish: being penetrated without fear, pain, or physical damage. This was his chosen reality and he did whatever was necessary to make it happen. In this regard, the Sun, like the ego, can exert a countercathexis to inhibit the expression of any contradictory or unwanted impulses.

Although ultimately the Sun must regulate the functioning of every planet, we can speculate that solar aspects are going to be especially pivotal to the identity of the native. The Sun will either embrace or resist those planetary energies. For example, if the Sun is square Uranus, the person may initially resist liberal, progressive views, forming an identity that struggles against Uranian impulses toward change and reform. Or, he may identify with progressive ideals and struggle against the egocentricity that is characteristic of the Sun. Either way, Uranus will be central to the formation of the native's identity and self-esteem. Solar aspects merely underscore that the nature of the aspected planets will have a greater bearing upon what the native ultimately expresses or suppresses. Again, however, a planet is subject to solar regulation regardless of whether that planet is aspected by the Sun.

The degree to which a planet functions in a balanced, integrated way is determined by how conscious the person is of that impulse. If a planetary impulse is repudiated, it is more likely to underfunction or overfunction, i.e., manifest in an unbalanced, dysfunctional manner. One cannot regulate the expression of something that operates outside of awareness. That is why the function of conscious will is so critical to the personality. Just as the astronomical Sun is the center of the solar system, so the Sun is the center of conscious awareness.

As the various subsystems of the psyche become increasingly differentiated, and as the Sun gains awareness of these planetary functions, the personality as a whole grows more balanced, unified, and synchronized. Psychic energy is more evenly distributed so that the parts of the psyche work together rather than separately.

DRIVING AND RESTRAINING FORCES IN ASTROLOGY

Recall that in psychoanalytic theory the ego has to find a balance between the id and the superego so that the personality is neither too impulsive nor too rigid. This is a relatively simple conception of what happens in astrology. Again, the difference is that the Sun must find a balance between a multiplicity of competing drives as symbolized by zodiacal signs and their planetary representatives.

Although the Sun is responsible for regulating the expression of each planet, some planets exert their own regulatory functions. Yin planets like Saturn exert a restraining, counterbalance to expressive, yang planets. Accordingly, there is a relative balance in the psyche between expressive yang forces (cathexes) and suppressive yin forces (anticathexes). To the extent that the psyche differentiates and actualizes its various potentials, intrapsychic conflict is reduced.

The primary division in astrology is between yin and yang, as reflected in the alternating sequence of signs—masculine and feminine. Also, the nature of the planets that rule them, the houses that correspond to them, and the corollary aspects between planets all can be understood in the framework of yin or yang polarity. We have six yang signs—Aries, Gemini, Leo, Libra, Sagittarius, and Aquarius—alternating with six yin signs—Taurus, Cancer, Virgo, Scorpio, Capricorn, and Pisces. The houses follow the same sequence as the signs, as do the angles that constitute the planetary aspects. Yang aspects are the conjunction (Aries), the opening sextile (Gemini), opening trine (Leo), opposition (Libra), closing trine (Sagittarius), and closing sextile (Aquarius). Yin aspects are the opening semi-sextile (Taurus), opening square (Cancer), opening quincunx (Virgo), closing quincunx (Scorpio), closing square (Capricorn), and closing semi-sextile (Pisces). There are four yang planets—Sun, Mars, Jupiter, and Uranus—and four yin planets—Moon, Saturn, Neptune, and Pluto. Mercury and Venus are bi-polar in that each rules a yin sign and a yang sign; that is, Mercury rules Gemini and Virgo, and Venus rules Taurus and Libra.

Yang energies are associated with extroversion, expressing themselves outwardly through physical and mental pursuits. In this regard, they are similar to what Freud would call the driving forces of the psyche. Conversely, yin signs are introverted, being reflective, suppressive, and oriented toward the inner world of feelings and sensations. They correspond to Freud's restraining forces.

Signs adjacent one another have a compensatory relationship similar to Jung's description of the compensatory relationship between conscious and unconscious. In effect, each sign is the unconscious of the sign that succeeds it; Pisces is the unconscious of Aries, which is the unconscious of Taurus, which is the unconscious of Gemini, and so on. Thus for every yang impulse there is a compensatory yin impulse to ground and regulate it.

Metaphorically, this is depicted in zodiacal images of archetypes that reflect the alternating rhythm of yang and yin. First there is the adventurous Aries pioneer who seeks new experience in uncharted territory. Aries will fight, if necessary, for the right *to be* and *to go*. After new territories are conquered, Taurean settlers move in to farm and develop the land. Taurus checks the outward expansion of Aries, grounding it in something permanent. When the lands are settled and crops planted, people naturally turn to education and communication—Gemini—as psychic energy moves outward again.

We can express this mythologically because it reflects what is happening psychologically. Yang energies tend to be spontaneous, active, and outgoing. Yin factors, on the other hand, constitute a controlling, restraining function and serve as a counterforce to yang energies. Because yin forces are inhibiting, they keep the psyche from overextending and flying too high or (worse) flying apart. Mythologically, the myth of Icarus captures this fundamental psychic reality.

> Icarus, the son of Daedulus, must flee with his father from King Minos on the island of Crete. Daedulus makes wings for himself and his son out of feathers and wax. Father and son intend to escape by flying away. Daedulus warns Icarus not to fly too high or the Sun will melt the wax, but if he skims too low the feathers will get wet in the sea. In other words, the advised course is the middle way. But Icarus ignores the advice of his father and out of the sheer joy of flight flies too high, so that the Sun melts the wax in his wings, and he falls headlong to the sea and drowns.

The story of Icarus seems to symbolize how uninhibited flight into the realm of air and fire (yang) leads to disastrous results. In seeking to escape the limits of the earth-water realm, Icarus flies too high and pays for it with his life; too much air (height) and fire (heat) prove his undoing. For his lack of restraint, yin energies must forcibly draw him back to the realm of earth and water. Likewise, each person must seek to find the middle way between yang and yin, neither flying too high nor too low. Imbalance will surely lead to disaster—which, quite appropriately, means "against the stars."

The story can also be interpreted in terms of the difference between youth and maturity. Although Icarus perishes in the sea, his father arrives safely on similar wings. Recall that psychoanalytic theory holds that the first few decades of life are characterized by instabilities between the competing systems of id, ego, and superego; the unconscious (id) predominates. However, as adulthood is reached, psychic energy gradually becomes more evenly distributed as the ego gains control over id and superego.

Likewise, in astrology each sign of the zodiac constitutes a developmental stage during which time the psyche is able to potentiate a new function. In the first two years, infants develop a capacity for autonomy and assertion (Aries). From two to five years the capacity for self and object constancy is realized (Taurus). The Gemini period from five to nine years represents a phase of unparalleled learning and cognitive development. As the psyche unfolds and its various sign-systems become differentiated from one another, psychic energy becomes increasingly stable and intrapsychic conflicts are more easily contained. Drives are gradually brought under control of the solar will, and the personality as a whole is characterized by a synchrony of functioning not possible in earlier years. Whereas Icarus symbolizes an immature solar will, incapable of regulating the impulses, Daedulus signifies the realization of a mature Sun that is able to express and suppress in accordance with the dictates of reality.

What I am saying here is that yang signs, planets, and angles are analogous to the driving, expressive forces of the psyche, whereas yin signs, planets, and angles signify restraining, suppressive forces. The exception is the Sun, which signifies a yang function yet can also be inhibitory. This may seem contradictory until one realizes that the Sun has responsibility to monitor and regulate the functioning of all the planets, both yin and yang.

While yin energies are generally inhibitory, they do have their own form of expression. Taurus expresses itself by holding on, Cancer by reflecting, Virgo by analyzing, Scorpio by penetrating, Capricorn by controlling, and Pisces by passively surrendering. In each case, the Sun can exert some degree of influence over these processes. For example, the Sun may allow Pluto to express an erotic impulse. Although Pluto is a yin planet, it has a form of expression that the Sun can allow, or disallow. No one gives in to every sexual impulse. The Sun must decide on the basis of assessing the social impact of the erotic impulse. Will it evoke approval or disapproval? A person may decide not to come on sexually to his best friend's wife because he determines that such advances would be inappropriate and socially damaging. Thus the Sun directs attention away from his sexual fantasy—suppressing it, as it were. Accordingly, the Sun's job is to be aware of each and every part of the psyche, both yin functions and yang functions, and strive to bring about a balanced, harmonious expression of opposing forces.

To the extent that the Sun can identify with every planetary function, the person attains wholeness. This is made easier, of course, by a sufficient integration of each planetary impulse. Planets not only occupy various signs and houses, they also have relations with each other. The relative distribution of yang and yin energies in the horoscope reflects the balance of cathexes and anticathexes.

Imagine a yang planet like Mars in the sign of Cancer in the 12th house conjunct Pluto and squaring Saturn. Every astrological factor involved with this Mars is yin. Accordingly, the anticathecting, restraining forces predominate over the Martian drive. We can anticipate, therefore, that the impulse for self-assertion may be overmodulated, i.e., rigidly controlled and repressed. If this is the case, then the Sun will have a difficult time regulating the expression of Mars because it is relatively inaccessible to conscious awareness. This is equivalent to the King not having access to his minister of war because he has been bound, gagged and imprisoned in the dungeon (12th house); thus if a situation arises that calls for aggressive action, the King will be at a loss. Repression of the Mars function breaks the unity of the psyche/kingdom. We will return to this topic in chapter five when we discuss how psychic energy can become frozen (imprisoned) as a consequence of emotional trauma.

ENTROPY

Just as Jung's principle of equivalence is borrowed from the first law of thermodynamics—the conservation of energy—so his principle of entropy is borrowed from the second law. It states, in effect, that the distribution of energy in the psyche is always moving in the direction of equilibrium or balance.

For example, if a person has a T-Square, the psyche will naturally strive for a balance of energy between the three planets. Recall Freud's chart in which Saturn squares both Jupiter and Mars. According to the principle of entropy, the psyche would strive to attain perfect balance between these three forces. Since Freud's Mars is inhibited by Saturn and contradicted by Jupiter, he might have felt both morally "imperiled" (Jupiter) and fearful of punishment (Saturn) whenever he experienced an aggressive impulse. In this case, his Saturnian and Jupiterian instincts would be strong at the expense of his Mars, which would be weak. Of course, the situation could be the reverse as well; Freud's Mars could be strong, and his Jupiter and Saturn comparatively weak. At different times and in different situations, Freud would have been more or less identified with any of these planetary functions.

Eventually, however, Freud might have succeeded in bringing these psychic elements into balance. His Mars might be disciplined and directed toward long-term goals by Saturn, which, in turn, could be energized by Mars. Jupiter would amplify Saturn's ambitions, while Saturn would organize Jupiter's speculations into a solid, defensible theory grounded in empirical research. Mars would remind Jupiter that the personal, primitive side of the psyche has its own truth, and Jupiter would inspire Mars to assert for what is ultimately right. To the extent that these energies are balanced, conflict is minimized and each planet enhances the functioning of the other.

As planets combine their forces to produce stable, integrated wholes, the hierarchical structuring of the psyche in enhanced. So long as Mars, Jupiter, and Saturn operate separate from one another, they function as quasi-independent systems. When they become integrated, however, then a higher-level system emerges from a synthesis of the three parts. Each planet is incorporated as a sub-system of the new whole. As a higher-level system, a Mars-Jupiter-Saturn T-Square will evidence certain emergent traits and behaviors that do not exist at the level of either planet individually.

Although perfect balance is never achieved in any permanent sense, this hierarchical restructuring is the ideal toward which the psyche naturally strives. The ideal state in which the total energy is evenly distributed throughout the various fully developed systems is the Self, which is realized only when there is a more-or-less perfect equilibrium of forces. Astrologically, we can imagine this as a situation in which every part of the psyche is perfectly balanced, coordinated, and in harmony with every other part. Out of this synthesis of many parts, the Self emerges as the ultimate, higher-level system made up of all the aspects, planets, and signs.

While a real astrological chart can never reflect such a state, as invariably there are unresolved conflicts and imbalances suggested by the distribution of planets in the signs, the point to remember is that balance is the ideal. A hierarchically organized wholeness is the psyche's goal. Accordingly, a strong Air-Fire type like Icarus is going to be drawn in the direction of Earth-Water, so to speak, for without yin to balance his excessive yang he will be forever causing himself trouble. This is why an inferior element is often that dimension of the psyche that becomes strongest over time.

Wherever the personality is one-sided or out-of-balance, there is likely to be conflict, tension, and strain, both internally and externally. The natural flow of energy in the psyche, therefore, is from a center of high potential to one of low potential. Jung's entropy principle means that a weaker system attempts to improve its status at the expense of a strong system. Imagine, for example, if a weak Venus was squared by a strong Mars so that the person was continually accused of insensitive, tactless social behavior.[5] In all probability, the troubles created by his aggression and lack of grace would eventually compel him to develop his Venus side more thoroughly. Otherwise, he would suffer a limited social life and rather rocky relationships. Whereas lack of balance creates internal tension and external conflict, a balanced de-

---

[5] By "weak" I mean a planet that is in an antithetical sign and/or house, and that it has few aspects to other planets, e.g., Venus in Virgo in the 12th house with no aspects.

velopment of the constituents of personality produces inner contentment and outer harmony.

In terms of intrapsychic conflict, the equalization of two values or structures that had very unequal amounts of energy—one very low, the other very high—can lead to a strong, durable synthesis of the values. When the conflict is resolved so that a balance is achieved, the balance will, according to Jung, be very difficult to disturb. The union of opposites will be a particularly strong one. Instead of being compulsively one way, the person will express a blend of two different qualities.

For example, once Mars and Venus become integrated, so that there is a relative balance between the two functions, Mars does not actually become weaker and Venus stronger. Rather, Mars becomes less aggressive but more functional by virtue of the fact that one is able to assert in a manner that is likely to arouse less resistance. Likewise, Venus becomes emboldened and encouraged by an infusion of Mars' energy. While the person is still able to compromise and appease when necessary, Venusian behavior is less compulsively oriented in this direction. Harmony is better managed and maintained by virtue of the fact that one is able to effectively assert in one's own self-interest, thus reducing the likelihood of being exploited, abused, or mistreated.

NEGENTROPY

Jung's application of the 2nd law of thermodynamics as an analogy for the psychological tendency toward equilibrium is not entirely right. Since psychodynamics is predicated upon movement of psychic energy as an inevitable consequence of conflict, and since the principle of entropy postulates that the distribution of energy in the psyche is tending toward equilibrium (cessation of conflict), then perfect balance would constitute a cessation of psychodynamics. The life of the psyche would come to an end. Fortunately, however, complete entropy can only occur in closed systems—that is, systems that are shut off from any exchange of energy or information with the environment. An open system, like the psyche, is one that is permeable to the environment.

Although general systems theory was not available to Jung during the time he was formulating his own theory of analytical psychology, he recognized that psychic energy—consciousness—is constantly being added to the psyche from outside sources, e.g., we learn from social (Venus) experiences. This added energy creates imbalances, which then must be resolved. In restoring balance, however, there is a certain amount of added growth and differentiation of psychic components. Psychic energy just doesn't become evenly distributed, it grows; consciousness evolves toward states of increasing complexity, integration, and awareness. In other words, the total amount of psychic energy—consciousness—available to the individual increases over time, at least potentially.

Conversely, when a system is unable to exchange energy or information with its environment, the total energy in the system gradually becomes uniformly distributed (dissipated), leading to the irreversible degradation of order in the system. In thermodynamic terms, this is actually what is called *entropy*. The degree to which disorder, uniformity, and randomness prevails is a measure of the system's entropy. According to the second law of thermodynamics, a closed system will move spontaneously toward maximizing entropy until it attains a condition known as "equilibrium." When there is no longer an orderly differentiation of parts within the borders that define the system, that system is said to be at equilibrium. Systems at or "near equilibrium" are by definition closed systems. The emergence of order in a closed system is not possible since dissipative processes lead invariably toward equilibrium.

Imagine a prisoner placed in solitary confinement for an extended period of time. Other than being provided minimal amounts of food and water, he has absolutely no contact with any outside source of information. Research indicates that when a person is denied physical, mental, and social contact with other beings he will deteriorate psychologically. In fact, he will gradually go mad. A relationship with the outside world is absolutely indispensable to maintenance of psychological health.

In an open (living) system at a purely physical level, the mass flow through the system is converted into a regular sequence of metabolic reactions that reproduce the system's structure. This ordering work is referred to as negative entropy, or *negentropy*, since it contradicts the dissipative processes predicted by the second law. Ordering work enables the living system to function "far from equilibrium," maintaining it there so long as the mass/energy flow is not interrupted. Thus, open systems maintain their form and chemical composition unchanged even while the flow through of matter/energy is continually changing, e.g., the foods we consume during the day are metabolized to maintain biological structure.

At a psychological level, human beings similarly maintain their psychic structure—mental health—through information flows provided by their relationships with the outside world, i.e., with friends, family, lovers, professional and group associations, nature, and so on. Individuals who are cut off from these informational flows are at risk to form any number of psychological problems, such as depression, paranoia, and psychosis. The more closed the system, the greater its tendency toward entropy; maximum entropy is the equivalent of complete psychosis, which is what happens when individuals cut themselves off from reality (feedback) and live in a delusional world. Astrologically, this is associated with the planet Neptune, a subject we will take up in greater detail in Chapter 6.

Jung's use of the term "entropy," therefore, must be understood in the context of his own theory of psychodynamics. Clearly, he was not using the term to refer to the degradation of order within the psyche, but to the gradual resolution of conflict and the development of an integrated, balanced whole. Had he known of the term "negentropy," he most surely would have used it. Put simply, negentropy is the utilization of energy to develop structure and prevent entropy (death) from occurring.

Negentropy is actually equivalent to what Jung refers to as *individuation* and what Maslow, Rogers, and others have called the tendency toward self-actualization. Whatever the term, living systems appear to have an intrinsic need for growth and development, moving from a state of relative globality, randomness of patterning and lack of differentiation to a state of increasing differentiation, articulation of parts, and hierarchical order. Astrologically, this means the optimal development and harmonious integration of planetary processes into a unified whole. In later chapters, we will return to the concept of negentropy in our discussion of how conflicts are resolved and growth is achieved.

SUMMARY

Psychodynamics concerns itself with the dynamic relations between various parts and processes of psychic structure. The relation between motivation, emotion, cognition, and behavior is the prime topic of psychodynamics. Whereas conventional psychodynamics is limited to an arbitrary, tripartite structure of id, ego, and superego, an astrological model is considerably more complex in that it presents a ten-planet, 12-sign model with clear external referents.

Psychic energy is postulated to be the carrier of all psychological activity. Astrologically, psychic energy is consciousness itself, which can be further defined as an evolutionary process of organized relations. The human psyche is a microcosmic reflection of a larger, transcendent, Universal Psyche that is immanent within all psychological processes. As a spontaneous ordering process, human consciousness is hierarchically structured, holographically organized, and evidences intrinsic purpose, intelligence, and creativity in its operations.

Not only does psyche conduct energy between its various energy centers—the planets—but it also interacts with external systems of consciousness. The relationship between inner and outer is synchronistic, meaning there is a circular relationship in which outer conditions define (mirror) the psyche, while also providing the necessary stimulus for the its further evolution. Character is fate; or, stated in the reverse, fate is soul spread out in time.

Freud's model of psychic energy was divided into two fundamental types: sexual energy (libido) and aggressive energy, both of which originated in the id. Psychic energy is invested in ideas, goals, and objects that are valued; that is, cathected. Astrologically, there are 12 fundamental types of energies as symbolized by zodiacal signs and their planetary representatives. Subjectively, these energies are experienced as feelings and impulses (drives). The placement of planets in signs, and the angular relations between planets, determine how psychic energy is distributed and what parts of life will be cathected. Those areas of a chart that are highly emphasized are said to be hypercathected.

In psychoanalytic theory, displacement refers to the movement of psychic energy from one interest to another that is more acceptable. This implies that psychic energy can be transferred, but not destroyed. Likewise, Jung's concept of equivalence states that psychic energy always remains the same because it moves from one activity to another that has equal value.

Astrologically, the twin concepts of displacement and equivalence are evident in the fact that planetary energies can manifest in a diverse number of ways. Each expression of an aspect, for example, is consistent with the meaning of that aspect, though manifestations will evolve over time toward more integrated, acceptable versions. What Freud called sublimation—displacement of a more primitive expression of psychic energy into a higher cultural achievement—is likewise evident in the tendency for aspects to gradually express themselves in more enlightened, culturally useful ways. Whereas displacement refers to the transfer of energy from a less acceptable to a more acceptable outlet, sublimation implies that some outlets represent higher, more integrated, and socially valued accomplishments.

Psychoanalytic theory postulates that psychic energy and psychic structure is relatively undifferentiated at birth. Thus, behavior tends to be relatively impulsive and unregulated in children. Over time, however, energy becomes bound and restrained from immediate discharge. These restraining forces are known as *anticathexes* in contradistinction to the driving forces or *cathexes*.

Likewise, in astrology the energies of the planets are relatively undifferentiated at birth, but gradually come under the influence of conscious control, as symbolized by the Sun (ego). This enables them to be restrained and regulated in accordance with what is socially appropriate.

In addition, there are yang signs, planets, and angles that correspond to the driving, expressive forces of the psyche, and there are yin signs, planets, and angles that signify restraining, suppressive forces. The Sun has a dual quality in that it not only symbolizes self-expression, but also self-suppression; it is both an activating and inhibiting agency by virtue of its capacity to direct attention toward or away from phenomena. As the various planetary subsystems become increasingly differentiated, and as the Sun gains awareness of each and every planetary function, the personality as a whole becomes more integrated, balanced, and unified.

Jung's principle of entropy states that the distribution of energy in the psyche is always moving in the direction of equilibrium or balance. Wherever there is imbalance in the psyche, e.g., one tendency is strong and another is weak, there is likely to be conflict, tension, and strain. Gradually, however, the psyche will bring about a synthesis of the two parts and thus produce a more stable and durable blending of opposing qualities.

Astrologically, Jung's principle of entropy is reflected in the observation that hard aspects between planets initially manifest as imbalance and instability between conflicting tendencies. That is, one planetary function is expressed while the other is repressed and projected. Gradually, over time, these processes tend to resolve themselves in the direction of a balanced wholeness. Each process is able to accommodate to the other and enrich itself by integrating qualities of the other into its own functioning.

Such an integrative process leads to an ideal state in which psychic energy is more evenly distributed throughout the various fully developed subsystems of the psyche. From the perspective of general systems theory, this spontaneous ordering process is known as negative entropy, or *negentropy*, in that it leads to a gradual build-up of order, complexity, and unity throughout the self-system. Astrologically, this means that the psyche, as symbolized by the chart, moves from a state of relative globality, randomness of patterning and lack of differentiation to a state of increasing differentiation, articulation of parts, and hierarchical order.

Chapter Three

AN ASTROLOGICAL THEORY OF MOTIVATION

In Chapter Two, we explored how psychodynamics concerns itself with four primary areas of human functioning: motivation, emotion, cognition, and behavior. The structure and dynamics of the psyche have to do with the relationships between these four dimensions. While they are inseparably related, we will now extend our analysis by exploring the concept of motivation in greater depth.

A ZODIACAL SYSTEM OF MOTIVES

Recall that psychic energy (consciousness) is intrinsically dynamic in that movement is its primary attribute, hence the term psychodynamics. But what determines movement? Our answer is motive forces. A motive is a desire, need, or impulse that acts as an incitement to action. In other words, a motive is a reason for a particular action; any need that prompts one to act is a motive. A need is experienced as an impulse, which is a feeling. The simplest way of putting it is: needs motivate. When awareness of a particular need occurs, a person is motivated to act and will persist in the action until the need is satisfied.

Motives, in short, cause motion; they compel us to act in the service of a goal that fulfills a need. For example, an individual might feel trapped by excessive responsibilities at work. Suffocated by his job, he experiences an impulse to take the day off and go hiking. His goal—hiking—satisfies a need for freedom, which is what motivates the action. Movement of psychic energy and thus all actual causes of behavior are rooted in motives. Needs are activated when a sufficient charge of psychic energy has accumulated vis a vis that need, which then impels (motivates) the appropriate behavior.

In the following sections, we will explore how the zodiac presents the ultimate taxonomy of motives. These motives are intrinsic to consciousness in that they are not derived from physiological processes. While zodiacal needs roughly correspond to Maslow's hierarchy of needs and various Jungian archetypes, they have certain unique properties that make them a superior system for classifying the core motivational drives of the human psyche.

EXTRINSIC VS. INTRINSIC MOTIVATION

In psychology, the concept of motivation has undergone a series of transformations over the past century. Early behaviorist theories, which were wedded to a mechanistic model of the psyche, postulated that motives were physiologically based. Needs for sex, food, and the like were the motive springs of behavior and all such drives were biologically determined. Organisms sought to maintain equilibrium in their physiological needs. Behavior was driven by whichever need was dominant in a given moment. Drives were forces that caused the organism to act in certain ways because those actions had become linked to the corresponding stimuli by reinforcement processes. For example, the need for nourishment may become associated with hunting deer simply because deer are plentiful in the region; deer hunting is reinforced by the satisfaction of eating venison.

Likewise, Freud's psychoanalytic theory postulated that instincts for sex and aggression were psychological representatives of biologically determined needs. Instinctual drives pressed to be "discharged" via gratification by a cathected object. While motives are preemptory and will persist until satisfied, behavior is flexible (selective) toward the desired object. This points up an important principle: behavior is characterized by fixed needs and flexible strategies. If the primary object is unattainable, the motive will be displaced onto a substitute object. Just as in behavioral theory, all of this operates mechanistically; that is, outside of personal choice.

In both Freudian and behaviorist models, human beings were thought to be *extrinsically* motivated in that they were passive agents of biological forces that operated independent of consciousness. These early passive-mechanistic theories held that since matter was the primary reality, all behavior was reducible to physiological drives stimulated by material events.

Eventually, however, extrinsic theories of motivation were replaced by concepts of *intrinsic* motivation that did not rely upon biologically based drives (Deci, 1980). Intrinsic motivation postulates that people engage in purposeful, non-random behaviors in a quest to actualize innate potentials. Humans are pro-active rather than merely reactive to stimuli; they are characterized by a variety of specific, quasi-independent psychological needs that have no actual physiological basis. Needs for achievement, meaning, and beauty (among others) are not wholly determined by biological or environmental events outside of consciousness. Rather, such needs are intrinsic to consciousness. Human motivations are self-activating processes that appear to derive from a level that transcends physical reality.

The concept of intrinsic motivation is important to astrology because it represents a significant departure from the reductionistic-mechanistic thinking that dominated personality theorizing during most of the 20th century. If Consciousness is the primary reality and permeates all dimensions of existence, then motivation for human behavior must necessarily be rooted *in* Consciousness. In other words, Consciousness has its own intrinsic motives that are irreducible. But from where do these motives derive?

ARCHETYPAL IMAGES OF NEEDS

Essential categories of motivation appear to be related to what Jung (1960) called *archetypes*—prepatterned impulses of an objective psyche that organize and animate life at all levels. Similar to Plato's concept of incorporeal forms or divine *Ideas* that serve as the models for all things having substance, archetypes not only constitute the basic structures of the human psyche, they are also the essential principles of reality itself. Seen in this light, a need is a psychological extension of a basic organizing principle in the Universe.

An archetype must be differentiated from the various images that symbolize it. As a dynamic pattern that exists without content, archetypes are like magnetic fields invisible to the human eye. Unless you place iron filings within a magnetic field, its organizing properties remain invisible. Similarly, an archetype represents only the possibility of a certain type of perception and action. Depending upon historical time, place, and circumstance, an archetype will manifest in a manner that reflects the nature of the people and situations that exist. The archetype of the warrior, for example, may manifest in contemporary American culture as a professional football player, in feudal Japan as a samurai, or in ancient Rome as a gladiator. Whereas the images of football player, samurai, and gladiator each give expression to the warrior archetype, the archetype itself transcends these various expressions. As a primordial form—a living idea existing everywhere and always—an archetype is determined as to its contents only when it becomes filled out with the material of conscious experience. While there is a basic theme and a recognizable pattern of variation, it will take a unique individual twist in each specific case. Not every gladiator is alike. Again, we return to the rule: fixed needs (archetypes) and flexible strategies (varying expressions).

Whatever the nature of the image, an archetype has a meaning that remains the same regardless of its changing forms. Jung referred to the archetype as "the self-portrait of the instinct" because as a primordial image it was symbolic of fundamental human needs as manifest in patterns of emotional and mental behavior. Each archetypal image symbolizes a different human need: the warrior symbolizes the Aries need for survival, the messenger symbolizes the Gemini need for communication, and the hero symbolizes the Leo need for self-esteem.

It is important to recognize that there is more than one archetypal image for each sign/planet. Multiple images reflect a planet's potentiality for manifesting in different ways depending upon how it is situated within the psyche as a whole, how it interacts with other sign-planet systems, and, most importantly, its degree of conscious integration. An unintegrated Jupiter might manifest as a demagogue, whereas its conscious, integrated form can be that of a guru or wise teacher. In fact, most manifestations of archetypal energies represent a blending of principles. For example, a Mars-Neptune aspect may manifest as a spiritual-warrior, as it did for Dan Millman (sextile) who wrote the book, *The Way of The Peaceful Warrior,* and Carlos Castaneda (square) who created the enigmatic character of Don Juan, a Yaqui Indian sorcerer in *The Teachings of Don Juan.*

SIGNS AS ARCHETYPAL MOTIVES

Astrology postulates that the Universal Psyche is divisible into two broad categories—the polarities of yin and yang. These are the most fundamental motive forces of Consciousness. As discussed in the previous chapter, yang signs/planets constitute a need for differentiation. These are the assertive, driving forces of the psyche that opt for separation and spontaneous expressiveness. Conversely, yin signs symbolize an integrative tendency. Their fundamental energy is inward; they are naturally inhibitory, restraining, and suppressive. A primary function of yin signs is to connect and combine the various differentiated parts of the psyche into a functional unity.

These two polarities can be differentiated into four elements—fire, earth, air, and water—that constitute more specific categories of motivation. Fire (yang) is the need to assert one's rights, intentions, and opinions, whereas Earth (yin) signifies the urge to ground oneself in the practical, "real" world and deal with material reality as such. Air (yang) motivates us to observe and

POLARITY MOTIVE	ELEMENT MOTIVE	SIGN MOTIVE
Yang differentiation, separation, spontaneity, expression	**Fire** action, affirmation, joy, faith, assertion	**Aries:** Survival, being, freedom, autonomy, independence
		Leo: Self-esteem, validation, approval, play, creative self-expression
		Sagittarius: Truth, meaning, wisdom, expansion, hope, justice
	Air communication, rationality, objectivity, detachment	**Gemini:** Information, knowledge, factual data, learning, language
		Libra: Relatedness, harmony, beauty, balance, intimacy, partnership
		Aquarius: Awakening, revelation, perspective, liberation, change, progress
Yin integration, uniting, control, inhibition	**Earth** practicality, grounding, productivity, conservation	**Taurus:** Constancy, safety, security, stability, pleasure, comfort
		Virgo: Service, competence, efficiency, improvement, health
		Capricorn: Perfection, success, structure, limits, order, mastery, authority
	Water emotional connection, love, unity, introspection, dependency	**Cancer:** Nurturing, belonging, tenderness, caring, protection, closeness
		Scorpio: Transformation, sex, healing, elimination, integrity, power
		Pisces: Transcendence, compassion, forgiveness, surrender, oneness

Figure 2: Three Categories of Motivation

communicate what we experience on a mental plane. Finally, water (yin) compels us to connect on an emotional level.

These four motivational principles can be further differentiated into twelve major categories—the twelve signs of the zodiac—each of which signifies a different motive/need. By observing behavioral attributes that characterize the twelve signs, one can discern the underlying needs that motivate behavior. In each instance the need of a sign can be inferred from behavior that characterizes that sign.

Note in Figure 2, column three, that there is more than one keyword for each sign-motive. As a category of need, a zodiacal sign constitutes a set of needs of which various motives are members. A set is a collection of distinct elements having specific common properties. Each need that belongs to a specific sign-set has something in common with every other need that relates to that sign. In effect, each need is co-dependent with the others for its fulfillment. To satisfy the Sagittarian quest for truth, for example, one must discern meaning and become wise. This, in turn, allows for expansion of awareness, gives occasion for hope, and inspires faith that justice will prevail. Each need—truth, meaning, wisdom, expansion, hope, and justice—is co-dependent with every other need of that set.

One might think of a sign-need as a diamond with various facets. Each side of the diamond is characterized by a specific keyword; yet, taken together, all the keywords contribute to an overall understanding of the core motivation that underlies that sign's behavior.

ZODIAC AS STRUCTURE OF NEEDS

Each sign of the zodiac is related to every other sign in a completely unique way as symbolized by the nature of the angles between signs. A key advantage of astrology is that it provides a structure for understanding how various human needs (signs) are related, thus allowing us to see the quality of energy flow between one part of the psyche and another.

For example, the sign of Aries forms an opening semi-sextile to Taurus, an opening quincunx to Virgo, an opposition to Libra, a closing trine to Sagittarius, and so on. Because each sign signifies a different need, their angular relationships symbolize how one motive relates to another. For example, the semi-sextile to Taurus means that the impulse for adventure (Aries) and the need for attachment (Taurus) are compensatory; one pushes forward and the other holds fast. An opening quincunx to Virgo denotes an incompatibility of motives. The Virgonian propensity for slow, systematic analysis is a problem for Aries, which operates on pure impulse. However, the Aries need for freedom is highly compatible with the Sagittarian quest for truth (closing trine), as expressed by laws to preserve freedom of religious faith.

It is not possible here to delineate the relationships of all the signs. Suffice to say that the zodiac provides us with a detailed map for understanding how different motives may conflict or combine. Depending upon the angle, the flow of energy between motives can be compensatory, stimulating, repressive, creative, problematic, polarizing, productive, and so on. The extraordinary potential this provides for insight into motivational dynamics is unparalleled by any other personality theory.

The founder of humanistic psychology, Abraham Maslow[6], provided a model of human motivation that does contain some similarities to astrology. Maslow (1968) theorized that basic needs are organized hierarchically and sequentially according to priority. At the bottom of the hierarchy is the first and most fundamental need, that of survival, which he defined as the need for food, water, and continuance of life. Next is the need for safety (security, order, protection from danger), followed by social needs for belonging, acceptance, and love. The fourth need is for esteem, which derives from validation and confers a sense of status.

Maslow's hierarchy roughly follows the sequence of signs in the zodiac. Aries corresponds to his need for survival, Taurus for security, and Cancer signifies social needs for belonging, acceptance, and love. Maslow's definition of social needs probably shades into Leo as well, although Leo most clearly symbolizes the need for esteem. While these four signs are covered in his schema, he seems to have ignored the third sign—Gemini—the need for learning. Figure 3 (see page 66) on the next page shows Maslow's hierarchy of basic needs and their astrological correlates.

One of the more interesting aspects of Maslow's theory was his claim that lower needs must be satisfied before higher needs assert themselves; thus, the need for survival must be met before the need for esteem will become conscious. Each need was an "impulse voice," said Maslow, which communicates itself through bodily feelings. While all needs are simultaneously present, the most pressing need is the one most clearly felt. If an earlier need falls below a certain minimal threshold level of satisfaction, the individual will regress to that level until satisfaction is re-established. For example, a person may be enjoying a family outing when suddenly a nearby volcano begins spewing lava. Since the need for safety (Taurus) has precedence over

---

[6] It seems befitting that as one of the founders of humanistic psychology and the originator of many new ideas, Maslow was a Sun sign Aries—a true pioneer.

social needs (Cancer/Leo) the person runs for cover (presumably with the rest of his family).

For this reason, Maslow termed the values that these needs signify as "Deficiency Values". If an earlier need fell below a certain threshold of satisfaction, which constituted a deficiency, it pre-empted satisfaction of a later need.

Whereas Maslow (1971) was able to organize basic needs in terms of a hierarchy, he admitted there were higher, transpersonally oriented needs that he could not organize hierarchically. These were called *metaneeds*, which included the need for service, beauty, justice, truth, goodness, order, unity, charity, and so forth. While basic needs operated on a deficiency basis, metaneeds did not. According to Maslow, one metaneed is as important as another and all are pursued more or less equally. These are the ultimate, highest values that are intrinsic to being human. Maslow termed them "Being-Values", of which he noted there were about fourteen. One need, however, transcended all other needs, and that was the need for self-actualization—the need to actualize one's fullest human potential.

The zodiac also recognizes higher needs that extend beyond the need for self-esteem (Leo). Maslow's metaneeds roughly correspond to Virgo (service), Libra (beauty), Scorpio (healing), Sagittarius (justice), Capricorn (order), Aquarius (altruism), and Pisces (charity). However, unlike Maslow's schema, astrology continues to organize these motives in a sequential, hierarchical fashion. Note in Figure 3 that Maslow's schema has the metaneeds jumbled together in random order. Conversely, the zodiac shows how the metaneeds can be hierarchically arranged. More so, it illustrates that what Maslow considered different needs may actually be related members of the same set of needs. His metaneeds for justice and truth, for example, both belong to Sagittarius.

Recall that the zodiac is divided up into three major time-space orientations, or perspectives—personal, social, and universal. The first four signs are personal, the second four social, and the final four are universal. Each group experiences time and space differently, which is the key to understanding the values that each group signifies. These categories represent a hierarchical prioritizing of needs as well as a developmental stage model that depicts the evolution of consciousness over the course of a lifetime.

Personal signs take precedence over social signs in that they are more basic, fundamental, and necessary for survival. Likewise, social signs take precedence over universal signs in that close, personal relationships generally precede concern for collective humanity. For example, a person may feel a greater loyalty to his best friend (Leo) or partner (Libra) than he would to colleagues that constitute an impersonal group association (Aquarius). Finally, universal signs represent needs that relate to concerns for humanity at large. Pisces, for example, symbolizes an altruistic impulse to relieve human suffering. As a person evolves, universal needs may ultimately assume priority over all other needs. In fact, the last two signs of the zodiac—Aquarius and Pisces—come closest to what Maslow called self-actualization.

A DEVELOPMENTAL PERSPECTIVE

The prioritizing of needs is even more apparent when we consider signs as twelve developmental stages. Each stage allows for the actualization of a new psychological function, the attainment of which constitutes the primary task of that period. Clearly, these tasks are arranged hierarchically. For example, if someone doesn't first learn to read and write (Gemini, stage 3), his options for work (Virgo, stage 6) may be severely compromised. Likewise, if a person doesn't develop a clear identity and self-esteem (Leo), her capacity to be emotionally vulnerable in close, personal relationships (Scorpio) will be sorely lacking.

Each sign-stage, in effect, transcends but includes the achievements of its predecessors (see Figure 3, p. 66). Successful negotiation of a given developmental period presupposes that the tasks of the preceding stages have been mastered. For this reason, each sign is progressively more complex. If one has not mastered the tasks of a preceding stage, the ability to negotiate succeeding tasks will be compromised. Part of consciousness, as it were, remains preoccupied with unfinished business. This is precisely what is meant by "developmental arrest" or "developmental fixation."

Sign-stages are increasingly longer as well, at least in terms of real time. That is, a given stage is approximately one year longer than the previous stage. However, because subjectively perceived time tends to accelerate as we age, each sign-stage is experienced as constituting equal time. This would mean, for instance, that a year to an infant (Aries stage) feels as long as ten years to someone in her late 40s (Sagittarius stage). Since each succeeding sign subjectively experiences time as passing more quickly, the actual length of time of each successive sign-phase is slightly longer: Aries lasts two years, Taurus 3 years, Gemini 4 years, Cancer, 5 years, and so on.

A corollary meaning of sign-stages is that each stage brings about an expanded perception of space. As time passes, consciousness expands; we see and understand more as we age. This implies that vision broadens as time accelerates. The ultimate goal, of course, is Pisces: to occupy all time and space simultaneously—the nirvana of enlightenment. A primitive forerunner

66 • DEPTH ANALYSIS OF THE NATAL CHART

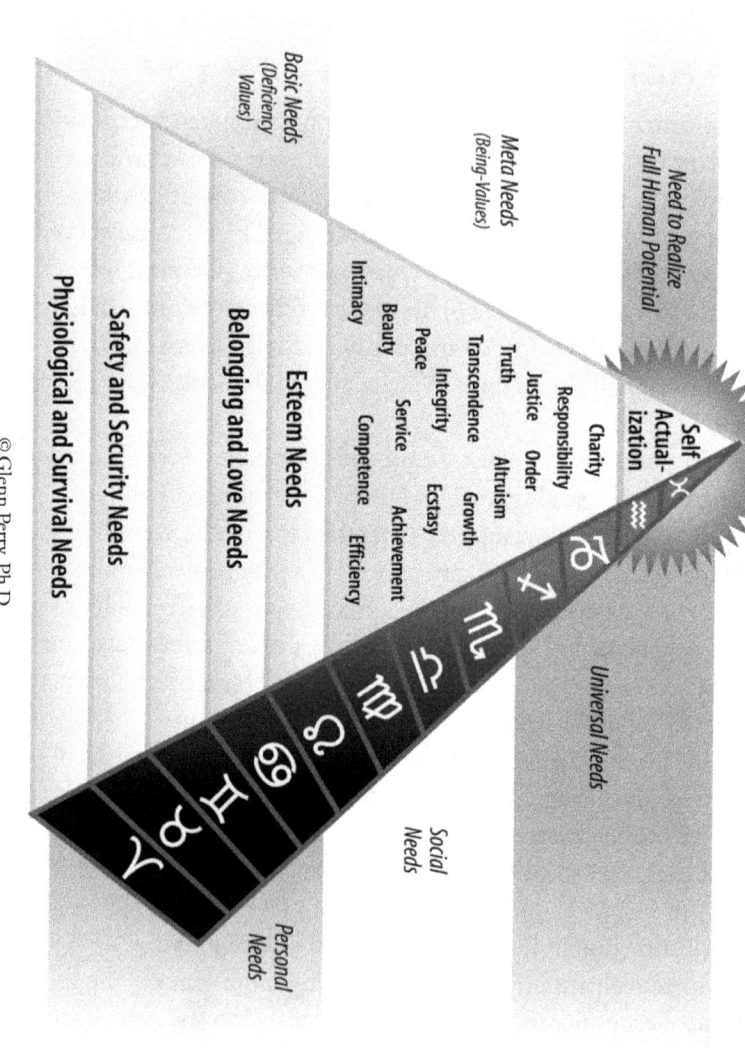

Figure 3: Pyramid Conceptualization of Maslow's Hierarchy of Needs with Corollary Signs

© Glenn Perry, Ph.D.

of this can be seen in the time-space disorientation that accompanies the senility of old age. A person in his 80's may relive memories that belong to earlier periods of his life, even infancy. Octogenarians slip in and out of the present moment as if unbounded by space or time.

To summarize, the sequence of signs in the zodiac constitutes a natural developmental cycle, from birth through old age. Each sign experiences time and space differently; the earlier the sign, the more constricted its vision of space and the slower its experience of time. The later the sign, the more expanded its vision and the more accelerated its time.

PRIORITIZING DEVELOPMENTAL TASKS

Because unfoldment of these capacities occurs sequentially, different motives assume priority at different stages (Figure 4, page 69). Generally speaking, the needs and aptitudes associated with one's current developmental sign-stage will assume temporary prominence, only to be replaced by concerns that belong to the succeeding sign-stage.

Hence at age 3 (Taurus stage), a toddler is preoccupied with ownership issues and personal security. By age six, after entering school (Gemini), the child's mind is awakened and suddenly every object has to have a name and every question an answer. In adolescence (Leo), the most important thing is popularity and development of self-esteem. By one's early twenties (Virgo), concerns about work and personal competence are in ascendancy. After one reaches the ripe old age of 50 (Sagittarius), philosophical and moral questions assume priority as individuals become preoccupied with passing on the wisdom gained through the years.

Every sign-stage, in effect, subsumes its predecessors and is characterized by a progressively wider and deeper understanding of what it means to be human. This is reflected in Figure 4 (page 69) by the fact that earlier stages are at the bottom and later stages on top. What is being built, in effect, is a hierarchy of capacities in which each new capacity both includes and is built upon the foundation of its predecessors.

All of this is consistent with developmental studies that detail the evolution of cognitive and moral capacities over the course of a lifetime. For example, Lawrence Kohlberg's (1976) study of the development of moral reasoning revealed that human beings restructure their thinking about social and moral questions as they develop their cognitive structure from the very concrete to the more abstract. In fact, Kohlberg's six-stage model of moral development very closely approximates our zodiacal twelve-stage theory. By assigning two signs to each of Kohlberg's stages—Aries-Taurus constitutes stage one, Gemini-Cancer stage two, and so on, parallels between the two theories are remarkable (Perry, 1998).

Of course, in real life, the needs that relate to each sign-stage are operating simultaneously and do not sort themselves out quite so simply. Invariably, there are conflicts that constitute core themes in a person's life story. For example, if a person has an opposition from Moon in Aries (personal) to Saturn in Libra (social), the planets occupy signs in different life-stage perspectives. A life issue may be that the person has to balance a need for protecting his own interests (Moon Aries) against the fulfillment of a social responsibility (Saturn Libra). Numerous conflicts of this sort can be evident in an actual horoscope.

As a person ages, the priority given to different needs will shift, thus allowing for a progressive integration of planetary aspects and the motivations they symbolize. For example, consider someone who has a quincunx between the Sun and Saturn. At age 16, he feels that romance and play (Sun/Leo) are infinitely preferable to the responsibilities thrust upon him by his father (Saturn/Capricorn). This is due, undoubtedly, to the fact that his current developmental stage is Leo, during which the needs for romance and play predominate. At age 60, however, while occupying the Capricorn stage of life, he might find himself working as a judge presiding over cases involving unruly adolescents who have run afoul of the law. Now he sees this Leo age group as undisciplined, narcissistically self-involved, and woefully irresponsible. Hopefully, he can recall his own experiences as an adolescent—anger at his father, resistance to authority, and so on—for this would allow him to integrate the aspect more successfully and thus find a compassionate solution to the Sun-Saturn quincunx that both he and his juvenile offenders must resolve.

In summary, the zodiac depicts a mandala of the motive structure of the human psyche. Not only are core archetypal motivations revealed, but their sequence and overall patterning are made clear. Each psychological need is related to the others in a unique way. The angular relationship between signs reveals the precise nature of their interaction. While the zodiac has certain features in common with Maslow's hierarchical model, astrology presents a more detailed and comprehensive catalog of motives. In addition, the zodiac also relates the twelve core motivations to specific developmental stages in the life cycle. This has the advantage of showing how different needs assume precedence at various stages, and how the psyche evolves toward balance and wholeness over time.

SIGN STAGE	BASIC NEED/MOTIVE	AGE	DURATION
Pisces	Transcendence, compassion, forgiveness, surrender, oneness	77–89	13 yrs. +
Aquarius	Awakening, revelation, perspective, liberation, change, progress	65–77	12 yrs.
Capricorn	Perfection, success, structure, limits, order, mastery, authority	54–65	11 yrs.
Sagittarius	Truth, meaning, wisdom, expansion, hope, justice	44–54	10 yrs.
Scorpio	Transformation, healing, elimination, renewal, integrity, power	35–44	9 yrs.
Libra	Relatedness, harmony, balance, intimacy, marriage, partnership	27–35	8 yrs.
Virgo	Service, competence, efficiency, improvement, health	20–27	7 yrs.
Leo	Identity, self-esteem, validation, play, creative self-expression	14–20	6 yrs.
Cancer	Nurturing, belonging, tenderness, caring, protection, closeness	9–14	5 yrs.
Gemini	Information, knowledge, factual data, learning, language	5–9	4 yrs.
Taurus	Constancy, safety, stability, comfort, pleasure, ownership	2–5	3 yrs.
Aries	Survival, freedom, independence, activity, adventure, novelty	0–2	2 yrs.

© Glenn Perry, Ph.D.

Figure 4: A Zodiacal Developmental Stage Model

Every astrological sign signifies a developmental stage with an associated task: to actualize one's human potential for satisfying the predominant need of that stage. Note that each sign is progressively longer in real time due to a natural acceleration of subjective time as we age. Just as each sign corresponds to a specific time-space phase of the earth's orbit about the Sun, so each sign in a psychological sense has its own unique time-space orientation or developmental perspective. Time and space are quite literally experienced differently for each sign of the zodiac, and this qualitative difference in perception is intricately tied to that sign's psychology or point-of-view. At earlier stages of development, vision is relatively narrow, and time moves slowly. At later stages, time seems to have accelerated, and concomitantly, vision has broadened. Two principles are worth repeating: (1) As consciousness expands with age, our subjective perception of time and space changes with it: we see more, and we see more quickly—or, put simply, vision broadens as time accelerates; and (2) signs appear to be time-space phases that holonomically symbolize the steps of the evolutionary process. Thus, the human life cycle recapitulates in microcosm the overall process of human evolution.

THE MASTER MOTIVE

While the zodiac describes a hierarchical sequencing of archetypal motivations, it is the psyche as a whole that describes the master motive—wholeness or unity. This has been variously referred to as *self-actualization* (Maslow, 1968), *individuation* (Jung, 1953), and *personal efficacy* (Deci, 1980), all of which imply that the psyche has a tendency to grow toward the fullest possible actualization of human potential. This tendency to develop in the direction of a stable unity is the central defining feature of Jung's psychology.

THE PROCESS OF INDIVIDUATION

Individuation, according to Jung, is an autonomous, inborn process. Development is an unfolding of the original undifferentiated wholeness with which humans are born. The ultimate goal of this unfolding is the realization of selfhood—the actualization of all psychological potentials in a state of cooperative balance and harmony. In order to realize this aim, it is necessary for the various systems of personality to become completely differentiated and fully developed. To have a healthy, integrated personality, every system must be permitted to reach the fullest degree of differentiation, development, and expression. Individuation, in Jung's view, is a kind of spiritual journey or religious quest, even though the individual may not consciously realize it.

Jung felt that wholeness was innate, a priori, and inborn. Yet, during infancy the archetypal components of the psyche operate unconsciously and independently as separate entities. The left hand doesn't know what the right hand is doing, so to speak. The personality is disintegrated and uncoordinated; one component does not influence another in a conscious way. This singleness of individual parts remains a characteristic of the psyche during the greater part of the infantile period. Gradually, however, through the agency of an organizing principle, the individual parts begin to differentiate and cooperate with one another. This harmonizing of separate parts is called *integration*—the act of bringing together the parts into an integral whole.

THE SELF

Jung called this integrating factor the *Self*. The *Self* not only signifies the union of opposites within the psyche but is also a God-image that symbolizes a wholeness toward which the psyche strives. The *Self* is the unity archetype, the organizing principle of the personality. As the central archetype of the collective unconscious, the Self is like the Sun at the center of the solar system; it draws to itself and harmonizes all the archetypes (planets) into an integrated whole. Because it signifies the totality of the psyche, the Self has a tendency to produce images of something "beyond" the ego (images of God, mandalas, or heroic personages). Such images symbolize the need for, and the possibility of, development toward an original unity.

Astrologically, we can think of this inborn unity as Pisces-like, an undifferentiated, unconscious wholeness. With birth (Aries), this Piscean unity gradually breaks up as experiences accumulate; yet, it serves as the template or blueprint for later experiences of wholeness and integration. Thus the psyche constitutes an original undifferentiated wholeness at birth, differentiates into parts over the first half of life (Individual signs), then reintegrates back toward wholeness during the second half of the life (Collective signs). Just as a seed grows into a plant, the individual develops into a fully differentiated, balanced, and unified personality—Pisces once again. That, at least, is the direction development takes. The goal of complete differentiation, balance, and unity is rarely if ever reached, except, as Jung (1953) observes, by a Jesus or a Buddha. Nevertheless, "The Self is our life's goal," said Jung, "for it is the completest expression of that fateful combination we call individuality" (Vol. 7, p. 238).

Although life begins and ends in wholeness (Pisces), one condition should not be confused with the other. The original, inborn unity is one of undifferentiated wholeness, a more or less total submergence in the collective. The path of individuation is to differentiate and make conscious every part of the personality. Before one can actualize the potential of a psychological function, one must be aware of it. Self-awareness is the path to self-realization. One must make conscious that which is unconscious in order to be in harmony with oneself. This means the various sign-planet systems must become increasingly differentiated and integrated. Each system becomes differentiated from every other system, but more importantly, each system becomes differentiated within itself. From a simple structure it develops into a complex structure, just as a larvae develops into a butterfly. Complexity means that a structure is capable of expressing itself in an increasing variety of ways.

For example, a person's Jupiter may evolve from a simple, childlike faith into a deep, sophisticated philosophy of life. One study (McAdams, 1993) revealed that human beings are capable of moving through at least four qualitatively different structures of religious belief. Stage one is characterized by a superficial morality combined with vague beliefs about God. Faith is limited to concrete behaviors such as saying prayers before meals. Stage one beliefs are extremely general, scattered, and diffuse. In Stage two, faith is organized around a systematic creed or conventional theory that is largely unquestioned. Beliefs are determined by an external authority such as the Catholic Church, an *Imam* (Islam) or a scientific fraternity.

In Stage three, however, a person moves beyond conventions and begins to fashion a personalized and unique faith structure. What one believes may encompass a variety of different doctrines. Such an ideology can account for the contradictions and complexities that are encountered in life. Ideas are questioned; some are rejected, while others are accepted. What remains is a self-constructed ideology that is tolerant of the tenets of other people's faiths. Finally, Stage 4 is characterized by an acceptance of irony, paradox, and ambiguity. The individual comes increasingly to accept that ultimate truth is beyond our ability to grasp with reason alone. Such a faith transcends belief and begins to merge with the object of its aspiration.

The point is that sign-planet systems evolve from simpler, undifferentiated, and unconscious expressions to more complex, articulated, and conscious ones. Only through awareness can a system of personality proceed to individuate, e.g., for Jupiter to individuate the person must become aware of, and begin to question, the nature of his or her beliefs. Ultimately, the goal is to become conscious of every sign-planet system and then integrate them into a single, conscious, unified whole—the *Self*. This is the *differentiated* wholeness of a fully mature Pisces state.

TELEOLOGICAL VERSUS EFFICIENT CAUSATION

I have stated that individuation can only proceed if there is awareness; that is, conscious recognition of one's feelings, thoughts, and beliefs. Awareness catalyzes the unfoldment of consciousness. The question arises, *why* does one become more conscious over time? What impels the evolution of consciousness? That we can describe the process of change does not necessarily explain why it occurs.

As we shall see, the answer to this question has important implications for astrology. It may be that the same forces that impel the evolution of consciousness also provide a basis for understanding how astrology works.

Such a possibility is important, for otherwise astrology tends to be evaluated through the lens of physical science, which invariably assumes it is based on astral determinism—the notion that mysterious cosmic "forces" determine the formation of personality and destiny. It is precisely because the theory of astral determinism is *not* plausible that astrology's credibility is damaged. Jung's theory of synchronicity provides a better explanation: one is born when the planets are arranged in a formation that reflects (not causes) the evolution of the soul. In other words, the relation between psyche and cosmos is acausal, or synchronistic. Consciousness is not the product of an externally originating cause; rather, each individual is his or her own cause. On the basis of past actions in past lives, we make ourselves, which is then reflected in the heavens at the moment of birth.

Over the centuries, there have been a variety of theories that purport to explain evolution and development. One of the first was Aristotle's theory of teleological causation. Aristotle distinguished "efficient" from "final" causes. Efficient causation is what modern science would consider a cause: linear, material causation based on the impact of matter and forces. This is the notion that all events are a consequence of antecedent causes that physically impact the entity in question, e.g., billiard ball "A" smashes into billiard ball "B" and sends it careening forward. A's behavior is thus the cause of B's behavior. Again, when this theory is applied to astrology, it presumes that personality and behavior are determined by cosmic forces that originate outside the consciousness of the individual.

Conversely, final causation is the idea that there is a particular end *(telos)* for which a thing exists and toward which it is inexorably drawn. This theory presupposes that all entities are in some sense alive and conscious and thus have an internal subjectivity—feelings, aims, and purposes, which enable them to be self-directed toward specific (final) ends. The power of attraction, thought Aristotle, was a better model for causation than propulsion; things are lured more than they are driven. Aristotle's notion of evolution being drawn forward by divine ideals is known as teleological causation. Divine ideals, archetypes, or Platonic *Forms* are implicit in any theory of final causation.

Almost every religion and philosophy has some variation on the theme of final causation. Whether we call these formative principles divine ideals, gods and goddesses, Platonic Forms, planetary archetypes, or morphogenetic fields, all such terms make the same claim: that the lower, denser world is an emanation of a higher, subtler one. According to Plato, the order and content of the world depends upon an intelligible sphere replete with the *Ideas* of all things. The visible Universe is a huge organism ensouled by a divine Mind, out of which emerge certain formative principles—Forms, or Ideas—that act as the generative matrix for natural phenomena. By combining and re-combining, these Forms give form and structure to the world below. And since they can only be known by their effects, the various qualities of the phenomenal world are thought to be derived from these Forms. Beauty, for example, can never be encountered as a thing in itself, but only as a property of some concrete thing that is beautiful.

Teleology, or goal-oriented behavior, is thus based on the idea that everything in the physical universe is a consequence of things superior to it. Causation throughout is downward—from superior to inferior, from what is more to what is less. Downward causation suggests that things move by being drawn toward that which fulfills them, fulfillment occurring to the degree that they refashion themselves to its likeness. For Aristotle, the entire universe was thus animated. Everything reaches toward its better in the effort to acquire for itself its virtues. What is better is what is more real in the sense of having more power, duration in time, extension in space, complexity, and overall importance in the grand scheme of things. Again, entities that fit this level of description are what Plato described as divine Ideas or Forms. These are the living templates or essential models for all things having substance. Atop Being's hierarchy, said Plato, is the Form of the Good, being both the cause of all subordinate things while also being the universal object of desire.

One of the advantages of the zodiac is that it not only depicts a system of basic psychological needs, but also of universal, formative principles. Because zodiacal archetypes are cosmic in origin and evident at every level of reality—physical, biological, psychological, cultural, and spiritual—they constitute essential principles of reality itself. An astrological sign can signify a psychological need, an affect state, a behavioral trait, a developmental stage, a body part, an event, a thing, an external character, a place, or an institution. As such, it would seem to signify a basic organizing principle in the Universe. In every sense, zodiacal archetypes are equivalent to Plato's concept of divine Ideas or Forms. We are not only animated from within by the archetypes but are also drawn inexorably upward toward higher expressions of the divine ideals that they symbolize.

Most of modern science has been a reaction against the theory of teleological causation. In contrast to teleology, modern science is deterministic. The prevailing assumption is that elementary objects have no hidden internal reality that impels them toward some future goal. Rather, the only kind of motion they can have is *loco*motion, motion through space from one locale to another. There can be no internal movement, such as internal becoming, which would involve the capacity for choosing from alternative possibilities. Determinism implies that all events, including moral choices, are completely determined by previously existing causes that preclude free will. These causes in the final analysis are material; that is, because no element of internal self-causation is found, all causation comes from external sources.

Applied to psychology, this view implies that so-called psychodynamics are a consequence of the brain's physiology and nothing more. In fact, by the 18th century, so complete was the extrusion of teleological reasoning from science that the mind was regarded as "epiphenomenal," which meant that it was a real phenomenon, but only as an effect, not a cause. The two most influential psychological models of this century, psychoanalysis and behaviorism, were both founded upon deterministic principles and both equally denied the possibility of genuine human freedom.

By contrast, Jungian psychology is steeped in teleological reasoning. Jung's concept of the *Self*, as the unity archetype, is analogous to Plato's Form of the Good. The *Self* is both the cause of psychodynamics while also being the ultimate end or purpose of psychic activity: Self-realization. In Jung's words:

> Life is an energy-process. Like every energy-process, it is in principle irreversible and is therefore directed towards a goal. That goal is a state of rest. In the long run everything that happens is, as it were, no more than the initial disturbance of a perpetual state of rest, which forever attempts to re-establish itself. Life is teleology par excellence; it is the intrinsic striving towards a goal, and the living organism is a system of directed aims which seek to fulfill themselves (*CW* 8: p. 798).

Jung's final goal has a spiritual connotation in that the Self signifies both the fully realized human being and also a God-image, as we will explore more fully in the next section. Suffice to say that our astrological theory of psychodynamics is likewise teleological. Planetary processes are motivated by needs, but these needs are rooted in planetary archetypes, which draw human behavior upward and forward toward an ideal state of satisfaction—what Jung describes as "rest." The ultimate expression of this state is *nirvana*, which has been described as an ideal condition of rest, harmony, stability, and joy.[7]

---

[7] In Buddhism, nirvana also signifies the ineffable ultimate, which is attained only when one has attained disinterested wisdom and compassion. Likewise in Hinduism, nirvana signifies the extinction of ignorance and the renunciation of all attachment.

While such a condition may be merely an ideal, the fact remains that human beings are motivated by target states of optimal need satisfaction. Anything that is done is done for a reason; behavior is goal-directed. And the goal of a behavior is an affect or feeling that signals when the target state has been reached, at which point one can "rest"—at least *vis-à-vis* that motive. In reality, a new motive will invariably supplant the former one. Every sign has a target state it strives to attain. The goal of Taurus is a state of comfort, the goal of Leo is a state of confidence, of Scorpio one of power, of Sagittarius faith, and for Pisces it's compassionate bliss. As soon as one need is satisfied, a new motive assumes priority. Whichever need is most dominant at the time is where psychic energy is directed.

To achieve a stable and enduring state of satisfaction requires that the relevant planetary function develop the necessary aptitude. Life necessitates that each planetary system keep evolving toward its fullest potential. A psychological need, therefore, acts as a lure that pulls us forward toward greater realization of an innate functional capacity. This is precisely what we mean by teleology—a final goal for the sake of which behavior occurs. A basic need is never completely fulfilled in the sense that we can never perfect our capacity to satisfy it. There is always room for improvement, as it were, and so the need inspires us to realize ever-higher expressions of functionality.

Taken collectively, the final goal is a state of optimal fulfillment of each sign-planet motivational system. When planetary functions have been fully developed, integrated, and harmoniously blended with all other planetary systems, then the final goal (telos) of psychological activity is attained: wholeness, or Self-realization. In spiritual traditions, such a state is described in terms that are consistent with Pisces—rapture, ecstasy, or nirvana.

SELF, MANDALA, AND ZODIAC

While Pisces may symbolize the final goal of individuation, the Self is perhaps best depicted astro-logically by the zodiac itself. Jung must surely have recognized that the zodiac is first and foremost a mandala image, which was his primary symbol for the Self. The Sanskrit word *mandala* means "circle" in the ordinary sense of the word. Likewise, the word zodiac is derived from the Greek, *zōidiakos,* which also means "circle". In the sphere of religious practices, as well as in psychology, a mandala denotes circular images that are drawn or painted. Again, the zodiac is a circular image, too, which symbolizes the psyche as a totality.

Because mandala images appear spontaneously in dreams and in certain states of conflict, Jung theorized that they represent an integrative factor.

This idea receives support from Buddhism where mandalas function as ritual instruments that assist meditation and concentration. Likewise, the horoscope, by objectifying the psyche through zodiac symbols, provides insight into the nature of consciousness. Integration is supported by study of the horoscope because it provides an image—a mandala—of the psyche as an integrated whole. Reflection and meditation upon such an image can promote the process of self-realization.

Mandala images often contain a quaternity or a multiple of four in the form of a cross, a star, or a square. In fact, the overwhelming majority of mandalas are characterized by the circle and the quaternity (see Figure 5, page 78). The circle and the square depict the inner and the outer aspects of life. The watery, fluid inner realm is round while the earthly world of substance is square.

The circle of the zodiac contains a fourfold structure, too, as determined by its four cardinal points that symbolize the beginning dates of the four seasons: Aries (Spring), Cancer (Summer), Libra (Fall), and Capricorn (Winter). Just as mandalas depict the inner and outer aspects of life, so each sign of the zodiac symbolizes an intrapsychic factor and a corresponding outer condition.

The circle of the zodiac contains a fourfold structure, too, as determined by its four cardinal points that symbolize the beginning dates of the four seasons: Aries (Spring), Cancer (Summer), Libra (Fall), and Capricorn (Winter). Just as mandalas depict the inner and outer aspects of life, so each sign of the zodiac symbolizes an intrapsychic factor and a corresponding outer condition.

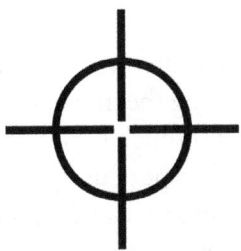

Figure 5: The Basic Mandala Image

In alchemy, mandalas represent the synthesis of the four elements to produce the *quinta essentia*, the "Incorruptible One," which represents the union of opposites necessary for the *Mysterium Coniunctionis*. As such, Jung considers the mandala image the preeminent symbol for the Self, the archetype of wholeness. The zodiac can also be viewed as a whole, with its four elements of fire, earth, air, and water—all opposites—that must be brought into balance by finding a center.

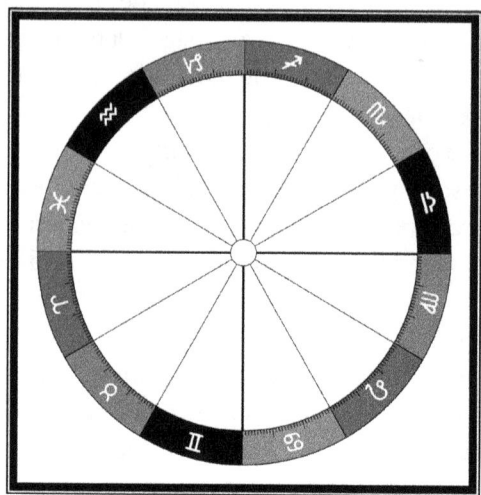

Figure 6: The Zodiac as a Mandala Image

Jung described the Self as both the center and the circumference of the psyche. Self-realization entails a centering of consciousness that involves the union of opposites; the Self incorporates within its paradoxical unity all the opposites embodied in the various archetypes. Likewise, the zodiac is comprised of six archetypal pairs of opposites—Aries/Libra through Virgo/Pisces—which, once integrated, enables the individual to find a new center, a point of balance that allows for harmony both within and without (see Figure 6, page 78).

Jung (1960) describes how centering brings about a shift of power from the ego to the Self, thus enabling the individual to more readily surrender to a higher power that works through him. Because the Self, of which the mandala is a symbol, is the archetype of unity and totality, it is, therefore, the God within. The individual, in seeking self-realization and unity, becomes the means through which "God seeks his goal." By fulfilling his own highest potential, the individual is also fulfilling God's will. This is why Jung felt that the individuation process was ultimately a spiritual journey.

All of this is implicit in the structure of the zodiac, which is a symbol both of microcosm and macrocosm, human and divine, part and whole. The prime dictum of astrology is, "as above, so below;" cosmos and psyche are mirror images. Jung noted that the "quaternity of the One," his mandala symbol for the Self, is likewise the schema for all images of God. Thus, the innermost divine essence of man is characterized by mandala images that can just as well express a God-image, the *atman* that is *Brahman*. An astrological chart is an image of Deity—the Universe as a whole—unfolding within the consciousness of an individual human being.

As symbols of the Self, mandalas seem to represent an integrating factor. Jung noted that when consciousness is confused, mandalas might emerge via dreams or fantasies as compensatory attempts at self-healing by imposing an ordered structure. When people are disoriented because of severe psychological conflict, the circular pattern of the mandala compensates the disorder of the psychic state—namely, through the construction of a central point to which everything is related. This can be interpreted as an attempt at self-healing on the part of Nature. The psyche instinctively produces a mandala image, which operates teleologically as a lure or a reminder of a potential wholeness yet to be realized.

Just so, the zodiac symbolizes a concentric arrangement of contradictory but reconcilable elements. It is precisely when people feel confused and conflicted that they often seek an astrologer. Like a mandala, the horoscope symbolizes the potential for integrating what appear to be irreconcilable parts into an ordered whole with a new center. For many people, the goal of a good reading is insight and integration, for the horoscope enables one to see that a disordered psychic state has a meaning that, once understood, can bring order out of chaos. Seeking a chart consultation may serve the same purpose as a spontaneous mandala image; it is the psyche's attempt at self-healing. Perhaps the astrologer is employed by the client's Self and used as an agent of the higher will.

THE TRANSCENDENT FUNCTION

The integration of personality is one of the prominent themes in Jungian psychology. We have seen that the first step toward integration is differentiation of all aspects of the personality. Differentiation and integration are co-existing processes in the development of the psyche. If one part of the personality is undifferentiated, this undeveloped part will still find ways of expressing itself, albeit in problematic ways. Personality remains fragmented; rogue systems operate independently and create problems for the whole person.

According to Jung (1960), once diversity has been achieved by the operation of the individuation process, the differentiated systems are integrated by the transcendent function. This function is endowed with the capacity to unite all the opposing trends of the several systems and to work toward the ideal of perfect wholeness. The transcendent function is the means by which the Self is realized.

An example of integration would be the Aries-Libra polarity. To the extent that these opposing principles remain unintegrated, the person is at war with himself. One part wants perfect freedom, the other perfect intimacy. Aries is the impulse to assert one's individual rights, whereas Libra is the impulse to consider the rights of others. Aries is assertive; Libra is cooperative. Such a person feels pulled in two directions that appear, on the surface, mutually exclusive. If he acts assertively, it is without grace or tact; thus he antagonizes others. However, if he behaves kindly, it is without strength or backbone; thus he loses other's respect. Either his freedom is compromised by an inability to get along with others, or his relationships are rendered superficial by an inability to assert. If he opts for freedom, he finds himself longing for relationship; if he commits to relationship, he finds himself yearning for freedom. Neither Aries nor Libra is fully satisfied.

If, however, these two complementary principles can be brought into balance, then both are enriched by the other's qualities. His capacity to assert himself is enhanced by awareness of how he will be received by others; boldness is thus tempered with kindness. By establishing cordial relations, he wins support for personal interests that he desires to pursue. He can be truly intimate because he is not afraid to lose himself in the process, and he can be separate without worry because he has earned the trust of his beloved. Instead of opposition or separation, there is a harmonious blend of Aries and Libran qualities. Such a person is *not* one whose behavior is sometimes in the Aries mode and sometimes in the Libra mode. Rather, a true synthesis between opposites has been achieved so that it may be said that he has transcended the Aries-Libra dichotomy and resolved what earlier appeared to be mutually exclusive instincts. Now his character reflects an interpenetration of Aries and Libra archetypes, like two primary colors joined to produce a beautiful hue that is both individual and unique.

EMERGENT PROPERTIES

In system theory, when two or more parts conjoin to produce a higher-level structure, this new structure would be called an *emergent property*, which is an attribute of character that emerges out of the integration of two or more sign-needs. A system is always hierarchically organized. Hierarchic theory is concerned with the fundamental differences between one level of complexity and another. A planet, for example, is of a lower order in the system than a planetary aspect that creates a compound structure out of two planets. A T-Square involving three planets is a yet higher structure.

As we move up the hierarchical structure of a given system, properties emerge which do not exist on lower levels. To use a common example, the property of "wetness" does not exist at the level of the hydrogen and oxygen atoms that make up the molecule we call "water". Processes and properties at higher levels of complexity are dependent upon the stability of elements that make up these levels. Yet, these emergent properties have no meaning at lower levels of description.

For example, at the first level of the psyche are the signs of the zodiac, which symbolize core motivations. A higher-level structure that emerges out of the zodiac is a planetary aspect that ties together two or more signs. This structure symbolizes behavioral attributes and experiences that do not exist at the level of the signs that comprise that structure. A bold and aggressive negotiator who talks to terrorists that have abducted hostages might have an integrated closing quincunx between Mars and Venus. This character structure is neither Martian nor Venusian, but a combination of both.

Each level of a system is progressively more complex than the one before and exhibits increasing degrees of freedom. An integrated Mars-Venus quincunx is free to pursue Aries and Libra needs in ways that are outside the behavioral range of either sign individually. Behavioral options open up that are non-existent at the level of Aries or Libra. In other words, there is more choice and flexibility; the individual can employ variable strategies within the context of fixed rules. The imperative of Aries is "you must assert to survive;" the canon of Libra is "you must compromise to relate." These rules are fixed and allow for little variation of behavior. However, once Mars and Venus are combined in cooperative harmony then behavioral patterns emerge that are less predictable and exhibit a larger variety of strategic choices.

As stated, each emergent level of organized complexity exhibits properties and attributes that could not have been predicted by the properties of its constituents at lower levels. These new emergent properties have no meaning at lower levels of the hierarchy. For example, "bold and aggressive negotiator" has no meaning at the level of Mars, which has nothing to do with negotiation. Likewise, it has no meaning on the level of Venus, which is the antithesis of boldness and aggression. Only by joining Mars and Venus together in a context of crisis resolution (quincunx) can a behavioral pattern emerge that exhibits the aforementioned properties of a "bold and aggressive negotiator who talks to terrorists that have abducted hostages." The higher level of organization includes characteristics from its lower levels—Aries and Libra—while at the same time adding something new.

Of course, the highest level of the psyche from an astrological perspective would be the horoscope as a whole. Accordingly, we can anticipate that personality at this level evidences certain emergent properties—traits, aptitudes, and life themes—that cannot be predicted by analysis of any one part alone. The best metaphor for this level of the system would be the concept of *story*. Planets constitute the characters of our story, both inner and outer. Houses provide contexts for action, and aspects symbolize the relationships between characters. Each chart, in effect, tells a story, which is the unfoldment of character over time. We will be examining this idea in more detail in later chapters.

URANUS AS TRANSCENDENT FUNCTION

According to Jung, the aim of the transcendent function is the revelation of the totality of the psyche as a single, integrated whole. Other forces of personality may oppose the operation of the transcendent function. For example, repression—withdrawal of attention from a feeling or impulse—divides and fragments the psyche. Nonetheless, the forward, unifying propulsion of development will continue to take place.

Astrologically, this process is best described by Uranus, which exhibits all the properties that Jung attributes to the transcendent function. Described elsewhere as "the observing self," Uranus signifies six distinct yet complementary actions—objectifying, detaching, awakening, liberating, changing, and progressing (Perry, 2000). Uranus is our capacity to observe the contents of consciousness from a detached (transcendent) perspective and allow them full emergence into awareness. This capacity to observe without judgment is precisely what enables integration to occur. When we relinquish attachment to a preferred way of experiencing, we allow the wholeness of the psyche to manifest. And by not identifying with one part of the self at the expense of another, we transcend limited perspectives and allow the totality of the psyche to be revealed. Uranian objectivity thus liberates the individual from rigid, dysfunctional patterns of behavior and frees the person to experiment with new possibilities.[8]

Consider, for example, an individual with Moon in opposition to Jupiter. She experiences a conflict between her need for belonging and her need for

---

[8] If we define transcendence as the spiritual impulse of reconciling duality and merging in oneness with the whole, then Neptune would best be described as "the transcendent function." However, what Jung meant by this term is closer in meaning to our concept of Uranus.

meaning. That Uranus is not aspecting either of these two planets does not prevent it from assisting their integration. Imagine that everyone in this person's family is a Christian fundamentalist; yet, she prefers Buddhist doctrines that abstain from fixed definitions of a transcendent deity. Not surprisingly, her family withdraws whenever she begins to espouse her beliefs. If she is overly attached to her religious convictions, she runs the risk of alienating her family. However, if she identifies so closely with her need for belonging that she denies her true convictions, she feels like a hypocrite. She might argue with family members in hopes of persuading them to accept her beliefs (and therefore accept her). In so doing, her conversations about religion are overly subjective, strident, and irrational because they inevitably stimulate fears of rejection.

If, however, she can activate her Uranus function, she will be enabled to view the conflict from a detached perspective and see that any attempt by one person to convert the other is doomed to failure. Realizing this, she may decide to try something different. Perhaps she begins to listen in a sympathetic way to the views of her family without judging them or challenging them. Likewise, she discovers she can sensitively express those tenets of her faith that are in keeping with her family's Christian values, thereby creating bridges between the two belief systems. One of her primary religious values (Jupiter) becomes a tender concern for loved ones (Moon), and her capacity for expressing her convictions is enriched by a subtle sensitivity to the emotional underpinnings of the other's personal beliefs.

Uranus, in other words, has enabled her to transcend the illusion of mutually exclusive opposites. By exercising tolerance, she can liberate herself from a fruitless conflict and realize that the Moon and Jupiter can be integrated at a higher level of complexity. By asking questions and listening to her family, she awakens to a deeper understanding of the historical antecedents of their faith. In effect, she changes her attitude, thus allowing progress toward wholeness—Moon *and* Jupiter—to resume. Even though Uranus was not directly involved in the aspect, it could still exercise an integrative function, helping her to see both sides and allowing the conflict to work itself out in the light of a higher, more objective and inclusive awareness.

Of course, when Uranus does aspect a particular planet, it will be more directly involved in processes that pertain to that planet. If it is a soft aspect, Uranus will enable that planetary function to operate in a more progressive, enlightened manner. However, if it is a hard aspect, then that planet may resist processes of change and is more likely to function in an erratic, unstable manner until it integrates Uranus.

It must be stressed that unless the individual has a relatively strong ego, he or she will not be able to attain the perspective of the observing self. Uranus requires one to temporarily detach from egoic concerns for approval and validation. To look at oneself in an objective, self-critical light presupposes that one has a relatively stable sense of self. If one lacks self-esteem, then it will be difficult to adopt a Uranian perspective.

Significantly, Jung (1953) describes the goal of the transcendent function—wholeness—in terms that are remarkably consistent with the properties of Uranus. The person who achieves the goal of wholeness, says Jung, "possesses an attitude that is beyond the reach of emotional entanglements and violent shocks—a consciousness detached from the world" (CW 13, par. 68). Likewise, when Uranus is integrated there is a capacity for radical objectivity, detachment, and tolerance. Liberated from egoic attachments and entanglements, such a person achieves equanimity and is, therefore, relatively unshockable. He or she is not only able to successfully resolve external conflicts, but, more importantly, internal ones as well.

Here again, astrology sheds new light on traditional psychodynamic theory. Not only is Uranus relatively synonymous with Jung's transcendent function, but its various, interrelated functions add insight and complexity to a psychological process of preeminent importance: how people evolve toward wholeness.

SUMMARY

Motivation in astrology is rooted in the zodiac, each sign of which symbolizes a basic need. While early theories of motivation postulated that all human motivation was biologically determined, later theories refuted this claim by showing that many needs have no clear physiological basis. By locating human motivation in archetypes, which may be essential principles of reality, one can argue that specific motives are intrinsic to consciousness; that is, core human needs are extensions of universal formative principles—archetypes, or divine ideals—that organize and animate life on all levels.

The zodiac provides a comprehensive cataloging of motives, showing how interrelated needs can be classified within a sign "set". It also depicts the quality of relationship between different classes of needs. Each sign is related to every other sign by virtue of a specific angle (aspect), thus revealing the intrapsychic relations between different motivations. Angles between signs depict how various motives may harmonize or conflict. The organization of the zodiac also illustrates how the twelve fundamental motivations are hierarchically related in accordance to their priority. Not only are needs prioritized, but they are associated with specific developmental stages. Each sign represents a developmental task, the achievement of which paves the way for the next sign. Different motives assume priority at different stages of life.

As an integrated totality, the zodiac itself symbolizes the master motive—wholeness or unity. The sequence of signs in the zodiac depicts what Jung called the process of individuation. The ultimate goal of this process is the realization of the Self, which Jung described as the actualization of all psychological potentials in a state of cooperative balance or harmony. To realize the Self, each sign (and its ruling planet), must become fully differentiated and integrated with every other sign and planet.

Planets, as the active agents of signs, represent psychological functions that are geared toward satisfying the needs of the signs they rule. Whereas modern science presumes that the development and evolution of the psyche is a random, matter-driven process devoid of any intelligence or over-arching purpose, astrology supports Aristotle's theory of teleological causation. Planets strive toward states of optimal need satisfaction; yet, the capacity to attain such states requires continuous development. This process is inwardly directed and animated by archetypes, or divine ideals, as symbolized by zodiacal signs. It is the allure of an ideal state of optimal need satisfaction that drives evolution forward. Optimal satisfaction has been described as a feeling of oneness, or bliss, which is the affective equivalent of psychological wholeness—simultaneous and balanced fulfillment of every need. It is precisely this innate striving to attain unitive consciousness that makes astrology a teleological model.

As the unity archetype, the Self is the organizing principle of the personality and has traditionally been depicted as a mandala image. Here again, astrology parallels perennial wisdom by virtue of the fact that the zodiac is itself a mandala image—a square within a circle that symbolizes the unity of inner and outer realities. The Zodiac is both a God image—the macrocosm—and an image of the psyche—the microcosm. As such, the zodiac is an appropriate symbol for the Self, a seed of God unfolding within the consciousness of the individual human being.

What Jung called the transcendent function is responsible for uniting the various differentiated subsystems of the psyche—signs and planets—into an integral whole. The transcendent function is the means by which the Self is realized. In astrology, this function is best described by Aquarius-Uranus, which is our capacity for detachment, radical objectivity, and liberation from self-limiting ideas toward a new, wholistic perspective.

As two or more planets become cooperatively linked via aspects, higher-level structures are born. These higher-level structures are characterized by emergent properties—traits and attributes that do not exist at the level of the planets that make up the aspect. The horoscope as a whole produces the ultimate emergent property, the personality, which is best described as a story that signifies the unfoldment of character over time.

Chapter Four

PLANETARY EMOTION & TARGET STATES

Chapter Three can be summarized by the simple assertion: *needs motivate*. Once a felt need begins to dominate awareness, that person is motivated to engage in behaviors that satisfy the need. A theory of motivation, therefore, must deal with human feelings and emotions. Feelings/emotions are inseparable from the motivational process. People act out of anger, fear, love, excitement, pride, shame, aesthetic pleasure, and so on. Yet, the exact nature of emotional responses is a complex phenomenon that has spawned a considerable amount of research over the last 100 years, including entire books dedicated to the subject (Jones, 1995; Goleman, 1995). In this chapter, we will explore the significance of emotion for an astrological theory of personality. I will propose that emotions are "archetypal voices" of sign-planet motivational systems and that they function as barometers of need satisfaction.

From the ancient Greeks to the middle of the 18th century, what we now call emotions were commonly referred to as passions. *Passion* derives from the Latin, *pati*, which in turn is related to the Greek, *pathos*, meaning suffering. Also related to passion are such terms as *passivity* and *patient*. Emotions are experienced passively in the sense that they are beyond the individual's control, as when a patient "succumbs" to illness. The term emotion comes from the Latin, *e + movere*, which originally meant to migrate or transfer from one place to another. It was also used to refer to states of agitation or perturbation, whether physical or psychological. Emotion thus emphasizes the often stormy or turbulent nature of emotional reactions along with their tendency to arouse and activate behavior.

Averill (1980) points out that at the root of these concepts is the notion that an individual is undergoing or suffering some change, as opposed to doing or initiating change. Colloquially, the experience of passivity during emotion is expressed in many ways. We "fall" in love, are "paralyzed" by fear, "plagued" with doubt, "haunted" by guilt," "torn" by jealousy, "carried away" with joy, "consumed" by envy, "seized" with remorse, and so forth. In archetypal psychology, one hears of "daimon possession," meaning the usurpation of the total personality by a split-off part. This way of speaking implies that emotions are something that happens *to* us, not something we do. It is as though emotions were alien forces that "overcome" and "possess" an individual.

Jones (1995) declares that emotions, or "affects" (the two terms being synonymous), are best understood as presymbolic representatives and governors of motivational systems. An emotion is presymbolic because it is a way of knowing that does not depend upon the symbol systems we call language, and it is the experiential representative of a motive because it conveys information about our state of being and what we need at any given moment. In other words, an affect is an analog of a psycho-physiological state.

Just as sense organs within the brain monitor the body's states and needs through feelings such as hunger, thirst, and temperature, so emotions provide a continuous readout of how the psyche is functioning. If a person's survival is jeopardized, he feels fear; if his desire for learning is stimulated, he feels curious; if his need for self-esteem is met, he feels proud. "Emotions are the experiential monitor of complex motivational systems," says Jones. "By cross-comparing the affective intensity of feelings from competing systems, the organism has a simple, effective way of prioritizing information and thus reaching a decision, which, in turn, initiates a course of action" (p. 45). It is in this regard that emotions are governors of motivational systems.

We can think of this astrologically by relating each sign-planet motivational system to a specific range of affects. Consider, for example, a young man with Mars square Moon who regularly experiences a simultaneous desire for freedom (Aries-Mars) and closeness (Cancer-Moon). As one motivational system is competing with another, the intensity of the competing affects allow for a quick means of prioritizing information and determining choice. If our young man recently spent a considerable amount of time alone, it is likely that his Cancer-Moon motivational system will have greater affective intensity, thus motivating him to seek closeness. However, if he just enjoyed an intimate weekend with his girlfriend at home, his Aries-Mars motivational system is likely to become dominant and he will feel an urge to separate.

The connection between emotions and motives is illustrated by the etymologic history of the terms; both words are derivatives of the Latin *movere* and its past participle *motivere*. In effect, emotions are subjective experiences that "move" us to action. Recall that Maslow referred to needs as impulse-voices. If sufficiently attuned to these archetypal voices, one can "hear" what they want. Asked to account for his sudden separation from his girlfriend, the young man might say, "Something was telling me to leave; I had to get away."

Affects are prime motivators of behavior. "Cross-sectionally, affects provide the principle means of identifying moment-to-moment shifts in motivational dominance" writes Lichtenberg (1989, p. 260). Emotions provide the affective signals indicating which motivational systems are predominant at a given moment. If planets could talk, each would have a characteristic imperative; each would have its own distinct internal voice.

Aries-Mars:	"Just do *it!* Go for it! It's your *right*."
Taurus-Venus:	"If it feels good, enjoy it. Pleasure yourself. Mellow out."
Gemini-Mercury:	"That's interesting; define and classify it. Put on your thinking cap."
Cancer-Moon:	"Listen, turn inward; what are you feeling now?"
Leo-Sun:	"Let it shine, baby. Express yourself!"
Virgo-Mercury:	"Be careful, there's a problem here. Figure it out."
Libra-Venus:	"Turn on the charm and *engage*. Consider, compromise, cooperate."
Scorpio-Pluto:	"Face your fear. It's do or die. Get down and dirty."
Sagittarius-Jupiter:	"Keep the faith, baby. God is good. Just do the right thing."
Capricorn-Saturn:	"Bear down and focus. Concentrate. Control yourself."
Aquarius-Uranus:	"Expect the unexpected. Stay open and detached."
Pisces-Neptune:	"Let go and let God. Surrender. Trust the Universe."

The above examples illustrate how we experience the planets as a form of self-talk. These are our inner voices, the archetypal imperatives that tell us what to do through specific emotional signals that are converted into language.

For example, we might feel angry (Mars) and then say to ourselves, "I've got to fight; he can't do that to me!" If we feel attracted (Venus), we might think: "Be nice; let them know you are interested." Each planetary state has its own agenda and behavioral imperative. One can also experience conflicting emotions and voices as evidenced by hard aspects between planets, a subject we will take up in later chapters.

Planets as Emotions
A Continuum of Emotional Expression

SIGN-PLANET	MOTIVE	A CONTINUUM OF POSITIVE TO NEGATIVE EMOTIONS	TARGET STATE
Aries/Mars	Survival, Freedom, Autonomy	Joyful, excited, enthusiastic, bold, brave, eager, desirous, impatient, annoyed, irritable, angry, fierce, rageful, discouraged, dispirited, timid, afraid, bored, dead.	Joy & Aliveness (vs. Deadness)
Taurus/Venus	Safety, Security, Constancy	Comfortable, pleasured, attractive, secure, safe, stable, calm, serene, mellow, at ease, lazy, lethargic, stubborn, grasping, greedy, insecure, unsafe, unstable.	Security & Comfort, (vs. Insecurity)
Gemini/Mercury	Knowledge, Communication	Informed, knowledgeable, proficient, educated, Interested, curious, inquisitive, wonder, restless, scattered, nervous, unsettled, jittery, uninformed, ignorant	Wonder & Informed (vs. Ignorance)
Cancer/Moon	Closeness, Caring, Belonging	Tender, loving, caring, sympathetic, understanding, warm, close, accepting, protective, maternal, sentimental, shy, disconnected, rejected, forlorn, abandoned.	Caring & Acceptance (vs. Rejection)
Leo/Sun	Validation, Approval, Self-Esteem	Proud, confident, self-assured, certain, happy, playful, worthy, romantic, willful, stubborn, defensive, disdainful, uncertain, unworthy, embarrassed, humiliated.	Pride & Confidence (vs. Shame & Doubt)
Virgo/Mercury	Productivity, Service, Competence	Productive, useful, helpful, competent, efficient, humble, modest, troubled, worried, skeptical, perplexed, critical, obsessed, incompetent, broken, useless.	Useful & Productive (vs. Incompetent)
Libra/Venus	Partnership, Social Relatedness, Beauty	Social, cooperative, agreeable, nice, affectionate, balanced, engaged, intimate, attractive, dependent, indecisive, hesitant, unresolved, uncooperative, separated.	Intimate & Harmonious (vs. Disharmony)
Scorpio/Pluto	Transformation, Power, Integration	Powerful, centered, intense, erotic, passionate, vulnerable, wounded, ashamed, ostracized, impotent, guarded, afraid, paranoid, possessed, vindictive, destructive.	Powerful & Centered (vs. Paranoid)
Sagittarius/Jupiter	Meaning, Truth, Justice, Expansion	Faith, hope, optimism, enthusiasm, jovial, expansive, benevolent, righteous, knowledgeable, euphoric, zealous, manic, hopeless, faithless, disbelieving.	Optimistic & Expansive (vs. Hopeless)
Capricorn/Saturn	Structure, Order, Perfection, Success	Successful, organized, focused, ambitious, determined, serious, grave, stressed, anxious, inferior, craving, inadequate, failure, gloom, isolation, guilt, despair.	Order & Success, (vs. Disorder & Failure)
Aquarius/Uranus	Perspective, Insight, Liberation, Change	Detached, objective, open, dispassionate, altruistic, tolerant, different, liberated, rebellious, agitated, upset, shocked, unstable, remote, cold, aloof, disconnected.	Objective (vs. Schizoid Detachment)
Pisces/Neptune	Transcendence, Unity, Charity, Altruism	Elated, cosmic love, compassion, oceanic oneness, bliss, inspiration, passivity, confusion, apathy, withdrawal, helpless, weak, fatigue, loss, despair, guilt, grief.	Bliss & Compassion (vs. Grief & Guilt)

© Glenn Perry, Ph.D.

Figure 7: Planets as Emotions

As analogs of psycho-physiological states, affects are experienced through a range of intensity. This intensity gradient can be described by pairs of words that represent opposite extremes of emotion along a continuum. In our astrological model, there is a different affective range for each planet. Mars is joy→deadness; the Sun is pride→shame; Neptune is elation→grief, and so on (see Figure 7, page 90). Experienced changes in intensity are the analogic representation of complex sensing systems that allow us to make quantitative distinctions, such as *how* angry is the person, *how* determined, or *how* proud. Intensity variations in affects provide the means for prioritizing needs: the loudest, most intense affect is the one that gains our attention and thus activates the behavioral sequences of that motivational system.

Planetary emotions also differ qualitatively. In Figure 7, this qualitative range illustrates various degrees of integration of sign-planet motivational systems. A well-integrated, fully functional planet will more often be experienced in terms of positive affects, which are listed toward the beginning of the continuum. A repressed, weak planetary function will more often be experienced in terms of negative affects, which are listed toward the end.

If, for example, an individual has difficulty with the Capricorn-Saturn motive, he is more likely to experience the negative end of Saturn's emotional continuum—despair, pessimism, and inferiority. However, if he overcomes this tendency and works to strengthen his Saturn function, he is more likely to experience its positive states—a feeling of control, success, and superior status.

CALIBRATION AND TARGET STATES

In systems theory, the relationship of emotion to motivation would be described in terms of calibration and target states. Every individual has a range of permissible feeling for a given motivational system. For Capricorn-Saturn, we tolerate a certain amount of failure or lack of success, beyond which we are motivated to achieve. For Aries-Mars, we tolerate a certain amount of restraint, beyond which we are compelled to break free. The term for this fixed range is the *calibration,* or "setting" of the motivational system, like a setting on a thermostat. Just as a thermostat automatically responds to temperature changes and activates switches controlling heating mechanisms, so human beings automatically respond to changes in affective states and respond by activating corrective behaviors.

With the Capricorn-Saturn system, if a person feels he is falling too far behind in his goals, he will tend to try harder; if he feels he is way ahead of schedule, he may, for the moment, relax and focus on some other need until he again feels an urgency to achieve. Each sign-planet in astrology has a desired state. Capricorn-Saturn would be a state of order, control, success, and so forth. Leo-Sun would be a state of pride, confidence, and personal happiness. The degree of realization of the preferred state is continually monitored by a reference signal—an affect—which specifies the amount of deviance from the "target state."

When a disturbance arises in the environment that has a destabilizing effect on the desired state, this effect is registered as a varying reference signal. The degree of variance from the target state represents a measure of error; the indication of error is then used to trigger a behavior that opposes the error. Thus, changes in action (output) are opposed to the effects of disturbance (input) in exact measure as to the degree of error from the target state.

To put this in astrological terms, imagine an individual with a strong Capricorn-Saturn component to his personality, the target state of which is a feeling of success and superior status. Of late, however, he has been underfunctioning on the job. Eventually his boss tells him that he is being demoted due to inferior performance. This is the disturbance; his affective response includes feelings of anxiety, guilt, and failure. As a reference signal, these affects vary markedly from the target state of success. To the extent that he feels unsuccessful, he is likely to compensate by working harder, staying focused, putting in extra time, and so on. His improved performance is calculated to counteract the feelings of guilt and failure that have been evoked by his demotion. His goal is to re-establish a feeling of success.

A primary goal of any system—human or otherwise—is to restore balance (homeostasis) by counteracting disturbance and re-attaining its target states. An emotional variable that has slipped out of its prescribed bounds is the system's equivalent of motivation in the sense that it leads the individual to search for a means to bring it back into line. The point here is that an organism does not simply respond to an environmental stimulus in a direct, linear fashion; rather it controls its responses by virtue of intrinsic reference signals—emotions.

Human beings have internal needs, goals, and purposes independent of environmental circumstances. A person controls inputs in accord with the effect these inputs are likely to have on desired states. An individual employs ego defense mechanisms to protect his self-concept and maintain his customary level of self-esteem (Leo). If a person's property is threatened, s/he may become possessive (Taurus). If survival is jeopardized, s/he is apt to fight (Aries). If one's religious convictions are challenged, one is likely to argue (Sagittarius). Again, the response is determined by the perception of disturbance. If the disturbing effect is great, the compensatory response is great. The determining factor, again, is not the stimulus itself, but the person's assessment of the effect this stimulus will have on his preferred state.

As living systems, human beings utilize feedback to regulate their functioning. A feedback loop is a process in which information about one's current state is continually compared with one's desired state as a way of keeping on track. It begins with some internal standard of comparison—a desired state of optimal satisfaction. In an attempt to achieve and maintain the standard, people compare where they are to where they want to be. If there is congruence, they terminate that set of behaviors; if there is incongruence, they continue to strive.

Miller (1960) conceptualized this as a TOTE unit, which stands for the sequence of *Testing* one's state against the standard, *Operating* if there is a discrepancy, again *Testing*, and finally *Exiting* when there is a match between the standard and one's state of being. If we were to analyze a Taurus-Venus motivational system, a TOTE unit would operate the following way:

1. **Testing**: A person experiences a need for security and is motivated to satisfy it. He has a standard, or preferred state—prosperity—and "tests" his current state against the standard. He then sets a specific goal that he hopes will satisfy the motive, and decides what behaviors are appropriate to achieve the goal. For example, he decides to embark on a savings plan of putting away $1000 per/month.
2. **Operation**: He then implements his savings plan to attain the extrinsic goal of saving $1000 per/month in hopes of satisfying the motivating need for increased security.
3. **Testing**: At completion of the behavior, i.e., after each month of successfully meeting his goal, he checks (tests) to see if accomplishment of the goal has led to the desired state of prosperity.
4. **Exiting**: If his need for increased security is satisfied from attaining the goal, that motive will cease to be dominant and a new motive becomes foremost. He may suddenly decide he wants to enjoy life more and plans for regular vacations with his wife (Leo-Sun motivational system). If, however, his savings did not lead to satisfaction, then he will have to "operate" again by coming up with a new plan.

In the above example, we can see how the Venus target state of prosperity becomes the standard for the operation of a TOTE feedback loop. Once the person becomes aware of the potential satisfaction, he engages in a behavior—saving money—aimed at achieving the satisfaction. Upon reaching satisfaction, his state of being will match the standard and the sequence will end or recede into the background. In other words, if the plan is successful, it will become habit and not need to be uppermost in his mind. Every sign-planet motivational system operates in a similar way. In later chapters, we will explore what happens when more than one motivational system is operative at the same time, i.e., when planets are in aspect.

The relative strength of a motive can be inferred from how a planet is constellated in the chart as a whole; that is, how many planets it disposes, its sign and house position, and the aspects it forms to other planets. Although these topics will be covered thoroughly in later chapters, a brief comment may apply here. If a planet receives many aspects, and/or is in its own sign or house, then the affects related to that planet will be strongly experienced and will constitute a dominant motive. One cannot tell merely by looking at the chart, however, whether the planetary function is well integrated, only that it will be a dominant affect. Such a planet may symbolize a chronic "mood," for a mood is simply a relatively stable pattern of feeling—a kind of global affective response pattern that is more diffuse and enduring than an affect. It may not be a response to a specific event, but rather expresses itself in certain qualities of feeling that saturate a person's every perception, thought, and behavior.

For example, if the planet is Jupiter, the person may be perpetually optimistic; if Saturn, the native could be chronically depressed, if Mars, continuously angry, and so on. These affects would repeatedly activate the corresponding planetary function to engage in some behavior that attempts to satisfy the need which the emotion conveys. Such a pattern of behavior would constitute a dominant trait.

To summarize, people become aware of basic needs through the processing of information from the environment and from their own physiology. They experience these needs as emotional states that motivate them to act in state-specified ways; that is, to choose behavioral goals that will result in the desired state of need satisfaction. They tend to persist until the goals are achieved and the needs are satisfied. If their behavioral strategies prove effective, then goal attainment will result in need satisfaction and termination of the behavioral sequence. Once a behavior becomes a successful habit-pattern, conscious awareness can shift to other concerns. Otherwise, individuals are compelled to reevaluate their strategy and decide on a new goal or a new approach.

Astrologically, this process can be understood by relating sign-planet motivational systems to specific affects that are experienced on a range of intensity. Each sign-planet system has a target state, or preferred feeling, that is experienced as a varying reference signal. Deviation from the target state evokes a disturbing affect, which, in turn, stimulates a corrective planetary action that is calculated to achieve the desired feeling. Planets, therefore, symbolize flowing goal-oriented movements that constitute a series of operations conducing toward an end. Such processes involve continuous change until the goal state is reached. In the next section, we will explore how planets can be correlated with specific kinds of psychological states.

PLANETS AS PSYCHOLOGICAL STATES

Planets not only symbolize a range of affects that are evoked in response to specific events, they also represent enduring psychological states. According to Horowitz (1987), a psychological state is characterized by a recurrent pattern of experience as reflected in mood, attitude, internal dialogue, facial expression, posture, voice tone, and what a person says and does. In other words, a state is reflected in virtually every aspect of a person's inner life and outward behavior. States common to most persons include those moments dominated by strong expression of emotions, such as anxiety, anger, guilt, sadness, shame, sexual excitement, surprise, and joy. However, a state is more complex than its emotional component, for it also includes an underlying motive, associated beliefs, self-talk, and an outward attitude. A person's dominant states are the behavioral manifestations of his character structure, which is reflected in the way specific planets are constellated in the birthchart.

In our astrological model, each planet can be associated with a range of states. Remember, a state is characterized by a recurrent mood, attitude, internal dialogue, and behavioral pattern. Consider, again, the planet Saturn. Wherever Saturn is located in the chart, we find a tremendous drive for perfection. But perfectionism can manifest along a continuum of states from suicidally depressed to supremely successful. Since perfection represents an absolute that can never be attained, it can result in perpetual anxiety if carried to a negative extreme.

This sort of mood is what we often find in people who are too Saturnian, or *saturnine*, meaning gloomy, pessimistic, cold, or depressed. The attitude symbolized by Saturn and evidenced in its melancholy behavior is negative; it is the fear that one will never be good enough. Good enough for what, we ask? For anything with which Saturn happens to be involved. To determine the specifics, we would have to look at Saturn's sign, house, and aspects. A strong possibility with any Saturn placement, however, will be an inferiority complex, fears of inadequacy, expectations of failure, depressive tendencies, and the like. The internal dialogue tends to be self-deprecating and predictive of failure. "I don't have what it takes. It's too hard, I'm going to embarrass myself," and so on.

Of course, this is but one way Saturn expresses itself. Just as often, Saturn goes to the other extreme by overcompensating, thus producing the chronic achiever. This person, through a combination of discipline, perseverance, and hard work, pushes himself to the top of his field. No matter how much status and honor are conferred, however, he will not be satisfied. Since perfection can never be attained, he can never stop striving to excel, to surpass himself, to be perfect. This Saturn mood is stressed, driven, and relentless. The attitude is ambitious and superior, "I am (have to be) the best." Self-talk focuses on setting the next goal, formulating plans, pressuring the self to improve, "You should have gotten the promotion; you can do better."

In both instances, Saturn is overfunctioning and unintegrated. When Saturn is operating in a balanced, harmonious manner, the individual is earnest, has a determined attitude, accepts responsibility, respects limits, and works systematically toward the achievement of long term goals. The difference with an integrated Saturn is that the person is more relaxed, patient, and flexible in pursuing aims, is less driven, and more capable of achieving and enjoying success.

States can usefully be divided into three categories: undermodulated, well-modulated, and overmodulated (see Figure 8, page 97). To modulate a state means to regulate and control its expression, just as one controls the tone and amplitude of one's voice. The impulse voices of sign-planet motivational systems can similarly be regulated. Planetary states occur along a continuum from positive to negative. Where on the continuum a person's experience falls is a function of how that planet is modulated.

Well-modulated/integrated states are spontaneous, openly expressive, and congruent in verbal and nonverbal communications. Impulses are well contained and controlled; there is a sense of being "in tune" with oneself. Because the person is relatively conscious of that planetary function, it comes under volitional control. There is flexibility and freedom of choice in expressing behavior appropriate to that function. One can turn it on, tone it down, or turn it off as the situation requires.

PLANETARY EMOTION & TARGET STATES • 97

MOTIVATIONAL SYSTEM	UNDERMODULATED	MODULATED	OVERMODULATED
Aries-Mars	Angry mood, hostile attitude, impatient, selfish, aggressive, impulsive, rude	Joyful mood, positive attitude, vital, alive, enthusiastic, assertive, spontaneous	Passive anger, hidden resentment, covert aggression, as if strong & bold, but scared
Taurus-Venus	Licentious mood, lazy attitude, possessive, self-indulgent, greedy, rigid, materialistic	Mellow mood, easy going, sensuous, calm, stable, patient, steadfast, secure	Uncomfortable with bodies, as if stable, anal-retentive, clinging, but insecure Unsensual
Gemini-Mercury	Nervous mood, glib attitude, restless mind, scattered, shallow, hyperactive, garrulous	Alert mood, keen mind, curious, wonder, eager to learn, observant, knowledgeable	Afraid to learn new things, rigid ideas, contrived knowledge, dis-interested, as if smart
Cancer-Moon	Moody, hyper-feminine, dependent, needy, overreactive, hysterical, effusive, maudlin	Tender mood, caring attitude, protective, vulnerable, sensitive, soft, sympathetic	Uncomfortable with feelings, as if caring, but shut down, shy, withdrawn, afraid of rejection
Leo-Sun	Inflated mood, egotistical attitude, vain, boastful, grandiose, exhibitionistic	Playful mood, confident attitude, creative flow, sunny, affable, generous, honorable	Defensive mood, as if special, hidden shame, false pride, affected, uncertain, uncreative
Virgo-Mercury	Critical mind-set, faultfinding, fastidious, troubled, worried, picky, carping, irritable	Modest, humble, conscientious, analytical, efficient, competent, helpful, useful	Uptight mood, overconscientious, obsessive, as if competent, fearful of making mistakes
Libra-Venus	Dependent mood, compliant, too nice, eager to please, syrupy, equivocating	Agreeable mood, cooperative attitude, charming, fair-minded, polite, engaging	As if nice, phony, uncomfortable with intimacy, rigid social style, disingenuous
Scorpio-Pluto	Fearful mood, dark mind-set, paranoid, distrustful; as if possessed, vindictive, evil	Intense mood, passionate attitude, deep feelings, powerful, regenerative, healing	Afraid of sex, death, and power; closed, invulnerable, rigid, uneasy with intense feelings
Sagittarius-Jupiter	Euphoric mood, pompous attitude, full of advice, blind optimism, manic, unrealistic	Jovial mood, positive attitude, optimistic, enthusiastic, hopeful, ethical, far-sighted	Narrow, self-righteous attitude, rigid opinions, lacks true faith, shallow religiosity, amoral
Capricorn-Saturn	Depressed mood, negative attitude, driven, pressured, anxious, pessimistic, gloomy	Serious mood, determined attitude, dutiful, responsible, disciplined, patient, realistic	Fearful of failure, lack of discipline, avoid hard work, as if responsible, pretense of success
Aquarius-Uranus	Shocked, detached attitude, aloof, remote; or agitated, unstable, odd & rebellious	Tolerant attitude, open minded, objective, impersonal, humanitarian, progressive	Afraid of change, rigid approach to progress, as if open-minded, reactionary, oppositional
Pisces-Neptune	Spacey mood, passive attitude, victim mentality, confused, helpless, sad, tragic, guilty, addicted, co-dependent, deluded	Blissful mood, deep trust in God, idealistic, empathic, compassionate, selfless love, yielding, spiritual	Fear of chaos, lack of true trust in God, as if spiritual, but can't let go; avoids tragedy and experiences of loss, uncharitable

© Glenn Perry, Ph.D.

Figure 8: A Listing of Planetary States

If a function is unintegrated, it may either be overmodulated, undermodulated, or vacillate back and forth. **Undermodulated** states involve experience and behavior that is not well controlled. The person tends to overfunction and express that quality to excess. Often, there is a sense of something "taking over" the person; behavior is characterized by intrusive moods and memories, irrational outbursts, and regressive immaturity. Feelings may "leak out" in the form of inappropriate comments or behavior. If the function tends to operate outside of awareness, it is usually expressed in a primitive, impulsive manner. On the other hand, undermodulated states may be quite conscious, but the person exaggerates and overidentifies with the planetary process that produces those states. A woman, for example, may be quite proud of her ability to behave in aggressive, competitive, and independent ways, yet she has difficulty toning down her Mars behavior in situations that warrant it.

Overmodulated states, on the other hand, seem to have rigid control features, sometimes leading to a sense of contrivance or pretense as well as restraint with regard to expression of that function. The person tends to underfunction in this area and appears uncomfortable with the motivating impulse. Because the function is repressed, behavior seems phony; the person acts "as if" they had the right emotion or attitude, but it appears ingenuine. A person with an overmodulated Jupiter, for instance, might have difficulty believing that justice will occur, that the Universe is lawful, or that ethical and moral precepts are worth following. His personal philosophy might appear well-reasoned, but in some way is compensatory to fears or doubts related to Jupiter matters. He is not likely to be open to revising his beliefs or considering alternative religious, philosophical or moral perspectives.

Typically, a planet may appear overmodulated one moment, and undermodulated the next. This is because when a function is repressed it builds up a charge and pushes against the defenses that oppress it. An archetype has its own autonomy and cannot be denied forever. When it finally breaks through, there is an excessive, irrational quality to its expression—like a damn breaking—and the person seems "flooded" with the planet's energy.

Every sign-planet motivational system is modulated to one degree or another (see Figure 8, page 97). How a planet is modulated is suggested by its position in the overall chart, especially its aspects to other planets. Some planets and aspects will stimulate a planet to excess (under modulation), while others will suppress it (over modulation). This will be explored in detail in later chapters.

Recall in the previous example of Saturn that it was undermodulated; Saturn was being expressed in an extreme, out-of-control manner that was characterized by blind ambition, unrealistic goals, a driven attitude, excessive self-criticism, and compulsive perfectionism. The person was possessed with a need to be successful yet couldn't control the function (Saturn) necessary to achieve it in a balanced way. If this individual experienced failure or defeat, it is likely s/he would overreact and collapse into depression, loss of conviction, gloom, and self-deprecation.

If Saturn were overmodulated, on the other hand, the person would tend to avoid behaviors that would lead to success. While the person may want to be successful, and may give an outward appearance of success, it is more pretense than real. There is an inclination to procrastinate, resist authority, reject limits, and avoid the planning and hard work that is necessary to achieve long-term goals. Again, if Saturn is unintegrated, a person can express both the undermodulated and the overmodulated versions at different times. By comparison, a well-modulated Saturn would entail a serious mood, a realistic attitude, and an internal dialogue that reflects a sober, responsible approach to achievable ends. Goals would be wellplanned and plans would be well executed, leading to eventual success.

There are several advantages to categorizing states. By labeling a state, one derives a name for a kind of experience that correlates to a specific planet. The label suffices to refer to all the patterns that cohere to form that state of mind—mood, attitude, posture, self-talk, and behavior. Delineating states allows for greater self-awareness and enables people to understand what triggers specific states—their various features, circumstances associated with them, and what can be done to maximize the occurrence of states that are desired and minimize the occurrence of states that are dreaded.

In other words, recognition of states increases efficacy and control. If a person becomes aware that his Mars is undermodulated as evidenced by a chronically angry mood, hostile attitude, belligerent posture, and an inflammatory internal dialogue, such as "I'm going to kill that guy," his awareness allows him to reflect on why he is expressing his Mars in this manner. Introspection may lead to insights that pertain to his need for freedom or survival.

For example, he may discover that he believes that other people have hostile intentions toward him. This belief, in turn, may derive from formative child-hood experiences where he was repeatedly abused by an older sibling. Realizing that he is projecting past images of his brother onto people in his current life may help him to become less hostile and more trusting. This example serves to illustrate the importance of becoming conscious of states—that is, developing awareness of what they are, what triggers them, their early prototypes, and how they can be better controlled.

To summarize, a psychological state is a recurrent pattern of experience as reflected in mood, attitude, self-talk, and verbal and nonverbal behavior. Each planet is associated with a continuum of psychological states ranging from well-modulated to over- or undermodulated. When a planet is well modulated, its function is openly expressed, relatively well controlled, and positively experienced. The underlying motive that fuels that planet's states tends to be easily satisfied. If a planet is undermodulated, it functions in an immature, impulsive, and primitive manner, as if the person is unable to control its expression or satisfy its motive. An overmodulated planet, on the other hand, tends to be *too* controlled, as if its expression were going to cause trouble or embarrassment. The motivation behind the planet's expression evokes anxiety and is not readily satisfied due to excessive behavioral restraints. Categorizing states increases conscious awareness of their nature, allows for more choice and control, and enables the individual to maximize the occurrence of states that are desired.

PLANETARY BEHAVIORAL GOALS

By now it should be apparent that when people become aware of motives through experiencing their corollary affects, they then must decide how to satisfy the motive. A lonely person (Venus) may decide to seek out a relationship; a curious person (Mercury) decides to study a subject; an ambitious person (Saturn) decides to redouble her efforts in pursuit of a goal. In short, people choose behaviors they expect will lead to outcomes that produce the desired satisfaction. The final phase of a motivational sequence, therefore, is some sort of action. Each planet symbolizes a different kind of action. The Sun expresses, the Moon listens, Mercury learns, Mars asserts, Venus attracts, Jupiter expands, Saturn orders, Uranus awakens, Neptune dissolves, and Pluto transforms. Of course, a planet's propensity for action can be described by more than one verb; each planet symbolizes a class of related actions, all of which are designed to satisfy a need and achieve a target state.

The goal of a behavior, however, is different from its motive. Again, motives are intrinsic and reside in zodiacal signs. Aries is the need for survival, which motivates the individual *to assert* (Mars). 'To assert' is the behavior that is designed to satisfy the intrinsic motive of survival. If the person succeeds in his goal, then a sense of having survived (or simply of having *the right to be*) is the intrinsic reward. But what is the actual goal of the assertion? A goal differs from a motive in that it has to do with an extrinsic reward, the attainment of which will hopefully lead to satisfaction of the motive.

For example, an individual may decide to assert in an effort to protect his loved ones (Mars in Cancer), or perhaps in defense of astrology as a valid belief system (Mars in Sagittarius), or in order to obtain a promotion (Mars in Capricorn). In each instance, he asserts his right to be; yet, in each case the goal is different—to protect loved ones, defend astrology, or obtain a promotion. Also, the extrinsic reward differs from the intrinsic one. In the Cancer example, the extrinsic reward is that his friends are protected, in the second example that his belief in astrology is successfully defended, and in the third that he obtains the promotion. These examples serve to illustrate how the object of a goal is often described by the sign the planet occupies, whereas the motivation behind the goal is described by the sign the planet rules.

In effect, planetary signs constitute the last phase of a three-part motivational sequence. The beginning is awareness of the emotion that conveys a need, which is followed by the impulse to behave in a way that satisfies the need. The third phase is the establishment of a specific goal for the requisite action. Very often, the goal—the extrinsic reward—has something to do with the planetary sign position.

With Mercury, for example, the individual may feel curious and thus become aware of a need for information (Gemini). But what kind of information? What does he want to learn about? If Mercury is in Scorpio, he might be curious about sex, death, crime, or the machinations of power. He then acts with this object in mind.

For example, he might decide to read about the life of Charles Manson, for the topics of sex, death, crime, and power would be strongly in evidence. If reading Manson's biography satisfies his desire to learn, then the behavioral sequence will be terminated. If not, he will have to set another goal based on his new awareness that the Manson biography was not adequate to satisfy his need. The point is that the sign that Mercury occupies, Scorpio, symbolizes the goal of the sequence—reading the Manson biography.

Of course, the goal of a planetary action is not always related to its sign position. A person may have Mars in Gemini and assert to protect his loved ones, which has nothing to do with Gemini. A sign position may merely describe the style or type of action that characterizes the planet. Mars in Gemini may assert to protect loved ones by giving the offending person a verbal tongue-lashing!

SUMMARY

A planetary archetype is a protean entity that can assume a variety of psychological forms—need, function, and emotion. Planets symbolize psychological functions that are oriented toward satisfying the needs of the signs they rule, whereas emotions serve as barometers of need satisfaction. Each sign-planet motivational system symbolizes a class of affects on a continuum from positive to negative. Affects are experienced along a range of intensity. When an emotion strays too far from its preferred (target) state, it activates the behavioral sequence of its sign-planet motivational system. The individual is then compelled to act in a manner that steers experience back to the target state.

Planetary states constitute a recurrent pattern of experience that involves mood, attitude, internal dialogue, and behavior. Such states can be undermodulated, overmodulated, or well modulated, depending upon the planet's degree of integration. Undermodulated states tend to spin out-of-control, whereas overmodulated states are too controlled. Well-modulated states are spontaneous, readily controlled, and lead to experiences of need satisfaction. When people become aware of motives through corollary affects, they establish a behavioral goal that is designed to satisfy the motivating need and achieve a preferred state. The sign the planet occupies often suggests the object of the goal. If the goal is achieved and it leads to the target state, the behavioral sequence is terminated.

Chapter Five

COGNITION IN ASTROLOGY

In the last chapter, we explored how emotions are the motive forces of psychodynamics. Every sign constitutes a distinct type of feeling, which impels planetary agents to act in accordance with the needs that these feelings convey. Actions are fueled by feelings, which are messengers of needs. In this chapter, however, we will explore how feelings are mediated by cognitions.

It has been said that behind every emotion is a hidden cognition. One of the hallmarks of late 20th century psychology is the recognition that emotions are not simply spontaneous reflections of reality, but are a consequence of habitual modes of thinking, usually at an unconscious level. The emotions that an individual experiences depend on how he or she interprets events rather than on the events themselves. This bears repeating: It is how we interpret events, not the events themselves that determine how we feel. Since emotions steer our actions, it would follow that behavior is directly influenced by the meanings that we attribute to events.

COGNITIVE ASTROLOGY

Cognitive science is that branch of psychology that presents us with theories about the acquisition, retention, and utilization of information for purposes of growth and adaptation. It is important to distinguish levels, forms, and ways of knowing, and to dispense with the idea that "thinking is knowing" or even the main way of knowing. Every planet in astrology constitutes a distinct way of knowing—intuition, sensation, empirical observation, identification, analysis, aesthetics, abstract reasoning, holistic awareness, psi abilities, and so on. Likewise, each planet specializes in a specific realm of knowledge. Mars knows about survival, Mercury is an expert with language, the Sun understands performance, Saturn specializes in success, and Neptune is an authority on dreams.

In this chapter, we will be exploring the importance of cognition and how it is reflected in the astrological chart. Specifically, we will examine how planetary aspects symbolize core beliefs that mediate perception and determine our thoughts, feelings, and behavior. Aspects are at the heart of an astrological theory of psychodynamics. Whereas signs signify needs and their emotional counterparts, and planets represent the active agents of these needs, it is aspects that represent the underlying beliefs that determine how and whether our needs will be fulfilled.

EARLY THEORIES OF COGNITION

In the early days of psychology prior to the 1960's it was assumed that all knowledge of the world was revealed through our senses—sight, hearing, smell, taste, and touch. What formed inside the mind were "traces" of sensory experience. Outer experiences and inner ideas about those experiences become linked together, or "associated". This model is what Karl Popper called "the bucket theory of mind". The human being was assumed to be a relatively passive repository of the aftermath of sensations. Perception was solely "stimulus-initiated," and memory was characterized by storage metaphors that emphasized "mental representations" of experience.

Because psychology was wedded to the physical sciences, the mind was considered to be merely another object to be studied from the outside in. Orthodox behaviorists completely ignored what mediated between stimulus (input) and response (output). So-called "consciousness" was causally irrelevant to behavior since it was thought to be merely an epiphenomenon of an externally originating, material cause. This traditional view, which is sometimes called *copy theory,* holds that the mind/brain "picks up" and "stores" information about the world. Mind is passive and mental operations are mechanistically determined by external stimuli.

Since the 1960's, however, mainstream psychology has reoriented toward those processes within the organism that contribute to the phenomenon of attention, perception, and learning. The cognitive revolution reflected the growing realization that behaviorist, stimulus-response models of learning were inadequate. Eventually it was recognized that something is mediating between stimulus and response. It was postulated that the mind/brain is populated with *schemas,* which refer to abstract "cognitive structures" that generate specific patterns of mental experience. Like cookie cutters of the mind that are impressed upon external reality, schemas provide a familiar shape and meaning to everyday experiences. This latter view is much more compatible with astrology, which postulates that what we see is unavoidably influenced by how we perceive.

Let's suppose that a person has Pluto in the 10th house opposing Saturn in the 4th. Based on past experience, he tends to regard people in authority as untrustworthy. This idea (cognitive structure) is not simply a passive response to prior experience, for it now affects how he perceives authority figures, how he feels and behaves toward them, and the kinds of responses he evokes from them. Hostility begets hostility; thus, the individual may unintentionally cause people in authority to respond in a manner that bears out his original premise that authority figures are untrustworthy. In other words, his actual experience with authority figures is going to be influenced, to an indeterminate extent, by his beliefs, expectations, and behavior, all of which are symbolized by the planetary configuration.

Conversely, someone else may have Sun conjunct Venus in the 10th with both planets trine Jupiter in the 6th. This person has an innate tendency to perceive people in authority as kind, generous, and magnanimous. Such a perception influences his feelings and subsequent behavior toward authority figures, which, in turn, affects their responses to him.

Now what if both people worked for the same company and had the same boss? Each person's experience is likely to be radically different. If they were asked to describe their boss they would offer conflicting testimony. So, who is the real boss? We can conclude from this hypothetical example that any objective description of the boss is impossible. Each person is going to see a different boss and behave accordingly. In turn, their behavior will affect how the boss responds to them, and each will end up having an entirely different experience. This illustrates how an astrological configuration symbolizes a schema, or cognitive structure, which depicts a way of knowing that underlies a perceptual, behavioral, and experiential pattern.

CONSTRUCTIVISM

Whereas modern epistemology was based on the assumption that there is an objective universe that exists separate from the perspective of the observer (objectivism), postmodern thinking in the cognitive sciences is called "constructivism" and emphasizes active (participatory) processes in knowing. Constructivism posits that any statement about reality is primarily a statement about the observer. The term "constructivism" derives from the Latin *construere,* which means, "to interpret." Emphasis is placed on a person actively "construing" a particular meaning to experience.

Person co-constructs reality. This is the meaning of constructivism reduced to its essence. The prefix "co" in "co-constructs" acknowledges that there may be a real, objective world that has a relative influence on one's thoughts and feelings, but we can never know it directly. We can only know it through the conceptual filter of our personal theory of reality. Accordingly, our perceptions of external reality are unavoidably mediated by our preconceptions. The individual is a "co-creator" of personal realities since there is an interactive interdependence between inner and outer conditions.

It is a tenet of constructivism that organic and cognitive structures evolve in a similar fashion. In each case, selection processes operate through trial and error. Experiences gained through action become hypotheses, which in turn serve to guide further action. While there is a beyond-our-constructions world that imposes constraints on what will "work" in a given environment (one cannot walk on water regardless of how one "constructs" it), there are innumerable ways to view the world, each having its own emotional, behavioral, and experiential consequences.

Again, there is a ready parallel with astrology if we consider that different planetary configurations will construct different realties. A planet in a house, for instance, not only describes a way of perceiving the phenomena of that house; it also describes the nature of the experiences that we encounter there. Imagine a woman with Mars in the 2nd who discovers early in life that if she wants something she is going to have to aggressively pursue it; there is no time for waiting and saving, because desirable commodities are in short supply and tend to quickly disappear. That is her experience. This person, therefore, is prone to impulse buying. The operative belief is: "Get it now or you may never have it."

Conversely, someone with Saturn in the 2nd may "construct" an entirely different reality. For her, things that are worth having are worth saving for; her interest is in quality not expediency. Experience has taught her it is better to have one good thing, which lasts, than many cheap things that don't. Patience and frugality are her operative strategy. She makes her purchase only after careful and lengthy consideration of the best deal for the best product. Since this strategy works for her, it gets reinforced over time.

In each case, the person perceives a 2nd house reality that is in accord with her pragmatic goals: get something while it's available (Mars), or carefully select the best possible product (Saturn). Accordingly, constructivism does not aim at knowing reality but only seeks to understand how models that serve differing pragmatic purposes are constructed. Because people differ with respect to their pragmatic goals, there exist nearly unlimited possibilities for the construction of diverse realities.

For the Mars person, her 2nd house reality was characterized by the dimension of "available versus not available." Desirable objects were either immediately obtainable, or they were not. For the Saturn person, her 2nd house reality was defined in terms of quality; there were superior and inferior products and only the best was worth having. Mars might worry that what it wants could be gone tomorrow; Saturn will worry that a better product could be purchased at a lower price if she is sufficiently patient to explore her options. In each instance, reality is constructed in accordance with the nature of the purposes symbolized by the planet-house combination.

One could argue that in each instance there was an entirely different external condition and that each person's perceptions and behavior was a logical response to a wholly objective reality as described by the planet in that house. Yet, it is impossible to know how much is perception and how much is reality. Subjective and objective are unavoidably blurred. Constructivism, therefore, holds that person and situation are inextricably related. How we perceive what we experience constitute a closed system in which "how" (inner) and "what" (outer) are not absolutely discriminated. Esteemed constructivist philosopher Paul Watzlawick (1976) asserts:

> Our everyday, traditional ideas about reality are delusions that we spend substantial parts of our daily lives shoring up, even at the considerable risk of trying to force facts to fit our definition of reality instead of vice versa. And the most dangerous delusion of all is that there is only one reality. What there are, in fact, are many different versions of reality, some of which are contradictory, but all of which are the results of communication and not reflections of eternal, objective truths. (p. xi).

PERSONS AS EMBODIED THEORY

What Watzlawick calls "communication" is described elsewhere as *confirmatory bias*—the tendency to twist the facts in order to make them "fit" our memories, preconceptions, and expectations. Individuals selectively attend to information that confirms their bias, while ignoring or distorting information that threatens it. Such cognitive patterning is a property of the mind, which has as its major task the ordering of the massive amount of data that are constantly absorbed through the senses. Lived experience contributes to the formation of hypotheses that guide further action. Human beings maintain order in their experience by projecting familiar categories—schemas—onto unfamiliar particulars.

Such habituated responses save time and energy in the multiple actions that an individual must undertake in different environmental (house) contexts—work, play, home, school, marriage, and so on. Messages or data that do not fit into already organized cognitive patterns are necessarily ignored as irrelevant or distorted to fit the procrustean bed of the organized patterns. In this manner, consciousness is not a passive mirror of an objective reality; rather, consciousness molds external stimuli according to its own nature. The psyche is an organic, formative force that independently changes information that has been appropriated from outside itself and converts this data into familiar categories of meaning.

Human beings, in effect, are embodied theories, or "stories". Epstein (1980) notes that people must have a theory to exist for they would experience chaos without one. Individuals are guided in their behavior by an implicit theory of reality, which has subsections consisting of a self-theory and a world-theory. One's self-theory consists of a hierarchical arrangement of major and minor postulates. Major postulates are broad, inclusive beliefs about the self, such as "I am a good person." Branching off from this are lower-order postulates, such as "I am a good astrologer," which contain yet lower-order beliefs such as, "I am skilled at understanding Pluto."

Likewise, a person's world-theory consists of a hierarchical ordering of beliefs about other people and external conditions. A person's total, embodied theory contains innumerable assumptions about how the two theories—self and world—interact with each other. How a person views himself is, of course, not independent of how he views the world. Self-concept and world-concept largely reflect each other. A negative self-concept, such as "I'm unworthy," will be mirrored by a corresponding world-concept, such as "people are rejecting."

THE IMPORTANCE OF CHILDHOOD

It is important to recognize that a person's implicit theory of reality is not necessarily conscious. The construction of meaning begins in infancy and continues throughout life whether we are aware of it or not. Concepts formed from emotionally significant experiences serve to organize and guide future behavior. These concepts constitute broad, general postulates that assimilate later experiences into themselves. Astrologically, they are symbolized by aspect configurations that describe the world of outer experience and its inner, psychic representations.

For example, a boy with Sun square Saturn might have a father who is perfectionistic, judgmental, and withholding of approval. Eventually the child comes to believe that he is undeserving of validation or praise. The concept that he develops about himself, "I'm unworthy of approval," is a corollary to the outer experience of a father who disapproves. When he grows up, he will expect the same kind of treatment from his superiors. He will interpret their behavior in terms that conform to his preconceptions, and he will behave in a manner that presupposes the outcome he expects. For example, he might procrastinate due to a fear of failure or overcompensate in an effort to avert the criticism he anticipates. All of this will be motivated from an unconscious level because the nature of his belief causes him anxiety and thus must be repressed.

Children make inappropriate generalizations from strong emotional experiences. They think "this will always happen," or "I'm no good," because they have limited conceptual abilities and a limited range of experience. Naturally egocentric, they tend to assume responsibility for everything that happens to them. If the parents of a three-year decide to divorce and the father subsequently moves out, the child is apt to think, "Daddy left because he doesn't love me," or "Daddy left because I'm messy." In short, children think that whatever happens to them is because *of* them.

The problem is compounded due to the naïve faith that children have in their caretakers. Kids assume that the way they are being treated is how they deserve to be treated. Even if the treatment is abusive, it is preferable for the child to believe that they deserve the abuse than otherwise, because at least then there is the possibility of altering the outcome by changing their behavior. To feel security as a child, one needs to believe that adults are good and that one can control their responses by behaving in ways that are acceptable. It is too terrifying for children to think that their parents are simply out-of-control, mean, or evil, and that there is nothing they can do about it.

Beliefs that result from emotionally charged experiences are prescriptive; that is, they are broad generalizations that stipulate how to behave in the future to maximize the pleasure/pain balance, assure approval, and maintain an optimal level of self-esteem. The earlier such beliefs form and the greater the trauma that underlies them, the more rigid they are apt to be. For our Sun square Saturn person, his experience might predispose him to develop a strict, behavioral rule: either be the best at something or don't bother at all. This prescription necessarily follows an implicit, associated belief that one is worthy only if one is superior—that is, *not* average, imperfect, mistake-prone, or deserving of criticism.

It is unavoidable for children to make sense of experience in egocentric, idiosyncratic ways, for a child does not have the mental ability to think in more flexible, abstract terms. They are apt to overgeneralize from limited experiences because for them the experience is not limited—*it's all there is*. Ideally, we develop more flexible rules and beliefs as we grow older. We learn that the same behavior can be "bad" or "good" depending upon the context; we recognize that sometimes it is necessary to break the rules in order to serve a higher principle. Beliefs that develop from repetitive, traumatic circumstances, however, tend to remain simple, fixed, and primitive. There is a developmental arrest or "fixation" in these areas.

Imagine, for instance, a girl who has Moon in Aries in the 2nd house square Uranus in the 11th. When she was two years old her mother took a fulltime job as an environmental protection lobbyist and left her with an indifferent babysitter. Initially conditioned to expect a mother who is at least somewhat responsive, she was shocked by the change of care. Suddenly she realized she can be hungry, wet, tired, or scared, and no matter how hard she tries to communicate her distress, no one comes. This continues for three years. By the time the child starts school, she has formed a theory about herself and the world that goes something like this:

> My personal, emotional needs are unimportant and no one particularly cares what I need to feel secure. Since others ignore my feelings, it's best that I ignore them, too. Otherwise I will be in constant pain. The world is full of cold, indifferent people who love you one moment and reject you the next; so, don't get attached to anyone. The only real security is what you can get for yourself.

As a child, this person formed a theory about herself and the world that was consistent with her lunar configuration. At five years old she couldn't possibly articulate her "story" as I have above; yet it is implicit in her behavior. To the extent that she remains unaware of the presuppositions that underlay her behavior, she will continue to have lunar/2nd house experiences that appear to be controlled by an external destiny that she is powerless to affect. Yet, this destiny will be determined to a large extent by her need to maintain a familiar world that is consistent with her personal theory of reality. In other words, the cognitive structure symbolized by her Moon-Uranus square will function as a self-fulfilling prophecy. Unconsciously she will seek out and create experiences that confirm her bias.

The tendency to selectively attend to data that confirms one's bias is alternately referred to as proactive knowing, feedforward, or biased anticipation. In other words, people are active participants in their knowledge acquisitions. Rather than just being a passive repository of relational experiences, the individual is a seeking, anticipatory, "embodied theory" that is constantly scanning the environment for data that confirms expectations. Such data is like food, or fuel, that keeps the theory alive; and since the theory is *oneself*, it *is* alive. The individual is an embodied, evolving, theoretical structure, a living story that actively feeds on confirmatory data to perpetuate its existence. Whereas "feedback" constitutes any experience that provides information about the consequences of one's behavior, "feedforward" actively anticipates those consequences, hungers for them, searches for them, and eventually brings them about.

Perhaps the woman with the Moon-Uranus square unconsciously believes that anyone she depends on will eventually turn a cold shoulder. This belief is rigid in that it's difficult for her to perceive (or even imagine) being treated any other way. Yet, she cannot entirely stop herself from wanting closeness. Since unconsciously she fears that she will end up alone, she behaves in an aloof, distant, and reactive manner whenever she becomes emotionally involved. Like a deer in the headlights, she is anticipating disaster and fearing what she anticipates, which unavoidably influences her behavior. Any action of her partner that even remotely conforms to her expectations—a glance away, a lateness, a preoccupation with another concern—is interpreted as evidence that what she anticipates is about to occur: *rejection*. So she cuts off her feelings and abruptly distances herself before the other person can do further damage.

Viewed objectively, her behavior makes sense in the context of what she is anticipating—a cold, abrupt, cutting-off of caring in the person upon whom she emotionally depends. Because this core belief was her way of making sense of the world at a young age, it was adaptive. Yet, now her expectation of rejection is so strong that it actually influences the reality of her partner who begins, in fact, to feel rejecting. She helps to bring this about by behaving as if it has already occurred. This is sometimes referred to as "projective identification"—behavior that evokes in others what is expected (projected). It does not occur to her that she is the one who is behaving in a cold, abrupt, emotionally cut-off manner.

Her partner regards her behavior as terribly unfair and hurtful, so he reacts defensively. Confused by her sudden change, he thinks she no longer cares. So he pulls away, thus bearing out her original premise. His behavior is a response to her behavior, while her behavior is a response to his behavior (remember, he glanced away). Unwittingly, she has allowed her fear to operate as a self-fulfilling prophecy. Her response has influenced in him a potential for behaving in a way that conforms to her expectations and actually increases the probability of the outcome she fears. Eventually he experiences an impulse to reject, which is really his defense. For he has a story, too, which he is projecting and helping to bring about by his own behavior. The relational system becomes so intertwined as stories begin to fuse into patterns familiar to each that often it is impossible to know which came first, "the chicken or the egg."

In leading their everyday lives, human beings function like scientists. They continuously formulate and test hypotheses at a subconscious level. The self-concept is a self-theory that individuals unwittingly develop because they need it to live their lives. This personal narrative begins in childhood and develops into more integrated versions as one matures.

A self-theory and world-theory together comprise an individual's personal theory of reality and total conceptual system. The theory has three basic functions: (a) assimilate the data of experience, (b) maintain a favorable pleasure/pain balance by behaving in need-satisfying ways, and (c) optimize self-esteem. To do this, the individual selectively attends to data that confirms his theory while distorting or ignoring data that disconfirms it. Thus, people appropriate certain features of their environment—partners, bosses, friends—and incorporate them into a pre-existing story, which seems to have a life of its own.

EQUIFINALITY OR STRUCTURE DETERMINISM

In general systems theory, the notion of confirmatory bias is implicit in the concept of *equifinality* or "structure determinism." Equifinality means a system's behavior is determined not so much by causes external to the system (initial conditions), as by the system's parameters, or organization. As an assemblage of parts that have relations with one another, a birthchart is a system. The way a chart is organized represents the system's parameters. Signs symbolize basic psychological needs, which constitute the first level of the self-system. These, in turn, are organized at a higher level by aspects, or cognitive structures, which reflect strategies for meeting needs. The chart as a whole depicts the final level of the self-system, which signifies the individual's total theory of reality, or personal myth/story.

How one behaves is determined less by the environment and more by the way one perceives the environment. Strategies for meeting needs are governed by a "steering property" in the psyche called equifinality. Simply put, equifinality [Latin *aequus,* equal; *finis,* end, goal] means that the final result of a person's behavior is more or less the same, or equal, regardless of environmental contingencies. This means that people behave in a self-consistent manner even when the external situation differs. For example, a woman with Neptune in the 7th marries three different men and treats them all pretty much the same. While the men and marriages are different, her choices, behavior, and subsequent experiences are the same, or equal.

Equifinality implies that it is not possible to make deterministic predictions about a person's behavior solely on the basis of initial conditions (external situations). Systems parameters predominate over initial conditions such that inputs are acted upon and changed by the self-system. For example, our woman with Neptune in the 7th may marry someone that is initially sober; yet treat him as if he were an alcoholic. She may even drive him to drink. Since a system is inherently active rather than merely reactive to external stimuli, an outer stimulus does not cause behavior but merely acts in relationship to an autonomous system. Thus the same results—behavior—may spring from different initial conditions.

Let's consider another example. Suppose a man has Mars in the 6th house squaring Pluto in the 9th. His employment history reveals a series of jobs and outcomes that reflect a consistent pattern. Reports indicate he is a loose cannon at work, difficult to control with a tendency to break rules and act unilaterally. If confronted by a supervisor, or forced to do something he doesn't like, he becomes inappropriately angry. His insubordination has resulted in frequent firings, to which he responds by filing lawsuits. It doesn't seem to matter where he works or for whom (initial conditions), the pattern keeps repeating.

It is not difficult to understand the pattern when viewed astrologically. Mars rules Aries—the need for autonomy. Mars is inherently aggressive and independent. Pluto rules Scorpio, or the need for power, and is inherently resistant to attempts at control. When combined in a stressful relationship (square), there is often a behavioral pattern marked by aggressive resistance to perceived attempts at domination. The houses—work (6th) and the department of justice (9th)—provide the context in which the struggle occurs. At work, the person fears being subjugated by an external power. Regardless of the specifics of the work environment (6th house), such a person will always behave in a manner that is consistent with the aspect. At his hearing (9th house) he might complain to the judge that his supervisors have all been power-mad, corrupt oppressors who attempt to degrade him—treatment that he won't tolerate! Hence, the lawsuit. Yet, his perceptions and experiences are a reflection of the way he is internally organized. Systems parameters predominate over initial conditions.

Equifinality implies that a system has an end in mind that regulates its internal functioning. The most basic goal of a system is simply to be itself; that is, to maintain its organization and survive. External manifestations of behavior are secondary to internal processes that, by comparison, are relatively enduring. Again, these internal processes are the organizational characteristics of the self-system.

Maturana and Varela (1980) refer to this as "structure determinism." Living systems are autonomous in that they are not caused or instructed by outside forces. It is the structural pattern of a system that determines its nature and behavior. Again, we can readily see this in the astrological chart. It has a dynamic structure made up of myriad aspect patterns that determines one's perceptions and behavior independent of external situations.

Equifinality also implies that different results may spring from the same initial conditions. Consider, for example, two politicians who live in the same state. One has Moon in Pisces in the 9th trine Jupiter in Cancer in the 1st. Deeply compassionate and enormously hopeful (an idealist more than a realist), he is elected on a platform of reducing poverty through government welfare programs—a classic liberal Democrat. Spread the wealth! Care for the people! The other politician, a typical conservative Republican, has Saturn in Taurus in the 9th forming a quincunx to Pluto in the 2nd. He was elected on a platform of reducing taxes by cutting back on wasteful, irresponsible spending that has precipitated a crisis in the state budget.

Given that their political goals are at cross-purposes, we can surmise that their realities are divergent as well; each will see evidence that justifies his values and political promises. Even though they live in the same state—same initial conditions—their behavior is going to vary markedly. The democrat will notice the poor and the dispossessed, and champion their cause. That is his reality. The republican will see the hard-working businessman who feels ripped off by excessive taxation and unchecked government spending. So, he devises legislation that he believes will heal the state economy. That is his reality. For practical purposes, each politician inhabits a different world—a world that is constructed by the organizing properties of their own minds.

CONTROL STRUCTURE OF THE PSYCHE

The human psyche, or self-system, can be depicted as a vertical chain of command, with executive or higher processing mechanisms coordinating operations that occur at lower levels in the hierarchy (see Figure 9, page 116). This model suggests that the mind is organized and managed hierarchically. For example, we can depict the psyche as a three-dimensional structure comprising three concentric circles, or levels. It looks a bit like a "top," a toy having one end tapered to a point, allowing it to be spun, like a solar system that rotates on its axis.

In Figure 9 of the model, the perspective is from the top down, looking into the structure's interior. For a side view, see Figure 12 on page 125. Each stratum of our "top" has a different meaning. At the very bottom, there is a hole with twelve portals that open out into a universe of possibilities. In other words, the hole is a kind of plane, with twelve permeable openings that signify the twelve signs of the zodiac. Each sign represents a set of self-consistent, interrelated needs. Our plane of the zodiac has an upper side and an underside, which allow for basic input/output processes.

The underside of the portals signifies the entry point into the twelve houses, which symbolize twelve sub-divisions of the environment. The signs, in other words, are superimposed over the houses, just as in the astrological chart. The upper side of the portals signifies openings into the world of the psyche where information about external events is metabolized and converted into psychic structure. Thus, the signs are a kind of filter that allows information about the outer world to activate basic psychological drives and processes, which are symbolized by the planets.

The second level of our model is divided into two parts, both of which are symbolized astrologically by planetary aspects. Unconscious core beliefs constitute the darker, inner rung, which are flanked above by automatic assumptions and thoughts that necessarily flow from these less conscious ideas. In other words, our conscious strategies for meeting needs are a product of unconscious, core beliefs. The third level of the self-system is the chart as a whole, at the center of which is the Sun, ego, self, or personal identity, which necessarily encompasses the whole chart. As a symbol of the will, the Sun constitutes the executive processing and decision-making level of the psyche.

Our top (self-system), as it were, is floating in psychic space, which is a kind of dreamscape or sea of possibility. The self-system is open at both the top and the bottom. Above the structure, opening out into yet higher realms of consciousness, is Universal Mind, of which the individual self is a subsystem. Each person, in other words, is an extension of a larger Self that subsumes us. This spiritual Self has its own nature and intentions, which it communicates through non-ordinary, non-sensory means, including dreams, telepathy, intuition, visions, synchronicity, and so forth.

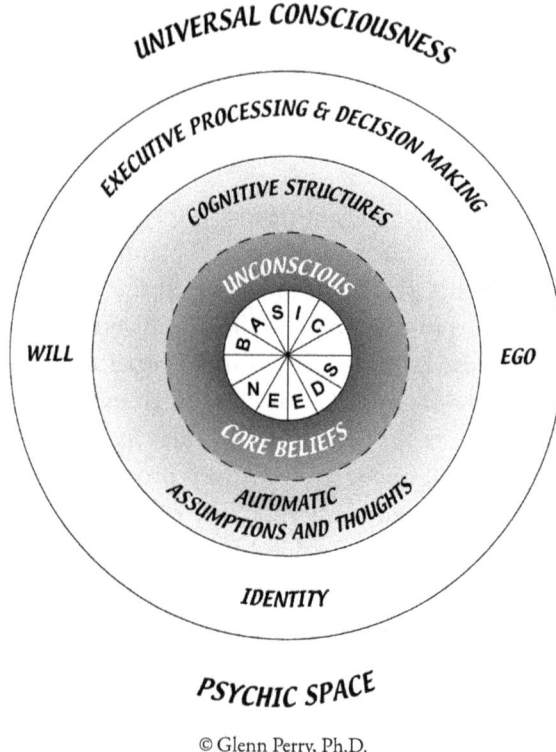

© Glenn Perry, Ph.D.

Figure 9: Top View of The Self-System

LEVEL I BASIC NEEDS

The realm of space that stretches out below the top represents the world of mundane experience. Again, we can think of it as divided into twelve subsections, or houses. Although this level is not physically part of the self, it provides the context within which the self functions.

Each house is itself a doorway into a separate world of experience—the world of survival (1st), personal security (2nd), work (6th), religion (9th), group affiliations (11th), and so on. Every experience of the self occurs in a specific social context.

Events enter the self-system through the twelve portals, or permeable membranes, at the bottom of the structure. These are doorways to the twelve signs. As information flows from the houses through these portals, it stimulates the needs that the signs symbolize.

For example, if the sign Aries is superimposed over the 10th house, then the need for autonomy is activated in situations involving career. The individual experiences this stimulation as a type of feeling, or impulse, such as the impulse to assert, to initiate, to fight, and so on.

Each sign signifies a distinctly different need, which, once stimulated, is conveyed via feelings to its planetary agent at the level above. Once that planet is stimulated, it strives to meet the need of its motivating sign in a way and in a context indicated by its sign and house position.

LEVEL II PROCESSES

At the second level of the psyche are intermediate mediational processes, or cognitive structures, which constitute beliefs and strategies for fulfilling the needs that have been activated. When needs are activated, so too are their planetary agents. Each planet signifies a psychological faculty with distinct functions that are geared to satisfy a specific need-set. At this level of the self-system, the individual must find a way of integrating the various planetary functions that have been stimulated. Invariably there is more than one planet activated at a given moment. Accordingly, different planets must combine with one another in various ways—aspects—to create higher order beliefs that prescribe the rules, strategies, and plans for coordinating the divergent needs that the signs symbolize.

We can imagine the self-system as a ceaseless, buzzing cacophony of psychic frequencies that are forever conveying impulses along familiar channels. Because this level of the psyche is continually processing information that has been generated by dynamic, multiple control centers—the planets—it is characterized by an internal dialogue, or self-talk, which is what the person says to himself or herself with regard to the dominant concern of the moment. These automatic thoughts, however, are just the conscious, self-aware portion of a larger organizational pattern that stretches down into the unconscious, like a building that has a basement.

In the basement of the psyche are implicit postulates that predict the likelihood of meeting core needs. These postulates begin to form almost immediately after birth. Like scientists in the crib, infants hypothesize on what to expect when impulses are expressed for food, affection, reassurance, curiosity, and freedom, to name a few. If basic needs are consistently satisfied, the child associates those needs with positive beliefs and feelings. However, if certain needs remain unfulfilled due to trauma or neglect, then the child develops negative beliefs and feelings around those needs. These experiences (both good and bad), and their corollary beliefs and feelings, gradually coalesce into a coherent story about the self-world relation.

If the lower, darker half of Level II is like a basement that contains unconscious beliefs, the signs below it are underground springs that flow up from the collective unconscious into the basement. Here, in the cellar of the psyche, deep core beliefs process informational flows and provide the foundational structures for the resulting self-talk above, which, in turn, filters up to the highest level of the system—the executive control center, or ego at Level III.

Level II implies that we are multi-selved. Every sign-planet is a sub-system, or sub-personality, a living, quasi-autonomous entity that inhabits the psyche and has its own agenda and goals. Yet, each sub-personality contributes to the overall self-concept, which is an emergent property of Level III. If a sub-system of the self is enhanced or diminished, a corresponding increase or decrease in one's self-assessment occurs.

For example, if we strengthen our Mercury function by getting an education, there is a corresponding increase in pride and confidence vis-à-vis our Mercury function. Accordingly, as planetary faculties find new ways to combine and coordinate their respective functions, there is an overall increase in self-esteem because such an integrative process enriches each planet and increases its functionality. Resultant feelings of exhilaration are adaptive because they reinforce motivation for further differentiation and integration of system components.

If Saturn squares Mercury, for example, and the individual begins his adult life believing he is intellectually inferior and a failure at his career, this will take a toll on his self-esteem. However, if he is able to integrate his Mercury-Saturn square by getting a practical education that increases his potential for career success, he will begin to feel and think about himself differently——perhaps as a bright, successful professional. Such thoughts, in turn, will elevate feelings of confidence and self-esteem.

THE SELF IS HIERARCHICALLY ORGANIZED

In systems theory, each higher level includes its lower levels as parts, or subsystems. Accordingly, each sign-planet is a system that contains its own parts—a set of needs and functions. Note in Figure 10 (page 119) that Capricorn needs provide the motivations for Saturnian functions. A sign-planet system is, in turn, a subsystem of a higher-level system, such as an aspect configuration. Saturn may be part of an aspect structure that includes Mercury, such as a square. Certain attributes such as mental discipline, good planning ability, and the belief that one can succeed in tasks that require focused learning are emergent properties that result from integration of these two structures (see Figure 11, page 120).

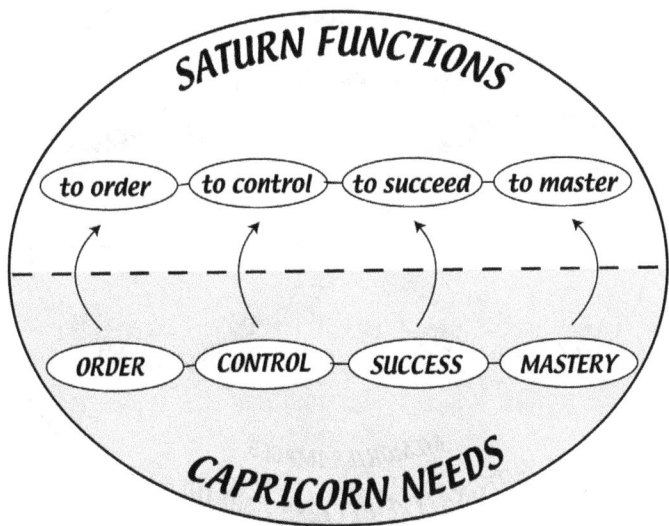

Figure 10: The Capricorn-Saturn System

At each level of the hierarchy, there are emergent properties that do not exist on previous levels. At Level I, for example, simple impulses or feelings serve as motivators of action. At Level II, however, there is the ability to attribute meaning to these feelings and impulses, and to coordinate them with other feelings/impulses. An additional property of this level is the ability to attribute meaning to the external events that stimulated the Mercury-Saturn response. These meanings and their derivative feelings constitute cognitive structures. As mentioned, an emergent property of a Mercury-Saturn cognitive structure might be mental discipline. Finally, at level III, there is the ability to choose a course of action or implement a strategy that was produced at Level II. Let's consider an example.

If a father tells his son that he is too stupid to succeed at a particular task, there are at least two parts of the son's psyche that are activated—Saturn, the need for success, and Mercury, the need for knowledge. He may interpret his father's admonition to mean, "I lack adequate knowledge to succeed at the present task." However, if the father's rebuke is repeated many times, the child may generalize these isolated incidents into an unconscious, core belief: "I am likely to fail in any situation that requires intelligence."

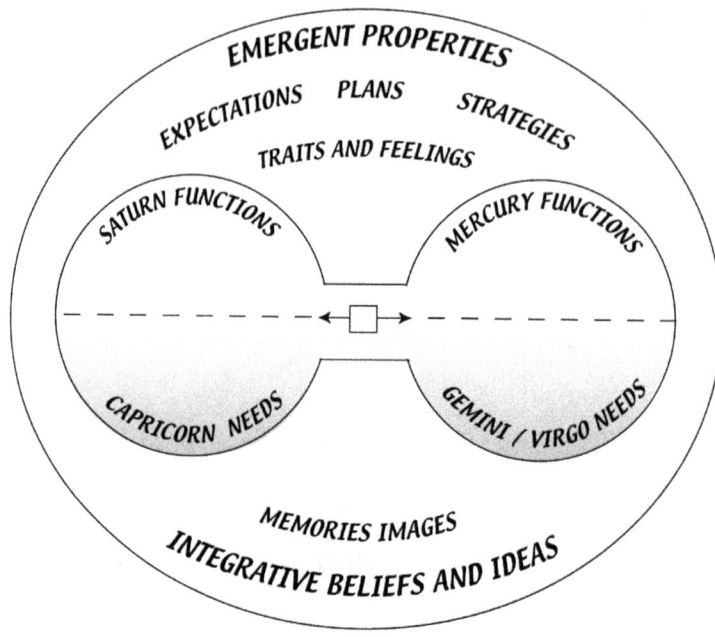

Figure 11: The Saturn-Mercury System

Subsequently, whenever he experiences a situation that requires him to demonstrate mental ability, he suffers anxiety due to an expectation of failure. His anxiety is a product of his belief; thus, it overlays the initial Mercury feeling of interest and the Saturn feeling of ambition. In response to this anxiety, an idea may arise: "if I can successfully avoid situations that test (Saturn) my intelligence (Mercury) I will not experience failure." This idea constitutes a strategy that flows directly from the core, underlying belief, "I will fail in attempts to demonstrate adequate knowledge," which is likely to be unconscious due to its grim, painful nature.

Level III receives inputs from Level II and must make a decision on the basis of the feelings and associated ideas that have been generated at that level. While there may be multiple thoughts, feelings, and strategies that pertain to a Mercury-Saturn square, he must choose a single idea with which to identify and a single strategy to implement. If he interprets the Mercury-Saturn events and corresponding thoughts-feelings to mean, "I am stupid," then he will have created an identity vis-à-vis his Mercury function. Again, this is not the only meaning that the event in question could have, but it is the one that he has chosen. Our capacity for creative decision-making is the primary emergent property of Level III, which must coordinate operations that occur below it in the hierarchy.

If he chooses to believe that he is stupid, he may further decide to avoid careers (Saturn) that require a high level of mental ability (Mercury). Recall that this is but *one* strategy (among several potential strategies) that developed at Level II. At Level III, however, a fateful choice is made, and the strategy is implemented.

It is possible that at a later date he may re-evaluate his original interpretation of events and decide, "No, I am not stupid. My father was hypercritical and projected his feelings of mental inadequacy onto me." This interpretation would enable him to change his identity vis-à-vis Mercury to something more functional. He might choose to believe, "I am uncertain of my mental abilities and need to test myself in a learning situation that affords me an opportunity for further development in this area." This new belief and strategy would also allow him to choose a career that is more challenging and, perhaps, more commensurate with his actual intelligence.

LEVEL III – THE EXECUTIVE CONTROL CENTER

One might ask what makes a person decide to get an education and pursue higher levels of career success? What motivates the integrative process? Again, the decision itself is a property of Level III, which is the executive branch of the personality, the control center, or what we would call the ego/Sun. A primary attribute of the ego is its capacity for choice; the Sun is will, volition, or intentionality. It is that part of the psyche which decides to pursue one course of behavior over another.

In this regard, the ego is creative. For it endeavors to create outcomes that are in accord with its values and preferences. Just as the Sun is at the center of the solar system, so the ego/Sun is at the center of the personality. In our model, however, the ego is not only at the center, it also constitutes the top level which, spreading out like a mushroom cloud, encompasses all the information that resides in the levels below. This image suggests we are solar *systems*, not just isolated solar entities without planets.

Recall that the cognitive structures (aspect systems) of Level II result from integrating the various sign-planets that constitute their subsystems. Just so, the self-concept is a system—a cognitive structure—albeit at a higher level of organization (Level III). The subjective experience of "I" can be understood as a higher order inference that encompasses all of its subsystems; that is, every sign-planet subsystem and every aspect subsystem.

In other words, "I" is an integrative structure that includes all the other selves—planets—as subdivisions of the total self-system, just as the solar system constitutes a Sun with planetary subsystems. To the degree that the individual is able to integrate all of his or her parts—all the signs and planets—into a functional, indivisible, harmonious whole, s/he attains the *Self*. This is what Jung meant when he said that the Self represents the center and the circumference of the psyche. As such, it is the supreme object of aspiration.

Again, an emergent property of Level III is the capacity to regulate the functioning of its lower order parts—that is, the capacity *to decide*. The Sun must decide when and how to express the impulses, ideas, and plans that constitutes the information of Level II. As a higher-level inference, or self-*concept*, it has a number of interrelated goals: (1) to assimilate the data of experience and give it a meaning, (2) to respond to this meaning in a way that satisfies the needs that are involved (maximize pleasure; minimize pain), and (3) to optimize self-esteem.

As an acronym, one's self-concept, or personal narrative, can be summarized as an AMO involving the following components:

A = assimilate the data of experience
M = maximize the pleasure/pain balance
O = optimize self-esteem

Just as exhilaration results from personal growth and resolution of conflict, so in a comparable but opposite manner anxiety occurs when one's self-theory is unable to assimilate information or establish internal consistency. Anxiety is adaptive in that it provides motivation for correcting the self-theory so that self-esteem can be optimized.

Imagine, again, our person with Mercury square Saturn. His initial belief that he was intellectually inadequate and unable to succeed is likely to have caused anxiety. As mentioned earlier, cognitions generate feelings that reflect the individual's appraisal of a situation. A strong mood, for example, signals that something important is happening or that the individual believes it could happen—in this case, that he will be judged incompetent and his success thwarted.

Such anticipation of an unwanted outcome is called *signal anxiety* and is a consequence of psychic conflict. In this case, the urge to succeed (Saturn) and the desire for knowledge (Mercury) are operating at cross purposes (lack of internal consistency). There is an internal self-perception that his knowledge is insufficient to assure success, which causes anxiety. If he strives for success yet avoids getting the education he needs to attain it, this constitutes a lack of internal consistency. The two functions are not working together; in fact, they are working against each other. Mercury is not giving Saturn what it needs, and Saturn is not able to provide Mercury with its gifts.

Saturn, in effect, requires Mercury to attain a high standard of knowledge, which the self experiences as a pressure to know more. If Mercury doesn't rise to the challenge, Saturn will increase its pressure until the person is forced to find a solution.

It is precisely this experience of stress, anxiety, and pressure that is conveyed to level III of the system. Now the individual has to make a choice, which, of course, is the province of the Sun. One option is to suppress the anxiety and avoid situations in which he might be intellectually tested. This strategy may result in a temporary lessening of his anxiety, but it will also assure that his success is limited—a self-fulfilling prophecy. He may decide to believe, "I'm not very smart; I can only succeed at a low paying, menial job."

An alternative, better solution is to use his anxiety as motivation for improving his intellectual capacities and acquiring knowledge (Mercury) that can be directly applied in his career (Saturn). To the extent that he does this, a new belief will supplant the old one: "I've taken advanced courses and now I know I can advance my career."

Of course, the individual has to coordinate Mercury and Saturn with multiple other functions and beliefs that vie for attention. Subjectively, this is experienced as the endless chatter, review, and preview that make up the content of our daily thoughts. Cognitions cannot be treated in isolation. Each belief helps to maintain a unified, internally consistent conceptual system. Deep beliefs are interlaced like a net that supports the self-concept; thus, they are not easily abandoned or replaced. Every belief must be understood in the context of the system as a whole.

The Sun is like the chairman of the board. Not only does it decide what to attend to, it also issues directives to the various planets with regard to preferred behavior. For example, it might instruct Mercury to cooperate with Saturn and get an education of practical value. It might tell Saturn to lighten up on the guilt factor and not be so perfectionistic. The person might then think, "I am not intellectually inferior; I am simply undereducated. By taking online classes I can alter this condition."

Imagine that Saturn in Pisces is in the 7th squaring Mercury in Sagittarius in the 4th. The person has to find a way to integrate a sense of responsibility

(Saturn) in a domain of compassionate service (Pisces) in the context of his social relations (7th) with a desire for knowledge (Mercury) about legal issues (Sagittarius) surrounding homes and families (4th).

Perhaps the person will decide to start a neighborhood e-mail message center discussing legal issues involving proposed changes to neighborhood schools, traffic lights, road reconstruction, new housing developments, and the like. Picture this decision emanating from Level III, informing Mercury-Saturn at Level II, channeled into planetary sign positions on level I, and flowing out through the portals into the mundane world of the houses. The outer world receives information from his behavior and responds, which provides new feedback to the self-system.

All of this implies that self-esteem is contingent upon two separate but related processes: (1) satisfaction of the Leo need for attention and approval; and (2) satisfaction of needs symbolized by every other sign-planet duo. In regard to the latter, it can be assumed that how a person expresses himself reflects, to a great extent, his overall level of differentiation and integration. In other words, the more one is able to actualize and harmonize all parts of the self, the more one is likely to express oneself in a manner that wins approval from others (satisfying the Leo-Solar need). Thus, integration of the chart as a whole has important consequences for self-esteem.

AN OVERVIEW OF THE SELF-SYSTEM

To summarize, the control structure of the psyche is organized hierarchically with lower levels being subsumed by higher ones (see Figure 12, page 125). The lowest level of the psyche is the zodiac itself, which constitutes basic needs. These needs are superimposed over an abstract plane that represents the houses—the mundane world of lived experience. Events stimulate needs, which are conveyed via feelings to their planetary agents on Level II.

Planets organize themselves into cognitive structures that must find a way to resolve conflicts and collaborate with one another. Ideas, strategies, and automatic thoughts are the emergent properties of this level, which are perceived by the next level (III) as internal dialogue. The content of Level II provides the psychic material for the primary emergent property of level III—a sense of self or personal identity, which is symbolized astrologically by the Sun and all the planets combined. At the heart of Level III (the Sun) are executive control processes. This is the decision-making center that determines how the various needs and strategies will be coordinated; some will be expressed, others suppressed, and so on. The Sun receives information from the strata below and conveys information as commands back down the

COGNITION IN ASTROLOGY • 125

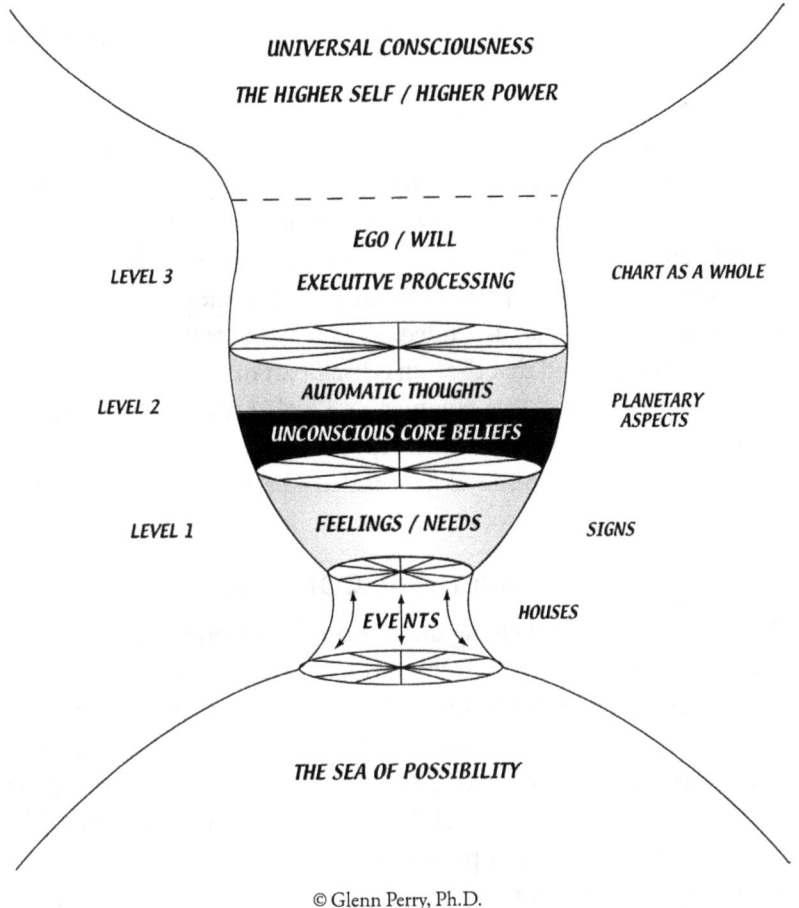

© Glenn Perry, Ph.D.

Figure 12: Side View of the Self-System

hierarchy. The psychic boundary depicted by the twelve portals is a semipermeable membrane that allows for input/output processes. Once a decision is reached, the information is eventually expressed as output, which stimulates a new environmental response (input) in an ongoing feedback cycle.

We can imagine the astrological chart, therefore, as a kind of top that becomes wider and more inclusive as we ascend its various levels. The divisions between levels are like one-way mirrors. Looking up, we see only reflections of the level we are on; looking down, the mirrors become plate glass and cease to exist. Each higher system includes the contents of its subordinate parts. Signs (Level I) contain a set of interrelated needs; aspects (Level II) contain multiple planets and signs to produce emergent cognitive structures, or strategies, for fulfilling needs; and personal identity (Level III) is a summary product of all the needs, beliefs, and strategies that originate at lower levels. Each new level produces emergent properties that do not exist at the previous level.

Our model shows that Level III—personal identity—includes Levels I and II as component parts. This expansion suggests a progressive increase of consciousness that results from the greater complexity and inclusivity of higher levels. When we look at an actual astrological chart, we have to image it as layered, and that the top layer constitutes an invisible entity that is greater than the sum of the parts we see displayed on the paper. This highest level—the self as such—is suspended on a plane above the chart.

We are also reminded that the Sun is itself part of a vaster system that we call the galaxy. By analogy, we can imagine a higher self that subsumes each and every individual, and which incorporates our individual selves into a kind of collective Self. This level may, indeed, be a Universal Mind that is both our source and object of aspiration.

COALITIONAL, HETERARCHICAL CONTROL

In the model offered, I am saying that the psyche is hierarchically organized with executive or central processing mechanisms coordinating operations that occur below them in the hierarchy. In truth, however, this model is somewhat inadequate for depicting multiple, simultaneously occurring processes that interpenetrate one another. I am speaking here of planetary aspects, or level II. Likewise, Level III is the summary product of multiple, parallel, and interdependent operations.

Current models depict the mind and brain as a complex unity of distributed systems and dynamic (ever shifting) control centers. This is a useful model for the astrological chart, too. Picture a three dimensional system with multiple connections through the interior (Figure 13, page 127). This is *heterarchical* control, a heterarchy being a system of distributed and interactive hierarchical subsystems. These coalitional or decentralized models of psychological functioning suggest that astrologers must address the dynamic complexities of conscious control, as well as the inescapable fact that unconscious processes are pervasive in human experience.

In an actual person, all planetary processes are operative to varying degrees simultaneously. For example, if a man is talking on the phone with his girlfriend, he may be asserting his rights (Mars), considering her rights (Venus), speaking (Mercury), listening (Moon), defending his pride (Sun), making a moral judgment (Jupiter), planning their future (Saturn), shocked by her attitude (Uranus), empathic with her suffering (Neptune), and penetrating her defenses (Pluto). While some of these processes are occurring within his conscious awareness, probably a greater amount of feeling and thinking is operating on an unconscious level. A person with Mars opposition Moon may, for example, be completely unaware of the fact that his anger and defensiveness is generated by an unconscious expectation that the other person will act without sensitivity to his feelings or emotional needs.

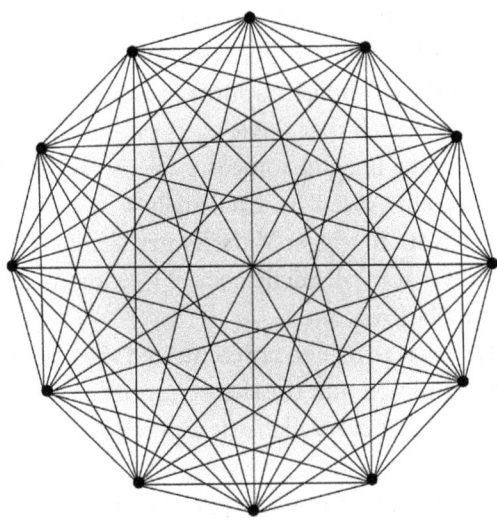

Figure 13: **Planetary Heterarchical Control**

Planetary processes are massively distributed in the sense that they are all going on simultaneously rather than sequentially, or linearly. Hierarchic theory rejects simple stimulus-response models in favor of multiplex parallel processing models. Parallel processing means that rather than a simple, linear chain of cause-effect, there are processes that are occurring simultaneously and that are massively distributed throughout the self-system. In our model, planetary processes are interactive but also semi-independent, which amplifies the power of the system as a whole.

In Figure 13, the yellow core that radiates out to the periphery symbolizes the Sun, which encompasses each and every planetary function. Even though the Sun at the center is the final decision maker, and thus each planet must ultimately subordinate itself to the solar will, planets retain a certain autonomy and influence of their own.

In addition, the various planetary processes are all connected. The strength and nature of the connections are influenced by the frequency of their co-activation. Depending upon aspects and dispositorships, each planet will be more or less involved with every other planet. The more aspects a planet receives, the more pervasive its influence. However, even without these more formal connections, every planetary process interpenetrates every other process. That is, they are massively distributed.

If a man's Saturn is activated and he is feeling the pressure of responsibility, this is eventually going to influence his Mars impulse for freedom even if there is no aspect between the two planets. For to the extent that he is obligated to others he is not entirely free to act in his own self-interest even if he might want to. A holistic approach to astrology implies that the chart works as a system such that single parts can never be entirely isolated from one another. Again, imagine someone who is stressed with the burden of excessive responsibility (Saturn). Eventually s/he's going to feel restless and trapped, which is apt to trigger Mars. Saturn is not activating Mars, but rather circumstances that entail a deficiency of freedom and spontaneity will eventually trigger a Mars response.

It may be, in fact, that all planets are connected via their angular relations. As Blaschke (2000) pointed out, the sheer number of minor and major aspects virtually assures that every planet is aspecting every other planet one way or another.

All of this is to say that astrology is a great deal more complicated than we might think. In attempting to interpret a chart, it is critically important to remember that the whole is always greater than the sum of its parts. This means that everything is affecting everything else. What we call personality is actually an emergent property of multiple, interpenetrating, autonomous control processes that must be integrated into a coherent whole. This underscores an important point: one cannot presume to know a person simply by looking at his or her chart. A horoscope is so maddeningly complex that there is an inescapable ambiguity to any single part. Only by listening, observing, and studying a person over time can one hope to catch a glimpse of what the chart actually symbolizes—a multidimensional, hierarchically organized, dynamic, and continuously evolving whole.

ASPECTS AS COGNITIVE STRUCTURES

At the heart of our theory of cognition is the claim that aspects are cognitive structures. A cognitive structure is an enduring idea or expectancy by which an individual interprets his world and guides his behavior. More simply, we can think of a cognitive structure as a **belief**, which is a conviction as to the truth or actuality of something. A person, for example, may believe that all politicians are corrupt, that marriage stifles one's freedom, or that work should serve a spiritual purpose. Many of our beliefs operate at an unconscious level.

The term "cognitive structure" derives from cognitive psychology and refers to a kind of mental habit or blueprint that shapes perception, generates feelings, and influences the direction of our thoughts. As beliefs, cognitive structures operate in the contexts of specific houses. A planetary aspect will tie together the houses that the relevant planets occupy. If, for example, there is an aspect between the 2nd house and the 5th house, this may emerge as a belief that one's security is affected by creative self-expression.

An alternative term for cognitive structure is *schema*. While cognitive psychology defines schema as a dynamic structure for organizing experience, it is interesting to note that the fifth definition of schema in my Webster's Dictionary states: "A representation of the aspects of the planets at a given time; a figure." So, the meaning of *schema* has come full circle; it was first an astrological term, then a psychological one, and now it is returned to astrology again enriched by its sojourn through cognitive psychology.

We can think of a schema as an innate, *a priori* pattern of perception with an attendant behavioral strategy. Racially motivated hate crimes are a dramatic example of schemas and serve to illustrate the general principle. Imagine a white supremist with Sun opposition Pluto who thinks: "blacks are inferior and should be subjugated." This schema implies a preconception of, and tendency to look for, confirmatory evidence of African-American inferiority. It also denotes an accompanying behavioral strategy—to subjugate blacks.

In less dramatic ways, but no less important, the mind of the average person is populated with schemas. They are, in effect, prejudices that, if unexamined, will influence our thoughts, shape our perceptions, and control our behavior. Ultimately, they determine our life pattern. As an aspect, a schema has an additional meaning that relates it to the external world. An aspect is not merely a belief or pattern of perception, for it will also tend to manifest as a real, objective event. An aspect's early manifestation in childhood is the prototype for later re-enactments.

Astrologically a schema, or cognitive structure, is a multifaceted entity that unites prototypical events, perceptual patterns, world-beliefs, self-beliefs, associated feelings, and behavioral strategies under one, all-inclusive heading. It can be defined in terms of six facets: 1) memory of a prototypical event-pattern that pertains to specific needs; 2) a recurrent pattern of perception vis-à-vis the outer world; 3) a belief about the world vis-à-vis the likelihood of satisfying certain needs; 4) a belief about one's capacity for satisfying certain needs; 5) a pattern of emotional response in relation to specific needs; and

6) a strategic pattern of activity that provides a means for resolving specific intrapsychic conflicts. We will now consider each of these in turn.

1. A cognitive structure is rooted in memory of a prototypical event-pattern that pertains to specific needs.
While certain parts of a chart more obviously pertain to childhood than other parts, it is important to recognize that the whole chart begins to manifest from the first breath. The first thing to consider when interpreting an aspect, therefore, is how it might have manifested early in life as a prototype; that is, as an event-pattern that establishes the aspect's initial meaning. Later, this meaning may change. However, the initial meaning of the aspect will leave a deep footprint on the child's psyche, influencing later thoughts, feelings, and expectations.

Since the planets that are involved in an aspect are striving to meet their respective needs, the prototypical event-pattern will necessarily bear some relevance to the needs that are involved. If Mars is squaring Pluto, there might have been some condition or event-pattern that involved an overly intense expression of anger by someone in the child's immediate environment. Perhaps there was a condition that felt life threatening, abusive, or that made self-assertion seem dangerous. In short, needs for freedom/survival (Aries) and healing/power (Scorpio) existed in a stressful relationship.

In one case involving this aspect, a woman reported that as a child she had a strange health malady that made strenuous activity and excitement (Mars) actually life threatening (Pluto). Her mother never let her play outside for fear that her heart rate would go up and she might die. In another case, a man watched his father abuse his mother and felt powerless to stop him. If he tried to intervene (fight) in her behalf, the father turned on him. Another woman reports an alcoholic father who was violently, sexually abusive toward her.

In all these cases, the surface particulars are different; yet, each case has a similar meaning and a similar effect—the perception that one's survival is jeopardized and that expression of Martian energies to combat this condition is extremely dangerous. It is as if Pluto has appropriated Mars, abducted it into the underworld, intensified it, and rendered it more explosive, violent, and reactive.

Whatever the aspect's prototype event-pattern, the individual internalizes it and subsequently carries the memory of it inside. This memory becomes the seedbed for emergent ideas and strategies that pertain to the needs that are implicit in the aspect.

2. A cognitive structure constitutes an underlying expectancy and recurrent pattern of perception vis-a-vis the outer world.

The subsequent history of the event-pattern is likely to involve recapitulations of the original experience. Once enough experience of sufficient affective intensity has accumulated, the individual comes to expect that the pattern will continue. The pattern of perception is well grooved, as it were, and is subsequently projected into virgin territory (biased anticipation). Any potential experience that could conceivably conform to the structure is expected to do so. Past experiences give rise to hypotheses about the probability of new experiences conforming to the old pattern. The individual then tests these hypotheses by looking for confirmatory evidence. In doing so, however, his internal psychological reality—perceptions, thoughts, and feelings—are partially determined by what he is anticipating. Internally, the person functions as if what he is anticipating has already occurred, which, in a sense, it has—inside his mind.

If someone with Moon conjunct Saturn is used to emotionally cold, withholding caretakers, then every time he experiences a need for nurturing he will anticipate a response that is in keeping with his primary pattern of experience. In this manner, people tend to see what they expect to see, which is what they have become accustomed to seeing. Biased anticipation is constructed on the basis of past experience. Human beings are fundamentally conservative creatures; people expect things to happen as they have happened before. We look for the patterns, the consistencies, in our experiences.

Imagine a young man with Saturn Pisces in the 9th opposed Pluto Virgo in the 3rd. When he was 8 years old, his parents placed him in a strict, Catholic boarding school, which was traumatizing. Afflicted with an undiagnosed learning disorder, he was shamed and pressured mercilessly by Catholic nuns during the 4 years that he attended the school. Now, as an adult, he unconsciously anticipates that if he makes a mental error he will be condemned to hell, so he reacts anxiously whenever he is in a situation that entails the acquisition or distribution of information.

If someone compliments him on a report he's written, he's likely to dismiss or minimize the significance of the remark, for it does not conform to his cognitive structure. In a very real way, he can't hear it. If such feedback continues, he is likely to be confused and uncomfortable until he alters his hypothesis to account for the new experience. But this may take considerable effort, for one does not easily alter a personal theory of reality, even a painful one.

It is important to recognize that an aspect (cognitive) structure is a dynamic, preconceptual ordering process. It is, in other words, a structure of activity that is active and malleable and that precedes any mental representations of experience. As process structures, aspects are dynamic and intentional. They are not merely receptacles into which experience is poured; rather, they shape perception and are the primary means by which we construct order. Mental representations—memories, images, and thoughts—are the products of our cognitive structures. The aspect exists *a priori* to any actual memories or beliefs that might become attached to it. As a congenital configuration, it generates internal experiences of specific thematic content from birth onwards.

Such a structure is malleable in the sense that many different kinds of content can conform to it. Relevant events are identifiable by virtue of having a similar meaning and feeling tone. Mars-Pluto events, for instance, may be perceived as dangerous and frightening. As Mark Twain is reputed to have said, "History does not repeat itself, but it does rhyme."

A core principle of constructivism is the primacy of the abstract. Learning and knowing necessarily involve predominantly tacit (beyond awareness) processes that constrain (but do not specify) the contents of conscious experience. The surface structure particulars—the momentary content of experience—are determined by a more basic deep structure of process that works to create order, relatedness, and meaning in experience. An aspect, therefore, is a tacit process that is capable of manifesting in a wide variety of ways while still being true to itself. As an archetypal compound made of planets, signs, and houses, it constrains but does not determine the particulars of experience. Momentary content is likely to change, yet still conform to the structure of meaning that the aspect entails. Again, different events are related to one another by virtue of having the same or similar meaning.

A woman with Venus square Saturn, for instance, was frustrated as a child in her need for physical touch. Her parents worked long hours and didn't have time to engage her or show her affection. As an adult, she unwittingly chose a career that involved the beauty industry. Her responsibilities necessarily entail the cultivation of refined sensibilities and superior aesthetic appreciation, which sometimes can be burdensome. She married a man who is controlling and withholding of affection. He favors his career over relationship, thus requiring her to work extra hard to achieve intimacy. Aspiring to climb the social ladder, she joins organizations that obligate her to network with successful people in hopes of courting their favor; yet she finds them snooty and snobbish. In her spare time, she likes to work with clay sculptures, molding them into lonely figures that reflect the anguish she feels inside. While the astute astrologer can see the handprint of Venus square Saturn in all these experiences, it might not occur to the woman that such an event-pattern is the product of a single cognitive structure.

This woman's experience suggests that the tacit rules by which we live—that is, the scaffolding of our personal realities, limit what we can experience. And because an aspect partially determines what we can observe and know, it helps us become more aware of our position as observer and knower. To the extent that we become conscious of our expectations and patterns of perception, there is a corresponding freedom in how one responds to experiences that conform to the nature of the aspect. It is precisely in this freedom to attribute alternative meanings that one has the power to change experience itself. Informed by her astrological chart, the woman might think: "Part of my work in life is to develop mastery in social skills, a highly refined aesthetic sense, and an enduring and excellent marriage. These goals may be difficult, but with discipline, perseverance, and determination, I can achieve all of them."

3. A cognitive structure contains a belief about the world vis-à-vis the likelihood of satisfying certain needs.

In response to every event, the individual attributes a meaning. This meaning is not in the formal nature of a theory or philosophy that purports to reveal higher truths and moral imperatives. Rather, these meanings are about the simple phenomena of everyday life. If I act in my own self-interest (Mars), how does the world respond? If I strive to acquire an object or attach myself to a person that I value (Venus), what is likely to happen?

In each instance of striving to fulfill a need, there is an environmental response that means something. The individual must interpret the response in terms that pertain to the need in question. Did my action yield the desired result? The meaning of the event, therefore, pertains to whether it frustrates or satisfies a specific need. If I ask my teacher a question (Mercury) and she looks blank, I am likely to construe that she does not have an answer for me. Since there are always one or more needs operating at any given moment, individuals are engaged in a continuous process of meaning-construction. Virtually every moment has a meaning of one sort or another, and usually more than one. We live suspended in a medium of meanings.

Repeated attribution of meanings of a similar nature constitutes not only a pattern of experience, but a cognitive habit. In regard to Gemini, for instance, imagine someone who rarely gets her questions answered. Each time she is frustrated in her attempt to learn, she attributes a meaning to that specific experience. Mommy doesn't want to read me a story, Daddy didn't hear my question, my teacher is too busy with the other students. Eventually these singular acts of meaning-making are consolidated into a core belief about the world. She doesn't have to start from ground zero every time her Gemini need is stimulated. If on a regular and recurrent basis she is unable to acquire adequate knowledge from the sources that are available, she is likely to construe that the world is information-deficient (at least for her). Saturn in the 3rd or Saturn square Mercury might signify the cognitive structure that underlies her experience.

For every aspect in a chart, there is going to be a belief that pertains to some feature of the world. Since the aspect constitutes a pattern of lived experience it also symbolizes a pattern of meaning. These patterns, or cognitive structures, invariably relate to the likelihood of meeting the needs that the operative planets are pledged to fulfill. By itself, a planet simply acts in accord with its own nature. If the world were nothing but Mars, it would be a constant battleground. Survival would be the sole need and the sole reality. However, unless one is a flaming sociopath, we know the world is more complicated than this. The need for survival has to be coordinated with multiple other needs or there is going to be a problem.

If Mars opposes Saturn, and the individual cannot accommodate to the rules and limits that characterize the society he inhabits, he is going to run afoul of the authorities. Those in charge will not be pleased and he will suffer accordingly. On the other hand, if he occupies a position of authority and strives to oppress fundamental freedoms, then he is going to have a problem and, again, suffer accordingly. Either way, Mars and Saturn have to accommodate one another.

As experience accumulates, certain complex beliefs begin to form that combine elements of both planets. With Mars opposed Saturn, these beliefs will pertain to the likelihood of Mars meeting its needs in relation to Saturn, and Saturn meeting its needs in relation to Mars. Since each planet constitutes a kind of sub-personality, or role identity, different but related beliefs will accrue to each planet. Mars might say, "If I act independently, somebody in control will try to stop me, but I'll fight them." Conversely, Saturn might believe, "If I'm going to achieve my goals, I'll have to watch out for reckless fools whose selfish acts of aggression will ruin my plans."

Note that both beliefs are predictive of negative outcomes in relation to needs that appear mutually exclusive—total freedom versus absolute control. In fact, neither extreme can lead to stable need satisfaction. Unbridled freedom will invariably have to be curtailed, whereas oppressive restraints will invariably be defied.

A common strategy for escaping the tension of inner conflict is to project one pole. At different times and places, the person may identify more with Mars or Saturn. Either way, the other side will take up residence in the environment and constellate an external conflict that intrudes upon the individual. In this way, projection leads to consequences that reinforce the nature of the original belief (self-fulfilling prophecy again). If Mars is projected, unruly combatants will challenge the person's need for control. If Saturn is projected, the right to act freely will be challenged by someone in authority.

The point is these conflicting beliefs are part of the same cognitive structure. I call such beliefs 'bi-polar' or 'doublethink' precisely because they constitute two, mutually exclusive ways of thinking that are wedded together, a matched pair. To the extent that the aspect is not integrated, mutually antagonistic beliefs will co-exist in the same person and will create a feeling of tension and inner conflict. Invariably, this inner conflict will be acted out in behavior that is self-defeating. If the person behaves in accord with his Mars convictions, "I should be able to do what I want," then he'll be in conflict with his Saturnian principles. If, however, he acts in accord with his Saturn belief, "people should obey the rules," then he'll be in conflict with his Mars' principles.

This lack of internal consistency between behavior and beliefs is also referred to as "cognitive dissonance." And dissonance is experienced as anxiety. More broadly, cognitive dissonance is the subjectively felt discrepancy between 1) two incompatible cognitions, 2) between a behavior and cognition, or 3) between an experience and cognition. Cognitive dissonance leads to attempts to resolve the dissonance/anxiety by changing or eliminating a cognition; changing one's behavior to conform to cognitions; or changing cognitions to conform to experience.

As aspects are integrated, previously bi-polar beliefs become more internally consistent. Rather than conflict with one another, the two beliefs will increasingly coalesce into a single pattern of thought that represents a balanced perspective. A seamless, interweaving of the two planetary functions operates to create a pattern of experience that satisfies both needs. One's perceptions of the world begin to reflect the new integration. A square between Mars and Saturn, for example, might manifest as a Mars belief: "The world is full of opportunities for independent, enterprising young men, if I persevere." Or "The boss will be impressed by my bold initiative."

Consistent with the Mars' beliefs, Saturn might say, "There is tremendous energy in the work force that, if properly harnessed, will enable me to build a company of strength and vigor."

The 19th century American author, Horatio Alger, had Mars Sagittarius square Saturn Virgo. Alger became famous for his formulaic novels about impoverished boys who rose from humble backgrounds to lives of respectable middle-class security and comfort via their hard work, determination, courage, and honesty. What became known as the "Horatio Alger myth" is the classic American success story that depicts a character arc from rags to riches. Alger wrote 120 books about young working-class males who, by leading exemplary lives and struggling valiantly against poverty and adversity, ultimately gained wealth and honor, thus realizing the American Dream. One can readily see the imprint of Mars Sagittarius square Saturn Virgo in Alger's novels. Significantly, his Martian characters—young men fighting to get ahead—often improved their social position through the aid of an older, kindly, wealthy helping person; that is, Saturn Virgo characters.

We can presume these Mars and Saturn characters were aspects of Alger's own psyche, subpersonalities that found a way to coordinate their respective gifts as expressed in the plots of his novels. This illustrates that regardless of whether the person is in a Mars role or a Saturn role, the beliefs they symbolize are mutually consistent when integrated; both are predictive of positive outcomes for the needs in question. In fact, the degree to which a belief is positive or negative is a primary indicator of an aspect's integration. If it is a negative belief that predicts need-frustration, this evidences an unintegrated, internal conflict, often symbolized by a hard aspect. To the extent that the aspect becomes integrated, it will manifest as a positive belief about the world vis-à-vis the likelihood of satisfying the relevant needs.

4. A cognitive structure contains a belief about the self vis-à-vis one's capacity for satisfying certain needs.
One's beliefs about the world are directly related to self-beliefs that pertain to one's capacity for need fulfillment. If a person learns that the world is such that certain needs will be difficult if not impossible to fulfill, this will directly affect his self-concept in relation to that need. Recall that the self-concept is not a unitary phenomenon. Ultimately the Sun has to identify with the qualities and attributes of every planet. To the extent that various planetary functions are integrated into the self-concept, the person develops an integrated, complex sense of self. That is, s/he becomes whole. It follows that there are self-beliefs in relation to every planetary function. A man, for

example, might think of himself as bright and knowledgeable (Mercury), but not very organized (Saturn). A woman might regard herself as strong and independent (Mars), but not particularly feminine (Moon).

Planetary aspects suggest the nature of these beliefs. While processes of identification are a function of the Sun, the Sun does not have to be in aspect to a specific planet for the individual to develop a self-concept in relation to that planet. A woman may have no solar aspects to her Jupiter, yet think of herself as wise, hopeful, and virtuous, qualities we normally associate with Jupiter. Jupiter's aspects will produce certain emergent ideas and beliefs with which the woman may further identify. For example, if Jupiter is in the 8th house sextiling Uranus in the 6th, a professor might believe that she is not only wise in general, but specifically insightful in understanding the meaning of sex, death, and power. Her theories about these topics are at the cutting edge and constitute a genuine advancement in her field (Uranus factor). The point is that the woman believes that she is capable of discerning a truth (Jupiter) about sex, death, and power (8th house) and of utilizing it in the service of a humanitarian objective (Uranus) that solves a social problem (6th house).

Beliefs, as we explored in the previous section, tend to fall along a continuum of positive-negative. At one end of the spectrum are negative beliefs that predict the person will fail in his or her efforts to attain a goal. At the other end are positive beliefs that predict the opposite, success! In most cases, a person's beliefs will be neither all positive nor all negative but will vary along this axis. Just as positive beliefs about the world reflect a successful integration of the relevant planetary functions, so positive beliefs about the self are a consequence of integration.

Imagine an individual with Moon forming an opening trine to Pluto. The Moon signifies one's capacity to receive nurturing and Pluto signifies our capacity to transform; thus, an easy trine between these two functions may combine to create a belief that self-disclosure of one's deepest, most personal feelings will not only facilitate a healing connection with others but can actually be fun (opening trine). I know a psychologist who has this aspect who lectures on the importance of self-disclosure. She tells personal stories to her audience, is able to model tenderness and emotional vulnerability, and has a transformative effect on her listeners. Other notable people with this aspect include the late psychologist Leo Buscaglia, Martin Luther King, and Milton Erikson (the great hypnotherapist), all of whom embodied a quality of "expressive emotional vulnerability."

At different times and in different situations, self-beliefs may momentarily shift. Thus, cognitive structures tend to operate along an axis of stability-instability. The more genuinely positive a belief the more stable it tends to be. Of course, some beliefs may appear positive when actually they are merely compensatory to a negative belief that has been repressed. Again, two planets in aspect can produce bi-polar beliefs that compensate one another. The famous daredevil, Evel Kneivel, had a conjunction between Mars and Neptune. He claimed he was capable of transcendent feats of courage, like jumping a motorcycle over the fountain at Caesar's Palace in Las Vegas. One might suspect, however, that underlying the grandiosity of his death-defying stunts was a corollary, negative belief such as, "I am too weak and cowardly to prevent tragedy." It is ironic that in seeking to transcend his physical limitations, Kneivel likewise succeeded in bringing about his own downfall—quite literally, in fact, when he crashed his motorcycle on twenty-four occasions, breaking thirty-six different bones over the course of his career.

A genuinely positive belief tends to remain stable precisely because it is adaptive. It leads to need satisfaction and enhances feelings of self-esteem and self-efficacy. Negative beliefs, on the other hand, tend to produce negative consequences that motivate the individual to reassess the belief; thus, negative beliefs tend to be less stable. Some theorists postulate that human beings are motivated at an unconscious level to test negative beliefs and will even develop complex plans in an effort to disconfirm them. There is a substantial body of clinical studies that support this theory (Sampson & Weiss, 1986).

5. A cognitive structure will manifest as a pattern of emotional response in relation to specific needs.
In Chapter 4 we explored how each sign-planet motivational system is associated with a range of affective states. If a person's attachment needs (Taurus/Venus) are frustrated, he might feel alone and insecure; if his desire for nurturance (Cancer/Moon) is stimulated, he may feel dependent or sympathetic; if his need for order (Capricorn/Saturn) is not met, he could feel disorganized or out-of-control. Emotions are experiential monitors of our motivational systems. That is, they serve as barometers of need satisfaction. Each sign-planet motivational system symbolizes a class of affects on a continuum from positive to negative.

Affects are also experienced along a range of intensity. By cross-comparing the affective intensity of feelings from competing sign-planet motivational systems, the individual has an effective way or prioritizing needs and reaching a decision, which, in turn, initiates a course of action. In this way, emotions are governors of motivational systems. When an emotion strays too far from its preferred (target) state, it activates the behavioral sequence of its sign-planet motivational system. The individual is then compelled to act in a manner that steers experience back to the target state.

In truth, however, the situation is more complex. Planets invariably are involved in aspects and thus form cognitive structures that involve multiple functions and feelings that cross-pollinate one another. As a result, simple feelings can join together to create compound feelings.

Recall that a cognitive structure can manifest as an emotionally significant event-pattern, beginning in childhood, which crystallizes into specific beliefs about the world and about the self. These beliefs predict the likelihood of satisfying basic needs that pertain to the aspect in question. While cognition refers to mental operations such as memory, judgment, and reason, one cannot perform such operations without at the same time generating feelings that correlate to the cognition. If I think, "I'm going to be hurt," I am likely to feel anxious. There is a Buddhist saying, "Emotions are the clothes on the bones of thought." Although feeling and thinking— *orexis* and *noesis*—are often viewed as separate processes, they are, in fact, two faces of the same phenomenon. Cognitions mediate initial emotional responses and change them in ways that are specific to the aspect. Accordingly, an emotional response is a necessary and inevitable component of a cognitive process.

I once had a client named Ruth whose Moon was conjunct Pluto and Mars in the 2nd house, all of which squared Uranus in the 11th. Ruth had a mother who was brilliant but emotionally unstable due to traumatic childhood losses that involved losing her own mother in childbirth, and later her father. Not surprisingly, Ruth's mother was afraid something terrible might happen to her daughter as well. Accordingly, she would overreact whenever Ruth was sick, upset, or troubled. Rather than contain Ruth's feelings in a sensitive manner, she would become upset, guilty, angry, impatient, intrusive, frantic, or some variation of all of the above. In addition, the mother was frequently distraught over small, relatively inconsequential things like her husband coming home 30 minutes late from work. Ruth described her mother as "scary" and "devouring" with huge, hungry eyes that burned with intensity.

The situation was complicated by the fact that the family frequently moved, and Ruth often felt like an outsider at her new schools. That Ruth's mother was often remote and unavailable due to an obsessive devotion to her career compounded the problem. All of this reflected the nature of the aspect. Ruth's mother was 1) emotionally aggressive and impatient, which reflects Moon conjunct Mars; 2) impinging and fearful, which corresponds to Moon conjunct Pluto; and 3) unstable and unavailable, as might be expected from Moon square Uranus. The latter also correlates to Ruth's experience of frequent moves that left her feeling alienated from her peers.

There were four notable consequences of this pattern of events, each of which is reflected by the Moon's position. First, Ruth learned to be extra sensitive to her mother's feelings of insecurity; thus, she tried not to say or do anything that might upset her. To the contrary, Ruth would calm and reassure her mother whenever it became necessary (Moon in the 2nd). Second, she came to regard her own needs for nurturance and understanding as potentially dangerous and harmful to her mother (Moon conjunct Pluto); thus, she avoided expressing them, preferring instead to take care of herself (Moon conjunct Mars). In addition, she anticipated that her emotional needs would be as unwelcome to others as they were to her mother, so she learned to distance herself affectively (Moon square Uranus).

On an emotional level, the situation is quite complex. Every time Ruth feels a need for closeness, it triggers the whole constellation of aspects to her Moon. Her underlying belief is that it is dangerous to reveal her feelings (Moon-Pluto); it is imperative she be strong and independent (Moon-Mars); and it is critically important that she remain detached since the people she depends on will invariably cut out on her (Moon-Uranus). Note that each of these beliefs operates as an injunction; each aspect not only constitutes a belief, it is also a strategy for dealing with her lunar needs.

While we could say more about the events and resultant beliefs that this cognitive structure entails, the point is that her thinking mediates her affective response. If she thinks it is dangerous to reveal her dependency needs, she will become **afraid** whenever she feels emotionally dependent; if she believes that others are too self-absorbed and reactive to adequately care for her, she's going to feel **angry** whenever she needs caring; if she perceives others as emotionally absent and disconnected, she will feel **detached** from her feelings, too. So her lunar needs and feelings are collectively mixed with fear (Pluto), anger (Mars), and detachment (Uranus).

At different times one feeling or another might predominate, but they are all there, a potent compound of emotional distress that flows directly from convictions that originated in childhood. Even though the circumstances of her life have radically changed and her mother has long since passed away, she still believes that everyone she meets and cares about will respond to her emotional needs the same way. Accordingly, she experiences more or less chronic anger, distrust, and hostility toward other people, especially woman. Finding it difficult to get close to anyone, she suffers from profound emotional alienation.

Ruth's case illustrates how beliefs that derive from childhood experiences mediate emotional responses. First, a person experiences certain affects in response to life events, and these emotional response patterns then become linked to memory traces. Familiar perceptual patterns become superimposed over current events, so that the present increasingly resembles the past. Since memory traces invariably involve persons with whom the individual was previously involved, such as a parent or sibling, affects are usually linked to object representations—intrapsychic images and fantasies related to an original caretaker or other important person. Ruth's Moon and its various aspects symbolize her object representation of "mother" and by extension "women." The Moon also symbolizes her self-representation vis-à-vis the need for closeness and belonging. Accordingly, when this need is stimulated, it also activates Ruth's "story" about how other woman will respond to her lunar longings.

This last linkage led Freud to state that affects are drive derivatives; that is, emotional responses derive from ideas associated with certain needs. Perceptions of immediate stimuli trigger corresponding intrapsychic representations. For example, Ruth's perception of a potential female friend, on whom she might depend for support, triggers associations to the intrapsychic concept of "mother." Hence, she tends to evaluate and respond to present situations along the lines of past experience. The same feeling state is evoked—fear, anger, and aloof detachment.

All of this underscores how emotions are not simply spontaneous reflections of reality, but are a consequence of habitual modes of thinking, usually at an intuitive, unconscious level. Emotions largely result from how one interprets events rather than on the events themselves. Astrologers can help individuals become aware of how thought patterns contribute to unpleasant emotions and problems in living. As clients learn to recognize and then correct biased hypotheses and maladaptive ways of thinking, they are increasingly able to profit from new experiences.

It is a revelation to many people to find that their cognitions, which determine how they subjectively perceive the world, also influence how they feel. People feel encouraged when they realize that these cognitions are directly under their control. Once an individual recognizes this, he or she no longer has to accept thoughts as automatic reflections of reality; rather, thoughts can be evaluated as destructive or constructive in accordance with their emotional effects.

Strong emotions tend to be aroused when anything of significance to an individual's self-theory occurs. For example, if a woman with Sun square

Saturn unconsciously believes that she will never be good enough to succeed in the real world, then every time her need for career success is stimulated she is likely to experience anxiety, which derives from her fear and conviction of imminent failure.

By noting the events to which a person emotionally reacts, important clues can be gained about a person's implicit postulates. In the above example, the woman's recurrent anxiety in career situations provides a clue to her Sun-Saturn beliefs. Emotions can thus be regarded as the royal road to an individual's implicit postulates.

Behind almost every emotion is a hidden cognition. Once it is recognized that implicit cognitions mediate emotions, it is evident that people who are frequently depressed, anxious, or chronically angry must have certain habitual thoughts that produce a disproportionate incidence of these feelings. Chronically negative feelings reflect chronically negative beliefs. Bringing these beliefs into conscious awareness is a first step in changing the moods and feelings that they habitually generate.

Astrologically, emotional response patterns can be modeled in terms of our hierarchy (Figure 12). At Level I, there is an initial emotional response to an event. This is a kind of basic, generic human response that is more or less universal. A man gets fired from his job and experiences disappointment (failure/Saturn), a woman is hurt when she discovers her husband's infidelity (betrayal/Pluto), or a car backfires and a child is startled (flight or fight/Mars). These emotions are connected in a more or less pure way to parts of the psyche symbolized by the relevant sign-planet system. In Chapter 4, an affective range of these states was listed Figures 7 and 8.

However, once these emotions are triggered, they are "picked up" or "received" by certain thought patterns as symbolized by the aspects that the respective planets form. They are, in effect, appropriated by the aspect patterns of Level II. The initial emotional response is then modified by the belief pattern through which it is processed.

Emotional response patterns may be suppressed, amplified, intensified, calmed, diffused, denied, or weakened—all depending upon the idiosyncratic meaning that the individual attributes to the event stimulus. These meanings, of course, will be rooted in the individual's cognitive history and personal narrative vis-à-vis the needs and functions activated by the event. So even though a sign is always associated with certain kinds of feelings, those simple feelings are going to be compounded by planets to which its ruler is in aspect.

For example, imagine that a woman with a Venus-Pluto square experiences a simple attraction (Libra). That feeling of attraction will not simply activate

Venus, but Pluto as well; the initial feeling of attraction may be compounded by fear, obsession, or passion. Feelings of attraction are intensified and deepened by Pluto. She might even feel in danger of losing control of her desires, as if the object of her interest could arouse overpowering feelings.

These compound emotions, which develop (emerge) at Level II, will then be picked up by Level III, the decision-making center. Here, feelings are evaluated, and the total feeling compound provides the motivational basis for a decision as to what one should do. Generally, the behavioral response will make sense in the context of the meaning or "story" attributed to the event stimulus, which will be attached to the accompanying feelings.

A woman with Venus square Pluto may feel aroused by the thought that a man is dangerous. Such thoughts and feelings may be conscious or unconscious depending upon the individual's level of awareness vis-à-vis that aspect. If the woman is relatively conscious of her Venus-Pluto beliefs and, thus, of the feelings associated with them, she may decide to articulate them to the object of her interest. Feelings of fear and vulnerability might be communicated in a way that allows for healing in the relationship. However, if Venus-Pluto ideas and feelings are operating outside of awareness, she may repress the initial feeling of attraction because of the dangers associated with it. Because the whole complex is operating unconsciously, she will not be conscious of her decision to avoid the relationship. Intense feelings of attraction-repulsion may then fester at an unconscious level.

Equally likely, she may at some point become compulsively attracted to individuals who are likely to provide painful, extreme kinds of emotional experiences. This would constitute an acting out of the negative, pathogenic belief associated with the aspect—a belief that likely derived from an original wounding. Such experiences can be interpreted as attempts on the part of the individual to remember the initial injury and become conscious of the pathogenic beliefs and maladaptive strategies that resulted, a point we will explore further in the next section.

6. A hard aspect will manifest as a strategic pattern of activity that provides a means for resolving an intrapsychic conflict.
Ultimately, an aspect is going to manifest as a pattern of behavior that constitutes a strategy—a schema—for satisfying certain needs. This strategy is a product of an underlying belief that predicts the likelihood of satisfying those needs. Accordingly, the strategy is no more effective than the nature of the belief that underlies it. If there is a conflict between the planetary

processes that make up the aspect, then the resultant strategy is likely to be maladaptive.

As stated, however, resultant experience can be useful to the extent that it provides an incentive for correcting the maladaptive belief. The individual will be motivated to find an outer situation that provides a vehicle for resolution of the conflict. Initially, this vehicle may not be particularly satisfying or enjoyable; yet, if the individual persists, eventually it will yield a quota of experience that serves to replace a negative belief with a positive one. In effect, the activity itself constitutes a process of self-healing.

Recall our earlier example of the man with Mars squaring Pluto from the 6th to the 9th. We speculated that his hostility toward supervisors was based on an expectation that he would be overpowered, subjugated, or even destroyed by an oppressive, unjust other. Underlying this expectation was probably a fear that he was comparatively impotent in the face of a hostile, destructive, and immoral force; in effect, he lacked sufficient power to resolve the injustice. To the extent that he feels disempowered, he overcompensates and thus succeeds in bringing about the very result that he fears—termination of employment, a kind of death—albeit one that is repeated from one job to the next. We might surmise that if he is to escape from this self-defeating pattern, he will have to change the belief that underlies his behavior; namely, the idea that he is powerless to resist a destructive force that he projects onto his supervisors.

Imagine that our Mars square Pluto man has been working as a paramedic at the same hospital for several years (they can't fire him because they know he'll sue). In addition to his hostile attitude toward supervisors, he also evidences certain other distinct behaviors. For example, he likes to do jobs that involve dangerous conditions that bring him close to death, such as stabbings, gunshot wounds, and automobile accidents; he is fearless in confronting situations that would intimidate others; he likes to drive ambulances and functions well in emergencies; and he is handy with tools and technology for medical crisis interventions. As a consequence of his training and accumulated experience, he gradually comes to feel powerful in relation to the most deadly force of all—death itself. His capacity to act boldly (Mars) in medical crises (Pluto) is helpful not only for his patients, but also for himself. His experience teaches him that he is not powerless and that he can directly influence what happens in his environment. Indeed, he can even save lives.

It is not difficult to see that his job provides a vehicle for resolving his Mars-Pluto conflict. As such, the pattern of activity constitutes a strategy for disconfirming a negative belief. With every successful crisis intervention he is provided an opportunity for re-authoring a negative story and turning it into a positive one. Experience teaches him to develop a new personal theory of reality with new, adaptive beliefs. This, in turn, may enable him to resolve his conflict with supervisors (6th house) and renew his faith in a moral order (9th house).

Because individuals are usually not conscious of the negative beliefs that underlay their behavioral strategies, they likewise are not conscious of their strategies. That is, their strategies are not consciously chosen. However, research suggests that people are nevertheless motivated at an unconscious level to devise plans for testing and disconfirming negative ideas that impair the realization of their human potentials. These plans bring about specific patterns of experience that recapitulate unfinished business from childhood. Regardless of the lack of conscious awareness and the sense that one has not intentionally chosen the experience in question, more often than not it is just what the doctor ordered—that is, the physician within. As an astrologer, one can only marvel at the consistency with which people hit upon ingenious strategies for resolving intrapsychic conflicts. Such behavior seems to reflect an innate, self-actualizing, evolutionary tendency in the human psyche.

REPETITION COMPULSION

Cognitive psychology teaches that in order to change negative cognitions it is necessary to learn to talk to oneself differently. However, this may first require corrective emotional experiences to counteract strong, self-limiting hypotheses that are deeply ingrained because of early conditioning. Negative core beliefs symbolized by difficult planetary aspects operate as self-fulfilling prophecies. This is referred to as repetition compulsion, the compulsion to repeat a pattern of experience that originated in childhood without recognizing one's own participation in bringing about the incident(s). Such re-enactments are regressive in that they activate repressed memories along with the feelings and behaviors contained in them. Regression can have adaptive significance, however, in that it not only brings into awareness memories and meanings that were previously unconscious, but also provides an opportunity to "redo" or "rewrite" a part of one's story with a new, more satisfying outcome.

A client, "Barbara," had Sun conjunct Saturn in the 12th house opposed Mars in the 6th. As a child, she grew up with a violent father who suffered from an apparent inferiority complex. This in itself is consistent with the aspect. In order to bolster his ego, he constantly criticized Barbara. Again, we see how an aspect can describe features of the environment and of typical characters that are symbolized by the relevant planets. Both Sun and Saturn are father indicators, while Mars is a symbol for combatants. Her father was a brutal tyrant whose rages seemed to be fueled by feelings of failure, impotence, and low self-esteem—all aptly symbolized by the aspect and its placement in the 12th. Recall that 12th house characters are frequently victims; in this case, Barbara was the victim of an abusive father, who himself felt victimized by life. Barbara's challenge would be to find a more successful resolution of the conflict than her father was able to achieve.

Forced to carry his unresolved feelings of inferiority, she grew up with the belief that men would abuse and degrade her unless she was perfect. Her strategy to avoid criticism was to "try harder" to measure up to her father's unrelenting standards. Try as she might, however, she could never please him, for he was psychologically invested in maintaining her feelings of inferiority by projecting his own devalued self into her, and then attacking it. Barbara's resultant belief had two components: (1) she was inadequate, inferior, and incapable of generating positive attention; and (2) efforts to stand up for herself would be met with fierce opposition. She would be attacked and subjugated if she attempted to act in her own self-interest. Again, this complex is precisely symbolized by Mars in the 6th opposed Sun-Saturn conjunct in the 12th.

As an adult she ended up working as a stockbroker in a male dominated office (Mars in the 6th). Despite the fact that she outperformed almost every person in the company, she was continually criticized for not measuring up to standards. Such treatment conformed to her internal story, as symbolized by the aspect. Accordingly, she resorted to her old familiar strategy of "trying harder" in compliance to the faulty belief that she was inadequate and inferior to her male bosses. However, she was also privy to statistical records that measured her performance relative to others and confirmed a dimly felt subjective sense of doing exemplary work.

At first she was confused by the reports, but over time it became obvious that something was wrong. If she accepted her boss's evaluation that she did not deserve a raise or promotion, she would have to deny the reality of her own superior performance as confirmed by the statistical reports. Finally, after several years of suffering, it occurred to her, "Maybe the problem is not me; maybe it's *them*."

Such cases demonstrate a principle that I call "amplification." The current situation amplifies a previous, childhood scenario and mirrors back a false belief in stark, exaggerated terms. In Barbara's case, her bosses were treating her more or less as her father had. She felt kicked around, beat up, and put down. No matter how hard she tried or how well she did, she was never good enough.

Eventually, the situation reached a point of *reductio ad absurdum*. If she were an inferior employee, this would be evident in measures of her work performance. In fact, her work performance showed just the opposite. The more she achieved, the more absurd became the proposition that she didn't deserve a raise, praise, or promotion.

The situation became so strained that something had to give. Either Barbara would have to deny the reality of her own superiority, or she would have to confront her bosses and, if necessary, leave the company. The real issue was her self-perception and beliefs about entitlement. As a child she had little choice but to accept her father's negative appraisal. Again, children believe that how they are treated is how they deserve to be treated. This led directly to the current situation, which activated her pathogenic belief of inferiority. Her bosses treated her like dirt, which was incongruent with objective indicators (statistical records) that indicated her performance was, in fact, superior to other employees.

Accordingly, there was mounting evidence that her pathogenic belief was false, and the external situation undeserved. Barbara was forced to conclude that her strategy of "trying harder" was maladaptive because it derived from a false premise that she was inferior. The problem was not her performance; it was her *belief* that her performance was inadequate.

So long as she held onto this belief, it would continue to generate circumstances that falsely defined her as inadequate and inferior. This points up an important principle: *A false belief will generate circumstances consistent with itself.* Eventually tension will arise between contradictory pieces of information (cognitive dissonance). On the one hand, a person or situation will define the person negatively and in a way that activates an old complex.

The native's defenses will be amplified and perturbed as the complex surfaces into awareness. Yet, evidence will also mount that the appraisal is invalid. Eventually, the evidence is so overwhelming that the native marshals the internal resources to reverse a decision (and meaning attribution) that was rendered long ago.

During childhood, Barbara could not speak in her own behalf because to do so was dangerous. Also, she lacked the capacity to understand that she was not the cause of her father's behavior. As an adult, however, the situation is different. Now she can look at an analogous situation—her boss's withholding of approval—from a more mature perspective. Now she can reassess the meaning that she initially attributed to the prototypical event-pattern of childhood. This means deciding that she is more than adequate; she is actually superior in some instances and, more importantly, she is entitled to respect and appreciation.

In effect, the current situation provides an opportunity for the person to re-evaluate an early decision by showing that how one is being treated is not necessarily how one deserves to be treated. When the situation reaches a point of absurdity, the individual is enabled to become conscious of the pathogenic belief that is responsible for maintenance of the problem. This is the moment of truth, the turning point. For inherent in the time is an opportunity to change a maladaptive strategy that derived from a childhood wound. It becomes painfully obvious that one is no more responsible for the situation *now* than one was responsible for the situation *then*. Finally, the self affirms that one *is* entitled to something better.

Resolution of Barbara's pathogenic beliefs can be summarized thusly: "I am a responsible, successful person that deserves respect and appreciation. More so, I can act in my own self-interest and triumph over those who seek to exploit me for selfish ends." Such a belief represents a healthy resolution of Sun conjunct Saturn opposed Mars. Barbara's case is an example of how adult situations can reenact childhood injuries while providing a vehicle for the resolution of resultant pathogenic beliefs.[9]

FILLING UP THE HOLLOW

In other instances, the disconfirmation of a pathogenic belief involves experiences in which the individual plays a role opposite the one that s/he played in childhood. I call this "positive reversal" or "filling up the hollow" because people find themselves doing for others what they needed done for them. In other words, a current situation or relationship offers an opportunity for developing the very quality that was needed yet missing in one's childhood caretakers. In so doing, a pathogenic belief can be transformed.

By way of example, I had a young female client with Moon in Cancer in the 9th square Uranus in Libra in the 12th. She was the product of an out-

---

[9] Of course, this explanation does not address the karmic implications of the aspect, which would suggest that, in fact, the person *is* deserving of the conditions symbolized by the configuration. This constitutes a different level of analysis, however, and does not necessarily contradict the points made above. It may be that an aspect initially expresses itself in painful or frustrating childhood conditions, which are later reenacted, until finally the individual learns the lesson and "lets oneself off the hook." To allow oneself to have a better outcome of the aspect in question and allow oneself full satisfaction of the requisite needs, may ultimately require an act of self-forgiveness.

of-wedlock birth. Her mother, who was married, had an affair and became pregnant by a man who was ten years younger. During the first three years of her life, my client, "Karen," was shopped around to various caretakers. These early years were extremely disruptive, upsetting, and traumatic because of constant change—a common theme with Moon square Uranus. Sometimes she would be with her mother and sometimes with her adoptive family who eventually fought the mother for custody and won. It wasn't until she was seven years old that Karen discovered that her adoptive parents were not her real parents.

Karen is now approximately 30 years old and works as a sales representative for a high tech college that trains people in the use of computers for medical and computer-related fields. She has to orient people to the programs and support them in obtaining the educational resources that will best serve their needs. In this regard, she functions as Moon Cancer in the 9th—a caretaker for people seeking higher education. However, many of these prospective students are casualties of technological innovations that made their jobs obsolete. Accordingly, they are feeling shocked and upset at having been displaced by radical changes in the workplace that revolutionized their fields. They are understandably scared, upset, and feeling unstable career-wise.

Again, all of this is consistent with the square from Uranus to her Moon. 12th house characters are often refugees or victims of one sort or another—in this case, Uranus victims. Thus Karen's job is to play the role of sensitive mother (Moon Cancer) in a context of higher education (9th house) to casualties of technological change (Uranus in the 12th). This requires her to be sensitive to their concerns and to basically take care of them. She is often the first person they talk to at the school. Her task is to orient them to what the school can provide and how it can nurture them back into the mainstream. Karen is sensitive to their worries about finding a place in the workforce so that they can, once again, "belong."

Note that Karen's role is reversed from the one she played in childhood. Just as she was upset by erratic, unstable, and tumultuous changes in her errant family, so her prospective students are upset by instabilities and changes in the workplace. Karen's job is to provide for them precisely what she needed but never received from her own mother—a caring, supportive, reassuring presence in the face of overwhelming change and instability.

Not surprisingly, Karen initially reported that she "hates" her job. And why wouldn't she? She is being asked to give precisely what she never received. The situation is regressive in that it activates in Karen the memory of what she experienced under similar circumstances as a child. If, however, she treats her callers with the same callous indifference that her mother treated her, she will lose her job. Here we see how prototypical childhood experiences of an aspect—Moon square Uranus—have later analogues that recapitulate the original pattern while also providing a vehicle for a higher level of integration.

Karen's predicament is an example of what I call "bootstrap recovery." She has to develop within herself precisely those qualities that were deficient in her early environment; this is the equivalent of pulling oneself up by the bootstraps. On some level, Karen knows the unintegrated version of the aspect—an erratic, emotionally absent mother—and so she is potentially able to have empathy for the students. To realize this potential, however, requires her to remember and to have empathy for her *own* suffering under analogous circumstances. To the extent that she is able to do this, and to provide others with a different kind of experience, she can vicariously identify with their good fortune. This can be healing for her because it demonstrates that a certain kind of caring is, in fact, available in the world. She is its best proof.

Karen's story illustrates how people often have to develop qualities that their caretakers most lacked in childhood. This may reflect an inborn (karmic) deficiency in those areas. Circumstances demand that the underfunctioning psychological part has to be developed over the course of the life. It initially shows up as a deficiency in one's early environment. Insufficient caretakers embody and reflect a wound that is also innate in the child. Later, during adulthood, the same aspect manifests as having to provide that quality to others. One is forced to develop, in other words, what one never internalized from a deficient environment. In so doing, an old maladaptive belief left over from childhood can be changed as a consequence of demonstrating its fallacy through one's own efforts.

Karen showed herself that one can be caring in the face of trauma brought about by an unstable environment. Pathogenic beliefs about unstable caretakers, which are the unintegrated version of Moon square Uranus, can then be adjusted to account for her own behavior. New, adaptive beliefs can take the place of the old. The person can now say, "Disruptive change can be contained; emotionally upsetting events can actually bring people together and provide an opportunity for loving." And because she has been able to do this for others, she begins to feel entitled to receive it from others.

In myth and fairy tales, this is breaking the family curse. The hero or heroine is able to do something that no one else in the family was able to do for untold generations. Astrology is advantageous in this regard, for it enables the protagonist—the native—to become conscious of precisely that myth that needs to be rewritten.

Jung defined neurosis as "suffering yet to find its meaning." If a difficult experience can be seen to have a redemptive meaning, then it becomes easier to endure and can even be made enjoyable. To the extent that individuals are conscious of the purpose of their suffering, evolution can be accelerated because they are empowered to cooperate with a change process inherent in life. This has been variously referred to as 'conscious myth-making' or 'conscious evolution' for it signifies an intention to collaborate with experiences that challenge and ultimately replace maladaptive beliefs. Otherwise, evolution may still occur, but it is likely to be slower and more difficult.

SUMMARY & CONCLUSION

In this chapter, we've explored how planetary aspects signify cognitions that mediate perception and determine our thoughts, feelings, and behavior. Astrology is consistent with a constructivist view that human beings organize their experience into familiar categories of meaning. Perceptions are inextricably related to schemas, or cognitive structures, as symbolized by planetary aspects. Cognitive structures constitute hypotheses about the self in relation to a world. Human beings, in effect, are embodied theories or stories.

The construction of meaning begins in infancy and continues throughout life. Stories, like people, evolve. Concepts that formed from emotionally significant childhood experiences develop into broad, general postulates that assimilate later experiences into themselves. A personal theory of reality has three main functions: to provide meaning to experience, to satisfy basic needs, and to optimize self-esteem.

The human psyche, or self-system, can be depicted astrologically as a vertical chain of command comprising three distinct levels. At the bottom of the hierarchy are basic needs, represented by the signs, which are necessarily associated with specific areas of life symbolized by the houses. At the second level are aspects, which constitute higher-level emergent structures or cognitions. The final level of the self-system is the chart as a whole, at the heart of which is the Sun. This is the executive branch and decision-making center of the personality.

As a cognitive structure, an aspect is an enduring idea or expectancy by which an individual interprets his world and guides his behavior. An aspect also constitutes an event-pattern that begins in childhood. Early manifestations of the aspect constitute the prototype for later re-enactments. Once the event-pattern is established, it crystallizes into an underlying expectancy and recurrent pattern of perception. The individual develops certain beliefs about how the world will respond to his or her attempts to satisfy basic needs.

These experiences, in turn, form the basis for self-concepts that pertain to one's capacity for need-fulfillment in specific areas of life. Positive beliefs are stable in that they lead to satisfaction and self-esteem. Negative beliefs, on the other hand, which are usually reflected by hard aspects, tend to be unstable since they do not lead to satisfaction or self-esteem. Negative beliefs produce negative consequences and associated negative emotional states.

While negative beliefs tend to be unstable, they can also be rigid. An unstable belief is one that continually generates painful experiences that cause one to be preoccupied with the belief; that is, to question, defend, and obsess about it. A rigid belief is one that is resistant to change because it is deeply embedded on an emotional level and associated with survival. A belief, therefore, can be both unstable and rigid. In fact, a colloquial definition of insanity sums up the matter: insanity is when a person does something that continually leads to the same negative outcome yet keeps doing it with the expectation that the outcome will change.

We call such behavior "insane" precisely because under normal circumstances people learn from their experience and make the requisite adjustments. This is what it means to be adaptive. Ideally, negative consequences are purposeful in that they motivate the individual to become conscious of maladaptive beliefs and strategies that developed from childhood experiences. Maladaptive ideas not only generate dysphoric emotional states, they also generate frustrating life circumstances that recapitulate early traumas and deprivations.

The individual then has the opportunity to reassess pathogenic beliefs that are responsible for maintenance of the problem. In effect, there is an opportunity to re-author one's story toward more positive outcomes. New, adaptive beliefs, which are self and life affirming, supersede dysfunctional strategies that kept one trapped in a repetitive cycle of frustration. Such beliefs represent a successful resolution of intrapsychic conflicts symbolized by hard planetary aspects.

Chapter Six

PSYCHOPATHOLOGY OF THE ZODIAC

In Chapter Five, we explored the nature of cognition and how it is displayed in the horoscope. Aspects were described as cognitive structures that screen, code, and evaluate lived experiences. An aspect also represents an event-pattern that begins in childhood and is repeated throughout the life. Schemas enable us to interpret experiences in a meaningful way. Meanings, however, can be adaptive or maladaptive. In this chapter, the reader is introduced to the nature of maladaptive schemas that distort the meaning of experience, create distress, and impair one's capacity for meeting basic needs. Maladaptive schemas are correlated with specific sign-planet systems and categories of pathology.

THE VALUE OF DIAGNOSIS

Over the last decade there has been a growing recognition of the importance of diagnosis for both clinical practice and research. It is widely accepted that human beings are prone to patterns of behavior characterized by specific symptoms organized around central themes. Each behavioral pattern constitutes a diagnostic entity with a predictable etiology, age of onset, prevalence, predisposing factors such as gender and familial patterns, along with distinctive impairments and complications.

Knowledge of these diagnostic entities provides clinicians and research investigators with a common language for communicating about the disorders for which they have professional responsibility. According to Maxmen and Ward (1995), psychopathology should be understood not just by psychiatrists, but also by physicians, psychologists, nurses, social workers, and psychotherapists and counselors of every persuasion. It is the view here that astrologers should be added to this list.

Conservative estimates are that mental and addictive disorders afflict between 40 and 50 million Americans, or roughly one out of five. Of these, over 20% go untreated. A National Comorbidity Study (NCS) established that 32-50% of adult Americans would at some time in their life experience a mental disorder. "That almost half of all Americans suffer or have suffered from some type of mental disorder is startling," writes Maxmen and Ward (1995). "What these studies make clear is that the essentials of psychopathology should be understood by health-care professionals of all fields" (p. 18).

It follows that if we are to champion astrology as a diagnostic tool then we, too, must be prepared to specify diagnostic categories that are implicit in our system. Not only will this sensitize us to common ailments that afflict the general population (thereby increasing our competence as helping professionals), it will also enable us to collaborate with colleagues in other fields that are treating patients. In the future, I expect that collaboration between psychologists and astrologers will be increasingly common.

In psychotherapy, planning a treatment program necessarily begins with a diagnostic assessment. However, the whole notion of diagnosis has been fraught with controversy. Many clinicians resist the concept because of a reluctance to place people in preformed categories. Diagnoses are regarded as too linear, static, reductionistic, simplistic, dehumanizing, and stigmatizing. Of course, these same criticisms have been leveled at astrology for its tendency to reduce people to one of twelve simple stereotypes, i.e., as *a* Capricorn, *a* Scorpio, and so on.

My personal view is that people should not be labeled "schizophrenics" any more than they should be labeled "Pisceans," however much the two labels may have in common. To do so is to reduce the complex nature of a human being to a misleading and demeaning singularity. The problem arises from the misconception that a classification system classifies individuals rather than the disorders (or signs) that individuals have. For this reason, care should be taken to avoid use of such phrases as "a schizophrenic" or "a Pisces," and instead use the more accurate, but admittedly more wordy "an individual with schizophrenia" or "an individual with Sun in Pisces." In other words, a sign or personality disorder should not be regarded as a type of human being, but as a type of human behavior.

THE PURPOSE OF DIAGNOSIS

According to Spitzer (1976), psychiatric diagnosis serves two main purposes. The first is to define clinical entities so that clinicians have the same understanding of what a diagnostic category means. While patients with a particular disorder will differ in some ways, they will have certain cardinal symptoms in common. Also, a given disorder will tend to have a similar history—a typical age of onset, life course, prognosis, and complications—regardless of the patient. The second goal is to determine treatment. Diagnosis influences biological treatments, such as medication, while also shaping the choice of particular psychotherapies.

For astrologers, the purposes for diagnosis are similar. First, the astrologer should have some understanding of diagnostic categories in order to communicate effectively with both clients and other helping professionals. A client with depression may be better helped by an explanation of how depression operates than a prediction of her next Jupiter transit. Second, the astrologer should know how a consultation might best be utilized for various clients. A provisional diagnosis will assist the astrologer in asking relevant questions and it will deepen his understanding of how clients are expressing their charts.

Clearly, the concept of treatment means something different in the context of a typical, one-time astrological consultation. However, just as a psychotherapist does not treat all clients exactly the same way, so astrologers need to alter their counsel in accordance with the client's condition. Differences in treatment may range from subtle adjustments in how one interprets the chart to referring the client to other professionals.

For example, if a client with a dependent personality disorder becomes over-reliant upon her astrologer for decision-making, the astrologer who indulges such a client is in danger of reinforcing her pathology. Astrologers should not allow themselves to be used in a manner that is counter to the client's best interest. Likewise, knowing when to refer a client to a licensed psychotherapist and how to make the referral is an important part of the astrologer's repertoire of skills.

A third reason for astrologers to know psychopathology is that it will deepen their interpretive skills. As will be discussed, there are many ways that a particular condition might show up in the chart. However, if one does not already have an understanding of the disorder, it is unlikely that the astrologer will see it in the horoscope. Diagnosis is always a joint product of listening to the client and examining his or her chart. Once a diagnosis is made, the astrologer with an understanding of psychopathology can interpret the chart at a much deeper and more meaningful level than an astrologer without such knowledge. A proper diagnosis greatly enhances the scope and impact of the astrologer's interpretations.

DEFINING PSYCHOPATHOLOGY

Before we can formulate a clear diagnostic system in astrology we first need a working definition of psychopathology, an ominous sounding term if ever there was one. Psychopathology, quite simply, is the branch of psychology that studies diseases (pathology) of the mind (psyche). Psychopathology means "sickness of the soul." It specifically is concerned with the nature and causes of mental disorders. A mental disorder can be defined as a clinically significant behavioral or psychological syndrome that is associated with (1) a painful symptom (distress), (2) impairment in one or more important areas of functioning (disability); and (3) deviation from a norm or from a socially acceptable standard of behavior (deviance).

One should be aware that the concept of psychopathology derives from the medical model and is based on a metaphor of physical disease. If a person suffers from a heart condition, there are specific causes, symptoms, impairments, and treatments. Likewise, it was hoped, if a person suffers from a mental illness, specific causes could be noted and treatments developed. Mental disease was conceptualized as analogous to physical disease. Unfortunately, as we shall see, the mind has proved a great deal more elusive than the body. Moreover, the metaphor of mental "illness" has blinded some researchers to alternative conceptualizations that yield different insights and conclusions.

Suffice to say here that the hallmark of psychopathology is some combination of distress and disability. There are a variety of ways that people can experience distress. Anxiety, depression, guilt, shame, rage, and painful shyness are just a few examples. Likewise, one can experience impaired functioning (disability) in a number of different areas, such as career, parenting, socializing, sex, or competition. For purposes of this chapter, impairment can be defined as difficulty in meeting one or more psychological needs as symbolized by sign-planet systems. For example, if Aries symbolizes the need for autonomy, someone who suffers from an impaired Mars function would experience difficulty meeting this need in a balanced way. Her Mars may over- or underfunction. A man with a dysfunctional Venus might suffer from social anxiety and feel impaired in his ability to form relationships (Libra need). In subsequent chapters, we will explore how each sign-planet pair is associated with different types of distress and impairment.

It should be emphasized that a mental disorder is not a discrete entity with sharp boundaries between it and other mental disorders, or between it and no mental disorder. It can be argued that the underlying cause of psychopathology is intrapsychic conflict, and this by definition implies lack of integration between two or more parts of the psyche on a continuum of severity. This, in turn, implies that psychological health exists on a continuum of functionality. There is no sharp dividing line between what is pathological and what is healthy.

The standard reference in the field, *The Diagnostic and Statistical Manual of Mental Disorders* (DSM), classifies mental disorders; it does not classify *individuals* with mental disorders. Patients who receive the same diagnosis are not the same in every respect. Just as the only similarity among Sun-sign Pisceans is having Piscean traits, so the only similarity among schizophrenics is having symptoms of schizophrenia. Otherwise, some schizophrenics are funny, some boring, some brilliant, and some stupid. The same could be said of Sun-sign Pisceans. Accordingly, when a client is diagnosed as having a particular disorder it should be understood that the disorder is an attribute of the person, and never his or her totality.

This becomes more obvious when we examine the astrological chart for indications of psychopathology. A client may have a difficult T-Square involving the Sun, Moon, and Saturn, with Saturn as the focal planet in the 12th house. Such a configuration could suggest a tendency toward depression and fears of inadequacy. This same client, however, may also have a grand trine in air signs in earth houses, suggesting an easy, intellectual brilliance in his career. Thus while he has trouble in some areas of his life, he does quite well in other areas. His Saturn problems do not define the totality of his character.

SYMPTOMS AND SIGNS

There are two ways that psychopathology manifests: *symptoms* and *signs*. Symptoms are experienced subjectively and cannot be directly observed. They constitute emotional and mental states, such as depression or paranoid thinking. To know the symptoms of a client's pathology, the astrologer would have to be told. The client, for example, might complain of a gloomy mood, fears of being followed, hallucinations of demons, or expectations of failure. Conversely, signs are apparent to an outside observer. These include things like crying, violation of social norms (stealing, speeding), avoidance of closed spaces, or a history of being fired from jobs.

Just as zodiacal signs have subjective and objective dimensions, so symptoms and signs constitute the inner and outer dimensions of psychopathology. In subsequent chapters, we will examine how different sign-planet systems correlate to specific symptoms (subjectively experienced states) and signs (objectively observable behaviors and events). With regard to events, astrology helps to make clear how a chronic pattern of negative experience can itself be a sign of psychopathology.

If someone exhibits a symptom or sign of psychopathology, this does not by itself constitute a mental disorder. For example, everyone at one point or another is going to experience anxiety, grief, or sadness. A symptom or sign reflects a mental disorder only when it is part of a specific constellation of signs and symptoms. For a diagnosis of anxiety disorder the individual would have at least six of a possible eighteen different symptoms as defined by DSM. Accordingly, even patients with the same mental disorder do not have identical clinical characteristics. Patients usually share one or two core features, but beyond that, have a variety of different symptoms that are all consistent with the disorder. Moreover, a mental disorder is characterized by a recurrent pattern of such symptoms. For example, an individual with dysthymic disorder would suffer chronically from a depressed mood for two years or more.

TWO DIAGNOSTIC APPROACHES

There are two approaches to diagnostic psychopathology: descriptive and psychological. In the descriptive approach, diagnoses are based on relatively objective criteria such as symptoms, signs, and natural history. Conversely, the psychological approach bases diagnoses on inferred causes and mechanisms. Whereas the descriptive approach relies solely on objective criteria, the psychological approach considers descriptive phenomena as merely superficial manifestations of more profound underlying forces. In effect, the psychological approach is moderately descriptive while being primarily explanatory.

Clearly, both descriptive and psychological approaches are valuable, since each addresses a different dimension of psychopathology. If the descriptive approach focuses on the what of behavior, the psychological focuses on the why. Generally speaking, it would be fair to say we are better at describing clinical entities than explaining their causes.

Traditional explanations of causality tend to be uniform according to the theory put forth. That is, different psychotherapeutic models are apt to claim that all disorders are more-or-less a consequence of one general thing—repression (Freudian), unresolved complexes (Jungian), pathogenic introjects (object relations), or maladaptive beliefs (cognitive-behavioral). In other words, the psychological approach de-emphasizes surface manifestations in favor of illuminating the underlying general cause.

The descriptive approach, however, adheres to a multiple model in which disorders are distinct and numerous. While explanations may differ as to the cause of a particular disorder, it is easier for clinicians to agree on what constitutes the disorder.

> **Explanations** of pathology tended to be *uniform*. For any disorder, there was assumed to be one general cause.
>
> **Descriptions** of pathology tend to be *multiple*. Disorders are distinct and numerous.

For example, when a therapist states that his patient meets DSM criteria for a major depressive disorder, clinicians know what is meant because DSM criteria for major depression are precise. For this reason, a descriptive rather than psychological approach is the foundation for modern diagnosis.

Suffice to say here that astrology's value in diagnosis is the obverse of psychology: it is better at explaining the underlying causes of a disorder than in predicting what the disorder may be. Like an X-ray in medical diagnosis, the birthchart shows the planetary configuration that underlies the presenting problem. However, the discernment of pathology must still come from objective indicators—symptoms and signs—and not from merely looking at the chart. The horoscope may deepen and further clarify our understanding of pathological behavior, but pathology itself can only be discerned from an objective assessment of the client.

This being said, it is worth mentioning that Gibson (1998) has done some interesting statistical work correlating astrological factors with clinical disorders. For any diagnosis, he cites a large number of potential astrological "markers" involving most of the planets one way or the other for every disorder that he cites. Allegedly, the more of these factors a chart has, the greater the likelihood that the person will exhibit signs and symptoms of that disorder. For a diagnosis of major depression, for example, Gibson notes 43 different configurations involving virtually every planet in the chart. While his work suggests that specific types of psychopathology may have astrological correlates, there is an easier way of making a diagnosis than memorizing and applying the benumbing complexity of Gibson's formulas: simply observe or talk to the person.[10]

The quickest way of making a diagnosis is to simply observe the person and ask the requisite questions during an initial interview, which might take 30 to 45 minutes of the typical 90-minute astrological session. If the client exhibits and reports the necessary symptom picture for a particular diagnosis, then that's their diagnosis. If astrology's value in psychopathology was limited to providing planetary correlates to empirically observable signs and symptoms, it is unlikely that mental health professionals will feel inspired to study it. And why should they? Their eyes and ears can tell them just as quickly, and more assuredly, what the chart only hints at with regard to a client's pathology.

This should not mean, however, that the astrological chart is without value as a diagnostic tool. Its main value, however, lays not so much in predicting psychopathology, as in explaining it. Again, there are two approaches to diagnosis: descriptive and psychological. The chart's value is that it illuminates the psychodynamics that underlie the client's presenting problem. Once a diagnosis is determined through observation and interview, the problem can be deconstructed by analyzing the birthchart. The archetypal components of the disorder are then more easily identified and understood. The reader should be warned, however, that the same disorder can show up differently in different charts.

A MULTIAXIAL SYSTEM

Before discussing astrological correlations of psychopathology, a brief review of psychological diagnosis is in order. In making a diagnosis, the clinician is required to evaluate her client along five axes, each of which provide a different type of information.

Axis I:	Mental disorders
Axis II:	Personality disorders
Axis III:	Pertinent medical conditions
Axis IV:	Psychosocial stressors
Axis V:	Psychosocial and occupational Functioning.

---

[10] A related problem to this method of diagnosis is the implication that the right combination of astrological factors is sufficient to cause the disorder. However, different individuals may express the same astrological factors at different levels of integration. Accordingly, psychopathology is not a consequence of astrological charts, but of how these charts are lived and expressed by the individual.

These include Axis I, which codes common clinical syndromes; Axis II, which codes personality disorders; and Axis III, which allows the clinician to note general medical conditions that might be pertinent to the case. Axis IV describes psychosocial and environmental stressors that might be contributing factors in the client's difficulty. These would include such things such as occupational or economic problems, loss of a job, a painful divorce, death of a loved one, or atrocities suffered in a war. Finally, Axis V enables the clinician to record their assessment of the client's current overall level of psychosocial and occupational functioning at the time of the evaluation.

A multiaxial approach provides a useful, comprehensive, and systematic overview of the clinical situation and assists the therapist in developing an appropriate treatment plan. However, perhaps the main reason for a multiaxial system is to underscore the distinction between a mental disorder and a personality disorder.

MENTAL DISORDERS

Mental disorders are common clinical syndromes and constitute the most common reasons that individuals come to therapy. If a person has a mental disorder, it would be listed on Axis I. These disorders tend to be acute, meaning they are characterized by a relatively rapid onset and follow a short but severe course. An impressive range of signs and symptoms are covered, including but not limited to depression, anxiety, substance abuse, sexual and gender identity disorders, learning disorders, eating disorders (anorexia, bulimia), sleep disorders, and impulse control disorders.

With mental disorders, symptoms are apt to be florid (subjectively intense and readily communicated), ego-dystonic (alien to how the person normally perceives himself), and non-psychotic (not characterized by delusions or hallucinations).

The exception is an acute episode of schizophrenia wherein the individual exhibits transient psychotic symptoms characterized by impaired reality testing. Psychosis entails an inability to objectively evaluate the external world and distinguish it from internal experience. Psychotic symptoms primarily involve (1) delusions, which are disorders of thinking—fixed, blatantly false convictions deduced from incorrect inferences about external reality, and (2) hallucinations, or disorders of perception, such as hearing or seeing things that are not based on external reality. While mental disorders do not normally entail psychotic symptoms, schizophrenia is not classified as a personality disorder because its symptoms are more often experienced as a distressful and alien (ego-dystonic) "state" rather than as a chronic, lifetime condition.

With the exception of schizophrenia, which is a psychosis, mental disorders are similar to what we used to mean by neurosis. While they can be very disabling, they generally do not paralyze the individual's functioning or violate social norms. In addition, they tend to be temporary and therefore readily amenable to treatment.

PERSONALITY DISORDERS

Personality disorders can be differentiated from mental disorders in several important ways. Personality, or character, refers to a person's longstanding and deeply ingrained traits. These include patterns of thinking, feeling, perceiving, and behaving. Personality traits are predominant behavioral features and are not necessarily pathological. However, when certain traits are so excessive, inflexible, and maladaptive that they cause significant distress or impairment, the individual is said to have a personality disorder, which is then listed on Axis II. A personality disorder is still a mental disorder, but constitutes a special category, or subset, of the more general class of mental disorders.

Personality disorders have been defined as deeply ingrained maladaptive patterns of behavior that an individual develops to prevent anxiety. They seem to derive from an immature, disordered personality structure characterized by a lack of balance and integration. Their core features include: (1) **rigidity** in that the person does not adapt to circumstances; (2) **excess** in the over-expression of a single mode of behavior; (3) significant, ongoing **impairment** in social and occupational functioning, and (4) resulting subjective **distress** even if not consciously recognized. In short, personality disorders are characterized by rigidity, excess, impairment and distress.

Whereas mental disorders (Axis I) tend to be acute, florid, and responsive to treatment, personality disorders (Axis II) are more chronic, consistent, and resistant to treatment. It has been estimated that personality disorders constitute up to 50% of all cases seen in psychotherapist's offices; yet, they are the most difficult and poorly understood disorders that clinicians are likely to face. There is little convincing data on their etiology (causes), and conflicting theories as to how to treat them.

As a rule, personality disorders are non-psychotic, but exceptions exist. The transient psychosis of borderline personality disorder is one such exception. Unlike mental (Axis I) disorders, personality disorders tend to be ego-syntonic; the individual's way of being "feels right" and there is often little motivation to change despite the interpersonal problems that inevitably accompany these disorders. An exception is the painful shyness of avoidant personality disorder. Again, knowing whether a patient has a mental or personality disorder (or both) helps clinicians determine the appropriate psychotherapeutic treatment.

ASTROLOGICAL CORRELATIONS

It is more difficult to correlate astrological factors with mental disorders than with personality disorders. The exception to this is learning disorders (Mercury), eating disorders (Moon/Venus), schizophrenia (Neptune), and the mood disorders—depression (Saturn) and mania (Jupiter). All these will be covered in detail in later chapters. The point is that DSM now lists some 200 diagnoses, most of which are Axis I mental disorders. They are simply too many and too varied to correlate neatly with astrological categories. The birth chart will generally provide some corollary to the intrapsychic conflicts and pathogenic beliefs that underlay Axis 1 disorders, but there are so many ways this can show up in a chart it would be difficult to formulate a precise natal configuration for any single disorder, Gibson's work notwithstanding.

Also, a mental disorder by definition is not a permanent feature of the personality. Mental disorders by their very nature are transient. Their transience, however, points to how astrology may be useful in this area, for transits are likewise transient, as the term implies. Once a diagnosis is made following the client interview, the astro-therapist merely needs to examine the astrological chart to determine the relevant transits and progressions that are currently operating.

There is an abundance of anecdotal evidence to suggest that specific types of transits, especially from Saturn and the outer planets, may correlate to intensely difficult periods during which clients are more likely to struggle with issues that correlate to the nature of the transit. For example, we might expect that an individual who is prone to manic episodes is more likely to become manic during the time that transiting Jupiter aspects his Sun. Similarly, if one is vulnerable to depression, the likelihood of becoming depressed is increased when Saturn forms a hard aspect to one's Sun or Moon.[11]

In this regard, astrology can be of tremendous value as both a diagnostic and prognostic tool. Not only can it help to explain the nature of the disorders with which one's clients are struggling, but it will also indicate what kinds of difficulties could occur in the future, what difficulties might have occurred

---

[11] Progressions operate in a similar way, although here it is the movements of the inner planets, especially the Sun and Moon, which are most important. Progressions of Saturn and the outer planets are generally too slow to signify challenging periods, as they will progress only a few degrees from their natal positions over the course of a lifetime.

in the past, a disorder's specific archetypal components, the type of challenge and opportunities for growth they present, and how long the condition might persist. In short, the nature, meaning, and duration of a disorder is likely to correlate with one or more planetary transits in combination with natal configurations that predispose the individual to that disorder.

Whereas transits and progressions are of singular importance in working with mental disorders, the natal chart itself is of greater value in working with personality disorders. Unlike mental disorders, personality disorders deal with relatively permanent features of an individual's personality. For this reason, they are sometimes referred to as character disorders, since character refers to the inherent psychological make-up of a person. The natal chart, of course, symbolizes one's inherent psychological make-up, or character structure.

Whereas there are over 200 categories of mental disorders in DSM, there are only 11 categories of personality disorders. Most of these connect rather perfectly with an astrological sign-planet system. In Figure 14, some correlations are listed between sign-planet archetypes and mental disorders. Note again that as a class, mental disorders subsume personality disorders. Accordingly, all disorders listed in Figure 14 (page 165) are mental disorders, but some are more specifically personality disorders, which are listed in bold.[12] Again, these will be explored more fully in subsequent chapters.

The twin hallmarks of a personality disorder are rigidity and excessiveness. In other words, a character disorder is characterized not so much by a particular type of behavior, as by an excess of that behavior. For example, Narcissistic Personality represents an extreme version of Leo-Sun. Moreover, individuals with personality disorders seem unable to adjust their behavior to accommodate to different situations. Instead, they rigidly adhere to one mode of behavior. Like the expression, "If all you have is a hammer, everything looks like a nail," someone with a personality disorder has one style and uses that style no matter what the situation requires. If aggression, for example, is expressed excessively and rigidly, the personality becomes lopsided and unbalanced in that direction. Whereas this mode of behavior may be appropriate in a football game, it would be inappropriate in situations that require tenderness, cooperation, or subordination—to list just a few.

Rigidity, in fact, is implicit in the term maladaptive, a word that is especially relevant to personality disorders. Maladaptive means marked by faulty or inadequate adaptation. The person does not adjust his behavior in response

---

[12] A given sign-planet system is not limited to only one mental disorder. Additional correlations will be covered in succeeding chapters. Figure 14 merely lists what I regard as the most obvious correlations.

to new or modified surroundings. This is why personality disorders can be associated with the extremes of a sign-planet system. While no sign-planet system is inherently pathological, it becomes so when the personality is fixed in that mode and when that mode of behavior is expressed excessively.

SIGN/PLANET	MENTAL DISORDER
Aries/Mars	Antisocial Personality
Taurus/Venus	Borderline Personality
Gemini/Mercury	Learning Disorder
Cancer/Moon	Histrionic Disorder
Leo/Sun	Narcissistic Personality
Virgo/Mercury	Obsessive Compulsive
Libra/Venus	Dependent Personality
Scorpio/Pluto	Paranoid Personality
Sagittarius/Jupiter	Mania/Hypomania
Capricorn/Saturn	Depressive Disorder
Aquarius/Uranus	Schizoid Disorder
Pisces/Neptune	Schizotypal Disorder

Figure 14: Mental & Personality Disorders

Insanity has been colloquially defined as doing the same thing with the same negative result yet doing it again and again with the expectation that the outcome will change. This is what in the vernacular we call "being stuck". Imagine that a planet becomes so predominant in the personality that it vampirizes psychic energy and locks the person into a rigid style of thinking, feeling, and acting. Despite the behavior consistently producing painful consequences, the person keeps doing it with the expectation that next time the outcome will be different.

For example, if Venus is a person's primary way of being in the world, he or she may be consistently and excessively compliant, accommodating, indecisive, placating, appeasing, and so on—qualities that typify Dependent Personality Disorder. Again, the lopsidedness that characterizes such a disorder may show up in a chart in a variety of ways. The patient, for example, may have a stellium of planets in Libra or the 7th house, or Venus as the focal planet of a Yod, or a preponderance of oppositions, or some combination of the above. Despite being consistently exploited and abused, she continues to be compliant—or, becomes even more compliant, with the expectation that this will make things better.

ADDITIONAL CONSIDERATIONS

In correlating personality disorders with the extremes of a sign-planet's functioning, a number of points should be kept in mind. First, a person can have both an Axis I and an Axis II disorder or more than one of each. Second, a person may demonstrate certain "traits" of a personality disorder, yet without sufficient severity to warrant an actual diagnosis. Many people, for instance, evidence narcissistic traits in their personality; yet, these traits do not cause the necessary impairments and distress to justify a diagnosis of Narcissistic Personality.

It must be emphasized, again, that personality disorders are not discrete entities despite constituting discrete categories of behavior. In real people, disorders overlap, intermingle, recede and advance, coordinate with healthy parts of the psyche, and so on. In short, every person is a unique blend of healthy and unhealthy parts and not easily slotted into a singular diagnostic category.

This is more readily apparent when we consider the complexity of the astrological chart. Since every planet correlates to one or more personality disorders, the fact that all planetary functions co-exist and interact in every person suggests a multitude of possibilities for dysfunctional behavior. By the very nature of its organization, the birthchart affirms there are no hard and fast categories of dysfunction; there are, in fact, no pure types, no monsters of the zodiac. It may be that disorders are simply emergent properties of specific planetary configurations that remain unintegrated. Of course, planetary combinations are legion and go far beyond the relatively simple categories of the DSM.

Controversies rage over whether some of DSM's diagnostic categories even describe genuine disorders. Critics charge that various alleged disorders are meaningless labels that no one cleanly and neatly fits. Moreover, proposed diagnostic categories are fluid, evolving, and subject to change as new research becomes available. What was a disorder in DSM-III—Passive-Aggressive Personality Disorder—was moved to the Appendix in DSM-IV because of questions raised about the validity of the diagnosis. It seems that passive-aggression may represent a single trait rather than a true personality disorder. Other proposed disorders have also been relegated to the Appendix. Self-Defeating Personality Disorder and Sadistic Personality Disorder are still being researched to determine their diagnostic validity. The authors responsible for DSM-IV have already completed DSM-V and no doubt there will be new versions to follow.

All of this underscores that the concept of mental disorder is merely a heuristic device; that is, it serves as a guide in the investigation and solution of problems that relate to psychological functioning. One must be careful not to reify mental disorders, for they constitute an abstraction and have no concrete or material existence. We are not talking about diseased livers here. Anyone who studies psychopathology knows that we are dealing with a mystery. While psychologists are increasingly able to differentiate and describe general categories of dysfunction, they still know very little about their causes and even less about their cures.

STORY CONCEPT AS ALTERNATIVE METAPHOR

Because typologies tend to reduce people to things—static characters—an alternative metaphor has been emerging in the mental health professions that views character in terms of a personal narrative or life script that unfolds over time. There is a growing recognition that people are more like stories than things (Freedman & Combs, 1996; White and Epston, 1990; Young and Klosko, 1993). A narrative metaphor allows therapists to see clients as separate from their problems. Instead of people being dysfunctional, people create stories that support dysfunction. They repeat a pattern of experience that is saturated with negative meanings that compel them to reenact the same pattern over and over, like a broken record. Such a pattern may constitute the dominant theme of a life.

Narrative approaches to therapy have shown that individuals can eliminate problems by discovering alternative meanings and creating new stories that empower them to take charge of their lives in their own preferred ways.

What we call mental disorders are simply clusters of observed symptoms that have been organized according to various themes. In fact, the underlying theme of a disorder is simply an implicit and recurrent idea that operates like a self-fulfilling prophecy. If someone makes up a story that his community is far more dangerous than it actually is, then this idea is likely to make him paranoid.

The term 'psychopathology' is a metaphor drawn from the biological sciences that suggests diseased mental organs. Conversely, a literary metaphor suggests that dysfunctional behavior is simply a by-product of grim stories that we tell ourselves. The person, however, is not the story, which is why a literary conception of the psyche is a more hopeful and empowering metaphor. Clearly, astrology is more compatible with this way of thinking. The chart can be viewed as a personal narrative and the person as an embodied life-script. It's not merely that every person has a story; every person *creates* a story.

If planets constitute the characters of these inner dramas, then the aspects they form to one another symbolize intrapsychic relations and conflicts. Each planetary character presents its own challenge and potential pathology. From this perspective, a pathological condition is the product of an internal conflict that is embedded within a larger story, and this larger story is symbolized by the chart as a whole. Diagnostic entities like depression can be reconceptualized as dominant themes in story constructions; stories are how clients organize their inner and outer lives. Rather than depicting mental disorders as things or illnesses like kidney failure, they can be described as pathogenic ideas that evolve and unfold as parts of stories. In this regard, they are more like dynamic, flowing process structures than static things.

Just as an individual can have multiple diagnoses on Axes I and II, so a story can have a number of dominant story lines, or themes, that intersect and overlap. A story can have a main plot and several subplots. All of this is beautifully illustrated in how the astrological chart is organized with its multiple planets and aspect configurations that interpenetrate and overlap with one another.

In the DSM, Axes I and II refer to specific behavioral attributes that have their corollaries in the astrological chart. As a kind of script, the astrological chart can be lived on multiple levels and admits of multiple stories. While psychopathology is not inherent in the chart, it can be potentiated in any chart at lower levels of integration. In cases of actual pathology, the horoscope will describe not only the internal processes (symptoms) and outer behaviors (signs) of the main character, but can also provide information about salient medical issues (Axis III).

The DSM recognizes that significant medical conditions are likely to have an impact on client's psychological well-being. However, astrology turns this around by revealing how psychological factors may have a significant impact on one's physical health. In other words, the birthchart symbolizes the intrapsychic conflicts and emergent negative ideas that underlay the client's pathology on both a behavioral and a physical level.

This kind of wholistic perspective is implicit in astrology since the same variables that symbolize psychic structure (signs and planets) also symbolize physical structure. Saturn, for example, not only symbolizes one's capacity for organization and career success; it also signifies the skeletal structure (bones, teeth) that determines the form of the physical body. I once had a client who had transiting Neptune squaring her natal Saturn. Neptune, of course, operates like a universal solvent. Not only was she feeling confused and depressed about her career (she'd recently lost her job), but a trip to the dentist revealed that her teeth were rotting and required a serious root canal. The same transit was operating on both a psychological, environmental, and physiological level.

Many physicians now regard medical problems as metaphors of processes that are occurring on a more abstract, intangible level of consciousness. This kind of thinking is especially prevalent in homeopathic medicine and wholistic approaches to healing. Likewise, astrology shows how medical conditions may be psychosomatically related to psychological issues reflected in the birth chart—pathogenic beliefs, imbalances, destructive attitudes, and the like.

A linear typology like the DSM does not see medical problems as related to the psyche except as causal influences. For example, hypothyroidism is sometimes presumed to be the cause of major depressive episode. This presumption is based on the fact that if the thyroid condition is treated, the symptoms of depression usually clear. What is not considered, however, is whether hypothyroidism has a psychic corollary such that physical and psychological factors are circularly related. Again, this is the advantage of using astrology as a diagnostic tool. The medical condition needs to be treated, of course, but it can also be seen as symptomatic of a psychological problem.

In all fairness, the relationship of psyche and soma (body) as explored in psychosomatic medicine has long been of interest to psychologists, even if this interest is not evident in conventional diagnostic procedures. Kandel (1983), for instance, demonstrated how psychosocial stress could alter the brain's anatomy and biochemistry to produce anxiety. In other words, not all biological changes have biological origins. Physical changes may be generated psychosocially, which then have psychological effects. It's a feedback loop beginning and ending with mind. Mental states influence behavior, which influences the nature of the events we attract and experience. Lived experience changes the body, and the body subsequently influences our mental states. For example, studies have clearly demonstrated that a person's inability to influence his surroundings—learned helplessness—can eventually induce biological changes resulting in depression. In effect, a person's brain does not mature or operate independently of the environment; rather, it continues to be influenced by the environment from the cradle to the grave.

Conventional psychology, however, has yet to fully appreciate Jung's contribution of synchronicity, which states that psychological states are not only mirrored in the body, but may be reflected in the environment as well—in an *acausal way*. In other words, the relationship between psyche and experience is not connected by linear causality in the conventional sense. Synchronicity implies a confluence of inner and outer events such that there is a circular, reciprocal relationship; inner and outer reflect but do not cause one another. Of course, this perspective is implicit in astrology, for every variable and configuration in the chart has both a subjective and objective corollary. If the individual is psychologically imbalanced, this imbalance will inevitably be reflected in some problematic external circumstance.

Such radical thinking is entirely absent in the DSM. Environmental experiences are depicted as psychosocial "stressors" on Axis IV. A stressor is defined as an event or situation that requires the individual to adapt, or cope. If the individual is overwhelmed by the severity of the stressor, it may cause him/her to feel, think, and behave in negative ways. Parental alcoholism may predispose a child to develop a conduct disorder, for example. The environmental condition is conceptualized as an independent, externally originating causal factor in the child's psychopathology. Again, this implies that the relationship between symptom and event is linear, or one-way: child behavior is an effect of (influenced by) parental alcoholism.

While one should not underestimate the impact of external conditions as predisposing factors in psychopathology, this conceptualization misses how an external event may mirror an intrapsychic, inborn predisposition. An astrological model does not presume that the relationship between inner and outer is linear; rather, it is viewed as circular. Psyche and environment are interdependent. That is, they are subjective and objective components of the same personal myth. For example, I grew up in an alcoholic family, but my mother's alcoholism is clearly symbolized in my astrological chart as a pre-existent, psychological configuration that has both inner and outer implications. In other words, my mother's alcoholism is part of my story, part of my karma if you will.

Astrology does not support the presumption that genetic and environmental factors are primary causes of behavior. More likely, the reverse is true: an innate, pre-existent consciousness generates appropriate physical conditions, both genetic and environmental, in which to manifest. Astrology suggests that medical and environmental problems are thematic components of a larger story. As such, they may have a purpose that transcends their surface features as mere (apparent) causal agents of psychological ailments. Just as stories have morals, so morals are implicit in the types of problems generated by a lack of integration. My mother's alcoholism, for instance, might have had the purpose of teaching me compassion for the suffering and havoc that alcoholism can wreak. As I develop greater compassion, so my psyche becomes progressively more integrated, balanced, and whole.

CENTRALITY OF BASIC NEEDS

As previously discussed in Chapter 3, Maslow (1968) theorized that human behavior is governed largely by basic needs, such as the need for survival, security, belonging, and self-esteem. These needs motivate the individual to behave in ways that provide for the satisfaction of these needs. If basic needs are not satisfied, says Maslow, sickness results. We can apply this model to astrology. The signs of the zodiac are reflective not only of basic psychological needs but also of psychological issues that may arise when these needs are denied satisfaction. Whereas psychopathology may present itself astrologically as a rigid, excessive, hyper-functioning of a particular sign-planet system, this implies that other sign-planet functions are comparatively under expressed.

PATHOLOGY OF DEVELOPMENTAL STAGES

Again, not only are signs symbolic of basic needs, they are also representative of developmental stages in the overall life cycle, beginning with the first stage, Aries, and proceeding sequentially to the last stage, Pisces (Figure 15, page 172). Each sign-stage seems to present certain lessons, or tasks, the completion of which paves the way for the stages to follow. The task, in other words, is to attain the developmental goal of that period. It follows that disturbances of development in earlier stages will be reflected in disturbances of expression in later stages. The creative self-expression characteristic of Leo/adolescence, for example, can be extremely problematic if one has not sufficiently developed a self *to* express.

This suggests that the qualities of a given sign are implicit in the personality even before the stage associated with that sign is reached. The stage corresponding to a particular sign merely indicates when the nature of that sign is in its ascendancy. Leonian qualities, for example, are most apparent during adolescence, even though rudimentary forms of creativity, volition, and pride are clearly apparent in earlier stages. We might say, then, that each sign rules a particular period of the life cycle.

Generally speaking, the nature of a developmental stage will bear some relation to the mental disorder(s) associated with the sign that rules that stage. For example, the mental deterioration/ego dissolution of very old age and the delusions of schizophrenia are characteristic of Pisces as a developmental stage and mental disorder respectively. Likewise, the "mid-life crisis," wherein one recognizes one's own mortality, and paranoia wherein one lives in fear of annihilation, are equally representative of Scorpio. Each sign of the zodiac appears to (1) constitute a developmental stage with associated tasks, and (2) can be correlated with one or more mental disorders if these tasks, or those of earlier stages, are mismanaged.

SIGN	STAGE	GOAL
Aries	0 - 2 yrs	Autonomy
Taurus	2 - 5 yrs	Object Constancy
Gemini	5 - 9 yrs	Factual Knowledge
Cancer	9 - 14 yrs	Emotional Security
Leo	14 - 20 yrs	Identity/Self-Esteem
Virgo	20 - 27 yrs	Competency
Libra	27 - 35 yrs	Social Relatedness
Scorpio	35 - 44 yrs	Transformation
Sagittarius	44 - 54 yrs	Wisdom
Capricorn	54 - 65 yrs	Authority
Aquarius	65 - 77 yrs	Perspective
Pisces	77 - 90 yrs +	Transcendence

Figure 15: Signs, Stages, and Goals

ETIOLOGY OF DISORDERS: AN INTRODUCTION

In subsequent chapters, we will explore etiological factors in psychopathology in greater detail. Suffice to say here that in astrology we have a system that strongly implies that the cause of a mental disorder does not originate in conditions outside the psyche itself. Inherent in the horoscope, from the moment of birth, is a symbolic portrait of the psyche that allows the practitioner to delineate the probable external factors that will reflect (not cause) this intrapsychic pattern. Accordingly, the triumphs and traumas of childhood appear to derive from a preexistent psychic structure. These external events can be conceptualized as feedback that activate this structure with memories that later appear to be the causal factors in the emergence of psychological problems. In actuality, however, the painful experiences that gave rise to these memories are merely secondary and not primary causes of the disorders that result.

In general, however, we can say that psychopathology has its origins in repression. If a basic need was denied satisfaction in childhood, for whatever reason, then the dissatisfaction of this need is going to register as pain. This pain is defended against by relegating the offending impulse into the unconscious where it will hopefully do no further harm. Such repression, however, is ultimately pathogenic. On a conscious level, the individual professes to be a certain way, but unconsciously the denied impulse is struggling to break free by pushing against and threatening the functioning of whatever has taken its place.

Denying a basic need is like trying to hold a beach ball under water. Just as the beach ball exerts continuous pressure upon the muscles that suppress it, so a repressed impulse creates psychic pressure. The difference is that with repression there is no conscious awareness of the conflict. Accordingly, the pushing from below causes unconscious perception of anticipated danger, which leads to the use of defense mechanisms that result in various types of mental disorders. The mind is disordered precisely because the order that would otherwise result from a proper balance of psychological functions has been thrown out of balance.

To summarize, we can say that a mental disorder results from (1) the denial of some basic psychological function; and (2) the subsequent exaggeration of some (usually) opposite function that tries to compensate for what is missing. This compensatory overfunctioning serves a defensive purpose while simultaneously causing the distress and disability we associate with psychopathology.

Looking at the zodiac, we can see a symbolic picture of this pathogenic neurotic process. Problems occur when a sign/drive is so minimized that its repression results in various types of dysfunctional behavior, or exaggerated to such an extent that it vampirizes the rest of the chart, sucking up psychic energy like a black hole. It must be emphasized, however, that the problems of any one sign derive not so much from its own nature, but more importantly from its lack of integration with other signs and with the whole of which it is a part.

If Virgo lacks the courage of Aries, the lighthearted curiosity of Gemini, the playful joy of Leo, the kindness of Libra, the faith of Sagittarius, the broad perspective of Aquarius, and the compassion of Pisces, then we are going to get that particularly virulent form of Virgo that we associate with Compulsive Personality Disorder. In other words, to the extent that these other signs are suppressed, Virgonian traits are going to be exaggerated. The exaggerated behavior is compensatory in that it tries to make up for, and assume the burden of, what is otherwise lacking in the personality.

Jung (1960) repeatedly stressed that when one part of the personality is repressed into the unconscious then the conscious attitude and behavior will reflect a pathological one-sidedness. In psychoanalytic terminology, this is referred to as a reaction formation. The formation of a conscious persona is a reaction to certain unconscious impulses that persist in the unconscious. Health is attained only by restoring the denied function to its rightful place in the overall psychic economy.

A reaction formation in astrology would take the form of a particular sign/planet overfunctioning. If a sign is overfunctioning, then the antidote is generally the sign that is its complementary opposite, which is probably underfunctioning. For example, the antidote to the pathological egocentricity of Aries would be the self-effacing love of Libra. Likewise, the antidote to the pathological dependency of Libra would be the healthy self-interest of Aries. This underlines the point that the problems of any one sign/planet do not operate in isolation from the rest of the chart. Health is wholeness, balance, and integration.

In order to avoid redundancy, I will limit myself in subsequent descriptions to only the pathology of a sign's overfunctioning, since its underfunctioning is generally represented in the problems of its opposite sign. For example, if Cancer is underfunctioning, then Capricorn is likely to be overfunctioning, as evidenced in a tendency toward perfectionism that may eventually lead to depression.

Also, the fact that I focus primarily on the pathology of zodiacal signs should not imply that I separate the problems of a given sign from its corresponding planet and house. The pathology of Aries necessarily implicates Mars, since Mars disposits any planet that is in Aries as well as signifying any house that has Aries on its cusp. In other words, the pathology of a sign and its ruling planet are inseparable. If Mars is under stress from hard aspects, then its difficulties are going to relate directly to the need of Aries that it is the function of Mars to satisfy. Likewise, the problems and challenges of the first house are in principal the same as those of Aries and Mars.

ASTROLOGICAL CORRELATES

The question as to how one spots pathology in the birth chart is not addressed since I will take this up in subsequent chapters. In a general sense, one is advised to follow the usual rules of chart interpretation.

1. A stellium in a particular sign/house suggests the person may be overfunctioning in that area.
2. An inner planet receiving a hard aspect from an outer planet may be undifferentiated, unconscious, and underfunctioning.

3. The focal planet of a T-Square or Yod tends to overfunction in the sign and house it occupies.
4. A singleton planet under stress (e.g., only planet in a given element) is especially prone to primitive overfunctioning.
5. An outer planet in a given house and forming a hard aspect(s) to another planet(s) can signal an area of potential trauma and repression.
6. Any planet in the 8th or 12th houses may be repressed, denied, sacrificed, or associated with shame and guilt.

Any of these chart factors, separately or in combination, can be indicative of psychopathology. There are no hard and fast rules for determining whether and to what extent a given area of the chart is going to be problematic. In fact, whenever a particular area *is* problematic it by definition is going to conflict with some other area of the chart since everything affects everything else. The quickest way of making a diagnosis is to simply talk to the person. The chart is merely a corroborative guide.

It should also be noted that the pathology of a given planet/sign takes different forms subjectively and objectively. For example, on a subjective level the Sun symbolizes the individual's creative, self-expressive function, whereas objectively it can signify the father as a primary source of validation and approval. I once had a female client who had Sun in Pisces in the 11th house square Uranus, which suggests a weak, underfunctioning Sun. In terms of her own personality, she was extremely humble, shy, self-effacing, self-sacrificing, and guilty about expressing her own worth. In therapy she acknowledged that she was afraid that if she expressed any pride she might become like her father, who she described as grandiose, self-aggrandizing, egocentric, and megalomaniacal. "He thinks the Sun revolves around him," she said, without realizing the astrological significance of her remark.

In effect, he embodied the overfunctioning, overcompensatory version of solar pathology, whereas she evidenced the underfunctioning version. Yet, it was her Sun in both instances. In trying not to be like her father, she had actually become like him, for she had identified with the hidden, devalued, and depreciated self that underlay her father's narcissism. She was, in effect, her father turned inside out.

A PROVISIONAL MODEL

I wish to emphasize that the examples to follow are by no means exhaustive of the possible manifestations of problems that may derive from a chart imbalance. My only goal here is to suggest how the 12 zodiacal signs can be viewed as predominant forms of personality organization or symptom formation. I want to reiterate that with the analysis of each sign I am not describing people who have their Sun in that sign. Again, signs are not human beings; they are behavioral patterns in the service of basic psychological needs. As a structural element of consciousness, each sign is present in every person to one degree or another.

My goal is to demonstrate how the extremes of each sign's dysfunction can be correlated with a specific mental disorder listed in the DSM *(Diagnostic and Statistical Manual of Mental Disorders)*. Although language requires that I sometimes use words like "they" in reference to people with a particular disorder, it should be remembered that what I really mean is "a person with this disorder." I also wish to emphasize that this model is provisional in that it provides only a very general outline illustrating how astrological terms might be integrated with modern diagnostic categories.

ARIES/MARS

The sign Aries can be associated with what Margaret Mahler (1975) calls the separation-individuation process, or the process of a child's initial differentiation of identity in the first two years of life. The basic need here is simply to exist, to emerge as a separate entity and to survive.

Initially, the child feels its will to be supreme and there is no differentiation of self from environment. If an infant could speak, it would say, "I am the world! Me, here, now!" In these words is revealed the totality of the infant's perception. Because the infant experiences itself as having complete control over its environment, there is an illusion of omnipotence. It has merely to scream to be picked up, fed, or comforted; its every need is satisfied on command. For the infant, there is no sense of "later." Only the present space and time exists. Accordingly, infants have no frustration tolerance or capacity to delay gratification. Unable to tolerate tension or manage anxiety, their every need must be satisfied the instant it occurs. If deprived of immediate gratification, they tend to react explosively.

Good and bad experiences are not integrated into a capacity for ambivalence since the infant can only experience the immediate present. If it is angry, it is completely angry, and the entire world is experienced as bad. If it is happy, it is completely happy, and the entire world is experienced as good. This splitting of the self-world relation into "all good" or "all bad" is characteristic of the period.

When the infant is adequately mirrored and gratified by its mother it achieves a healthy narcissistic self-love, or self-valuing—what Erikson (1963) calls "basic trust." It is filled with a sense of entitlement—of having the right and ability to survive. The infant learns to trust that it can satisfy primitive needs for food and comfort by communicating these needs to a responsive other. What is important to recognize is that the infant can experience itself as "real" only if there is someone "out there" who engages the infant and responds to its communications. If, however, the mother does not adequately mirror the child, then it fails to develop a healthy narcissism and basic trust. Later, this can manifest as assertion of the self in exaggerated, pathological forms—egocentricity, conduct disorders, impulsivity, rage, and the like. This behavior seems to be predicated on the assumption that in order to illicit a response the person has to make his presence known in a BIG way—so big, in fact, that it eclipses other people. What is missing, in other words, is a capacity for relationship, or Libra.

It is not difficult to see Aries behavior in the above description. Aries, in effect, *is* the psychology of the infant. As a psychological drive, it symbolizes the need for survival, existence, or simply *being*. Evidence of this drive is apparent in classic Aries behavior—assertive, aggressive, independent, alive, spontaneous, fresh, innocent, and childlike. Like an infant, Aries is prone to temper tantrums if frustrated. Yet, just like an infant, the mood quickly passes—especially if the frustrated impulse has been gratified as a consequence of the tantrum. In general, Aries anger is short lived. The archetype that best exemplifies this pattern would be the warrior who exults in the struggle for survival and is willing to engage any enemy who poses a threat. We could also call Aries the noble savage, or the pioneer who yearns for adventure.

When unintegrated or compensatory, Aries behavior again parallels the infant in almost every respect. Because the self is not adequately differentiated from other people, Aries acts as if other people either do not exist or exist only for the gratification of Aries' impulses. Again, we are familiar with the usual Aries descriptors in this regard—aggressive, egocentric, selfish, rude, inconsiderate. Also, because Aries' perception of time and space is limited to the immediate present, there is very little capacity for patience or self-restraint. Every desire and impulse must be satisfied *now*, for the present is all that exists. In this regard, Aries is impulsive, impatient, rash, reckless, infantile, primitive, and immature.

These patterns are typified in Antisocial Personality Disorder. The essential feature is a history of hostile and aggressive behavior in which the rights of others are violated. Sometimes this condition is referred to as "impulse disorder" or "sociopathic personality." Almost invariably there is a markedly impaired capacity to sustain lasting, warm, and responsible relationships with friends, lovers, or employers. The need for immediate gratification and a failure to accept social norms with respect to lawful behavior are hallmarks of the syndrome. The individual is prone to antisocial actions that frequently are grounds for arrest: illegal occupation, willful destruction of property, theft, aggravated assault, spousal or child abuse. Like Aries, antisocial personality disorder is typified by reckless behavior and accident proneness, as indicated by driving while intoxicated or recurrent speeding.

Irresponsibility is a central feature of the syndrome. The employment history is marked by an inability to sustain consistent work behavior, repeated absences from work, frequent unemployment, and abandonment of jobs without realistic plans for others. Also, the individual repeatedly fails to honor financial obligations, such as paying taxes, bills, or child support. There is frequently a devil-may-care, "live for the moment" philosophy that justifies a tendency to act on impulse. These individuals will travel from place to place without a clear goal and will not have a fixed address for months at a time. Not surprisingly, they have great difficulty sustaining a monogamous relationship. There is an aversion to intimacy with a tendency toward unfaithfulness and promiscuity. These people are prone to repeated lying, use of aliases, and the "conning" of others for personal profit or pleasure. Usually they will not tell the truth unless it is expedient.

One cannot really say that such people "suffer" from their disorder or that they are motivated to get better. For it is the nature of antisocial individuals to have little or no concern for the pain their behavior has inflicted upon others. Almost invariably they will feel justified in having hurt or mistreated someone. An absence of "conscience" and a complete lack of remorse is a hallmark of the syndrome. A good example of antisocial personality is the character played by Alec Baldwin (Sun Aries) in the film *Miami Blues*.

TAURUS/VENUS

As the sign that succeeds Aries, Taurus signifies the developmental period from two to five years. At this stage, the infant has lost its illusion of omnipotence and awakens to the realization that it is merely one person among many. There is a firming up of personal boundaries as the child comes to realize the essential "otherness" of the world at large. Piaget (1926) introduced this concept as *object permanence*, the knowledge that there are entities that have a reality of their own and that continue to exist even when the child cannot see, hear, or feel them. The child gradually comes to understand that his actions on the object are separate from the object itself. Thus, he begins to discover the limits of his own body and sees himself as merely one object in a world of objects.

The awareness of "ownership" and the capacity to hold and possess objects are developmental hallmarks of this period. At the most basic level, the child possesses a body, and thus an identity separate from the external world. The ability to retain and possess enables the toddler to learn bladder and bowel control for the first time, for now the child can "hold it." It also enables the child to possess objects and form attachments that assure its continued safety in the world. Some of these early possessions are "transitional objects," intense attachments to a favorite blanket or Teddy Bear, which provide a soothing function for the child.

Recall that in the Aries stage the infant had no capacity for self-soothing. If development proceeds normally, however, then by the time the child reaches three years it will have developed a capacity for *self and object constancy*. This means that the child will have successfully internalized a stable mental representation of the mothering figure that it can use as a resource to soothe itself in the face of mildly frightening or frustrating experiences. By "holding on" to a positive self-image (self-constancy) and positive object-image (object constancy) despite momentary experiences of displeasure, the child attains a capacity for self-soothing.

It is precisely because the child can hold in awareness a memory of the "good" self and the "good" mother that it can tolerate negative experiences without collapsing into an all bad self-other state. Thus, the capacity for ambivalent feelings toward self and other is born during this period. Experience is no longer split into "all good" or "all bad" but is a mixture of both. Likewise, a capacity for delayed gratification and for frustration tolerance are hallmarks of a successful resolution of this period.

It is not difficult to see that the attributes and personality characteristics of the toddler are precise correlates to the traits typically ascribed to Taurus. The Taurean tendency to resist change, pursue pleasure, and secure possessions can now be understood as the expression of an underlying need to feel permanent, real, and solid in a world of objects that are constantly changing and no longer entirely subject to one's will. A key word here is *retentive*. With Taurus is born the capacity to retain, to hold on, and to possess. The need for stability and sameness, the cautious but steady manner, the love of comfort and pleasure, and the compulsive acquisition of goods and property are Taurean qualities that are exemplified in the behavior of the toddler.

Likewise, Taurean excesses—hoarding, clinging, possessiveness, and rigidity—mirror problems that seem to derive from developmental failures at this stage. If the child does not develop self and object constancy, it remains preoccupied with issues of safety, attachment, and security. In extreme cases, the individual develops a borderline personality disorder. This condition represents the pathological extreme of Taurus. According to developmental psychologists, borderline personality traits are a response to failures of attachment during the subphase of development called "rapprochement," approximately 2 to 3 years, at which time the child is working through its discovery of having a separate existence from the mother. Predictably, children become very insecure at this stage. If the child's environment and attachments to caretakers is not sufficiently predictable, stable, and safe, this will later be reflected in psychological issues involving instabilities of behavior, mood, and self-image. One's body awareness may be diminished, sense of physical boundaries overly permeable, and self-image uncertain. Underlying all of these instabilities is a perception of the world as unsafe and unpredictable.

The consequence of not having attained self and object constancy leads to a key feature of borderline personality: *insecurity*. The borderline attempts to compensate for insecurity through a variety of means—binge eating, substance abuse, shoplifting, gambling, promiscuity, endless pursuit of sensual pleasures, compulsive spending and shopping, and a tendency to develop intense attachments to people, even to the point of wanting to "merge" with them. Underlying all of these behaviors is a tremendous fear of being alone, of being unattached. The individual is prone to chronic feelings of emptiness and boredom, which can result in a pattern of unstable and desperate interpersonal relationships characterized by possessiveness, jealousy, and manipulation. The tendency to cling to things and people operates as a defense against the pain of loss of attachment. In fact, much of borderline behavior can be understood as a frantic effort to avoid real or imagined abandonment. Borderlines crave attachment to things and bodies—the external world—precisely because they never developed stable self and object images.

This lack of stability is evident in almost every area of the borderline's life. In relationships, they shift from overvaluation to devaluation of the other person, seeing people as "all good" or "all bad." They experience constant cravings for objects or substances that they imagine will satiate their feeling of emptiness—food, drugs, alcohol, possessions, people. Affectively there are rapid shifts from one mood to another, such as from calmness to anxiety, or from happiness to intense, inappropriate anger.

Because borderlines do not have a stable self-image they attempt to gain one by identifying with the object(s) of their attachment. Their identities change in accordance with whoever is most influential in their lives at the time.

This can manifest as fluctuations in religious affiliation, career orientation, clothing style, haircut, and personal values—anything that the borderline can incorporate that characterizes the other person. When all else fails, the borderline may resort to suicidal or homicidal threats in a desperate attempt to avoid abandonment. A good example of borderline personality is the character "Alex" played by Glenn Close in the film *Fatal Attraction*. Another is the character played by Jennifer Jason Leigh in *Single White Female*.

GEMINI/MERCURY

Gemini represents the need for learning, mental stimulation, and communication of factual knowledge. For this reason, Gemini is related to the acquisition of language. This phase of the zodiac roughly corresponds to what Piaget (1926) calls "preoperational thought" (5-9 years), as opposed to Aries and Taurus, which in Piaget's model correspond more closely to the "sensori-motor stage" of development. Prior to the age of four, information is coordinated and integrated primarily through the five senses. At the Gemini stage, however, there is born the capacity to detach from the senses and move onto a mental level where perceptions can be organized into discrete categories and sequences that represent the phenomenal world. Although thinking is still very egocentric at this stage, the child is now adept at using symbols (mental images and words) to signify objects and events.

Like Gemini, children between ages five and nine are characterized by an insatiable desire to learn, which is why they enter school during this period. Kindergarten, for example, begins at age 5. Research indicates there is a greater capacity to assimilate information at this stage than at any other time in the life. A six year old child is constantly asking "why this, what's that?" And when it is not asking questions, it is reporting what it has learned. By the time the child reaches seven it has attained a capacity for what Piaget calls "concrete operational thought," which is the crowning achievement of this period. Concrete operations means that the child has developed the logical structures that enable it to perform an ever-increasing variety of mental operations.

In general, children between five and nine are classic examples of Gemini behavior. We have all read how "Gemini's" are eager to learn, inquisitive, curious, precocious, bright, knowledgeable, glib, chatty, communicative, and so on. In fact, there is virtually no difference between behaviors we normally ascribe to Gemini and those that typify the average six year old. Even the problems are the same—distractibility, lack of focus, inability to sustain attention. Lack of proper mental stimulation during the Gemini stage can contribute to communication problems and "learning disorders," although this is neither a necessary or sufficient cause of the disorder. Symptoms usually show up by the time the child enters school. Many individuals continue to show some attenuated signs of the disturbance in adult life. Invariably there is some impairment in academic functioning not accounted for by intelligence, chronological age, or inadequate schooling. In "dyslexia," for example, faulty oral reading occurs, often characterized by omissions, additions, and distortions of words. Reading is slow, and there is reduced comprehension.

As an archetype, Gemini is often associated with *Puer Aeternus*, of which "Peter Pan" is fairly representative. The problem with Puers is that they tend to be fickle, frivolous, silly, flighty, ungrounded, restless, changeable, distractible, scattered, and shallow—all negative Gemini traits. If carried to an extreme, we have "Attention Deficit Hyperactive Disorder" (ADHD), the essential feature of which is difficulty concentrating and impaired capacity to learn. ADHD by definition implies an academic skills disorder. Although ADHD may not last beyond childhood, there is increasing evidence that one third to one half of all people who were diagnosed as ADHD in childhood continue to experience an attenuated form of the disorder in adulthood.

People with this disorder are described as inattentive, impulsive, unable to sit still, fidgety, restless, and overactive. The main problem is that they are so flighty and distractible that they cannot sustain attention long enough to complete a given task. A child with ADHD appears nervous and agitated. Because they are so easily distracted by extraneous stimuli, they experience great difficulty in listening or following directions. Any task that requires focused concentration, like schoolwork, causes distress. The individual often acts without thinking, shifts excessively from one activity to another, and has problems organizing thoughts and perceptions. Work that requires sustained thinking is usually performed in a sloppy, careless, impulsive, or superficial fashion. Children with ADHD will often interrupt the teacher and disrupt the class with incessant questions and chatter. In effect, the mind of the ADHD person is so over stimulated that they cannot acquire the necessary focus to effectively learn or communicate. A good example of ADHD was the character, Dory The Blue Fish, played by Ellen DeGeneres in the Pixar animated film, *Finding Nemo*.

CANCER/MOON

Cancer symbolizes the need for nurturing, unconditional love, emotional sustenance, and sympathetic understanding. Most fundamentally it is associated with the need to belong, to be cared for and protected. Cancer seems to signify the latency period of development (9-14) when the child first begins to reflect upon feelings and derives an identity primarily from the family to which they belong. If there is sensitivity to the child's feelings, and an adequate amount of love and support, the child grows up with a strong sense of emotional security. He or she feels deeply rooted in themselves and develops a capacity to be vulnerable, which enables them to both express and respond to emotional needs.

If the child did not experience the warmth and closeness of a caring family then this will be reflected in their capacity to feel emotionally connected to others. There is likely to be significant anxiety around dependency needs as expressed, for example, in Histrionic Personality Disorder. The essential feature in this Disorder is the tendency to enter into overly dependent relationships and to demand constant reassurances of love. Individuals, both male and female, are caricatures of femininity. Yet, the shallowness of their emotions, helplessness, incessant drawing of attention, impressionability, seductiveness, clinging behavior, superficial warmth and caring, irrational outbursts, and overreaction to minor events all betray a desperate need to be loved combined with the fear of not attaining this love.

Perhaps the most extreme expression of Cancerian issues is reflected in Avoidant Personality Disorder. The essential feature here is hypersensitivity to potential rejection. Although there is a deep yearning for close personal attachments, the individual is unwilling to enter into relationships unless given strong guarantees of unconditional acceptance.

LEO/SUN

Leo symbolizes the need for validation of perceived identity. As a developmental stage, it closely corresponds to the period of adolescence (14-20). The basic task of this stage is to integrate the various identifications of childhood into a more complete, coherent identity. Accordingly, the focus is on differentiating a conscious self from the family matrix.

Leo issues are reflected in the self-consciousness of adolescents and their constant need for approval, attention, and admiration. Most fundamentally, it is associated with the need for self-esteem; that is, to feel oneself to be a person of worth and value. If separation from the family is supported and the individual is encouraged to be their own unique self, a cheerful confidence develops. Out of confidence comes a capacity for creativity, joy, playfulness, exuberance, and the ability to express oneself in a spontaneous, uninhibited manner.

If there is failure at this stage, this will be reflected in issues of self-image and self-esteem. This sign in general exemplifies ego defense mechanisms. The individual with a fragile self-image experiences great difficulty in being able to tolerate failure, admit wrongdoing, and accept human flaws and limitations without shame.

Paradoxically, low self-esteem often takes the form of self-centeredness and an exaggerated sense of self-importance. Here we have what might be called "the divinity complex," the "big shot" who is always right and never wrong, arrogant, prideful, obstinate, and willful. Such people often appear overconfident, abrasive, and energetic. They may be "big spenders" or have a tendency toward pathological gambling. The need to "look good" results in their evaluating things predominantly in terms of their own personal interests and how it reflects upon them personally. Another variation is the "playboy" who is forever seeking sexual conquests, self-gratification, and self-aggrandizement. Sometimes there is a compelling need to deprecate others in an attempt to look and feel superior. Again, all of these traits are compensatory to a poor self-image and low self-esteem.

The extremes of Leonian dysfunction are reflected in Narcissistic Personality Disorder. Narcissistic traits seem to compensate for an unconscious fear that one has no value, importance, or worth. These traits include a grandiose sense of self-importance or uniqueness; preoccupation with fantasies of unlimited success; an exhibitionistic need for constant attention and admiration; and disturbances in interpersonal relationships characterized by feelings of entitlement, interpersonal exploitiveness, and lack of empathy. There is a tendency to exaggerate achievements and talents (boasting), and a desire to be noticed as special without appropriate achievement. Not surprisingly, the narcissist is preoccupied with feelings of envy, which are a consequence of projecting his idealized self onto others. Self-esteem is extremely fragile and the narcissist may respond to criticism either with cool indifference or marked feelings of rage, inferiority, shame, humiliation, or emptiness.

VIRGO/MERCURY

Virgo symbolizes the need for efficient functioning or what might simply be called *competency*. As a developmental stage, it seems to correspond to the period following adolescence—from 20 to 27—when the individual joins the work force and focuses on developing a skill that can be of some service to the community. Emphasis is on problem solving, employment, and being useful. It is primarily a time of apprenticeship. The need for efficient functioning also extends to the body; thus Virgo is concerned with matters of diet, exercise, health and hygiene.

Virgonian gifts are pragmatism, discrimination, and caution. One could say that Virgo represents the repair and maintenance system of the psyche. Focus is on the detection and correction of mistakes that may impede efficiency. A system is broken down into its component parts and analyzed to determine how it works. Accordingly, there is a natural talent for detail and precision. When this need to improve a system's functioning is turned inward upon the self, it has a humbling effect. Thus, Virgo is also associated with modesty and self-restraint.

Virgonian overfunctioning is typified in Compulsive Personality Disorder, the essential features of which are (1) perfectionism that interferes with the ability to grasp "the big picture," e.g., preoccupation with trivial details, rules, order, schedules, and lists; (2) criticalness toward others if they do not conform to his or her way of doing things; (3) excessive devotion to work and productivity to the exclusion of pleasure and value of interpersonal relationships; (4) indecisiveness and inefficiency because of an inordinate fear of making a mistake; and (5) impaired social functioning due to a restricted ability to express warm and tender emotions. For example, the individual is overly serious and formal, stiff, stingy, and unduly conventional.

LIBRA/VENUS

Libra represents the need for harmonious relations with an equal other, thus partnerships, marriage, and intimacy in general. In a more abstract sense, Libra is related to the principle of cooperation, balance, and fair play. It is the sign most concerned with matters of etiquette, which assure that conduct among members of society conform to what is generally agreed to be in good taste and considerate of the needs of others. Developmentally it seems to signify that period between 27-35 when the individual emerges into full adult status as a "social equal."

When this sign is overfunctioning in the personality there is a tendency toward compliant, appeasing, conciliatory behavior in which the individual's true thoughts, feelings, and wishes are denied "for the sake of the relationship." Real intimacy is impossible because the individual is incapable of taking a stand that may conflict with the interests of his or her partner. Paradoxically, such behavior actually produces the very outcome it is designed to avoid—disrespect and aggression in the partner. Relationships are hurtful, dishonest, superficial, and ultimately dissatisfying for both parties.

The extremes of Libran dysfunctionality are best exemplified in Dependent Personality Disorder. In this Disorder, the individual passively allows others to assume responsibility for major areas of his or her life because of an inability to function independently. There is a marked tendency to subordinate personal needs to those of others on whom he or she is dependent in order to avoid any possibility of having to be self-reliant. Major decisions are left to others and there is an unwillingness to make demands on the people they depend on for fear of jeopardizing the relationship. For example, a wife with this disorder may tolerate a physically abusive husband for fear that he will leave her if she sets appropriate limits.

SCORPIO/PLUTO

Scorpio symbolizes the need for transformation and is thus associated with that part of the psyche that is dark, wounded, and unintegrated. Jung (1960) called this the "shadow." There is a natural tendency to fear and avoid these darker areas of the psyche and to this extent they are imbued with power. Their power derives from the fact that to encounter this aspect of the psyche could potentially alter one's very identity; that is, destroy who one conceives oneself to be. Such transformative processes are natural, however, and ideally lead to empowerment, healing, and self-renewal. Developmentally, this stage of the zodiac is associated with the mid-life crisis (age 35-44) when the individual must come to terms with his or her own mortality, re-examine deeply entrenched beliefs, and confront potentials that have gone unrealized.

Almost by definition there is going to be repression of those aspects of the psyche that Scorpio symbolizes. Under ideal circumstances, the task of integrating these split off functions occurs intermittently throughout the life. These are the regular and inevitable crises that provide opportunities for growth. Occasionally, however, the pain and suffering that such processes entail is overwhelming to the individual. When this occurs, the rigid defenses that are erected prevent the assimilation of those very psychic contents that are necessary for the life to evolve. The individual becomes a "closed system" and to this extent begins to rot, metaphorically speaking, from within.

Coincident with repression of the shadow is its projection outwards as the enemy. In projection, internal tension is transformed into tension vis-à-vis the external world, into biased anticipation of the external world, and, finally, into conviction about the external world. As Jung put it, "projections change the world into the replica of one's unknown face." In the milder forms of this disorder we have control issues—individuals who attempt to master their fears by manipulating, intimidating, oppressing, coercing, and otherwise seeking power over the object(s) of their distrust. These "power trips" may operate through political, economic, social, or sexual relations.

The extremes of scorpionic dysfunction can be seen in Paranoid Personality Disorder, the essential feature of which is pervasive and unwarranted suspiciousness of people and a hypervigilance against any perceived threat. They are often viewed by others as guarded, secretive, devious, and scheming. Ever alert to trickery and betrayal, they continually question the loyalty of others, are frequently hostile, and subject to fits of pathological jealousy. Individuals with this Disorder are keenly aware of power and rank and are usually envious of those in a dominant position. Fear of and resistance to their own inner life is evidenced by their inability to accept criticism even when warranted.

SAGITTARIUS/JUPITER

If one successfully negotiates the mid-life crisis, wisdom is born (age 44-54). Life is seen as a journey from that which is less to that which is greater, an ever-expanding process of personal growth. This is the essence of Sagittarius. Reduced to a basic need, Sagittarius represents the search for truth, meaning, and purpose. Research indicates that optimal psychological health requires that the human being believe in something greater than himself (Maslow, 1968). Generally this means faith in a religion, philosophy, or metaphysical system that provides hope for the future and guidelines for proper conduct along the way.

When the sign is operating properly there is the capacity to synthesize facts (Gemini) into a general statement or theory. To truly believe something requires trust in one's capacity to make meaning out of random pieces of information and vague hunches. Once convinced of the rightness and truth of a particular view, there is the impulse to spread the word. Thus, Sagittarius is associated with teaching, preaching, and proselytizing in general. Its deep faith in the goodness of life and the transcendent purpose behind everyday events infuses the personality with an infectious enthusiasm.

Occasionally, however, this process gets out of hand. The wise teacher becomes the demagogue who seeks to influence others for political, economic, or personal gain. Possessed by missionary zeal, an individual may suffer an inflated and totally unrealistic image of his or her capacity for knowing what is true, right, and proper. Opinions are dogmatic and unsupported by evidence, and advice is frequently given that is both unsolicited and foolish. Actions that are ill advised are undertaken without forethought of consequences. There can be grandiose schemes, exaggeration bordering on deceit, reckless extravagance, a pollyanna naiveté born out of blind optimism, and a tendency toward excesses of every known variety.

Extended to its logical end and we have a major affective disorder known as mania (or hypomania, which is the milder version). The essential feature is an expansive, elevated mood combined with symptoms that include hyperactivity, inflated self-esteem, distractibility, and excessive involvement in activities that have a high potential for painful consequences. Manic speech is typically loud, rapid, and difficult to interrupt. Flight of ideas is expressed in a nearly continuous flow of accelerated speech with abrupt changes from topic to topic (mutability gone wild). Advice is given on matters about which the individual has no special knowledge, and frequently there are grandiose delusions involving a special relationship to God or some well-known figure from the political, entertainment, or religious community.

CAPRICORN/SATURN

Having moved through the period of personal expansion represented by Sagittarius, one arrives at the zenith of one's existence (age 54-65). Capricorn represents that stage of life when one can hopefully look back and see that one has made an impact and successfully achieved something of lasting value. As a basic need, Capricorn can best be summarized as the desire for perfection. To perfect something is to attain ultimate success, the highest possible degree of excellence. Success can be defined as the realization of a goal on the material plane. To achieve success, one must be able to formulate a plan and apply it persistently over time. In this regard Capricorn represents the need for structure, order, and control, for without these little can be accomplished. Generally, people work to accomplish something where they feel a lack, a limitation. Thus, Capricorn is also associated with the pressure to overcome an inherent sense of inadequacy. Simply put, the goal is to attain a status of superiority where was once felt the pain of inferiority.

When integrated, Capricorn's gifts are substantial. Discipline, patience, perseverance, and eventual mastery all accrue from this drive for success. Capricornian overfunctioning, however, can be exquisitely painful. As perfection is an absolute that is unattainable, the individual may never feel good enough. There can be a grim, dutiful approach to life that negates any possibility of enjoying the fruits of one's labor. Or there can be a ruthless, driven need to succeed that thinly veils an underlying fear of failure and humiliation.

The individual may suffer intense feelings of guilt for not being able to live up to standards that are impossibly high. Unable to love themselves unconditionally (Cancer), they are cut off from their internal world of feelings, and this causes them to overvalue the external world of rules, codes, and status symbols. Yet, it is precisely one's subjectivity— hunches, feelings, and impressions—which serves as a reliable guide in navigating the changing currents of life. Divorced from their own insides, such individuals live a haunted, doubting existence plagued with loss of conviction.

Although there are a variety of ills associated with this sign, including workaholism, pessimism, and negativism, the extremes of Capricorn dysfunction is most clearly seen in depression. The essential feature is a deflated mood combined with loss of interest or pleasure in one's usual activities and pastimes. There is decreased energy, difficulty concentrating or thinking, and pervasive feelings of worthlessness, self-deprecation, failure, inferiority, and despair. All are symptomatic of an internalized conviction that one is inadequate.

AQUARIUS/URANUS

Developmentally, Aquarius seems to signify that period around retirement when the individual, having passed beyond the pinnacle of career success, steps back and considers the ultimate significance of his or her life (age 65-77). At this stage, there is a detachment from the external symbols that previously had defined one's identity. The wisdom gained over the years has given one a broad perspective. In this regard, Aquarius represents the tendency toward enlightenment, or breakthrough into a more inclusive awareness. It is fundamentally associated with the need for progress and reform. There is a natural ability for perceiving things whole (holistic thinking). This kind of objective overview affords the individual a capacity for seeing how all things change and are but transitional states in an eternally unfolding universal process. Accordingly, there is an abiding concern for the future welfare of collective humanity.

Properly integrated, Aquarius is broadminded, non-judgmental, and impartial in its perspective. There is a talent for seeing true because the vision is not clouded by personal motives and concerns. While the Aquarian dominated individual may want to change the world, the more significant function of Aquarius is that it provides us with the capacity to consciously and willingly change ourselves. Aquarius is the objective witness that enables us to observe ourselves without judgment or criticism. In psychoanalytic jargon it is the observing ego, although this is actually a contradiction in terms since the essence of Aquarius is that it is a decentralized, non-egoic perspective. Unlike Leo, which is concerned with will and self-image, Aquarius is a choiceless awareness having no fixed character or identity. The concern is always with the whole and the inevitability of change.

Not surprisingly, the pathology of this sign has to do with lack of identity. If ego is sufficiently de-emphasized, there may be no center left from which one can relate to the world. This is reflected in a condition known as Identity Disorder, the essential feature of which is an inability to reconcile aspects of the personality into a relatively coherent and acceptable sense of self. Such individuals are uncertain about a variety of issues relating to self-image, including long-term goals, career choice, friendship patterns, religious identification, moral values, sexual orientation, and group loyalties.

In effect, there is a disorder of will; the individual cannot decide what to do, what he believes, whom he likes, and so forth. Behavior is unpredictable, with difficulty either in making choices or erratic experimentation. Negative or oppositional patterns are often chosen in an attempt to establish an independent identity distinct from other individuals. Such attempts may be manifested as transient experimental phases of widely divergent behavior as the individual "tries on" various roles. Mild anxiety is common and the native is plagued with self-doubt. Frequently, the disturbance is epitomized by the individual asking the question "Who am I?"

A yet more extreme version of Aquarian pathology is expressed in Schizoid Personality Disorder. In this Disorder, there is a defect in the capacity to form personal relationships. This is the "social misfit," the loner, oddball, or "weirdo" who marches to the beat of a different drummer. Such individuals generally appear cold and aloof, preferring to pursue solitary interests and hobbies rather than involve themselves with other people. There is an absence of warmth or interest in the feelings of others, and they may appear equally indifferent to praise or criticism. Often, they seem absentminded and detached from their environment, "in a fog". Individuals with this disorder are usually unable to express legitimate anger. Similar to Identity Disorder, they may seem vague about their goals and indecisive in their actions. Because of a lack of social skills, they frequently never date or marry. Again, the core of the problem is a lack of ego or, more accurately, a denial of ego; the individual has no need to express or seek validation of an identity that is not consciously felt.

PISCES/NEPTUNE

Finally, with Pisces, we come to the end of the life cycle (77-90 and beyond) as the individual prepares for that final surrender to the greater whole of which he or she is merely a part. Expressed as a need, Pisces represents the yearning for transcendence of duality. There is a desire to merge, to melt, and to flow back into the source from which one has come. In this regard, Pisces represents the collective unconscious, or what some people call God, Tao, Spirit, or Brahman. This ineffable whole is not merely outside of one, but infinitely diffused throughout all creation and thus immanent within the human psyche. To identify with this ultimate reality is to renunciate oneself as a separate ego and surrender in selfless love to the Universe.

Properly integrated, Pisces softens the individual so that psychic boundaries are fluid and permeable. This bestows sensitivity and empathy; hence, the native feels at one with others. Piscean love is all-inclusive, impersonal, and indiscriminate. Compassion for suffering is frequently expressed as a penchant for self-sacrifice in a desire to save the fallen. By dissolving into the collective, the individual becomes receptive to images and impressions that may be transmitted by that larger consciousness in which all lesser minds reside. Thus, the psychic and intuitive faculties are strongly accented.

As is true with all signs, the gifts of Pisces become its liabilities when exaggerated beyond the point of balance. For example, the Piscean longing for transcendence makes it difficult to be grounded in mundane reality. Pisces problems are the opposite of Virgo in that they take the form of inefficiency in work related tasks, such as getting and keeping a job, solving problems, doing chores, and the like. Difficulties can also be reflected in an unhealthy life style as evidenced by poor dietary habits, insufficient exercise, and inadequate personal hygiene. The desire to escape reality can be expressed as muddled thinking and self-deception. Thirsting for the spirit frequently takes the form of alcoholism and drug addiction. The search for God can be perverted into an attempt to play God by martyring oneself to others, as exemplified in the co-alcoholic or co-dependent syndrome. And, finally, lack of discrimination and poor judgment can result in experiences where one is victimized and/or abandoned with associated feelings of loss and grief.

Schizotypal personality disorder is entirely consistent with Pisces and operates on a continuum. Its most extreme form is Schizophrenia proper. Characteristic symptoms involve hallucinations, illogical thinking, and multiple delusions such as the belief that others can hear one's thoughts. Cognitive style is characterized by a loosening of associations in which ideas shift from subject to subject in a way that is often incomprehensible. The sense of self that gives the normal person a feeling of individuality and self-direction is blurred. There tends to be a loss of ego boundaries accompanied by extreme perplexity about one's identity. Lacking initiative and unable to choose between alternative courses of action, there is a paralyzing ambivalence that can lead to near cessation of goal-directed activity. Frequently, there is a tendency to withdraw from involvement with the external world and become submerged in fantasies in which objective facts are obscured, distorted, or excluded.

SUMMARY AND CONCLUSION

The DSM is based on a medical model, which implies that mental disorders are akin to diseased organs that reside within the individual. Physical and environmental factors are construed as independently originating causal influences. A story metaphor, on the other hand, allows for a more integrated, holistic perspective based on synchronicity and circular causality. The astrological chart depicts psychological, biological, and environmental factors as interrelated, thematic elements of a single story. The view here is that horoscope as story provides a more hopeful and empowering model than one based on a medical metaphor of diseased organs afflicted by external forces. Psychopathology, in the final analysis, may simply be a consequence of impoverished ideas that generate negative conditions on behavioral, physical, and social levels.

A story's primary theme is a recurrent idea that entails a moral teaching. In stories, protagonists are expected to change and evolve—thus displaying a character arc—by learning lessons created by their own self-defeating behaviors. Herein lies the reason that a story metaphor is ultimately more hopeful than a metaphor of diseased organs. People are not their ideas; rather, they have ideas—or, perhaps, their ideas have them. Either way, an idea is separate from the person who has it. More importantly, negative ideas can change and evolve into more constructive, self- and life-affirming beliefs. It is one of the prime values of astrology to point the way toward this kind of psychological transformation.

It follows that psychopathology is not inherent in the astrological chart. No matter how difficult a configuration might appear, there is no way of determining where on the continuum of health/pathology the person might be expressing that configuration. It cannot be overemphasized that the astrological chart symbolizes a journey of unfoldment, not a static map of character. As such, every sign and symptom of psychopathology contains a seed of potential, which Jung called the *lapis philosophorum*, the philosopher's stone that with sufficient effort produces "the pearl of great price." Just as the pearl is formed through suffering in the heart of the oyster, so the suffering wrought by psychic friction may bestow a gift of profound and enduring value to the soul. Without anguish as a catalyst, there can be no transformation of the self into a more integrated totality.

I have also tried to emphasize the importance of developing a diagnostic system in astrology that is compatible with modern classification systems. The success of this enterprise will contribute to astrology's acceptance in the psychological community and further its use in clinical settings. Subordinate to this main point were several related ones: 1) A classification system should not be used to classify people but rather to classify the disorders that people have; 2) Mental disorders are not discrete entities but tend to overlap and mingle with both healthy and unhealthy aspects of the total personality; 3) Zodiacal signs can be conceptualized as basic needs that underlay and govern our behavior; 4) When these needs are denied satisfaction, disorders result. Such disorders are a consequence of non-integration in psychic functioning. That is, psychopathology results from a lack of balance and coordination between various parts of the psyche.

This last point deserves further emphasis. Psychopathology has its roots in repression that, in turn, is a manifestation of intrapsychic conflict. The denial of one part of the psyche usually results in the exaggeration of another part, a process referred to as overcompensation. It is precisely this under- and overfunctioning that constitutes the symptoms of psychopathology. The problems of a given sign-planet system, therefore, result from its lack of integration with other planets/signs and with the whole of which it is a part.

While these descriptions of psychopathology are necessarily incomplete, it should be clear that the extremes of a sign-planet's dysfunction can be correlated with one or more mental disorders. This helps to bridge the gap between astrology and modern diagnostic categories. Again, however, it must be emphasized that signs or mental disorders are not people; rather, people have the characteristics and tendencies associated with the various sign-categories depending upon their unique psychological makeup.

Generally speaking, the behavior of a sign-planet exists on a continuum of functionality, with health at one end and pathology on the other. The problems of a given sign-planet system reflect a failed attempt to satisfy the needs that sign symbolizes; sometimes the individual overshoots the mark. A sign's pathology, as represented by a particular mental disorder, is simply an exaggerated version of typical problems associated with that sign-planet. Pathology exists on a continuum of severity.

It cannot be stated too strongly that pathology is a consequence of intrapsychic conflict. Thus, a given disorder seldom exists as a discrete entity with sharp boundaries between it and other mental disorders. Just as planets and signs are blended together in unique combinations, so various clinical syndromes can overlap and interact in the same individual.

One client whom I was treating, for example, had his Sun conjunct Uranus in Cancer in the 2nd house, with both planets squaring Neptune. The clinical picture reflected multiple, interrelated conditions. He was diagnosed as suffering from Borderline Personality Disorder (Sun in 2nd house), with Avoidant Personality traits (Cancer), schizoid tendencies (Uranus), and transient psychotic symptoms (Neptune). Further, these different conditions shifted and changed over time, with first one syndrome in ascendancy and then another.

Clearly, astrology's potential as a diagnostic tool is significant. Perhaps its main value is that it shows how mental disorders are not isolated diseases that attack the individual like a virus, but extreme manifestations of otherwise normal psychological processes. Any behavior, no matter how disturbed, represents an attempt to satisfy some basic need (sign). The therapeutic goal, then, is not to rid the individual of the disorder but to bring the psychological processes represented by the disorder into a more integrated, balanced, and functional expression.

Chapter Seven

ASTROLOGY AND THE ORIGINS OF SUFFERING

Subsequent to making a diagnosis of one's client, the clinician develops a biopsychosocial formulation. This entails a full discussion of the etiology and pathogenesis of the client's current difficulties. The term *etiology* refers to the origins of a disorder, whereas *pathogenesis* refers to the processes that produce and maintain it. Etiology is the more general term, and encompasses pathogenesis and anything else that might be contributing to the client's presenting problem. In this chapter, we will be focusing mainly on the origins of psychopathology.

An understanding of etiology is critically important for the astrological consultant, for otherwise there is a tendency to formulate interpretations in a way that implies the client's problems are entirely determined by planetary "influences". What the chart actually symbolizes is the internal, psychological factors that are the true, underlying determinants of behavior. In other words, the planets are not causal agents in themselves, but merely pointers to inborn, intrapsychic processes that generate lived experience.

The ultimate origin of these inborn, intrapsychic processes (and associated mental disorders) may reside in the murky depths of the soul's history. Eastern theories of karma and reincarnation directly imply that mental disorders are a consequence of previous choices and actions in prior incarnations. Whether this is true or not may never be proven scientifically. However, so far as astrology is concerned, it provides an intelligible solution to a dilemma that begs for an answer—namely, how does astrology work?

While etiology plays a central role in psychotherapy, it is worth stating at the outset that we are entering a territory that is as mysterious as it is vast. Indeed, a major reason the DSM is based on a descriptive rather than a psychological (explanatory) model is because the etiology of most mental disorders is *idiopathic*, meaning 'of unknown causation'. Maxmen and Ward (1995) state the matter plainly: "Psychiatry is the only medical specialty that, virtually by definition, treats disorders without clearly known causes or definitive cures" (p. 57).

Certainly, we know more about etiology than ever before. The complexity of the subject is slowly beginning to unravel itself. For example, during the latter half of the 20th century, dramatic advances were made in psychobiology—the study of the interaction of mind and body. Likewise, there has also been a growing appreciation of how intrapsychic, familial, and social factors intersect with biology to produce psychopathology. This is why the clinician's old "psychodynamic formulation," which was limited to intrapsychic processes, has been superseded by a new "biopsychosocial formulation" which synthesizes biological, psychological, and familial/social factors as contributing causes in psychopathology. In this chapter, I will attempt to show that modern and karmic/astrological formulations of psychopathology are complementary and mutually enriching.

DIMENSIONS OF CAUSATION

The very concept of causation poses problems since almost all theorizing in psychology is wedded to a scientific, mechanistic paradigm in which linear, physical causation is presumed (Lowry, 1971). Psychological theories of causation traditionally fall into two camps: *nature* and *nurture*. Causation of the nature variety refers to genetic and biological determinants, whereas causation that derives from nurture refers to familial and social influences. Whether one favors nature or nurture theories, both are equally deterministic; each implies that the individual is not responsible for the conditions that afflict him. By removing any sense of personal responsibility for the suffering that one endures, psychological theories of causation create an inherent moral problem. They directly imply that (1) human beings are victims of forces beyond their control, and (2) the solution to psychological problems resides not within the self, but in the manipulation of material (biological) and social conditions.

Griffin (1988) has remarked that orthodox science can only be applied to that which has been deanimated. To deanimate is to remove all anima or soul in the Platonic sense of a self-moving thing that determines itself, at least partly, in pursuit of particular values—autonomy (Aries), security (Taurus), knowledge (Gemini), and so on. From a strict scientific perspective, persons can only be understood in purely impersonal terms, as embodying no self-determination and nothing that could be considered divine. Well versed in this perspective, it is easy for moderns to believe that an individual is the product of external forces—genetic and social determinants. What is most difficult for them to believe is that human beings may be products of themselves; that is, of their own choices and actions (karma).

As we explore the subject of etiology, the reader should keep in mind that while I am not endorsing either nature or nurture theories, it would be shortsighted to leapfrog over them into a strictly spiritual, reincarnationist perspective. A full account of etiology should be organized hierarchically with biological, social, psychological, and spiritual levels of explanation integrated into one unified framework.

It bears repeating that current theories of causation no longer ascribe to the notion that there is a fundamental, root cause of pathological behavior. Modern formulations assume that, at most, there are roots, with many sprouting, variegated phenomena. In other words, there are diverse etiological influences. This chapter will proceed along similar lines of thinking with the caveat that I believe there is a root, but it is not to be found in one life or a single body, but rather in something more permanent—soul. In this view, what we call character is a manifestation of soul in the present life.

TRANSPERSONAL ETIOLOGIES

An astrological formulation of psychopathology is necessarily transpersonal in that it goes beyond the human body-mind and has cosmic or spiritual implications. The very existence of the astrological chart requires it, for implicit in the chart are all the components of causation that are normally attributed to external determinants—the constitution of the body (nature) as well as one's relationship to parents, siblings, and society at large (nurture). Because every variable in the chart correlates to a biological, psychological, and social factor, one is almost forced to conclude that something exists that transcends the dichotomy of nature and nurture.

We know the birth chart prefigures any actual lived experiences, and is even implicated in the physical features of the native (Hill, 1993). Saturn square Moon symbolizes that a child is apt to feel deprived of nurturance and will be vulnerable to depression as an adult. If the child's subsequent experience actually conforms to this interpretation, what does this imply? Surely we cannot say that the child's vulnerability to depression is merely a consequence of being deprived of nurturing, for that condition was predictable before it occurred.

Accordingly, we must consider the possibility that higher-order causation exists that precedes biological (nature) and environmental (nurture) influences. Astrology suggests a causal mechanism that transcends the nature-nurture dichotomy by postulating that both biological and environmental "influences" may be crystallizations of a single psychic pattern that exists *a priori* to birth. One thing is certain: appearance, character, and destiny are prefigured in the chart. This can be established on the basis of observation by anyone who chooses to study the subject. Yet, nothing *per se* influences the chart to be what it is; the birth moment seems to be entirely random. And since the horoscope comes into being with the baby, one is left in a quandary as to explain how astrology works.

There are at least three theories of astrological causation. Although they are not mutually exclusive, they proceed from very different assumptions about the nature of the relationship between psyche and cosmos. We will now review each of these in turn.

Astral-Determinism: According to this conception, the child's fate—physical, psychological, and social—is determined at the moment of birth for reasons that are entirely independent of the entity being born. This suggests an impersonal, mechanistic cause. Some kind of subtle force that is linked to the rhythms and cycles of the planets imprints itself on the genome of the child and shapes it in a particular direction. Presumably, external planetary forces also determine the child's subsequent experiences with parents and society. This theory implies that chance alone—the moment of birth—is responsible for the child's fate.[13]

Astral-determinism also implies that the soul's fate has no particular purpose or evolutionary intent. If one presumes that psyche begins at birth and has no prior existence, then the human infant has not yet done anything that would warrant a consequence; thus, its fate has no basis in a character already established. The individual may be self-determining within the parameters that his chart establishes, but he is still limited by those parameters, and for reasons that are independent of the individual himself. The set of experiences and the particular conflicts and traits indicated by the chart are not intelligently designed to provide a corrective experience. That is, they are not purposeful in the sense of having a basis in the history of that soul, or intended to forward an evolutionary aim specific to that soul. Rather, one's

---

[13] British astronomer Percy Seymour (1988) has collected some scientific evidence to substantiate his claim of magnetic resonance between the solar system and the magnetic field of the human infant at birth See his book, *Astrology: The Evidence of Science*.

experiences appear to be randomly determined by a mechanistic universe that imprints its pattern upon the human infant at birth.

Personally, it is hard to believe that a mechanistic universe devoid of purpose or intelligence could by chance have created a system in which the psychic and physical anatomy of human beings, along with the unfoldment of their individual life stories, are precisely linked to the rhythms and cycles of the planets. Moreover, it is difficult to fathom how merely physical planets could have discernible, non-physical qualities that are linked to core values and properties of human consciousness, such as courage, pleasure, learning, caring, play, work, beauty, integrity, justice, order, altruism, and charity. That all this could have arisen by chance from a merely material, mechanistic universe stretches credulity to the breaking point.

Divine Determinism: This is still astral-determinism but with the addition of a divine component that uses the mechanism of the planets to administer or convey Its will. In this view, an inscrutable Creator that is omniscient and omnipotent determines the child's fate, which is then reflected in the heavens by the positions of the planets at birth. This one-life theory is consistent with most versions of Christianity (minus the astrological component), which vary only in the degree to which they assume God determines the choices and ultimate fates of individual human beings.

A more full blown conception of astral-determinism can be found in Hellenistic astrology, which borrowing from Platonic philosophy posits the cosmos as a living being that determines events on earth including the human personality and "the inner events that human beings experience" (Schmidt, 2004, p. 28). This does not entirely preclude the individual from influencing his or her fate after birth; however, the conditions of birth itself—genetic inheritance, the child's parents with their varying assets and liabilities, and the social level into which one is born, are all presumed to be determined by a supernatural power for reasons that, again, have nothing to do with the entity being born.

It is certainly plausible that some kind of higher power could arrange the Universe such that celestial forces from above determine the unfoldment of terrestrial events below—including the birth and subsequent life of an individual human being. It could even do this in a way that incorporates a resonance or phase-locking effect between the collective, magnetic symphony of the solar system and the magnetic field of the human infant, which is what Seymour (1988) suggests. Once this resonance is established at birth, the ongoing movements of the planets are synchronized to a complex matrix of biological cycles that regulate the human mind and psyche. "As above, so below."

However, as long as this view is limited to a one-life scenario, it still implies that one's soul is the divine play of an inscrutable Creator who has brought it into being and assigned to it a particular fate for reasons that are unfathomable. While divine determinism is somewhat more credible than mere planetary determinism and can subsume the former theory, I find it hard to believe that a Creator arbitrarily creates souls and fates such that the soul created bears no responsibility for the fate to which it has been assigned. This conception depicts God as a kind of monster scientist that throws human beings into painful and difficult circumstances merely to satisfy His curiosity as to how they might respond. Not only is this inherently immoral, it is also illogical. For what purpose could such a design serve? One could argue that a person must do the best they can with their fate, and perhaps that is part of God's plan, but why that particular set of challenges rather than another?

Karmic *Self* Determinism: According to this model, a child's fate, including the moment of birth, is inextricably entwined with previous choices and patterns of behavior that derive from prior incarnations. That is, consciousness is continuous from life to life. This view implies that one's constitution, character, and fate, as reflected in the chart, are at least partially earned on the basis of accrued karma. The child is born when the planets are arranged in a manner that is resonant with the consciousness of the incarnating entity. As this idea has its roots in the perennial philosophy, it is to that doctrine that we now turn.

THE PERENNIAL PHILOSOPHY

It is possible to reconcile our three theories into a single, integrated model. To do this necessitates consideration of a creed that predates science and that is at the heart of all the great religious and spiritual traditions throughout history.

In science, particularly evolutionary biology, it is widely accepted that living systems evolve by experiencing feedback that has been created as a consequence of the system's own behavior. Feedback is that effect of a system's output which is reintroduced to the system as information about the output. As this principle applies at every level of Nature, it is worth considering that it may also apply in the soul's evolution over a succession of lives. Such a claim is at the heart of what has commonly been called the perennial philosophy. While a full exposition of the doctrine is beyond the scope of this chapter, we can nevertheless consider certain key precepts that are relevant to our discussion of astrological causation.

The perennial philosophy is a spontaneously emerging core doctrine that keeps appearing, in one or another form, in all places and at all times. Leibniz was the first to give it a name, "The Perennial Philosophy," though he, Hegel, and others were simply the carriers of this tradition at particular periods of European philosophy. As Schuon (1984) pointed out in *The Transcendent Unity of Religions*, the various guises and distortions of the perennial wisdom are pointers toward a core truth that transcends any single doctrine. It is, as it were, a meta-doctrine that unifies the central concepts of virtually every major religion, philosophy, and metaphysical system that has exerted influence throughout recorded history. Huxley (1944) defined it as "the metaphysic that recognizes a divine Reality substantial to the world of things and lives and minds; the psychology that finds in the soul something similar to, or even identical with, divine Reality; the ethic that places man's final end in the knowledge of the immanent and transcendent Ground of all being" (p. vii). Among its exponents, Wilber (1981) cites

> the great majority of the truly gifted theologians, philosophers, sages, and even scientists of various times. It forms the esoteric core of Hinduism, Buddhism, Taoism, Sufism, and Christian Mysticism, as well as being embraced, in whole or part, by individual intellects ranging from Spinoza to Albert Einstein, Schopenhauer to Jung, William James to Plato. (pp. 3-4)

Ancient esoteric religions are founded on the premise that the human being is the Universe, the anthropomorphization of the divine thought. The core insight of the wisdom traditions is that Man's innermost consciousness is identical to the absolute and ultimate reality of the Universe. This absolute reality, or Universal Consciousness, is said to be immanent in all things and infinitely diffused throughout existence. According to Lawlor (1982), "The first principle of this theory is that Man is not a mere constituent part of this Universe, but rather he is both the final summarizing product of evolution and the original seed potential out of which the Universe germinated" (p. 91). In Hindu traditions, *Atman* is the term used to refer to the Brahman-nature at the core of the human being that, unfolding through degrees of realization (over a series of lifetimes), slowly blossoms into the full awareness of the individual. Atman, therefore, emerges from Brahman and implies wholeness as a transcendent self that is the revelation of totality (Brahman).

Based upon the direct experience of those who have committed themselves to the realization of such knowledge, this teaching is expressed most succinctly in the "great dictum" of the *Upanishads, Tat tvam asi* ("That art thou"); the Atman, or immanent eternal Self, is one with Brahman, the Absolute Principle of all existence. Significantly, this idea is repeated in the Hermetic doctrine of the macrocosm and the microcosm, upon which astrology is based. According to Smith (1976), the entire body of ancient teachings can be summed up in three important words: Man mirrors cosmos. Man is the Universe in miniature. Such is the bare statement of the doctrine.

Hall (1954) writes, "The human capacity to experience eternity results from the presence in one's own nature of an extension, or condition, of absolute consciousness" (p. 1). Accordingly, the anthropomorphic vision underlies the concept of knowledge by identity. Above we have a vast, immaterialized, resonating, spiritual energy field which the ancients called the Cosmic Man, and below a coagulated substance which is in direct correspondence with this higher field and is able to receive, embody, and implement impulses from this abstract realm. A harmonic relationship exists between Cosmic Man, the macrocosm, and incarnate man, the microcosm. The human being resonates to the Cosmic Being precisely because s/he was made in the *image* of God.

Astrologically, this is symbolized by the horoscope, which is a snapshot of the Universe from the perspective of the incarnating entity. Just as the human psyche mirrors Universal Consciousness in its basic structure and intrinsic dynamism, so it also embodies God's purpose for all life: conscious union with the Divine Ground. In Huxley's (1944) words, "The last end of man, the ultimate reason for human existence, is unitive knowledge of the divine Ground—the knowledge that can come only to those who are prepared to 'die to self' and so make room, as it were, for God" (p. 21). In this view, the astrological chart represents the required path of unfoldment for that particular soul, at least for the current life.

THE SIGNIFICANCE OF KARMA

The process by which this occurs is a creative one. As Teilhard de Chardin (1959) put it, *creation is evolution*. God embodies creativity and God resides at the deepest core of the individual. Inherent with the human psyche, therefore, is a capacity for both self- and world-creation. The individual, of course, does not create the whole world, only the one which he or she experiences. In astrology, the human capacity for creativity—for will and intentionality—is symbolized by the Sun, which aptly resides at the center of our psyche just as it resides at the center of the solar system.

The basis for the evolutionary process hinges on the claim that self and world are but two sides of a larger, transcendent Self, the Atman that is Brahman. Realization of this great truth, however, occurs only by degrees over a series of lifetimes and is intimately linked to the creative process of action. This is the eastern doctrine of *karma*. Karma has two complementary aspects: (1) as a behavioral pattern (action), and (2) as an environmental event (reaction). The relation between action and reaction is linked through the concept of creativity. According to this doctrine, an individual's behavior creates the world which he or she experiences, and it is through this self-created experience that the individual comes gradually to learn that self and world are one.

Chapple (1986) asserts that popular usage of the word karma in Western culture has come to be understood as equivalent to fate and associated with forces beyond human control. In its pure sense, however, karma simply refers to action (*karman*). Every action leaves its residue (*samskara*) in the memory of the person, and these residues collectively form habit patterns (*vasana*) that dictate personality. The roots of karma, therefore, are in what modern psychologists would call beliefs or cognitive structures, which astrologically are symbolized by planetary configurations. The process is self-creative in that action creates memory, memory coalesces into guiding beliefs, and beliefs determine further actions. Psychologically, it is a closed, self-perpetuating loop.

Entering into this loop, however, and becoming part of it, are the environmental consequences of actions. Habitual actions function like seeds, impregnating the world with the essence of one's being. These seeds become one's fate, ripening when the time is right. As Christ said, "as ye sow, so shall ye reap." It is one's actions alone that make up the code of fate. The seed produced bears the same structure as the one who produced it; thus, the conditions that result will mirror the psychic structure of the person who produced the original seed. As within, so without. Action and event, psyche and environment, have the same or similar quality. In a word, they are *isomorphic*. Astrologically, this is implicit in the birth chart. The same variables—signs and planets—that symbolize internal processes also represent outer events that correlate to these processes.

In the perennial tradition, all action ultimately leads to the realization that Atman is Brahman, self and world are ultimately inseparable. The identification with ego (separate-self sense) is transcended in exchange for identification with the whole of Universal Life. "Man can think of his own life," says Hall (1954), "either as the fulfillment of himself, or as the gradual completion of a greater existence of which he is a part and with which he is indissolvably associated" (p. 1).

This implies that ultimate reality is both within and without; Atman is that condition of Universal Consciousness that resides at the deepest core of the human psyche as well as in every situation the individual may encounter. All human relations occur within the context of the larger Consciousness that subsumes them, and are subordinate to the evolutionary intent of this Consciousness. This further implies that a divine purpose is immanent in the karmic feedback processes that occur between the individual and his environment. This process begins at birth and extends throughout life. So-called "formative events" of childhood do not happen randomly, but are concrete derivatives of psychic patterns that originate in the soul/psyche of the incarnating entity. By encountering self as it is symbolically reflected in the guise of external conditions, the individual is afforded the opportunity to correct intrapsychic imbalances that may be generative of interpersonal problems.

To say that one creates the experienced world should not imply that the individual creates experience in the way that a carpenter makes a piece of furniture. The subject does not give the object its existence. Neither, however, am I saying that the individual creates the world merely via his perceptions, meaning attributions, and behavioral responses. This would constitute idealism—the doctrine that ideas, or thought, are the fundamental reality, and that we can never know a thing as it is in itself but only as it appears to us after passing through our perceptual apparatus.

While idealism (or constructivism) is no doubt partially true, it does not constitute an adequate account of reality from the perennial perspective. The human psyche is creative in at least three distinct ways: dominant attitudes and beliefs are going to (1) affect the way the world is perceived and interpreted; (2) determine behavioral responses, which often influence others to respond in a way that confirms the original perception; and (3) attract people and situations that mirror psychic structure. This latter point is crucial, for it implies that the objective quality of the people and events one attracts are meaningfully related to one's own consciousness.

Aurobindo (1972) affirms that the individual is subject to a progressive evolutionary process and that karma is the mechanism whereby growth and progress is achieved. In Hindu traditions, the doctrine of karma was associated with various liberative techniques for overcoming bondage due to past actions. The central premise of such techniques is that karma is associated with affliction (*klesa*). Again, every decision or action leaves a residue (*samskara*) in the memory. These memory residues build up to form certain repetitive patterns of thought (*vasana* or cognitive structures). Such cognitive patterns are habitual and self-confirming; they dictate how one perceives and reacts to the world and, in turn, how the world reacts back. What one expects to experience generally determines what one does experience. In effect, karma constitutes a sort of addiction to the effects of habitual action. Inherent within some of these cognitive structures are limitations and distortions that induce suffering.[14] In this sense, each person is a prisoner of his own thoughts, held in bondage to a world of his own making.

The process of self-realization is generally considered to be a life-long endeavor of attempting to dissolve one's identifications with the ego by breaking its attachments to various physical, emotional, and mental states—the goal being to attain that highest state of pure, selfless awareness variously called nirvana, samadhi, or enlightenment.[15] The key to enlightenment is vulnerability, or non-attachment. This can be defined as a willingness to change by observing the contents of experience yet without identifying with them. Through spiritual practices (meditation, yoga, prayer), the individual can become progressively non-attached. And by surrendering attachment and performing action in a selfless manner, a person can become free of the binding influence of past karma (Chapple, 1986; Creel, 1986). Gradually the individual recognizes that the world of experience is created by his or her own thought structures, and that the purpose of all experience is for learning. Thus, when difficulties arise there is a willingness to surrender old perspectives to allow for the emergence of new experience and a new, transformed identity.

INTEGRATING TRANSPERSONAL ETIOLOGIES

If we are to integrate our three theories of astrological causation—Planetary determinism, Divine determinism, and Self-determinism—the perennial philosophy points us in the right direction. Far from being a blind, mechanical

---

[14] Not all *vasana* are negative. Some cognitive structures constitute integrated, harmonious relations between different parts (planets). Again, astrological aspects are the most obvious corollaries to core beliefs, or *vasana*.

[15] It is worth noting that the process of soul evolution is analogous to the physical evolution of our Sun. Just as the human soul is said to be indissolvably associated with the soul of the Universe, so the actual Sun is made up of atomic elements that were produced by the Universe at large. Like the psyche, suns (stars) go through various stages of birth and death until, ultimately, they reach the supernovae stage—a massive explosion—in which they expand indefinitely outwards, reuniting with the source from which they were born—the Universe itself. The process of enlightenment is similarly described.

universe ruled by chance alone, the cosmos is animated by a supreme intelligence. The physical universe—stars, planets, organisms, cells, molecules, and atoms—is but the visible expression of an immaterial consciousness infinitely diffused throughout nature.

According to the perennial philosophy, the Universe and everything in it is ensouled. The structure of the cosmos resembles that of a great organism composed of hierarchical levels of purposeful energies. Each level and part is interdependent with every other level and part. The stars and planets are expressions of the functions of this organism, just as the various organs of the human body are expressions and instruments of its functions.

The astrological maxim, "as above, so below," defines the essential relationship between the macrocosm, the Universe as a whole, and the microcosm, the individual human. Man, as the little world, reflects by virtue of his inner constitution, the greater world of which he is a component part. Every aspect of our physical and psychic anatomy has its counterpart in the celestial realm. This hierarchical conception of the cosmos is based upon the concept of "similars" and "sympathies". Similars are those structures that agree in design though they may differ in magnitude. For example, the structure of the atom is "similar" to the structure of the solar system. Sympathies are resonant bonds of vibratory frequencies that unite all similars. Thus, the ancients conceived of the Universe as a great system of similars decreasing in magnitude as we descend the orders of life, and united by resonant bonds of sympathy.

This notion of the Universe as an unbroken whole in which different systems combine and overlap in mutually conditioned relations has important implications for our theory of astrological causation. When subjected to analysis, the human body turns out to be mostly a vast matrix of interacting energy fields, not really solid at all. These energy fields, in turn, are measurably responsive to the fields and rhythms of the external environment, such as the geomagnetic field and the fields of Sun, Moon, and planets. Such interactions between the electromagnetic field of the individual and that of the cosmic environment have been shown to have a marked influence on human behavior, moods, and physiological processes (Playfair and Hill, 1978). This is what the ancients meant by "similars" bound together by resonant bonds of sympathy. Microcosm and macrocosm are internally related.

While the above might imply a cause-effect relationship in which cosmic energies impact the human body and brain, we must remember that, according to spiritual traditions, the greater part of the Universe is composed of a subtle, immaterial consciousness that unites human and divine; atman is Brahman, the human soul is a derivative of the Universal Soul. That brain and body register changes in the cosmic environment need not imply that this is the mechanism whereby astrology works. More likely, there is a deeper, subtler connection that is merely analogous to what occurs on the physical level. Because there is no ultimate separation between psyche and cosmos, there is a potential resonance. In effect, the human soul partakes of the intelligence of the larger cosmos and yearns to be reunited with it.

According to esoteric philosophy, the means by which this occurs is through a series of incarnations in which the evolving soul is born at a time when its vibratory frequency comes into sympathetic resonance with the harmony (or disharmony) of the planetary spheres. The nature of the relationship is not one of linear, material causality, but of synchronicity. The entity that incarnates—the birth event—is the effect of causes set into motion in prior lives. Karma, the law of compensation, controls the actual phenomena of birth itself. Individuals are born at the time that they have merited, into conditions that they have merited, and into opportunities suitable for their next state of development.

In this view, the Universe is eternally building and constantly improving vehicles for its own betterment. Since all karma, both good and bad, leads finally to enlightenment through experience, the conditions of one's birth are meaningfully and purposefully related to the consciousness of the incarnating entity. Birth is the ultimate example of synchronicity—a confluence of inner and outer events that links psyche to cosmos. When a sympathy occurs between these similars, the individual soul is swept into existence. He or she embodies the quality of the moment. As Jung (1945) said, "The form of the world into which he is born is already inborn in him as a virtual image" (p. 188). Thus, one's genetic inheritance, one's parents, and the immediate local universe, are symbolic of the consciousness of the person born at that time. Hall (1960) describes it thusly:

> Astrology is the mechanism that administers the law of karma. The universe is vibration. The interaction of heavenly bodies is constantly setting up fields of specialized vibrations. The incarnating entity of man is also a rate of vibration, modified by the karmic factor within itself. The incarnation of the individual is determined by these vibratory factors. He is born into circumstances consistent with the karmic modifications of his own nature. He is born when the planets are arranged in a pattern consistent with his own karma. (p. 35)

Such a view integrates the three theories of astrological causation advanced previously. Each theory is subsumed by the one that follows. The mechanistic view of physical causes and effects—planetary determinism—is subsumed by the theory of divine determinism, which states that all measurable, physical processes, such as electromagnetic fields, are animated and directed by an indwelling Consciousness. Divine determinism, in turn, is subsumed by Karmic self-determinism, which states that there is a seed of divinity (soul) within every human being that works in conjunction with the larger consciousness for its own betterment. Man, the microcosm, not only reflects the Macrocosm in his psychic structure, but also in his temporal becoming.

Because physical reality exists at a lower rate of vibration than psychic reality, the quality of the birth moment congeals into character and fate, which are mirrors of one another on the material plane, and unfold in synchrony. The incarnating consciousness is a vibratory causal field that sets into motion an effect consistent with itself. One's fate, as reflected in the moment of birth, reflects one's character and is diffused into a slowly unfolding series of events that provide opportunities for the further maturation of the soul.

A HIERARCHY OF CAUSES

The above discussion indicates that there should be no simple, unicausal explanations for psychopathology. Rather, there is a hierarchy of interdependent causes that link the various levels of the psyche together. This hierarchy can be illustrated in Figure 16 (see page 209). Note that each higher level subsumes and incorporates the causality of its lower levels; thus, causality as a whole starts at the top and works downwards. In this regard, the model I am presenting is one of downward causation; that is, from higher levels to lower.

Level I karmic inheritance is the highest level because all subsequent experience conforms to the pattern of the astrological chart. The first manifestation of the chart is the body (Level II) into which one is born—a body that is going to reflect the inherent soul properties of the incarnating entity. According to Hill (1993), correlations between the horoscope and the body go all the way back to Ptolemy's "The Form and Temperament of the Body," which was a chapter of his *Tetrabiblios* (140 A.D.). It is believed that at least some of Ptolemy's material came from still earlier sources at the great Library of Alexandria.

Hill maintains that, "Planets and signs describe but do not cause physical appearance" (p. 3). Genetic inheritance is an incontrovertible scientific fact and is certainly not being challenged here. However, as Hill suggests, it is likely that our genome takes the path of least resistance relative to the horoscope. "The features, forms and coloration suggested by the planetary birth chart," says Hill, "respond along a path of least resistance to the material available within an individual's gene pool" (p. 5). A planet, for example, will only express physically what is within the possible genetic range of the individual. This is analogous to an artist assigned to draw the face of a famous personage. If she has only pencil and pad, the sketch will appear one way; if she has a paintbrush, canvas, and full palette of colors, the portrait will appear another way. The artist's rendition is at least partially determined by the materials with which she works.

Level I:
Karmic Inheritance as Symbolized by the
Astrological Chart. Innate Psychology.

Level II:
Genetic Inheritance.
Biological Predisposition.

Level III:
Formative Childhood Events.
Adult Experiences.

Figure 16: A Hierarchy of Causes

If the soul is the artist of the body, it can only work with the materials—genetic endowment—with which it is presented. The soul may be akin to an archetypal field that permeates and shapes bodily tissue in a direction that conforms to pre-existent, psychic tendencies. Past life theorists attest that the soul is a kind of "subtle body" that exerts its own force upon the genetic material with which it comes into contact, presumably at some point before birth (Cerminara, 1950; Weiss, 1992; Woolger, 1988). One's genome, in other words, may be a kind of clay that is molded in accordance with a pre-inherited psychic pattern that inhabits the physical material of the body. This may explain why the appearance of a child clearly reflects the physiology of its parents while, at the same time, is consistent with the physiological attributes of dominant astrological factors in its chart.

It is also possible that the particular genetic endowment of the child is in some way resonant or compatible with the pattern of the subtle body that animates it. Like a key and a lock, there is a fit. In other words, genetic, physical inheritance and psychic, karmic inheritance may be complimentary processes. However, the psychic pattern must be the dominant influence since it precedes the physical body. The body, in effect, is a coagulation or crystallization of consciousness.

Medical astrology, of course, goes far beyond astrophysiognomy since every part of the chart conforms not only to an outer body part, but also to an inner organ and function. Mars, for example, not only rules the eyes and upper jaw, but also the adrenal glands; Venus rules the neck region but also the kidneys; Pluto corresponds to the genitals, and also the colon and processes of elimination. While use of astrology in medical diagnosis was common right up to the 17th century, it was gradually replaced by more scientific methods. Nevertheless, contemporary astrology continues to demonstrate that difficult planetary configurations predispose individuals to pathologies that correspond to those planets/organs. Astrology can also provide information about periods during which individuals are most vulnerable to certain kinds of illnesses (Tobyn, 1997; Nauman, 1995; Tyl, 1998).[16] The critical point is this: If the horoscope is implicated in physical pathology, it may also symbolize psychopathology that has a biological or genetic component.

Again, however, it is important to remember that the causal factor is not the chart itself, but the soul it reflects. Vulnerability to specific types of pathology may be inherited from past lives. Certain archetypal patterns that derive from the history of the soul could be encoded within the psyche and passed on from body to body in successive lives. Anecdotal evidence for this is contained in much of the literature on past-life regression therapy (Weiss, 1992; Woolger, 1988).

Roger Woolger, a graduate of Oxford University and certified Jungian analyst, sites a typical case of a young woman with lupus who suffered from severe arthritis-like pains in the joints of her arms and legs. In one particularly crucial past-life session, the woman experienced herself as a vengeful anarchist who was killed when a bomb exploded that blew off her arms and legs. According to Woolger, the imprint of this event seemed to be recorded in the subtle body and imprinted on the young woman's physical body in this lifetime. The lupus symptoms of pain in her joints were an echo of the past

---

[16] Any practicing astrologer can attest to this. Recently I had a client whose Sun was being squared by transiting Saturn. She developed a heart condition (Sun) that was stress related (Saturn). Another client with transiting Saturn squaring her Neptune discovered she had massive tooth decay, which necessitated an emergency root canal. Her teeth were literally dissolving. Saturn, of course, rules bones (teeth), whereas Neptune rules processes of decay and dissolution.

life trauma. Her cure required a cathartic release and working through not only of the bodily sensations of the past life trauma, but also of the destructive rage that precipitated her death in the prior life. Woolger (2000) continues:

> Letting go of the physical memories also entailed for her letting go of the vengeful feelings she (he) had carried as a young anarchist, which had symbolically turned against her as "explosive" rage. What is remarkable is that after this one session all the arthritic-like symptoms disappeared. Her doctor, who was present at the session, attests that the symptoms have not returned—over two years later. (p. 11)

Like Woolger, the psychiatrist Brian Weiss (1992) also cites hundreds of clients he has treated for psychosomatically related illnesses. A man, for instance, with chronic back pain, relived an experience under hypnosis in which he was mortally wounded from a lance puncturing his back during a 14th century battle. "Past physical trauma seems to leave present physical residue," says Weiss (p. 69). Echoing Woolger's findings, Weiss alleges that once the emotional impact of the trauma is released, the patient recovers—often in a single session.

There is even evidence to suggest that past life trauma can materialize in the form of birthmarks. Dr. Ian Stevenson (1997), a psychiatrist and chairman of neurology and psychiatry at the University of Virginia, notes that birthmarks seemed to have a peculiar relationship to the "prior" personality. Stevenson interviewed thousands of children who had apparent memories of past lives. In several of these cases the children "remembered" violent deaths. For example, they described being shot in particular parts of the body, and these remembered wounds corresponded in location to scarlike birthmarks. One boy, among twenty-six items that he "remembered," claimed robbers had slit his throat in his previous life. In the present life, he was born with a scarlike birthmark around his neck. In several cases, Dr. Stevenson was able to find the medical records covering the death of the previous personality and confirmed that the location of the wounds did indeed correspond to the child's memories as well as with the locations of the birthmarks.

All of this is interesting in light of the fact that modern scientific research has established that genetic factors are prerequisites for many mental disorders. Schizophrenia and manic-depression, for instance, have a clear genetic component. It has also been demonstrated that heredity contributes to panic and obsessive-compulsive disorders, alcoholism, phobia, and antisocial personality disorder. These conclusions derive mainly from researching twins and adoptees. However, even when genes are implicated, it is not clear what is being inherited. Is it a predisposition to a particular trait, such as shyness or aggression? Or is it a vulnerability to certain psychosocial stressors such as a chaotic family life or loss? Regardless of how these questions are answered, past life research suggests that genetic and biological determinants are not primary causal factors in psychopathology; rather, they may be facilitating agents that derive from karmic factors originating in past lives.

Further support for this line of thinking comes from the field of psychoendocrinology, which is the study of the interrelationships among the brain, hormones, neurotransmitters, and behavior. As stated in the previous chapter, biological changes do not necessarily have biological origins. The brain's anatomy and biochemistry can be altered by psychosocial stress. Mental states, for example, have been observed to have measurable physiological effects. The very term *psychoneuroimmunology* expresses the conviction that mind, or psyche, is implicated in biological functioning and propensity toward specific types of disease (Cunningham, 1986; Pert, 1987). This is likewise what past life research suggests. Actual traumas could be registered upon the psyche (soul) as specific kinds of imprints, which are transferable to the next life as a genetic predisposition toward related physical and mental illnesses.

In effect, the question of causality has come full circle. Intentions and actions result in certain kinds of experiences that feedback upon the individual; these experiences evoke mental and emotional states that have corresponding physiological effects; physiological effects register upon the subtle body (consciousness) as specific kinds of imprints, which are transferable to the next life as genetic propensities toward certain mental disorders. These, in turn, influence behavior, and so the cycle continues. It is a closed, self-perpetuating loop that begins and ends with psyche. This kind of feedback cycle, which presumably extends over the course of multiple lives, is exactly what the doctrine of karma implies. Whatever it is we are inheriting may not simply be from our parents, but from ourselves.

CONSCIOUSNESS AS CAUSAL REALITY

The theory of reincarnation presupposes that consciousness survives the death of the physical body and can operate independent of a physical substrate. There is a multitude of scientific and anecdotal evidence to support this requirement. In modern consciousness research, for example, neuroscientists are increasingly questioning the traditional positivist doctrine that (1) consciousness is an epiphenomenon of brain chemistry; and (2) neurophysiology is the cause of action rather than consciousness itself. Nobel Prize laureate Roger Sperry (1981) comments:

> Current concepts of the mind-brain relation involve a direct break with the long-established materialist and behaviorist doctrine that has dominated neuroscience for many decades. Instead of renouncing or ignoring consciousness, the new interpretation gives full recognition to the primacy of inner conscious awareness as a causal reality. (p. 2)

The recognition that consciousness is causal rather than merely the effect of a material substrate calls attention to the question of how mind and body are related. Various theories have attempted to describe the mechanism of mind-body relations, but most of these are either dualistic or materialistic. That is, consciousness (mind) is either presumed to emerge out of the organized complexity of bodily matter and subsequently comes to influence the brain (dualism)—or, consciousness is assumed to be "nothing but" and thus identical to the physical states of the central nervous system (materialism/identism). In both these theories, mind is still dependent upon a material substrate.

Griffin (1988), however, argues that the mind-body relationship constitutes a false dichotomy. The bulk of the evidence suggests that mental and physical states simply constitute different aspects or hierarchical levels of a single, unified reality. Mental and physical are flip sides of one another; mind is the subjective component of matter, while matter is the objective component of mind. Matter is simply consciousness that has crystallized onto a physical plane at a certain level of complexity. The greater the complexity, the higher the consciousness. Battista (1978) has suggested that consciousness is best defined as a general term that refers to all forms of experience and awareness. This would include the experience of non-human systems throughout the hierarchy of Nature, such as cells, molecules, and atoms. While matter is itself an embodiment of consciousness, the reality of consciousness is not dependent upon matter anymore than the existence of H^2O is dependent upon ice.

Many studies suggest that consciousness can function independent of brain and body. Tart (1981) claims that there is a substantial amount of high quality scientific evidence in support of psi phenomena—clairvoyance, telepathy, precognition, and psychokinesis. Psi phenomena can be defined as organism-environment interactions in which it appears that information has been transmitted or influence has occurred that cannot be explained through science's understanding of sensory-motor channels. Individuals are able to view events at a distance (remote viewing or clairvoyance), receive information from another person some miles away (telepathy), perceive events that have not yet occurred (precognition), and cause motion in physical objects merely by willing them to move (psychokinesis). Psi phenomena seem to violate the principle of linear, materialistic causality since they occur in the absence of any known form of energy and/or receptor to convey the information/influence. All of this suggests that consciousness is not limited to what occurs inside the brain. Rather, it is implicit in exchanges of information that occur between systems that are not in spatial contact.

Scientific evidence also suggests that consciousness can withdraw itself from the body, at least temporarily, and function independently. Again, Tart (1981) has chronicled extensive reports of individuals who have had out-of-body-experiences (OBEs) during which they were able to obtain information and report events under controlled scientific conditions. For example, he recounts an experiment involving a young woman who spent four nights sleeping in a laboratory while her EEG,[17] eye movements, blood pressure, and skin resistance were all monitored on a polygraph. She slept in an ordinary bed with short electrode cables that prevented her from sitting up or getting out of bed. Placed on a shelf seven feet above the bed was a series of numbers that could only be viewed from the perspective of the ceiling, looking down. During her reported OBE, she was able to float above her body and see the five-digit target number, which she reported in perfect sequence.

Her EEG pattern during the OBE was unique in that it constituted a mixture of Stage-1 EEG such as would be found in conjunction with REM sleep that accompanies dreaming, but in this instance there were no rapid eye movements recorded that would normally accompany dreaming.[18] This was explainable in light of the fact that what the subject was seeing was not her dreams, since she did not inhabit her body at the time. Rather, she was completely awake and aware outside her body while performing the task assigned her. The body, meanwhile, was in a state of dreamless sleep and recorded brain wave patterns that were discrepant with those that would normally accompany a thinking, seeing, intentional consciousness.

---

[17] An EEG is an abbreviation for "electroencephalogram", which is a graphic record of the electrical activity of the brain as recorded by an electroencephalograph.

[18] REM stands for "Rapid Eye Movement," which is what occurs when a person is dreaming.

Moody (1975), Sabom (1981), Ring (1998), and many other researchers have recorded similar observations regarding individuals who have had near-death-experiences (NDEs). Individuals who were pronounced medically dead—without heartbeat or brain waves—later reported floating above the death scene for up to twenty minutes and witnessing detailed events and conversations taking place around their body. Since the brain was not involved in witnessing and recording these events, there were no brain waves produced by neuronal firings. And since the person was able to recall events that were completely outside the auditory and visual field of the dormant body, the evidence suggests that consciousness can function and exist without a physical medium.

In both NDEs and OBEs, once consciousness reinhabits and reanimates the body, it can induce physiological changes that record an accounting of its disembodied experiences. So far as reincarnation is concerned, this is the crux of the matter: when psyche reinhabits soma following an OBE or NDE, it imprints itself upon the brain and central nervous system, which is able to register and encode information that was derived while in a non-physical state. Otherwise, the person would not be able to remember and communicate what s/he witnessed during an OBE or NDE. Such experiences encapsulate, in microcosm, what the doctrine of reincarnation requires. Psi phenomena, OBEs, and NDEs are all consistent in suggesting that human consciousness is able to function in ways that appear to be independent of brain and body. More importantly, consciousness is able to subsequently reinhabit and imprint itself upon the body and induce neurophysiological changes. If this can occur in measurable ways during a single life, it increases the plausibility that it might also occur from life to life.

REINCARNATION AND GENETICS

Opponents might argue that even if psyche can affect soma after periods in which it has apparently been outside the body, this does not necessarily mean that it can alter genetic structure. Yet, any theory of astrological causation that involves reincarnation must account for genetics. Through longitudinal studies of identical twins raised in separate environments, scientific research suggests that genetics may have a stronger impact on personality than the family environment. Such traits as intelligence, coordination, extroversion, religiosity, aesthetic preferences, artistic talents, as well as a propensity for particular types of mental disorders, have all been clearly established as having a genetic component.

Accordingly, if reincarnation is valid, there must be some kind of connection between consciousness and genetics from life to life. Presumably, lived experiences in a prior life might somehow alter the genetic code of the individual during that life and subsequently become imprinted upon the subtle body, which then serves as the organizing matrix for the genetic structure of any successive body in a future lifetime. But is there any evidence to support this?

An early dogma in genetic theory presupposed that the so-called "germ plasm" of sperm and ovum was totally isolated from the rest of the body. Hereditary DNA encoded in chromosomes was thought to be unaffected by anything that happened to the transient individuals who harbored the immortal plasm in their ovaries and testicles. Unless altered by noxious agents—cosmic rays, chemical shocks, and other unpredictables of nature—the DNA chains of heredity were presumably passed on, in unaltered form, from generation to generation. The fact that the genetic blueprint was isolated from other physiological processes meant that anything the organism experienced would have no bearing on subsequent generations. The DNA code could not be altered by what someone might have learned, or felt, or wanted during his or her lifetime. Thus, evolution as a whole was undirected.

Obviously, any research that indicates the genetic structure is not stable and static, that it is not isolated from feedback processes occurring in the mind and body, and that it is capable of being influenced by the organism's efforts to adapt to a changing environment, would have radical implications. It is surprising how much information is available that points in just this direction. Research over the past several decades indicates that, far from being static, genes are highly dynamic processes that are continually monitoring, responding to, and directing the various processes of the body. For example, Leder's research at the National Institute of Health established that genes function in conjunction with the immune system, and that they actively combine and recombine to function in the production of antibodies to combat viruses that have invaded the body ("Genes That Move," 1980).

Chambon (1981) reports that the mammalian genome has been found to contain long stretches of superfluous "nonsense" DNA, the function of which is unknown, between genes. When the genes are transcribed into RNA, which in turn makes proteins, the nonsense areas are clipped out by a special enzyme that appears to function as an intelligent editor, cutting away whatever is unnecessary to the needs of the organism. This is analogous to a musician having access to every note played on every instrument imaginable, such that all notes are available to be combined into whatever melody the musician wishes to create. Presumably, the musician would utilize notes in a manner that conforms to his musical needs and interests. Likewise, the intelligence within our genome utilizes superfluous DNA molecules in a manner that conforms to pre-established patterns and emerging needs.

Also revolutionary is the discovery of "jumping genes" that involve segments of the genome that can actually leave their original positions and insert themselves somewhere else, thereby turning themselves or other genes on or off. Such movements, which appear to be ongoing with the genome, create new proteins and alter an enormous number of gene products in the cell. Again, all of this appears to be intelligently directed toward specific ends.

The emerging picture of the genome is that of a self-regulating, evolving system equipped with feedback devices from a hierarchy of environments that surround every cell in the body. Genetic mechanisms appear to be in some sense self-aware, flexible, and purposeful rather than mere mechanical automons of fixed and invariant operation. Feedback devices make the genome capable of self-repair and self-organization, just like other natural systems. Regulator genes originating at higher levels of the hierarchy switch genetic processes on and off, transpose certain genes from one location to another, eliminate harmful mutations, coordinate the effects of useful ones, and even create whole new programs out of superfluous DNA, all in the service of the adaptive needs of the organism.

The molecular revolution in biology has established that genes are not the stable and immutable structures that neo-Darwinism assumed. Instead, they are controlled by other agents in complex, feedback processes that involve continuous information flows between the genome and the rest of the organism. Intricate chemical-neurologic networks form a relationship between the brain, the limbic system, and the genetic system via hormonal mediation.

The implications are radical, for it directly supports a "mind-body" mechanism of evolution. We know that inheritance is controlled, in part, by nuclear DNA, which can be regulated by external agents, such as proteins and hormones. Brain structures and hormones closely interact. Experiences conducted through sensory channels impact the brain and limbic system; thus, a person's experiences—thoughts, feelings, and perceptions—have an effect upon these brain structures. The brain is capable of activating a hormone chain that ultimately regulates gene expression through proteins; that is, the brain and limbic system influence the genome through hormonal "informational" molecules. Thus experience and genetics appear to be linked through complex, biochemical feedback processes. What an individual learns and experiences can be transmitted directly to the genome.

All of this implies that consciousness predominates over matter; psyche shapes soma. If lived experience can alter genetic structure, which, in turn, is imprinted on the subtle body (soul), then when the soul reincarnates it downloads its entire history into a new genome, like software into hard drive memory. In effect, we may actually inherit from ourselves.[19] Admittedly, the doctrine of reincarnation may never be proven scientifically. However, I merely want to establish that there is a plausible mechanism for the transmission of genetic patterns from life to life. The history of the soul may not only be reflected in the heavens at birth, it may also be reflected in the genetic blueprint of our bodies. Perhaps the astrological chart is an encoded map of past life patterns in the same way that the genome is an encoded map of heredity. In short, genetics and astrology may turn out to be complementary theories of causation.

PSYCHOSOCIAL THEORIES OF CAUSATION

Thus far, I have described a hierarchy of interdependent causes that link the various levels of the psyche together. Each higher level subsumes the one's below it, such that causality as a whole starts at the top and works downwards. Whereas Level I karmic inheritance subsumes genetic inheritance at Level II, in this section we will examine how Level II processes subsume formative childhood experiences at Level III. This is the end of the line, the psychosocial level of causality. Astrology established that the infant is already predisposed to experience his or her parents (and subsequent others) in particular ways. S/he is not a blank slate waiting to be imprinted by the vicissitudes of external experience; rather, there is a pre-existing psychobio matrix—a mind-body unity—that is programmed to generate, receive, and interpret social experiences in an idiosyncratic manner.

The age-old debate over whether nature (genetics) or nurture (family) is the more dominant causal factor in personality is coming down heavily on the side of genetics. According to studies, genes account for 70% of the intelligence quotient (IQ). The innate quality, pattern, and level of the child's thinking largely determine how s/he interprets external events. As we discussed in Chapter 5, experiences that do not fit into already organized

---

[19] Past lives research indicates that individuals are often born into the same ancestral line. If so, then perhaps we inherit genes that we ourselves helped to make. Anecdotal evidence seems to support this. I knew a little girl who at four years old demonstrated knowledge of being her great grandmother, who died some years before she was born.

cognitive patterns are necessarily ignored as irrelevant or distorted to fit the procrustean bed of the organized patterns, for good or ill. Consciousness is not a passive mirror of an objective reality; rather, consciousness molds external stimuli according to its own nature. Just as the soul may reincarnate and mold the physical matter of its new body into familiar patterns, so it can appropriate information from outside itself and convert this data into familiar categories of meaning. The psyche is an organic, formative force that independently changes information that has been appropriated from its environment.

This should not mean, however, that environment plays an inconsequential role as a causal factor in psychopathology. From a perennial perspective, it may not be a primary causal factor, but it is a causal factor none-the-less. Maxem and Ward (1995) remind us that, "Genetic theory is not equivalent with behavioral predestination" (p. 69). If a person inherits the genotype for a mental disorder, biological and psychosocial interventions such as diet, exercise, stress reduction, psychotherapy, or a spiritual practice can still alleviate or prevent it.

Social factors that can influence the course of a mental disorder can be divided into five general models—developmental, stress, behavioral, family systems, and sociocultural. We will now examine each of these in turn.

1. Developmental models are of particular etiological significance. Various developmental theories postulate a series of overlapping stages (or "passages"). These models uniformly claim that an arrest or crisis at any stage may produce associated psychopathology. For example, disturbances in attachment and bonding during the first four years of life may produce insecurity, anxiety, depression, distrust, and/or fear of loneliness (Erikson, 1968; Stern, 1985). A significant loss during childhood, usually of a parent, may be of special etiological significance, especially in depression.

Yet, development does not stop with adolescence; it continues through life. The patient's presenting problems may result not only from a historical precipitant, but also from a phase-of-life, or developmental, crisis. A 40 year-old man may be fired and develop acute, overwhelming anxiety. Losing his job may be the primary precipitant, yet why he was fired and why he is that devastated may be secondary to a "mid-life crisis" (Kegan, 1982; Sheehy, 1974).

If signs constitute generic developmental stages as discussed in previous chapters, then houses may correlate to stages as well. The first house is birth to 2 years, the 2nd house 2 to 5 years, and so on, just like signs. Whereas the zodiac signifies a generic developmental model, the houses may represent life stages in a more individualized sense. I am still experimenting with this line of investigation, but it is worth considering further.

For example, I've noticed that planets in houses often seem to correlate with the general quality of the person's experience during that life stage. A typical example involves the life of Charles Dickens. When Dickens turned twelve in 1824, a singular event occurred that was to irrevocably change his life. His father, who had a poor head for finances, found himself imprisoned for debt. His wife and children, with the exception of Charles, joined him in prison. Charles was put to work at Warren's Shoeblacking Factory, a grim and horrific industrial plant that utilized the shameful practice of child labor. Charles was required to work 16-hour days under atrocious conditions. Hence, not only did he lose his parents during this period, but he was also burdened with responsibility for paying off his father's debt. When the family finances were put at least partly to rights and his father was released later that year, Dickens, already scarred psychologically by the experience, was further wounded by his mother's insistence that he continue to work at the factory. His father, however, rescued him from that fate and eventually allowed him to enroll in school.

Dickens' chart reveals Saturn in Capricorn in the 4th house squaring Mars in Aries in the 7th. The 4th house, being associated with Cancer, symbolizes the period of approximately 9-14 years of age. Saturn's placement precisely corresponds to the year Charles was forced to work in the Shoeblacking Factory (age 12). Note that Saturn's placement is in the opposite house of that which it rules; thus, it is ill placed by house yet strong by sign (Capricorn), which perhaps only accentuates the misfortune of its placement in the 4th. Saturn represents responsibility and hard work, yet occupies a house that signifies the warmth and support of a loving family and the last bastion of childhood. Accordingly, Saturn in the 4th can describe a depressing family life, a stern mother, a weak father, and a period of time (9-14) that is likely to be characterized by excessive responsibility. Clearly, the potential for such experiences were most acutely manifest during Dickens' 12th year.

The square to Mars suggests Charles probably experienced seething resentment over being denied his freedom during this period. Alexander Welsh (1987), a Dickens biographer, explains that the dark side of many Dickens novels betrays his angry feelings toward his parents. According to an autobiographical fragment cited by Welsh, Dickens once stated in reference to his parents forcing him to work: "I do not write resentfully or angrily: for I know all these things have worked together to make me what

I am: but I never afterwards forgot, I never shall forget, I never can forget, that my mother was warm for my being sent back" (p. 4-5).

In fact, Dickens brief stint at the Blacking Factory haunted him all of his life. According to Welsh (1987), the dark secret was the source of his preoccupation with themes of alienation and betrayal that continually emerged in his greatest works. For more than a half-century, students of Dickens have emphasized the crucial importance of this traumatic period in his life when his parents suddenly were imprisoned and forced him into premature employment. Dickens' novels of orphans and persecuted, abandoned children—most notably Oliver Twist, and Smirke and Jo, in *Bleak House*—clearly hearken back to the numbing despair he must have experienced at 12 years old.

It is also worth noting that Mercury is placed right at the cusp of the 5th house, or at about the period of 14 years old when Dickens was allowed to return to school by his father. One can only imagine the joy (5th house) Dickens must have felt over this development. I suspect he embraced school fervently as if reunited with a long lost love—an apt symbol for Mercury (education) in the 5th house of romance.

Very often the crises of a later developmental stage will trigger an emotional trauma that originated at an earlier stage. I recall a case in which this showed up astrologically as a difficult transit to a planet in the 8th house, which corresponds to the "mid-life" (Scorpio) period of 35-44 years. My client, Tom, who was experiencing a mid-life crisis, had Pluto in the 2nd opposed to Saturn in the 8th. Tom's experiences during the Taurus/2nd house stage of 2 through 4 years correlated to this natal aspect. There was a rupture of attachment involving the father (Saturn), who left the family when Tom was 3. Pluto symbolizes a rupture (wound) to a paternal (Saturn) figure in a context of attachment (2nd house). In fact, Tom's father was wiped out financially due to an economic recession and a series of bad investments (Saturn in 8th), which left his family destitute (2nd house). The mother became depressed and withdrew from her son, which aggravated Tom's loss of his father. All of this was profoundly wounding, yet it was perfectly symbolized by his chart.

Again, the original trauma occurred during the period that correlated to Tom's 2nd house—2 to 5 years—and it culminated at approximately the time that corresponded to Pluto's natal placement in that house. As his 2nd house started at 3 degrees Leo and ended at 2 degrees Virgo, and Pluto was at 23 degrees Leo, Pluto was about 2/3 of the way into the 2nd house. If the 2nd house represents a period of 3 years beginning at age 2 and ending at 5 years, then Pluto's actual position in the house would be at 3 years—precisely his age when his father left. The pathogenic belief symbolized by Pluto's opposition to Saturn probably formed around this time when Tom's trust in a secure attachment, and faith in his capacity to retain control over his environment, was injured. His primary models in this regard—father and mother—both failed to provide him with the security that he needed.

Later, when Tom grew up and attained mid-life, the consequences of the Taurus stage was revisited, except this time the issue was experienced primarily through Saturn in the 8th. During his Pluto square Pluto transit at 39, his natal Pluto-Saturn opposition was activated, thus stirring up unresolved issues from his toddler years. He suffered deep pangs of inferiority and insecurity during this period, which interfered with age-appropriate developmental tasks such as making his mark financially, attaining economic power, coming to terms with his own mortality, facing his shadow, and going through a death-rebirth process of self-renewal—all 8th house experiences. His anxiety and depression led to underfunctioning on the job and he was subsequently fired. As painful as this event was in itself, his complete "devastation" derived not only from the present experience, but also from the period that correlated to his 2nd house and the pathogenic beliefs that formed during that stage. In other words, memories of that stage were activated in response to the loss of his job, which paralleled the loss of his father at age 3.

The above example illustrates how astrology can be a useful tool for linking the developmental experiences of a later stage to those of a preceding stage (diachronicity). In succeeding chapters, we'll examine this developmental approach more fully.

2. Stress. The body-mind's response to a demand for adaptation is called *stress*, which is an environmental factor of etiological significance in psychopathology. A *stressor* is any situation that calls for adaptation. For example, a man's wife threatens to divorce him if he does not learn to be more considerate; a woman's boss pressures her to sleep with him if she wants to get promoted. Recall that adaptation is the capacity to cope appropriately and effectively with environmental demands. While adaptation requires the ability to adjust to the reality of the external world, this may entail behavior directed at changing or influencing the environment. An adaptive response for the woman in the above example may mean confronting her boss and threatening to sue him for sexual harassment.

A certain amount of stress is necessary for growth. Without stress, people stagnate and atrophy. Too much stress, however, can cause a person to become overwhelmed. Stressors may be acute or chronic, mild or severe. Horowitz (1988) asserts that when a stressor is acute and severe, people generally respond along a continuum of affect states ranging from sadness, fear, and anxiety, to overwhelmed, dazed, and confused. This, in turn, may precipitate a range of affect states—from guilt, rage, shame, or fear, to panic, exhaustion, or dissociative symptoms such as psychic numbing and denial.

If the person is so overwhelmed that the full emotional impact of the experience is denied, a number of related symptoms and defenses will come into play, including repression, minimization, sleep disturbance (too much or too little), depression, substance abuse, reaction formation, or psychosomatic symptoms such as headaches and fatigue. Eventually, this will lead to the return of the repressed: intrusive, unwanted thoughts of the stressor-event accompanied by anxiety, decreased concentration, spacing out, inattention, and/or insomnia during which the person is consumed with thoughts about the event. More serious complications include hypervigilance, paranoia, obsessions, emotional lability (overreactions), symptoms of flight or fight readiness (nausea, sweating), impaired functioning in related tasks, and compulsive re-enactments of the trauma.

If a stressor is chronic, such as a failing marriage or growing up in an alcoholic family, the pressure may be less severe at any one moment; however, chronic stress tends to wear a person down and can lead to a deteriorating mental state in which any of the above symptoms and defenses come into play.

Stress can be symbolized in the astrological chart in any number of ways. In fact, it is not uncommon to hear astrologers talk about "a planet under stress." The most typical symbolization of stress is a hard aspect between two planets, such as a square, quincunx, or opposition, especially if one planet is an inner planet and the other an outer planet. However, there are additional planetary factors that can compound stress. The planet may be: (1) a singleton; (2) the focal point of a T-Square or Yod; (3) located in the 8th or 12th house; (4) located in a sign with which it is incompatible; (5) located in Scorpio or Pisces; (6) located in a house with which it is incompatible; or (7) forming a hard aspect to Saturn. Later, we will explore these factors in greater detail. Suffice to say the more a planet is characterized by the above factors, the more likely it will be involved with stress and potential psychopathology. A planet under optimal stress—not too much, yet not too little—has the best chance of evolving toward its full potential.

The doomed starlet, Marilyn Monroe, exemplifies a situation of too much stress. Marilyn had Saturn in Scorpio in the 4th house, which was the focal planet of a T-Square involving Moon in Aquarius in the 7th opposed

Neptune in Leo in the 1st (see Figure 17, page 226). One could argue whether Saturn or the Moon was under more stress, but it doesn't really matter; the whole configuration is stressful. Additionally, both squares are opening squares, which are Cancerian angles. All of this underscores that the real issue was a Cancer/Moon one, since the Moon not only squares Saturn, but it is an opening (Cancer) square with the added factor of Saturn being in the Moon's house—a house with which it is inherently opposed. Thus, as in the example of Dickens, this aspect can correlate with experiences of emotional deprivation and a general obstruction of lunar needs.

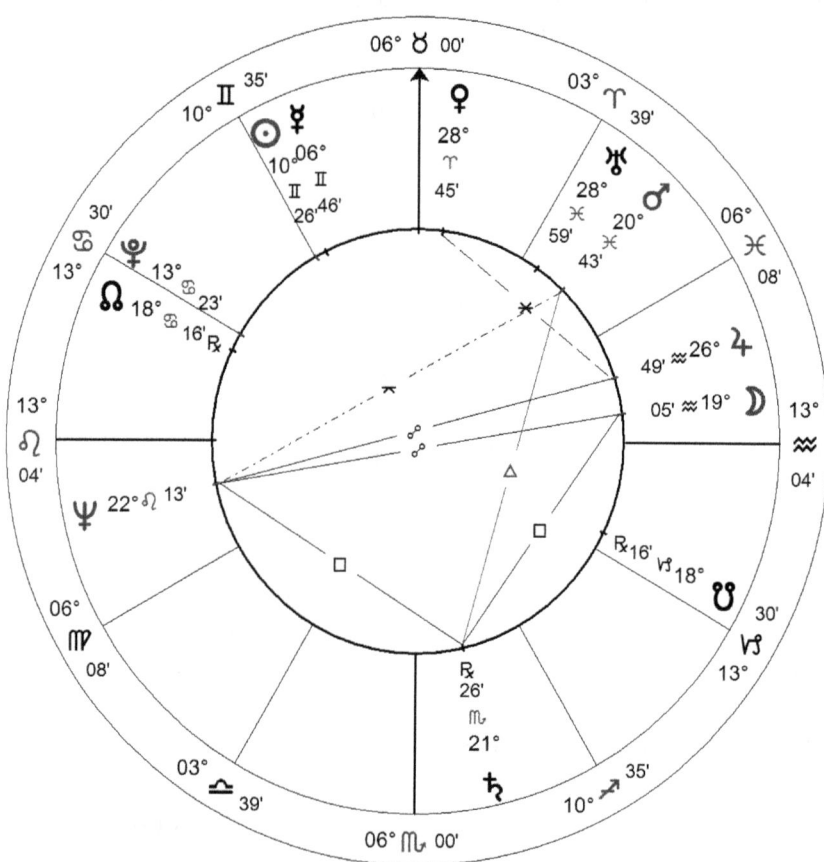

Figure 17: Birthchart of Marilyn Monroe, 6/1/26, 9:30am, Los Angeles, CA

Added to this rather grim scenario is the fact that both planets form a hard aspect to Neptune, which adds a likely dimension of tragedy, loss, confusion, and escapism through drugs or alcohol. Moreover, Moon in

Aquarius constitutes an incompatible placement, since Cancer (which the Moon rules) and Aquarius are naturally quincunx. To compound the problem, the Moon is in the 7th house, with which it is naturally square.[20] In short, we should expect to find substantial difficulty in all matters connected to the Moon and the 4th house—the need for belonging, unconditional love, nurturing, emotional security, close family ties, and the like.

We know that Marilyn was born out of wedlock and that her mother was institutionalized due to schizophrenia when Marilyn was still an infant. This would correlate to the Neptunian factor (☽ ☍ ♆). Marilyn never knew her father, and even after she achieved fame he cruelly rejected her one attempt to contact him. This would correlate to the Neptune square Saturn factor (a missing father). Never feeling that she truly belonged, she grew up unloved and unwanted in a series of foster homes. Throughout her childhood, men molested her and woman abandoned her. Later in life she recalled her childhood, "I knew I belonged to the public and to the world, not because I was talented or even beautiful, but because I had never belonged to anything or anyone else." Yet, despite being loved by millions, and numerous affairs with powerful men (including both Kennedys), Marilyn never achieved any real sense of emotional security.

Her symptoms of stress have been well chronicled in numerous biographies and documentaries. These symptoms included insomnia, depression, substance abuse, fatigue, anxiety, decreased concentration and attention, emotional lability, symptoms of flight or fight readiness, and compulsive re-enactments of the original trauma of sexual abuse and abandonment. In fact, after the Kennedys rejected her and declared her *persona non grata* at the White House—which was perhaps the ultimate, ideal home (♆ ☍ ☽) to which Marilyn aspired but could never attain—she died tragically in her own home of an overdose of sleeping pills, an apparent suicide. All of this illustrates how a planet, i.e., the Moon, can correlate to experiences of stress vis-à-vis those needs and areas of life that the planet rules.

3. Behavioral. Early formulations of behaviorism focused more or less exclusively on how specific environmental factors help to create, shape, or change observable behavior. In regard to psychopathology, the chief focus of behaviorism is whether the client's difficulties are positively reinforced (encouraged) or negatively reinforced (discouraged) by the environment.

---

[20] Compatibility of planetary placement by house is deter-mined by the angular relationship between the sign ruled by the planet and the sign associated with the house the planet tenants. Cancer/Moon and Libra/7th = square.

While astrology does not dispute that the environment can be a powerful force in shaping behavior, an astropsychology perspective would regard such a formulation as incomplete and one-sided. What is missing is how consciousness has a pre-existent organization that selectively attends to certain features in the environment, evokes particular kinds of responses, attributes idiosyncratic meanings to events, and magnetizes specific kinds of experiences that are necessary for the further evolution of that consciousness. All of this would be pre-figured in the chart.

The cognitive-behavioral revolution in psychology moved in this direction, for there was a new emphasis on how habitual thoughts and automatic assumptions are primary determinants of both outer and inner experience (Beck, 1995; McMullin, 1986). Cognitive approaches recognize that environmental factors may initiate the problem, but these experiences become internalized such that a person's subsequent thoughts ultimately provide their own reinforcement and punishment. Accordingly, behaviorism has expanded to consider how thoughts mediate between environment and response.

Astrologically, the relationship between various outer and inner factors is symbolized by planetary configurations. For example, I have a client, Bob, who has Sun in Pisces in the 12th house squaring Saturn in Sagittarius in the 9th. His childhood was marked by a problematic relationship with his father, who was both deaf and a remarkably successful doctor. Bob's father spent most of his time reading or working since his deafness precluded him from activities that he might otherwise have enjoyed with his son, such as bantering, playing, and engaging in a more personal, contactful relationship. Instead, the father's role was reduced to two areas: (1) giving his son tasks to do, and (2) pressuring Bob to measure up to an unrelenting high standard. Not surprisingly, Bob was conditioned to perceive his father (and authority in general) as onerous, demanding, grim, perfectionistic, and no fun. As he matured into adulthood, he found himself resistant to everything associated with authority—ambition, discipline, duty, hard work, perseverance, and so forth. His resultant lack of success aggravated an already low self-esteem and made him vulnerable to depression.

A behavioral formulation would say that Bob's negative attitude toward career was precipitated by a demanding father whom he could never please. Since Bob's experience with his father was not balanced by more enjoyable interactions, he associated his father solely with a suffocating burden of responsibility. By extension, he developed an automatic assumption about any authority figures that he might subsequently encounter in his career—ergo, that (1) he would be weighed down with endless tasks that would totally deprive him of any enjoyment in life; and (2) he would never measure up to their expectations. Bob acted out this belief by working in a lowly job presided over by a perfectionistic boss who relentlessly criticized him.

In short, work for Bob was negatively reinforced. Accordingly, he avoided doing the hard work necessary to advance his career (♄) and sought instead to maximize his enjoyment of life (☉) by dropping out of college, traveling, and procrastinating vis-à-vis everything associated with long-term goals. In so doing, however, he triggered the internalized voice of his father that persecuted him from within. As Bob's self-esteem suffered accordingly, he was frequently depressed. His external conflict with his father had become an internal one.

Thus far the astrological chart is perfectly in accord with the above behavioral formulation. The aforementioned aspect (☉ ♓ 12th □ ♄ ♐ 9th) corresponds to a childhood environment involving a dutiful, workaholic father (☉ □ ♄) who functions in a savior role (☉ ♓) at the hospital where he works (12th house). As someone who is hearing impaired, the father is also suffering and withdrawn (♄ □ ☉ ♓ 12th). There is a conflict (□) between the father's dual role as chief playmate/admirer (☉) and stern taskmaster (♄). Planets in the 12th house often seem to "disappear". In Bob's case, this correlated to a father (☉ 12th) who literally could not hear him; thus, to a large degree, Bob was invisible to his father. His low self-esteem was shaped by a lack of positive reinforcement (play, attention, approval), whereas his attitude toward work was negatively reinforced by an imposition of excessive responsibility

Once Bob's relationship with his father was internalized, it continued even in the father's absence. Thus the same aspect has both an objective and a purely psychological (subjective) meaning. Just as Bob tried to avoid his real father, who attended to his son only when he had a task for him, so Bob avoided his internalized father—the voice in his head that relentlessly pressured him to achieve a superior standard. Thus Bob suffers a psychic split (square): his Sun is operating on the assumption that he can only have fun if he shuns responsibility (Saturn), whereas Saturn believes he can only succeed if he renounces frivolity. So long as Bob remains unconscious of this inner conflict, he will continue to act it out in ways that perpetuate his problems. That is, he'll resist authority, avoid responsibility, retreat into fantasy, and end up relegated to subordinate positions for which he is overqualified. At the same time, he is apt to work *too* hard in a situation that is harshly demanding and inadequately rewarding. Rather than confront the problem with his boss by either (1) standing up for better treatment, or (2) pursuing more satisfying employment, Bob tolerated the situation because it felt familiar and deserved.

From a behaviorist viewpoint, Bob's problems clearly originated in a deficient environment, which he subsequently internalized. If Bob is to resolve his problems, he must disconfirm a network of pathogenic beliefs—that self-enjoyment and self-discipline are mutually exclusive; that duty will predominate over fun; and that he doesn't have the "right stuff" to succeed. Not only does Bob have to disconfirm these beliefs, he has to do it on his own, for until he changes his internal ☉ ☐ ♄ "story" it is unlikely that he will create new experiences with his environment, such as a boss who validates and appreciates him. Bob first has to give to himself what he never got from his father: validation for being a likable and worthy individual, and approval for having the necessary qualities to succeed.

Clearly, astrology can be utilized in a manner that is compatible with a behavioral formulation. However, it goes further in asserting that Bob's challenge constitutes a fate that at a deeper level originates within Bob himself. His experience with his father is not necessarily the true cause of his problems; rather, it is the first and thus prototypical experience of a pattern that precedes his relationship with authority. Moreover, it would be important for Bob to discern the purpose of this fate, for then he could work with it in a conscious, intentional way.

What might be the purpose of such a fate? Admittedly, we are entering speculative territory here, for the question presupposes that there is a purpose behind what the chart presages. From a reincarnationist perspective, the chart symbolizes a karmic inheritance. While there is no way to know specific details about Bob's past lives, we can conjecture that Bob's experience with his father, and his subsequent experiences with other authority figures (bosses, superiors), provide him with an opportunity to develop qualities and resolve problems that constitute unfinished business from a prior existence. Maybe he needs to learn the importance of a balance between work and play. Perhaps he needs to realize that creativity is not mutually exclusive with responsibility. Perhaps, too, Bob needed to experience the pain of insufficient attention and validation from his father in order to understand, at a deep personal level, how profoundly important a father's encouragement and approval can be.

While it is not the focus of this chapter to discuss how such challenges can be met, it is worth noting that Bob developed an avid interest in scuba diving and eventually became an instructor. This is significant in that it actually represents an integrated version of the Sun-Saturn square. His Sun Pisces in the 12th is certainly consistent with scuba diving into the "ocean of the unconscious," as it were.[21] This became an enjoyable and constructive retreat from the pressures of the real world from which Bob wished to escape. By integrating Saturn, he became an authority in precisely this 12th house activity.

More importantly, his job required him to give to his students precisely what he didn't get from his father—a sense of validation and encouragement that they've got the "right stuff" to succeed (in scuba diving).[22] Saturn's location in Sagittarius in the 9th suggests a capacity for developing mastery as an instructor (teacher). Saturn's square to Sun Pisces qualifies what he will teach—in this case, scuba diving, a Pisces/12th house recreational activity. Thus Bob's work (♄) became his play (☉) when he developed his own business as a diving (♓) instructor (♐) for hobbyists who traveled (9th) on vacation with him to various tropical paradises around the world.

4. *Family Systems* is yet another alleged source of psychopathology. General Systems Theory (GST) defines a system as a complex of interacting elements, such as an astrological chart. The psyche, or self-system, is a system made up of planetary functions with relations (aspects) between them. GST holds that one cannot fully understand an individual system without examining the context—the suprasystem—in which the individual system is embedded. Systems, in other words, are hierarchically ordered. Each system contains its own subsystems, while also being a subsystem of a larger (supra) system.

Applied to family therapy, systems theory would describe the family as a system with component subsystems (individuals) that have relationships with one another. At the top of the hierarchy is the family as such. Branching out from the family are its subsystems, comprising mother, father, and one or more children. This final level of the family system constitutes the intrapsychic world of each individual. Each individual is a system in his or her own right and has subsystems made up of planetary (psychic) functions (see Figure 18, page 230).

---

[21] Pisces and the 12th house are associated with the deepest level of the unconscious, which to access requires a willingness to submerge, to delve, to sink into the depths of oneself. Analogously, scuba diving entails a willingness to plunge the depths and submerge one's body into a greater whole—the ocean, which is a common symbol for water sign Pisces.

[22] Note that a karmic debt often requires that we give to others the very thing that we did not receive, i.e., we must give in the area where we were wounded or deprived. This, in effect, is what it means to be a wounded healer.

In GST, all levels and parts of a system are interdependent. For example, what happens to any one person in a family eventually reverberates and affects all the others; no person is an island. Accordingly, intrapsychic disturbances often have their roots in intrafamilial conflicts. A confluence of forces within the family can maintain, exacerbate, or even initiate the mental illness of any one member.

> **Family Suprasystem**
> (all members of family)
>
> **Individual Self-systems**
> (mother, father, child)
>
> **Intrapsychic system of each person**
> (planets in aspect)

Figure 18: The Hierarchical Structure of the Family System

Systems theory implies that what is going on within the self-system reflects what is going on without in the family system. In other words, there is a basic isomorphism—a similarity in form—between the structure of the individual and family psyches. The family is a system comprised of subsystems at lower levels—father, mother, children—all of whom have relationships with one another. Each individual is a subsystem of the larger family system; yet, each individual is also a system that contains its own parts (needs and functions), which have relations (aspects). The systems concept of isomorphy states that analogous structures and processes occur at different levels of a system. For example, a father may be very strict and oppressive toward his children, whereas the mother is permissive. The parents fight over how to raise their kids. This conflict within the family may show up as an intrapsychic conflict within one of the children; one part of the child's psyche is wild and unrestrained, another part feels guilty and fearful. Accordingly, the child's intrapsychic relations are isomorphic with the interpersonal relations of the family.

It follows that these isomorphies will be symbolized by the astrological chart. Because every planetary aspect symbolizes both an intrapsychic and interpersonal relationship, the chart as a whole can symbolize the child's character structure and his experience of the family—the suprasystem in which the child is embedded. Imagine, for example, that a child has a

ASTROLOGY AND THE ORIGINS OF SUFFERING • 231

three-planet aspect involving Mars in Leo, Moon in Aries, and Saturn in Scorpio (see Figure 19). Mars trines the Moon but forms a square to Saturn, which forms a quincunx to the Moon.

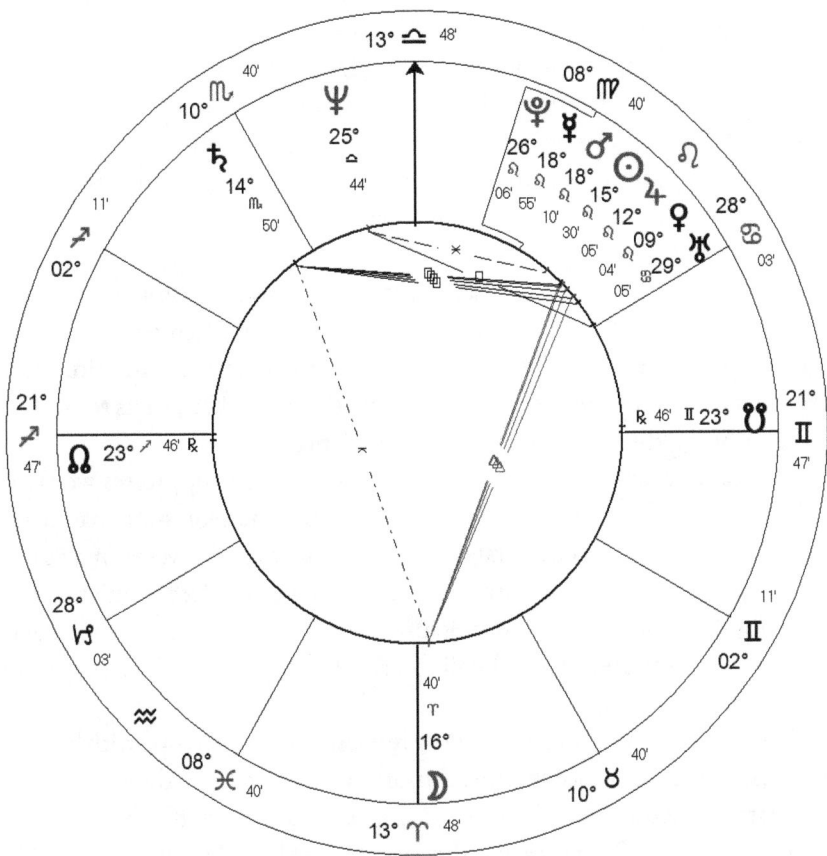

Figure 19: A Systemic Conflict

This configuration describes the child's interpersonal relations with his mother and father *vis-à-vis* his Mars function. If he acts in a spontaneous, impulsive, and assertive manner (Mars), his mother (Moon) encourages him. "Go out and have fun; you're only young once!" The father, however, is neither happy with his son nor his wife. He may restrict his son's freedom with threats of physical punishment (♄ ☐ ♂), and withdraw from his wife in stern disapproval (♄ ⚻ ☽). In fact, this may eventually precipitate a crisis

(⚻) in the parental relationship that derives from their different attitudes toward their son's Mars—trine and square respectfully.[23]

This type of outer, familial experience seems to activate the nascent potential of the child's internal structure as reflected by the horoscope. A psychodynamic formulation would describe it as a process of internalization. That is, the child introjects his experience of mother and father and subsequently develops conflicting beliefs about assertion. While this may be true, the conception misses the pre-existent synchronistic relationship between the child's inner and outer experience. In other words, there is a karmic fate operating here, which has a purpose.

5. *Sociocultural* factors can also contribute to psychopathology. Various social, cultural, political, economic, religious, racial, and gender aspects can all play a pathogenic role. Of course, it is not necessarily the outer situation itself that causes psychopathology, but how the individual reacts to it; that is, the meaning they attribute to their experience.

For example, an individual may live in a society that oppresses woman, such as occurred in Afghanistan under the Taliban. The depression that many Afghan women felt was understandable. One woman, however, may defy her oppressors and look for opportunities to assert her freedom; another, believing she is powerless, may collapse in hopelessness and despair. Each woman's attitude and internal beliefs are a factor in how she experiences her predicament.

The human being is extraordinarily resilient and able to cope with almost any torment, at least potentially. An oft-cited example is the case of the psychiatrist, Victor Frankel, who was imprisoned in Nazi death camps for five years during WWII. During this period Frankel endured unspeakable horror. While many of his fellow Jews struggled to find a reason to live, Frankel survived by attributing a redemptive meaning to his experience.

Aspects between inner and outer planets can symbolize a person's relationship to the larger sociocultural matrix within which his life is embedded. Uranus, Neptune, and Pluto are generational significators; their sign positions describe the cultural zeitgeist of a particular period. If an inner planet is in hard aspect to an outer planet, the function symbolized by the inner planet

---

[23] The fact that the Sun, Jupiter, and Mercury in Leo are all trine the Moon in Aries gives added weight to the "fun/wild" aspect of this chart. Clearly, these fire planets are all in conflict with the restraining, controlling aspect of Saturn. Not surprisingly, this person was later diagnosed with manic-depression.

will in some way conflict with the collective mind-set of the larger culture. Ultimately, this conflict will have to be lived out.

A woman may, for example, have a conjunction between Moon and Venus in Libra with both planets squaring Uranus in Cancer. Accordingly, her way of striving for intimacy (Libra) may conflict with certain cultural changes involving belonging (Cancer). The Uranus in Cancer generation saw the break-up of the nuclear family, followed by a growing reliance upon daycare centers for raising children. In recent decades, this has become increasingly part of the cultural landscape even to the point of normalizing single parenthood.

Imagine that our Moon-Venus square Uranus woman finds herself pregnant and unmarried. She doesn't want to be a single mother that has to work while her child grows up in a daycare center. Yet, her parents are divorced, live in separate states, and have no interest in helping her raise a fatherless child. Her boyfriend fears taking on the responsibility of supporting a wife and raising a family. She is reluctant to have an abortion or give the child up for adoption.

This kind of scenario might typify the aforementioned aspect. Her Moon-Venus wants to be a stay-at-home Mom and raise her children with the support of a loving husband and supportive extended family. Yet, cultural changes that typify Uranus in Cancer—fragmentation of the nuclear family, the collectivization of child rearing, and the normalization of single-parenthood—are experienced in a way that conflicts with her Lunar and Venusian sensibilities.

Another example of socioculturally induced stress involves the legendary German singer-actress, Marlene Dietrich, who has a Sun-Neptune opposition. Outraged by the specter of Nazism, she refused Hitler's 1933 invitation to come to Berlin to be the "queen" of German films. Instead, she fled her homeland and became an American citizen.

Shortly thereafter she joined the war effort against Germany by entertaining Allied troops on front lines throughout Europe, an act that Dietrich regarded as the single most meaningful of her life, and for which she received the U.S. Medal of Freedom, the French Legion of Honor, and the Belgium Knight of the Order of Leopold. Germans, however, viewed her as an unconscionable traitor.

The opposition between Dietrich's Sun and Neptune shows her conflict with German ideals (♆). Her Sun is in Capricorn in the 5th, which symbolizes her desire to perform (☉) a serious (♑) role—that of inspiring the troops (☉ ☍ ♆). Neptune, on the other hand, is in Gemini in the 10th, which symbolizes Germany's transcendent vision (♆) for a new world order as articulated by the government controlled media (Ⅱ) and its support of Hitler's Aryan quest for world domination (10th house). This was the dark dream that Dietrich willfully opposed. Accordingly, her films were banned in Germany during the war and she was savagely attacked in the press. Her expatriation and subsequent vilification were profoundly distressing to Dietrich. Yet, onward she performed, eventually marching with the Allied troops right into Germany to free her mother.

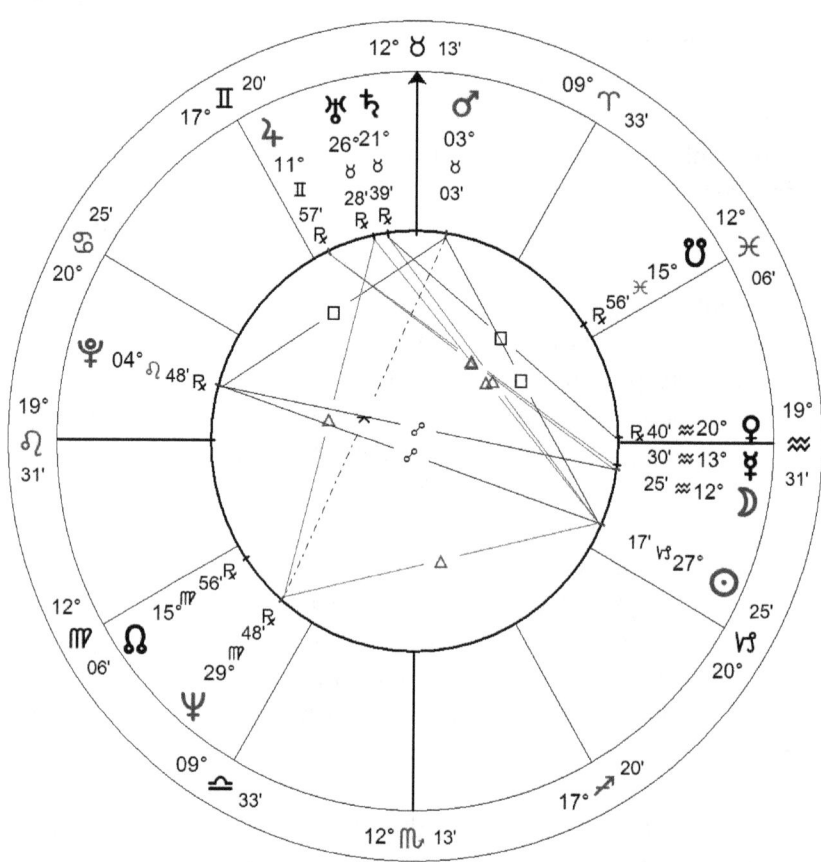

Figure 20: Birthchart of Muhammed Ali, 1/17/42, 6:35pm, Louisville, KY

The life of the boxer, Muhammed Ali, provides a good example of sociocultural stress involving Pluto. Ali's chart reveals a powerful T-Square with Sun opposing Pluto and both planets squaring Mars in Taurus in the 9th (see Figure 20). Pluto can signify the collective shadow in a culture. For many white Americans living in the sixties, the pain and frustration of black Americans was simply outside of their awareness. Racism (and its progenitor, slavery) was America's secret shame, symbolized by Ali's Pluto in Leo in the 12th house. Pluto in Leo suggests a period of transformation of the culture's collective hero-identity (Leo), something that was clearly happening in the turbulent sixties when Ali was fighting the U.S. Government. Of course, Pluto was not in Leo during this period, but it was the Pluto in Leo generation that was fated to ultimately transform the ethnocentricity (Leo) of a culture that was blind to its own shadow—racism.

When the young and newly crowned heavyweight champion, Cassius Clay, joined the black Muslims, changed his named to Muhammed Ali, and refused induction into the military on religious grounds, many Americans were outraged. Ali was widely persecuted, stripped of his crown, and threatened with imprisonment. Yet, we can see a kind of fate operating. With Ali's Sun opposing Pluto and Mars squaring it, the ferocious intensity of his struggle against the national shadow is aptly symbolized. Ali was willing to risk everything—his heavyweight crown and life purpose (Sun), along with his freedom and very survival (Mars)—in an effort to combat what he regarded as a collective evil (Pluto).

Various sociocultural factors during the sixties—political, economic, religious, and racial—placed Ali under tremendous stress. In fact, they nearly destroyed him. The identities and names of blacks abducted from Africa were completely lost as a consequence of slavery; thus, Ali was attempting to recover his identity as "African" by changing to an Islamic name. Islam was the religion of his ancestors, not Christianity. Again, this would be consistent with one meaning of Pluto opposed the Sun—violation and destruction of one's very identity. Ali was willing to die to get it back. It would be easy to understand if he demonstrated symptoms of anxiety, depression, rage, or paranoia during this period. Yet, his life demonstrates how an individual can triumph over adversity by attaining a level of integration and integrity that completely reverses a previous condition. Far from being a symbol of national shame, Ali now symbolizes our national pride.[24]

Muhammad Ali's life throws into relief an important though subtle implication of the perennial wisdom. In this section, we've been considering how a variety of social factors—developmental, stress, behavioral, family systems, and sociocultural—can influence the course of a mental disorder. From a

---

[24] A (2000) film, *Ali*, celebrates the boxer's victory in the United States Supreme Court. Ali was also our country's representative in the lighting of the torch to inaugurate the 1996 Olympics in Atlanta.

strictly scientific (mechanistic) perspective, such factors have no meaning beyond being potential causes of psychopathology. However, in the context of an astropsychologial perspective, the same causes take on a new meaning. The wisdom traditions hold that consciousness is intentional; the soul actively seeks experiences that will enable it to grow toward wholeness. We should not presume, therefore, that negative experience lacks a transcendent purpose or that it is merely punishment for some misdeed in a prior life. Rather, it may be that a certain amount of difficulty and suffering is essential for all human beings, without which our journey toward enlightenment would be stalled in the backwaters of complacency.

SUMMARY & CONCLUSION

Etiology refers to the origins of mental disorders. Causation in astrology can be explained in three different ways: planetary determinism, divine determinism, and self-determinism. Only self-determinism places responsibility for causation within the individual. In addition, it resolves the nature-nurture controversy by showing how both genetic and environmental factors are secondary, derivative causes that are subsumed within a reincarnational framework that places consciousness as causal reality.

Social factors that can influence the course of a mental disorder were divided into five general models—developmental, stress, behavioral, family systems, and sociocultural. Each of these was demonstrated to have astrological correlates. More importantly, each model is provided greater explanatory depth by postulating that external, social conditions are purposive, synchronistic reflections of inborn psychological factors.

Chapter Eight

PLANETARY CONFLICT, DEFENSE AND INTEGRATION

In the previous chapter, we explored the etiology of mental disorders from two complimentary perspectives: (1) reincarnation and its connection to genetic predisposition and inborn character structure; and (2) familial, sociocultural, and other environmental stressors that negatively impact the individual's capacity to satisfy basic needs. The second factor is, in effect, an outgrowth of the first. From a reincarnational perspective, an individual's innate, pre-existent psychic structure generates external circumstances that reflect its degree of integration and, further, provide the impetus for its evolution.

This suggests that we can differentiate the causes of psychopathology into two categories—*primary* and *secondary*. Primary causes are those that originate within the individual, and secondary causes refer to environmental stressors. Primary and secondary causes are equally symbolized in the birth chart since the same chart variables reflect both subjective and objective conditions. Note I am not referring to genetic/physiological factors as secondary causes, since if one accepts the perennial assertion that consciousness predominates over matter, there is no need to differentiate psychic structure from genetic structure so far as causes are concerned. All physical processes *embody* consciousness. As Teilhard de Chardin put it, "Matter is spirit moving slowly enough to be seen." Alleged body-mind dualisms constitute a false dichotomy. Karmic tendencies from a prior life, genetic predisposition, or current psychodynamics are all variations on the same principle: the primary cause of psychopathology resides within the person.

If primary causes are inherently internal, secondary causes are inherently external; that is, secondary causes derive from primary causes and manifest as events and relationships that the individual is fated to experience. Fate is a vehicle for the unfoldment of character. Just as character is symbolized in the birth chart, so, too, is the fate that flows from this character. For every piece of psychic structure, there is a corollary event, situation, or relationship.

ETIOLOGY

Etiology primarily refers to the origins of a disorder. These include outer, historical events and circumstances that overwhelm the individual's capacity to adapt—in other words, secondary causes—as well as *pathogenesis*, or primary causes, which constitute all those processes within an individual that produce and maintain psychopathology.

Etiology can be delineated into four levels that include both primary and secondary causes:

1. Predisposition (primary cause)
2. Initiation (secondary cause)
3. Perpetuation (primary cause)
4. Exacerbation (secondary cause)

While an environmental condition may activate an innate propensity (predisposition) toward a mental disorder, and therefore can be regarded as an initiating factor, what initiates a disorder usually differs from what perpetuates or exacerbates it.

A *predisposition* is a latent susceptibility to a disorder, which may be activated under stressful conditions. Almost invariably this is reflected in the birth chart by a particular configuration. Sun square Neptune, for example, can manifest as a susceptibility to Narcissistic Personality Disorder. Neptune often requires that the Sun/Ego sacrifice its need for recognition and self-importance. Since this natal aspect is operative from birth, it constitutes an innate predisposition to feel unworthy, unimportant, or unappreciated, which is precisely the condition that underlies narcissistic disorder. Narcissistic traits of grandiosity, self-importance, and pathological feelings of entitlement are compensatory to a weak, confused, and empty sense of self.

For this condition to be fully activated, however, requires an *initiating* event or pattern of events. Here astrology shows its diagnostic flexibility, for the same aspect that symbolizes a predisposing condition also symbolizes an initiating condition. Sun square Neptune, for instance, can symbolize a child's relationship with a narcissistic father. Consider, for example, that a boy with Sun square Neptune has a father that does not recognize or validate his individuality, but instead appropriates the child to enhance his own self-esteem. Accordingly, the boy's latent susceptibility toward self-doubt and unworthiness will be activated by his father's failure to recognize him as a separate individual in his own right. He may eventually compensate his father's neglect by exaggerating his worth through various forms of self-aggrandizement—bragging, posturing, grandiosity, and other ploys for attention typical of narcissism. The point is: the childhood environment initiates a predisposition toward the disorder.

What initiates a disorder is different from what perpetuates it. Frustration of the need for self-esteem (Leo/Sun) eventually gives rise to pathogenic beliefs that predict that expressions of this need will result in pain and/or danger. Such a deep-seated, unconscious belief operates like a self-fulfilling prophecy. If our Sun-Neptune man unconsciously expects that his value will be discounted, he may overcompensate by tooting his horn too often and too loudly. Yet, the more egocentric, obnoxious, and demanding he becomes, the more people turn off to him; thus, his worst fears—that he'll be ignored—are confirmed. His behavioral strategy both reflects and perpetuates his disorder.

Sometimes situations occur that can *exacerbate* a disorder. Imagine, for instance, that a woman with Sun square Neptune joins a college sorority in which some of the girls are invited to be "little sisters" of a male fraternity, a prestigious honor that confirms one's good social standing. Yet, with transiting Saturn opposing her Sun and squaring her Neptune, she is passed over.[25] This event constitutes a narcissistic wound and reinforces her inner image of unworthiness, which, in turn, gives rise to feelings of acute envy and hostility. She may subsequently act out these feelings through an assortment of obnoxious behaviors that offend her peers and deepen her sense of alienation and rejection. Thus a vicious cycle ensues that actually serves to exacerbate her disorder.[26]

---

[25] As mentioned in Chapter 5, a difficult transit to a sensitive natal configuration may correspond to an acute episode of the disorder that is immanent and potentiated by that natal configuration. Usually, such transits will correlate to social stressors that activate and exacerbate the natal situation.

[26] This type of experience typifies a certain percentage, though certainly not all, individuals with Sun square Neptune. The life stories of Dorothy Dandridge, Dylan Klebold, Douglas McArthur, "Neon" Deion Sanders, and Howard Stern all exemplify this pattern to lesser or greater degrees.

INHERENT AND CONSEQUENTIAL FACTORS

Astrologers should also distinguish what is inherent to a disorder from what is a consequence of it. An inherent quality is an essential constituent of a disorder that is the same in all cases. A consequence, however, is not inherent, but derives from an individual's capacity to integrate, manage, and express the conflicting functions that underlay the disorder. The same principle applies to aspects. For example, an opposition between two planets symbolizes a conflict between two antithetical needs and functions. Tension and conflict is inherent within the aspect. However, there are a variety of ways this conflict might be handled, each of which is likely to produce different consequences. In effect, behavioral and experiential manifestations are not inherent in the nature of an aspect, or a disorder, but are rather a consequence of the way the aspect/disorder has been managed and expressed.

There are at least three levels of interpretation implied in the above: (1) the archetypal core processes symbolized by the planets, signs, and houses that make up the aspect; (2) the lived experience that emerges from this archetypal level; and (3) the meaning that the individual creates from his or her lived experience. This final level of meaning-making entails making predictions as to what is likely to occur from future expression of the planets in question. These predictions derive from core convictions, or *stories*, which are constructed by the individual and determine his or her subsequent behavior. Behavior, in turn, influences subsequent experience and so on in an iterative cycle. Again, the meaning that one attributes to experience is not inherent to the nature of an aspect. As such, it cannot be predicted on the basis of the chart; yet, it may be the most important dimension so far as determining how the aspect is expressed and experienced over time.

Consider, for example, an opposition between Sun and Pluto. Inherent to this aspect is a conflict between the need for validation (Leo) and the need for death/rebirth (Scorpio). The aspect suggests that one's will (Sun) is at odds with the chthonic powers of the underworld (Pluto) that seek transformation and renewal. Because Pluto wants to tear down and reform what the Sun wants to defend and build-up (self-image), this aspect can correlate to Paranoid Personality Disorder, or simply paranoid traits. Intrinsic to the aspect could be a conviction that it is risky to express oneself and that efforts to be authentic might trigger animosity in others. Knowing this, however, does not tell us anything about how the individual manages this inherent conflict. Accordingly, one cannot predict the aspect's behavioral and experiential consequences except to say that whatever happens will fall within the range of possibilities indicated by the planets and angles in question.

By way of illustration, two famous people, Dorothy Stratten and Ricardo Ramirez, were both born on February 28, 1960. Both have Sun in Pisces in opposition to Pluto in Virgo.[27] Stratten, a playboy centerfold and Hollywood starlet, was brutally murdered at the age of 20 by her estranged husband, Paul Snider. She was described by those who knew her as "angelic, sweet, innocent, and pure"—all distinctly non-Plutonic qualities. Stratten seems to have managed her opposition by projecting its dark half onto Snider, who by all accounts was a thoroughly reprehensible character—a "pimp" who was obsessed with the money and status he could gain from Dorothy's career. His one attempt to make money independent of Dorothy involved the creation of a bondage bench for sadomasochistic sex, which he attempted to market. According to reports, Snider was a virtual embodiment of Pluto. He controlled and exploited Stratten, poisoned her dog out of jealousy, stalked her when she tried to leave him, strapped her to his bondage bench during their final encounter, and murdered her with a shotgun blast to the head.

What Snider did to Stratten, Ricardo Ramirez, alias "the night stalker," did to some twenty or more victims during a killing rampage that spread between the summers of 1984-85. Ramirez was described as the personification of Satan and an alleged devil worshiper. He stalked his victims, overpowered them, then raped, sodomized, and killed them. Whereas Stratten was a victim of a sexually crazed murderer who stalked her, Ramirez was a sexually crazed murderer that stalked his victims. It is rather chilling that these two individuals were born on the same day. Their stories are similar save for one important difference: Stratten projected her Pluto; Ramirez identified with it.

We can speculate that at some point in her life Stratten decided that real power was outside and could be attracted and harnessed only through partnership. In other words, Stratten disidentified with her Plutonic potentials; whatever was bad, or powerful, or dangerous, was in other people, not her. When oppositions remain unintegrated, however, the disowned planet can come back with a vengeance, as it did in the person of her husband, Paul Snider.

Ramirez, on the other hand, was in and out of juvenile detention centers most of his life before ending up on death row in San Quentin at age 25. We can speculate that some sort of abuse might have occurred to Ramirez that was consistent with the nature of his Sun-Pluto opposition. Research indicates that sex offenders are re-enacting a situation in which they were once

---

[27] Stratten was born February 28, 1960, 10:58pm in Vancouver, Canada. Ramirez was born February 28th, 1960, 2:07am in El Paso, TX.

themselves victims. Perpetrators almost universally report having been sexually, physically, or emotionally abused as children. Carnes (1983) puts the figure at 97%. Perhaps Ramirez was shamed, raped, or otherwise humiliated during his gang experiences growing up in the barrio of El Paso, Texas, or perhaps he was sodomized during one of his sojourns in jail. Whatever happened, Ramirez must have responded to his experience by identifying with it; thus, rather than projecting badness outward, as Stratten did, Ramirez collapsed into his bad experiences and became them. He no longer waited for others to plutonize him. Instead, he did it to them first—that is, attack, degrade, humiliate, overpower, and destroy. Geringer (2001) describes him thusly:

> He had but three interests in junior high and cared about little else—martial arts, marijuana and heavy metal. "He loved Black Sabbath and Judas Priest," remarks a friend from his teen years. Another interest grew from the sort of music he listened to—that which glorified cultist practices. He seemed preoccupied with Satanism and stories about black magic, demons and dragons. While his mother sent him to Bible studies, hoping he'd learn the Christian ways of life, Richard took the lessons to heart, but learned them in reverse. That is, after class he would go to the library and read up on Satan and the fallen angels, the characters that his teachers merely skipped over while exemplifying Jesus Christ and the twelve apostles. (p. 1)

The twin cases of Dorothy Stratten and Ricardo Ramirez underscore why it is important to distinguish what is inherent to an aspect from what is a consequence of it. Both Stratten and Ramirez were fated to experience an inherent conflict between their need for self-expression and their need for death-rebirth, or transformation. Stratten made decisions that resulted in her attracting Plutonic experiences via her partner that were ultimately disempowering and destructive. Ramirez made decisions that overpowered and destroyed others. Clearly, their joint experiences of sex, power, and evil were a *consequence* of how they managed their Sun-Pluto oppositions. However, neither person's experience was inherent to the aspect. In fact, there are many, constructive ways to express the aspect that neither Stratten nor Ramirez were able to achieve. To appreciate this, we need to revisit the concepts of displacement and sublimation, which were introduced in Chapter Two.

Recall that displacement refers to a defensive maneuver wherein the interest or intensity attached to one idea, or behavior, is shifted to another idea or behavior that is associatively related but more acceptable to the ego. Displacement underscores how the consequences of an aspect can manifest in diverse ways. Each expression of an aspect is consistent with the inherent meaning of that aspect, though manifestations may evolve toward more integrated, acceptable versions over time. When planetary energies are displaced from more primitive, destructive forms to more evolved, constructive, and culturally useful ones, then sublimation has occurred. The same aspect has manifested in the form of a higher, more socially valued accomplishment.

With regard to Sun-Pluto oppositions, examples of sublimation abound. Muhammed Ali has already been mentioned, but there is also Theodore Roosevelt, hero of the Spanish-American War and 26th President of the United States. Roosevelt's administration was marked by the regulation of trusts (a Plutocratic phenomenon)[28], reformist policies, and a foreign policy based on the motto "Speak softly and carry a big stick"—in other words, *be respectful but assert your power*. Authors Mary Shelly and Peter Blatty both wrote best selling books, Frankenstein and The Exorcist, which featured characters that embodied death and evil (Monster & Devil). Likewise, Goethe (who has the square), in his famous work, Faust, depicted a magician who makes a deal with the devil, Mephistopheles. In each of these creative works, evil/death/devil has to be faced and overcome.

Another sublimated version of a Sun-Pluto opposition was the philosopher, Friedrich Nietzsche, who asserted that a fear of death was implicit in Christianity's emphasis on the afterlife. According to Nietzsche, a religiously conditioned fear of hellfire and damnation made believers less able to cope with earthly life. Nietzsche argued that the ideal human being would be able to channel passions (Pluto) creatively (Sun) instead of suppressing them. This is an admirably concise description of a Sun-Pluto sublimation.

Nietzsche's written works include *Beyond Good and Evil* (1886), a title eerily echoed 100 years later by Ricardo Ramirez on the day of his sentencing, "You maggots make me sick," he cursed the jury, "one and all…I am beyond your experience, I am beyond good and evil" (Linedecker, 1991). Needless to say, Ramirez, unlike Nietzsche, did not sublimate his Sun-Pluto passions into creative and culturally useful ends. Still, his Nietzschean utterance of

---

[28] A trust is a combination of firms or corporations for the purpose of reducing competition and controlling prices throughout a business or an industry. Such abuse of plutocratic power, widespread at the turn of the century, was precisely what Roosevelt challenged and defeated.

being "beyond good and evil" reminds us how an aspect can be expressed in forms that are both similar and radically different at the same time.

NECESSARY AND SUFFICIENT CAUSES

In astrology as in psychology, causes of psychopathology can be categorized as: (a) necessary and sufficient; (b) necessary but not sufficient; and (c) facilitating or predisposing but neither necessary nor sufficient. Few diseases have causes that are both necessary and sufficient. This would require that a single factor, such as an errant gene, is both necessary and sufficient to cause the condition.

Alcoholism illustrates the second type. Alcohol is necessary to become an alcoholic, but is not sufficient to cause the condition, since many people drink without becoming alcoholic. Most causes fall into the third category of facilitating or predisposing but neither necessary nor sufficient. For example, loss of parents during childhood can be a contributing factor to most mental disorders, even though such a loss is neither necessary nor sufficient to produce any of them.

Probably all astrological configurations can be understood as facilitating and predisposing causes. For example, Moon square Uranus may predispose one to schizoid disorder, but is not sufficient by itself to cause this condition. In fact, there is probably not a single astrological factor that is necessary and sufficient to a particular outcome. One cannot say, "If you have this aspect, you will have this personality disorder or experience this particular outcome." At best, we can predict with relative certainty that a particular process or conflict will be inherent in the person. How they express it behaviorally and how it manifests externally is going to vary within a range of possible outcomes.

While a planetary aspect can symbolize a contributing dynamic to an existing condition, it is never in itself a determining factor; that is, a single aspect is unlikely to be the sole corollary to a mental disorder. There are always multiple, contributing streams to what ultimately emerges in character and in fate. That is why it is critically important to see any part of the chart as polyvalent, capable of manifesting in a wide variety of ways depending upon the nature of the whole of which it is a part, and the relative integration of that whole (psyche).

INTRAPSYCHIC CONFLICT

We have seen how claims that psychopathology originates in outer, historical events are necessarily speculative. However, we are on even more uncertain ground when considering the pathogenesis of mental disorders. Pathogenesis, again, constitutes all those processes within an individual that produce and maintain psychopathology. Whereas secondary causes can be observed in external conditions, primary causes—pathogenesis—must be inferred since they necessarily reside within the psyche itself.

In terms of the ultimate origins of psychopathology, it may be that we need look no further than the structure of the individual's psyche. The essence of psychopathology is intrapsychic conflict, and conflict is inherent in the psyche. To the extent that opposing forces are brought into balance, the individual's capacity to satisfy basic needs is enriched. Unresolved conflicts, however, produce a variety of adaptational maneuvers and defense mechanisms that compromise functioning and weaken the individual's capacity to satisfy basic needs.

Intrapsychic conflict refers to the struggle among incompatible forces or structures within the psyche. Freud was the first theoretician to emphasize the importance of conflicting internal forces. Conflict can be analyzed in terms of states of mind. Wishes are desired states of mind and fears are dreaded ones—sadness, pain, shame, or guilt. The mind anticipates future possible states that may result from attempts to gratify needs. Anticipation of negative outcomes can lead to the employment of defenses against resultant dreaded states of mind. This is what produces compromise states, which are likely to arise when attempts to achieve a desired state could have negative consequences. If the anticipated risk is too great, the person will ward off both desired and dreaded states by maintaining a compromised level of experience and style of behavior.

In psychoanalytic theory, conflict occurs when instinctual wishes come into conflict with internal or external prohibitions. The ego is threatened and produces signal anxiety (a negative feeling such as fear or guilt), which is accompanied by a fantasy of an unwanted consequence in which either the self or a loved one is hurt. In other words, the anticipated undesirable outcome—the dreaded state—is believed to be a likely consequence of pursuing some basic need. In response to signal anxiety, the ego's defenses are mobilized, and the conflict is resolved via compromise formations that show up in symptoms and signs, character changes, or adaptation.

Compromise formations can be adaptive if the behavioral strategy actually leads to satisfaction of needs that were previously in conflict. However, if the compromise formation produces undesirable consequences (symptoms and signs of pathology), or allows for the satisfaction of one need at the expense of the other, or allows for only a partial satisfaction of needs, then the strategy is maladaptive.

An intrapsychic conflict may show up initially in terms of an external conflict; that is, one that is between the individual and some aspect of the outside world. Conflict develops within the child as a consequence of (1) a wish for a desired state; and (2) a fear of the dreaded consequence that results from attempts to attain the desired state. For example, when environmental forces, such as a punitive father, oppose the child's aggressive drive, resolution of this external conflict becomes internalized. The child identifies with the parental prohibition; thus, it becomes an aspect of his own conscience. What Freud called the superego develops as a force within the psyche in opposition to his aggressive impulses. Astrologically, this generic intrapsychic dynamic is depicted by the square between Aries and Capricorn in the natural zodiac.

In the early days of psychoanalysis, the so-called "Oedipal conflict" was generally regarded as the core conflict in the human condition. It entailed the child's wish to possess the opposite sexed parent combined with a fear of injury (castration) as a consequence of the same sex parent's retaliation. In effect, the child thinks, "If I possess Mommy for myself, Daddy will cut my penis off." We now recognize, however, that Freud was obsessed with this conflict precisely because it was central to his own psychology (Atwood and Stolorow, 1993).[29] In fact, there are many types of conflict to which the human psyche is subject. There is no single or uniform cause at the root of psychopathology.

Maslow (1968) reminds us that human behavior is governed largely by basic needs, such as the need for survival, security, belonging, and self-esteem. These needs motivate the individual to behave in ways that provide for the satisfaction of these needs. If basic needs are not satisfied, says Maslow, sickness results. Just as an organism has physical needs for food, water, oxygen, and the like, so it has needs that are purely psychological. Psychopathology is "deficiency based" in the sense that whatever compromises the wholeness of the psyche causes distress and impairment. We know this intuitively, as expressed in such statements as, "he's not playing with a full deck," or "she's missing a few marbles."

---

[29] In chapter 1, Freud's castration anxiety was discussed in terms of his Mar–Saturn square, which recapitulates the Aries-Capricorn square of the natural zodiac. His erotic overinvolvement with his mother would seem to correlate with his Moon in the 8th square Neptune in the 4th.

As a child grows it learns which thoughts, feelings, and behaviors are met with approval and which are not. Because all behavior is in the service of underlying psychological needs, those behaviors that evoke parental disapproval tend to result in repression of the needs that motivate them. For example, if a child's spontaneity (Mars) is threatening to Mother (Moon), who reacts in a hurt, punitive, or rejecting manner whenever the child asserts, the child may associate spontaneity with harming the mother and subsequent punishment.

In this scenario, it is likely that all Mars impulses and feelings (autonomy, assertion, aliveness) will come to be regarded as dangerous and incompatible with the need for closeness and belonging (Moon). Feeling guilty for behavior that the child believes is threatening to his mother, the underlying drive for autonomy is repressed. The self-concept emerges from such processes and constitutes that portion of the total experiencing organism available to consciousness. The individual identifies with certain parental values and develops various ideas that permit only the expression of impulses that are likely to be accepted. In this case, a positive self-image may necessitate repudiation of Martian impulses.

A compromise formation might entail only allowing oneself to be aggressive when protecting loved ones. When engaged in the care of someone or something, the person is fiercely loyal and ready to fight against any perceived threat. Otherwise, he may alternate between repressing either his urge for autonomy (Mars) or his need for dependency (Moon). Depending upon which side is most repressed, certain moods will arise that are leakages of unwanted emotions or needs. When close (Moon), he may feel irritable (Mars), yet not know why. When acting independently (Mars), he may worry that he is neglecting loved ones (Moon). Various compromises will be attempted to satisfy both sides and reduce his anxiety, irritability, and guilt.

Let us consider another example, a conflict between Mars and Saturn. If a person anticipates that expression of his aggressive impulses (Mars) could result in retaliation by a more powerful entity (Saturn), the individual may compromise by developing a passive-aggressive style of behavior. The desired state, satisfaction of the aggressive aim, and the dreaded state, humiliating subjugation, are both avoided by indirectly expressing aggression. For example, he defies authority by appearing to forget something. This apparently innocent mistake, however, frustrates the aims of the dominant other (Saturn) and indirectly expresses aggression (Mars).

SINS OF OMISSION & COMMISSION

Disapproval can be communicated to a child in many ways. Roughly speaking there are "sins" of **commission** and sins of **omission**. Any caretaker can be implicated in such sins—sibling, parent, grandparent, aunt/uncle, babysitter, coach, or teacher—so long as that person has a significant relationship with the child. The greater the involvement, the more important the relationship.

Sins of **commission** involve overt acts that are excessive and in some way destructive to the child. These include harsh and relentless criticism, shaming, rejection, verbal or physical abuse, intrusion, rape, molestation, and other acts that overwhelm the child's capacity to adapt. Sins of commission are always damaging to the child's capacity to meet one or more needs—for survival, security, learning, belonging, self-esteem, competence, and so on. In each instance, the act carries a message that is devaluing, such as "you're incompetent" (criticism), "you're disgusting" (shaming), "I don't love you" (rejection), "I don't care how you feel" (abuse), and so on. Eventually, these messages are internalized so that they become part of the child's self-concept. To the extent that such ideas are too painful and overwhelming for the child to admit on a conscious level, they are repressed into the unconscious. Here, they reside as grim, pathogenic beliefs that predict harm to one's self or others whenever one strives to satisfy the relevant need.

For example, if a child tries to help his father with a task, and the father criticizes the child harshly and tells him to go away, the message is: "You're incompetent and I don't want you around." If this sort of thing occurs again and again, eventually the child will come to believe, "My need to be useful (Virgo) results in distress and pain." A Square involving Saturn and Mercury (or the Sun) might symbolize this astrologically.

Sins of **omission** entail a lack of support or modeling for certain functions. Very often what frustrates a child's need is not what *is* done, but what is *not* done. Many children grow up in environments that are markedly deficient in some way. There may be a pervasive disregard for the child's interests, or an inability to meet his or her needs. This might manifest as a chronic lack of approval, attention, support, encouragement, validation, caring, stability, structure, limits, or affection. Sometimes parents are too narcissistic, wounded, sick, alcoholic, disabled, handicapped, missing, overwhelmed, or busy to provide children with what they need. Parental deficiencies also prevent them from modeling healthy behavior for the child.

Neglect and abandonment are typical sins of omission and may be experienced in relation to any need. If a basic need is consistently frustrated, the child may conclude that need is excessive, unwarranted, or simply "bad".

Again, this may be too painful to admit on a conscious level, so the conviction is repressed and becomes a grim, pathogenic belief that influences behavior from an unconscious level. The child avoids expression of the need (planetary function) without being aware s/he is avoiding it.

The need, however, does not go away, but continues to press for fulfillment from an unconscious level. Dysfunctional behavior can be traced to a basic incongruence between self-concept and the experiencings of the total organism. Impulses that are discrepant with the way the person believes himself to be (or should be) are likely to be distorted or otherwise denied to awareness.

For example, if a boy has Sun square Uranus, he may grow up feeling that he is not particularly important. Perhaps his father is neglectful as a consequence of the father's involvement with an important cause. If the boy presses for attention (Sun), it may be responded to with cold indifference (Uranus). Consequently, the boy may try harder to gain attention, perhaps by acting out his attention-seeking impulses in a flagrant, obnoxious manner, thus assuring a punitive response. Fearing further punishment and pain, the desire for validation is subsequently repressed. However, while it may be down, it is not out. Eventually the boy may hit upon the strategy of behaving as if he does not care what other people think; he behaves oddly and unpredictably, constantly changing his style of presentation. This compromise formation partially satisfies his need for attention (Sun), while also expressing a radical detachment and flaunting of convention (Uranus). The outrageous and eccentric Dennis Rodman, former pro-basketball player and sometime actor, typifies this strategy.[30]

In short, psychopathology has its origins in repression, which derives from perceptions that certain impulses are either forbidden or futile within the family to which one belongs. If a basic need was denied satisfaction in childhood, for whatever reason, then the dissatisfaction of this need is going to register as pain. This pain is defended against by relegating the offending impulse into the unconscious where it will hopefully do no further harm. Yet, it does do harm, for if a need/function is not regulated on a conscious level, then it is apt to be expressed in a manner that is archaic, unregulated, and dysfunctional.

Repression is ultimately pathogenic because it drains the psyche of energy and weakens the overall integrity of the self-system. On a conscious level, the

---

[30] For a more detailed analysis of Rodman's Sun square Uranus, see my book, *From Royalty to Revolution*, Chapter 3, pp. 34-35.

individual professes to be a certain way, but unconsciously the denied impulse is struggling to break free by pushing against and threatening the functioning of whatever has taken its place. Repression is analogous to holding a beach ball under water; it requires force. Yet, pressure from below causes unconscious perception of anticipated danger (signal anxiety), which leads to the use of defense mechanisms that result in various types of mental disorders. The mind is disordered precisely because the order that would otherwise result from a proper balance of psychological functions has been thrown out of balance. This is evident in the tendency for dysfunctional behavior to be characterized by extreme emotional states—obsessive preoccupation, reactive anger, anxiety, antagonism, fearful resistance, harsh judgments, and other affective responses out of proportion to the situation.

CONFLICTING BELIEFS

Repression derives from a conviction that some kind of negative outcome will inevitably follow expression of the feared impulse. The belief holds the conflict in place, even though the belief may be unconscious and instinctive. For example, someone with an opening square between the Sun and Jupiter might unconsciously believe that conformity to moral postulates (Jupiter) is antithetical to self-enjoyment (Sun). Personal preferences might conflict with what is good and right for the community at large.

In the cult film, *Footloose* (1984), a city teenager moves to a small town in the Midwest where rock music and dancing have been banned. His solar impulses (for performance, romance, and play) initially require him to repress his Jupiterian impulse to behave morally. In so doing, however, he experiences guilt and a fear that unbridled self-enjoyment is ultimately uncaring and insensitive (opening square) in that it entails a failure to "do the right thing" and may result in his rejection by the community. How he resolves the conflict is the basis of the film.

Anyone with Sun square Jupiter may find himself periodically possessed by a moralistic impulse with which he gets carried away. He becomes hyper-moral, judgmental, and self-righteous, which contradicts his usual self-serving behavior. If this becomes a habit, he will be possessed periodically by his solar needs. They might erupt in flagrant self-centeredness and intemperance, which contradicts his customary ethical behavior. Either way, the likelihood of hypocrisy is great. The individual will seem to be inhabited by separate belief-systems that are mutually exclusive.

Kelly (1955) pointed out it is more or less normal to hold contradictory beliefs. The process of integration, which leads to integrity, is a matter of reconciling mutually exclusive constructs into a higher order unity. Most of us are internally fragmented to varying degrees. The challenge is working toward greater internal consistency. This means integrating our various roles and functions at a higher level where they become complementary and mutually enriching.

Ultimately, the solution to a Sun-Jupiter conflict will require some sort of compromise, for both the Sun and Jupiter will continue to exert a pressure upon the psyche. One way or the other, both impulses have to be expressed. Again, in psychoanalytic theory, character traits that emerge from such an attempt at integration constitute "compromise formations," which can be adaptive or maladaptive depending upon the degree of integration of the respective functions.

For example, I had a client with an opening square between Jupiter in the 10th and the Sun in the 12th. She ended up working as a counselor at a camp for troubled teens with drug and alcohol problems. The structure of the camp combined Jupiter and solar functions into a mix that was ultimately supportive for the adolescents that lived there. A Jupiterian focus on values clarification and moral guidance helped teens develop sound ethical principles (many of them had been in trouble with the legal system). At the same time, it was a camp, a solar "place" for having fun, recreation, and opportunities for theatrical performance and creative self-expression. The opening square (Cancer angle) was evident in the camp's function as a container, or home, for nurturing moral strength and self-esteem. It was also a retreat for reflection, contemplation, and recovery from substance abuse, which is a standard meaning of the 12th house.

My client's employment at this camp actually provided her with a vehicle for integrating her Sun-Jupiter opening square. The nature of the camp and the teens that lived there was a synchronistic reflection of her own internal struggle. Her job as a teen counselor required her to integrate conflicting impulses and arrive at a compromise formation that expressed the best of both planetary functions. Ultimately, she modeled for them how to successfully embody a Sun-Jupiter square—that is, to have fun and do the right thing, to be creative and wise, playful and righteous.

INTRAPSYCHIC CONFLICT IN THE ZODIAC

Astrology underscores that there is no single or uniform cause at the root of psychopathology. This is especially apparent when we consider intrapsychic conflict from the perspective of the zodiac, which depicts the psyche as comprised of twelve fundamental needs, or drives. As symbols of these drives, signs have specific relations with one another on the basis of their position in the zodiac. Intrapsychic relations can be conceptualized in terms of polarity, element, modality, and perspective. Because every yang sign is in conflict with every yin sign (by ⚻, □, or ⚻) in addition to every sign being in conflict with its opposite sign of the same polarity (by ☍), the number and types of intrapsychic conflicts is legion. In fact, there are forty-two different types of conflict implicit in the zodiac alone, whereas only 24 harmonious connections (✶ and △). These generic archetypal conflicts can be further compounded by aspects and combinations of aspects, such as T-squares and Yods, which involve endless variations of planets, signs, and houses. In comparison to such richly textured, multi-layered complexity, conventional models of psychodynamic conflict are misleadingly simplistic.

By examining the relationship of various signs, one can determine the type and degree of conflict. Type of conflict between signs is reflected in the nature of the angle between them—square, quincunx, or opposition—whereas the degree of a conflict can be measured in terms of polarity, modality, element, and perspective. The fewer factors two signs have in common, the more severe the conflict. The opposition constitutes the bare minimum of conflict, for the signs involved are of the same polarity and modality. Squares are moderately conflictual because they involve signs that have nothing in common except modality. Quincunxes constitute maximum or severe conflict because there is literally nothing in common between the signs. They differ in polarity, modality, element, and perspective. So, angles between signs tell us both the type of conflict (☍, □, or ⚻), and its degree (minimum, moderate, or severe). Hard planetary aspects highlight these innate, intrapsychic conflicts. For with each hard aspect, the planets occupy signs that naturally clash.

The conjunction can sometimes be considered a hard aspect, even though it is generally between planets that are in the same sign. The specific nature and meaning of a conflict is implicit in the sign to which an aspect corresponds in the natural zodiac. The conjunction, which has an Aries quality, can be the conflict of no-conflict. That is, sometimes it is the absence of conflict that produces a problem. Conjuncting planets have a tendency to act rudely, aggressively, or offensively precisely because there is insufficient restraint and awareness of others. If there are inadequate controls on two planets, they are apt to embolden one another in ways that cause impulsivity and insensitivity. The rest of the personality may be forced to compensate and correct for the excesses of the conjunction.

Conversely, yin angles, like the square and quincunx, have an innately restraining quality. This is because their corollary yin signs are naturally suppressive. An opening square between two planets, for example, will have a Cancer quality. There is an inhibited, suppressed relationship between the two planets, like a pressure cooker. Certain types of Cancerian themes will be evident in the way the planets interact and struggle to integrate. Consider the basic need of Cancer, which is for closeness and belonging, along with its corollary functions of caring, nurturing, and protecting. Stated in the reverse, Cancer is the fear of rejection and of not being cared for, nurtured, or protected. Experiences in this latter regard can result in a self-perception that one is unloving or unlovable and thus unworthy of closeness and belonging. For someone who has an opening square, this may actually be true to some extent, depending upon the degree to which the individual has been able to integrate the planets in question.

Every sign has a primary relation with Aries, the beginning of the zodiac. To some extent, a sign can be defined in terms of its relationship with Aries. If Aries is simply the impulse *to act,* how does the other sign mix and combine with the Aries principle? Signs that form hard angles to Aries—Taurus, Cancer, Virgo, Libra, Scorpio, Capricorn, and Pisces—are in conflict with the Aries impulse; assertion (Aries) is contraindicated from their point of view. The result is conflict and friction. This is classically represented in the closing square between Capricorn and Aries. Capricorn discourages the unrestrained aggression of Aries, whereas Aries chafes against the excessive controls of Capricorn.

Aspect theory follows the same logic as applies to relationships between signs. Any two planets during their synodic cycle have a beginning to their relationship. This is the conjunction, a time when something is being born; a new action is taking place. This outward thrust characterizes the conjunction and Aries. By the time the cycle reaches its opening square, however, the combined energy of the two planets is undergoing a transition inward. Something is deepening and becoming more reflective, contained, and aware on a feeling level. It has to be consecrated to caring in some way, rather than just acted out. This Cancerian/yin impulse necessarily inhibits the spontaneity and impulsiveness of the original planetary synergy of the conjunction.

To the extent that one fails at this, there is a tendency to "act out" impulses and feelings without reflection or conscious awareness. Recall that an opening square generates a concern that expression of the respective planets will be hurtful to others. As a consequence of poorly integrated impulses, one may actually hurt someone physically or emotionally. This, in turn, may result in personal rejection—the ultimate Cancerian fear. For the person with an opening square, there is anxiety that the combined expression of the two planets will cause one to be shunned. In an effort to compensate for these fears, the individual is compelled to utilize his emergent traits more sensitively. Dichotomous energies must be contained, controlled, and combined such that new traits emerge—compromise formations—that enable the planetary synergy to express love, caring, and protection in ways that are consistent with the nature of the respective planets.

Whereas the type and degree of a conflict is depicted by the nature of the angle itself, the intensity of the conflict can be measured by determining whether the aspect is applying or separating, as well as by its degree of exactitude. Consider, for example, an opening quincunx between Moon in Pisces at 22°41' and Saturn in Libra at 24°39'. Since the Moon moves faster than Saturn, it is an applying quincunx within two degrees of exactitude. Anything within four degrees would generally be considered a quincunx. The closer to exactitude, the stronger the aspect. Since applying angles are thought to be stronger than separating ones, a one or two-degree applying quincunx is fairly intense.

DECONSTRUCTING THE CONFLICT

Let us deconstruct this aspect more precisely. There are many ways to describe the conflict inherent in Moon Pisces quincunx Saturn in Libra. Considering the signs first, Pisces is the impulse to sacrifice oneself for the good of others, whereas Libra is the impulse to cooperate for the sake of mutual harmony. Pisces is compelled to rescue those who are helpless, as in acts of pity, whereas Libra wants an equal partnership based on fairness and mutuality. Clearly, these are not compatible drives.

When we combine signs with the planets that tenant them, we move to a higher degree of complexity in deciphering the conflict. Accordingly, the consequences of the aspect become harder to predict. One manifestation of Moon in Pisces would be a child's attempt to obtain caring (Moon) through compassionate concern (Pisces) for her mother's disability. Perhaps the mother is fragile and unable to cope with her family's demands; thus the child strives to relieve the mother's suffering by denying her own need for maternal supplies (caring and nurturing). Saturn in Libra, however, wants to achieve perfect harmony through a disciplined approach to human relations. In the house that Saturn tenants, there may be a felt pressure to master Libran pursuits, such as art, etiquette, diplomacy, and the like.

With an opening (Virgo) quincunx between these two planets and signs, the conflict is likely to manifest as a problem, or dilemma, which will show up in some type of symptom and external predicament that is difficult to resolve. Since the Moon and Saturn rule opposing signs (Cancer and Capricorn), these planets already constitute an archetypal conflict of their own. Accordingly, this fundamental, archetypal conflict is likely to be activated in a quincunxial way.

Saturn's effect on the Moon is to initially deprive it of any satisfaction. This might show up externally in the form of a parent who withholds nurturance for some reason. The mother, for example, may be depressed, or burdened with too many responsibilities, or feeling pressured and disorganized in her own life. She may respond to the child's emotional needs with an implicit disapproval. Once internalized by the daughter, however, this external frustration becomes an internal prohibition against dependency needs. She may say to herself, "My wish for nurturance constitutes an unfair burden upon my family; thus, I need to assume responsibility for my own emotional needs and not impose them on others." Her external conflict has become an internal one.

In an effort to adapt to this untenable state of affairs, she may develop certain character traits and symptoms. For example, she may feel compelled to assume responsibility as a caretaker (Moon) in response to some problem (quincunx), such as disorganization or stress, which is afflicting one or more members of her family. In so doing, however, she implicitly rejects her own emotional needs, effectively reversing roles with her parents. She assumes the parental role and takes care of them at her own expense. As a belief, this might be voiced as, "I am not deserving of love and closeness (Moon) unless I can solve problems that stem from a lack of responsibility and control (Saturn)." The nature of this belief would reflect the quincunxial (Virgo) quality of the aspect, as well as the planets involved. Given that the problem is beyond her capacity to solve as a child, she may feel varying degrees of failure, incompetence, guilt, loneliness, and sadness. In other words, our Moon quincunx Saturn child is a prime candidate for depression.

A BRIEF CASE HISTORY

In an actual case of a woman that had this aspect (see Figure 21, page 256), she grew up in a family that was very cultured and refined. In fact, her Saturn in Libra was in the 4th house, signifying a somewhat rigid, controlled family atmosphere that placed a high value on art, etiquette, and similar Libran virtues. It was very important, for instance, that the family seem harmonious to the outside world, with everyone behaving perfectly. All of this is consistent with Saturn in Libra in the 4th. Unfortunately, however, the father was periodically depressed and would self-medicate through alcohol (☽ ♓ 10th ☌ ♄ ☌ ♆ ♎ 4ᵗʰ).

Imagine Beethoven is playing on the family stereo, fine art all around, while her father is sprawled out in a drunken stupor on the expensive leather couch. And as a consequence of his alcoholism, he would frequently lose his job, which necessitated the family continually move from one state to another (note that her natal Uranus squares Neptune-Saturn in the 4ᵗʰ).

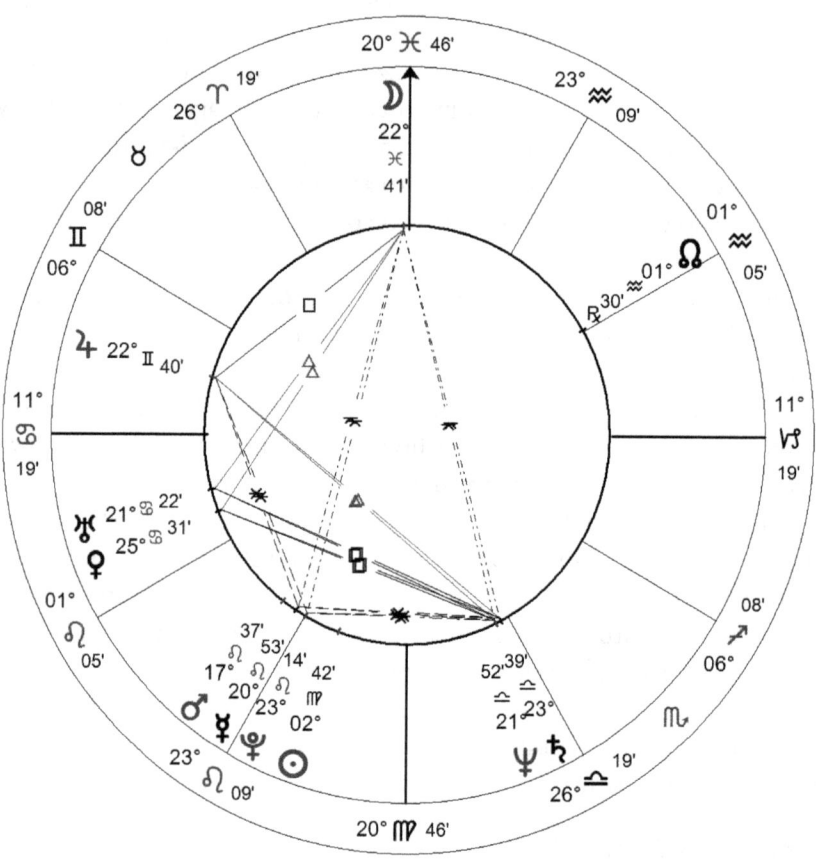

Figure 21: Birthchart of Moon Pisces Woman

My client's Moon Pisces was in her 10ᵗʰ house. By itself, Moon in the 10ᵗʰ can signify a mother that was responsible for the family and had to work. Addition of the Pisces factor, however, conforms to the fact that she was compensating for the father's childish irresponsibility and was burdened, overwhelmed, and frequently on the verge of collapse—a classic martyr.

All of this is consistent with Moon Pisces in the 10th quincunx Saturn. The theme is underscored by virtue of Neptune being conjunct Saturn in the 4th; in effect, not only is the Moon in the sign ruled by Neptune in Saturn's house (10th), but Neptune is conjunct Saturn in the Moon's house (4th). When a theme is repeated like this in a chart, it suggests something major. Of course, this same configuration also represents the immature, depressed father who was dependent upon alcohol, nursing himself at the bottle like a deprived child.[31]

The quincunx between Saturn and the Moon therefore symbolizes the essential dilemma that was both in the family and in my client. On the one hand, she had to play a Saturn in Libra role—a happy, perfect, cultured, well-mannered child that was kind and responsible beyond her years. At the same time, she was painfully aware that her family was crumbling as a consequence of her father's alcoholism and abdication of parental responsibility. Far from being happy, she felt profoundly deprived of the understanding that she needed in order to cope with a tragedy that threatened to engulf her. Her Moon in Pisces was constantly on the verge of tears, yet she dared not ask for support for fear that her mother would collapse from the additional burden. Thus, she denied her feelings, feigned maturity, and pretended that she was beyond needing care. Inside, however, she felt depressed, alone, scared, and out-of-control—feelings that haunted her right into adulthood when she finally sought therapy.

In the simplest terms, her conflict was between her dependency needs (Moon) and her sense of responsibility and self-control (Saturn). The particulars of her conflict, however, were further articulated by the nature of the angle (quincunx) and the specific signs that were involved (Libra and Pisces). The quincuxial dilemma entailed being raised by a family that necessitated she appear perfectly balanced and serene while, at the same time, struggling with a tragic, alcoholic mess that evoked overwhelming feelings of grief and despair. This paradoxical situation, or dilemma, caused her to feel incompetent and useless within her family, for there was nothing she could do to solve the problem.

The above case also illustrates how external and internal conflict overlaps. Initially, her conflict was an external one. If she depended upon her mother or father for emotional support, she received consistent messages that her needs were "too much." Father was too busy nursing himself at the bottle

---

[31] When the Moon (mother) is in the 10th (father), the same configuration can symbolize both mother and father, i.e., mother operates in a context of responsibility, and father is characterized by lunar attributes.

to be sensitive to his daughter's needs, while her mother was overwhelmed with having to carry the burden of the family; thus, she had nothing left to give her daughter. Frustrated by this external lack of support, my client interpreted and internalized her experience in an egocentric manner typical of children—namely, if her family rejects her dependency needs, it must mean that such needs are excessive, burdensome, and unwarranted. So, she should inhibit and control them, which is precisely the function that Saturn symbolizes.

The point is her lunar impulses did not disappear, but continued to conflict with her Saturnian restraints. They emerged into awareness through a variety of symptoms, such as psychosomatic ailments and obsessive fears—both of which typify the Virgonian nature of the opening quincunx. As a child, she would scratch her legs until they would bleed, thus necessitating a trip to the doctor, who was infinitely more tender and caring that either of her parents.[32] As an adult, she manages anxiety and nurtures herself by overeating; thus she is significantly overweight. Also, she developed an obsessive-compulsive perfectionism with regard to any caretaking role she assumed. Overprotective, overfunctioning, and over controlling of her children, she consistently relates to them as if they are a problem (quincunx) that needs to be managed. Her negativity is so annoying that her children criticize her and push her away, thus bearing out her original premise that she is unworthy of love. These symptoms, character developments, and maladaptive strategies, which are generated and maintained on an intrapsychic level, are compromise formations that produce the distress and impairment that is the hallmark of psychopathology. Overwhelming stress, however, can be managed and regulated over time through the employ of defense mechanisms. It is to this subject that we now turn.

DEFENSE MECHANISMS

Psychological processes that protect us from being overwhelmed by pain, stress, or worry are called defense mechanisms. According to Maxmen and Ward (1995), defense mechanisms are "relatively involuntary patterns of feelings, thoughts, or behaviors that arise in response to an internal or external perceived psychic danger in order to reduce or avoid conscious or unconscious stress, anxiety, or conflict" (p. 74). In effect, defenses are designed to maintain stress within bearable limits.

---

[32] It is interesting to note in this regard that Saturn rules the skin in medical astrology. Thus scratching at her skin, and the misery it caused her, could actually be symptomatic of the internal persecution she was experiencing from her Saturnian instincts.

Let us deconstruct that definition into more palatable bite-size pieces:

1. A defense constitutes an involuntary pattern of feeling, thinking, or behavior.
2. Such a pattern arises in response to a psychic danger that may be internal or external.
3. The purpose of a defense is to reduce stress, anxiety, or conflict, which may or may not be in awareness.

Defenses can be adaptive or maladaptive depending upon the circumstances and the extent to which the defense is utilized. Some periods of avoidance are healthy and permit a kind of dose-by-dose working-through process. Periods of restoration alternate with periods of high turbulence. If a defense is over utilized, however, so that there is a more or less complete avoidance of reality, it can have maladaptive consequences.

Intrapsychic conflict by definition implies a conflict between goals that exist in stressful relationship to one another. In the typical hard aspect, there are competing schemas that accrue to separate planets, each of which predicts a negative consequence if the other planet achieves its aims. If Mars squares Venus, for example, a Mars schema might predict: "if I commit to relationship I will lose my freedom," whereas a Venus schema predicts: "if I assert my rights I will lose my relationship." The apparent irreconcilability of the competing beliefs causes stress, which creates an additional conflict: one goal is to master the stressful situation, the other is to stay within tolerable levels of emotion and avoid becoming overwhelmed or demoralized.

A person wants to master threats and stressors, for mastery leads to a sense of self-efficacy and positive self-esteem. This requires allowing the conflict to be in conscious awareness. Conversely, the individual also wants to avoid painful states of mind such as occur when he or she realizes the emotional implications of a serious event. Protecting oneself from unwanted emotions requires keeping the conflict out of awareness.

For example, a woman with Mars square Venus may not allow herself to recognize the significance of lipstick on her husband's collar because unconsciously she fears being overwhelmed by the prospect of losing him to another woman. Thus she represses her anger in the relationship (Mars), and attends only to her love for her partner (Venus). However, if she continues to deny the significance of such telltale signs of infidelity, she will be unable to confront problems in her marriage that may be contributing to her husband's unfaithfulness. In such a case, her defense of denial is extreme and clearly maladaptive. Two former first ladies, Jacqueline Kennedy Onassis and Hillary Clinton, each had Venus square Mars, and each experienced difficulty in confronting their husband's extramarital affairs.

ARCHETYPAL DEFENSE MECHANISMS

Defense mechanisms can be matched with astrological archetypes, which include sign-planet systems and their corollary aspects. For example, Mars/Aries and the conjunction equate to the defense of *acting out*. In an actual chart, however, there is not a clear-cut one-to-one correlation between a defense and a sign-planet system, as any defense by definition involves a conflict between two or more parts of the psyche. Whereas the conflict activates the defensive actions of each planet against the other, at the heart of the conflict is the angle that defines the relationship between the two planets. This suggests that defenses primarily correlate to specific angles/aspects, and secondarily to the signs/planets that comprise the aspect.

Defenses that are implicit in aspects can be understood on the basis of the sign-planet system that corresponds to that angle. The defense mechanism that correlates to the opening square, for example, also correlates to the Moon and Cancer, since Cancer is the sign that signifies the opening square. This point may warrant further explanation. Recall that Cancer is a receptive, sensitive, introspective sign; it symbolizes shyness, inhibition, and reserve. Likewise, the Moon signifies a containing, holding capacity, as when a mother holds her baby and contains the baby's feelings. In so doing, however, the mother must suppress her own needs and feelings, and attend primarily to her child. The Moon, therefore, is naturally inhibitory and suppressive. Correspondingly, the opening square has this exact quality. Regardless of the planets involved, opening squares are containing and restraining. If 'holding back' is carried to an extreme, however, we get the defense of repression, which is the tendency to withhold from conscious awareness any idea, feeling, or impulse that is distressing.

Because repression is one of the major defenses, there is no one aspect that correlates to it. Like a primary color of the spectrum, repression of one sort or another is a potential with all yin angles—semisextiles, squares, and quincunxes. Accordingly, there can be a variety of issues involved with repression depending upon the aspect.[33] In general, repression simply means that a certain psychic content—a feeling, memory, idea, or wish—has become restrained to such a degree that it is held out of awareness. In other words, a

---

[33] Other major defenses include denial and projection.

given state of mind is sufficiently dreaded that it is more or less completely avoided. Repression simply means that attention is directed away from a given state, and toward states that are compensatory to the one dreaded.

With the opening square, for example, the unconscious conviction is that expression of the repressed material could lead to rejection (aloneness, unlovability), which is the state most dreaded by Cancer. Thus the opening square often correlates to repressed memories that involve hurtful experiences. With the closing square, the dreaded state is failure, which is the state most feared by Capricorn. With the opening quincunx, one avoids feelings of incompetence (Virgo), and with the closing quincunx (Scorpio) the primary fear is of violation or annihilation, which can lead to feelings of shame.

All of this suggests that pathological defense mechanisms are actually coping processes that have become rigid and excessive. However, just as there is nothing inherently bad about Cancer, Virgo, Libra, Scorpio, or Capricorn, so there is nothing inherently bad about a hard aspect. The critical factor in any aspect is the degree of integration between the planets involved. For example, if a closing quincunx is not integrated, the planets are apt to regard one another as shadows and thus see one another as destructive. Each reacts to the other in an extreme manner. The same aspect when integrated, however, can have a powerful, transformative quality. A closing quincunx between Venus and Jupiter suggests intense feelings and deep insights associated with the ethical dimension of personal relationships.

Again, although categories of defense can be primarily linked to specific aspects, we must also assume that the participating signs, planets, and houses are implicated in defenses, too, making any defensive process a compound made up of multiple, interacting variables. Recall that an astrological archetype can express itself in at least four ways: planet, sign, house, and aspect. Thus, the planet Neptune rules the sign Pisces, the 12th house, and the closing semi-sextile. The more a specific archetype is stressed, the more likely the corollary defenses are operative. Imagine, for example, that an individual with Sun in Pisces in the 12th has a closing semi-sextile to Neptune on the Ascendant. In addition, he has several other planets in the 12th, and additional planets in Pisces as well, each of which is forming hard aspects to other planets. Since all factors associated with a single archetype are present to a significant degree, and since that archetype is under stress, we can hypothesize that Neptunian defenses will be strongly evident in the personality. These would include *denial, altruism, fantasy, idealization, regression,* and *undoing,* as explained in the next section.

ASTROLOGICAL CORRELATES TO DEFENSES

It must be emphasized that defenses operate between planetary functions as a way of mediating conflicting aims. Accordingly, defenses do not operate in a singular, independent fashion; rather, they work in relation to one another just like with planetary aspects. A defensive formation is a compound mix of interacting planet-sign configurations that entails multiple, overlapping processes. No summary of defenses can be complete since virtually any psychological process can be utilized defensively. This means that the traits of any sign-planet system can serve a defensive purpose. Any listing of defensive operations from the range of existing possibilities must therefore be somewhat arbitrary. Different writers emphasize different types and styles of defense, and may even utilize different terminology.

SIGN-PLANET	ARCHETYPAL DEFENSES
Pisces-Neptune	Denial, Altruism, Fantasy, Regression, Undoing, Turning-against-the-self, Dissociation
Aquarius-Uranus	Minimization, Disavowal, Detachment
Capricorn-Saturn	Repression (of Capricorn feelings and impulses), Devaluation
Sagittarius-Jupiter	Generalization, Rationalization, Moralization, Advising
Scorpio-Pluto	Repression, Projective Identification, Humor, Reaction formation
Libra-Venus	Projection, Compliance, Appeasement, Ingratiation
Virgo-Mercury	Repression (of Virgo needs and impulses), Somatization, Compulsion
Leo-Sun	Exaggeration, Idealization, Identification, Introjection, Suppression
Cancer-Moon	Repression (of Cancer needs and impulses), Passive Aggression
Gemini-Mercury	Distractibility, Isolation (of affect), Intellectualization
Taurus-Venus	Resistance, Splitting (Black & White Thinking and Feeling)
Aries-Mars	Acting out, Displacement, Omnipotent Control, Counterdependency

© Glenn Perry, Ph.D.

Figure 22: A List of Archetypal Defenses

It should be kept in mind that defenses associated with astrological archetypes are invariably linked to the disorders that result from the extreme expression of those archetypes. In this regard, a mental disorder can be regarded as a chronic defense that has metastasized into a full-blown illness. Over utilization of the Martian defense of 'acting out', for example, would be consistent with antisocial personality disorder. A person who over relies upon the solar defense of 'exaggeration' would be narcissistic. Chronic use of the Taurus-Venus defense of 'splitting' is associated with borderline pathology, and so on.

The following are common defense mechanisms, which can be correlated with sign-planet systems and their corresponding aspects as summarized in Figure 22 (page 262).

Mars/Aries—Conjunction

Acting-out is the direct expression of impulses in response to stress or conflict. By acting without any apparent regard for consequences, good or bad, action substitutes for thoughtful and patient consideration of one's feelings; thus, emotions are not contained and actions are not regulated with regard to desired outcomes. Sometimes feelings are displaced from one area to another. For example, a man who is angry with his boss comes home, yells at his children, and picks a fight with his wife.

Displacement is the discharge of pent-up emotions, usually anger, onto objects, animals, or people perceived as less dangerous than those that originally induced the emotions. The classic example is a man comes home after a bad day at work and kicks the dog. In displacement, the avoided ideas and feelings are transferred to some other person, situation, or object. The defense of somatization (focusing on physical symptoms) is a form of displacement, even though it is primarily a Virgo defense. Displacement can also be a form of acting out.

Omnipotent Control is utilized to defend against the stress of having others neglect or fail to attend properly to one's desires. To compensate for the sense that one cannot do or get what one wants (impotence), the person acts from an attitude of having total control of the object (omnipotence). If one fears that the environment will be completely indifferent or unresponsive to one's actions, the primitive defense of omnipotent control may include attitudes of an irrational nature in which the person believes that actions (often violent), rituals, or incantations will bend people and circumstances to his or her desires.

Venus/Taurus—Opening Semi-sextile

Resistance occurs when one deals with emotional conflicts, or internal or external stress, by stubbornly clinging to the known and familiar. It takes the form of attitudes and actions that prevent awareness of unconscious conflicts. As a general term, resistance encompasses all of a person's efforts to avoid pain associated with change. It is regularly encountered in psychotherapy when the patient attempts to circumvent any knowledge about the self that might be distressing by clinging to the known. Accordingly, it has much in common with denial and repression.

Splitting is the viewing of oneself or others as all good or all bad, as opposed to being a mixture of positive and negative attributes. Splitting is a primitive defense that mimics how toddlers experience the world. In splitting, one deals with the tension of ambivalent feelings by repressing one side and expressing the other. Rather than struggling to integrate positive and negative qualities into cohesive images, objects are alternately idealized and devalued. Likewise, one sees the self as either all good or all bad. Splitting is related to a cognitive style called *centration,* which is the tendency to attend to one salient feature of an object or event and ignore other features. By keeping things simple and one-dimensional, the individual avoids the anxiety that naturally accompanies a more complex, yet less certain, view of self and the world.

Mercury/Gemini—Opening Sextile

Distractibility occurs when one deals with emotional conflicts, or internal or external stress, by allowing one's attention to be drawn to unimportant or irrelevant external stimuli. By focusing on tangential, superfluous matters, one successfully avoids attending to distressing ones.

Isolation of affect is the compartmentalization of painful emotions from the events associated with them, thus allowing the recollection of an emotionally disturbing situation without the anxiety that would otherwise be experienced. Essentially, isolation consists of splitting ideas and feelings. For example, one may have an obsessive idea of "killing" someone, yet without feeling anger, fear, or guilt toward the object. As a defense, isolation is characterized by flatness of affect and seeming indifference.

Intellectualization is the overuse of thinking in an attempt to reduce psychic discomfort. The person avoids the emotional implications of a topic by dealing with it on a purely ideational level. Alcoholics may use intellectualization when they quibble over the definition of alcoholism as a way of avoiding feelings associated with their drinking problem.[34]

Moon/Cancer—Opening Square

Repression consists of withholding from conscious awareness a distressing idea, feeling, impulse, or wish.[35] Whereas conscious expulsion of thoughts from the mind is suppression and thus an act of will, repression is relatively involuntary. It may operate to exclude from awareness something that was experienced. Rather than the event becoming an actual memory, it is held in suspended animation. With the opening square, there is anxiety about caring, closeness, and belonging. Ideas and impulses associated with actual or potential rejection are likely to be repressed. For example, a girl may repress a wish to join a sorority due to a fear of rejection. Also, one may repress impulses that might hurt someone else's feelings, such as the wish to exclude someone from a group.

Passive Aggression entails the indirect expression of aggression toward others. Anger is repressed due to a fear that its direct expression could result in rejection. When direct expression of anger is feared or otherwise regarded as unacceptable, it will tend to seek an outlet in an indirect, passive way. For example, a boy who is angry with his father may forget to do a chore that is important to his father.

Sun/Leo—Opening Trine

Exaggeration of certain meanings is used to protect self-esteem or emotional balance. For example, personal strength can be appraised in an exaggerated way to avoid fear before a fight. Or, one may exaggerate the significance of a boss's greeting to offset fears that one is expendable at work.

Idealization (a.k.a. "bragging") is the unwarranted praise of another or oneself by emphasizing or exaggerating certain virtues. Idealization is used to compensate threatening negative ideas by accentuating positive ones. For example, a woman may idealize her husband rather than criticize his flaws and end up a lonely divorcee.[36] Or, a man may boast about his intelligence to compensate for a fear that his lack of education will be exposed.

---

[34] A related defense, generalization, entails dealing with topics at an abstract rather than a personal level to avoid excessive emotion (see Jupiter/Sagittarius).

[35] As stated, there are several varieties of repression, each of which is associated with a different hard aspect. For variations, see also the opening quincunx, closing quincunx, and closing square.

[36] Idealization of the beloved at the beginning of a relationship is so indispensable to the maintenance of romantic feelings as to be almost the defining attribute of courtship.

Identification is the unconscious modeling of another's attributes to increase one's sense of self-worth, cope with possible separation or loss, or minimize feelings of impotence. For example, a girl might identify with a famous actress to boost her self-esteem. Or, a boy might identify with his mother to defend against a fear of abandonment. Identification with the aggressor is yet another example, as when concentration-camp prisoners assumed the mannerisms of their Nazi guards as a defense against fears of annihilation.

Another meaning of *identification* is when the individual identifies with the experience of someone with whom s/he is in dialogue rather than simply remaining receptive to it. In so doing, the individual defends against certain uncomfortable feelings that are being evoked, such as anxiety, helplessness, sadness, incompetence, inferiority, or uncertainty. Identification includes distracting from the other's experience by 'one-upping' them; that is, by sharing something that is more (entertaining, embarrassing, painful, disappointing, or frightening) than what the other experienced. In so doing the individual shifts the focus of attention from the other to the self.

Introjection is the incorporation of other people's values, standards, or traits to prevent conflicts with, or threats from, these people. For example, a captive may introject certain ideas and values of her captors to prevent further abuse. Introjection may also help a person retain a sense of connection to a lost loved one, as when people adopted John Kennedy's accent after his death.

Suppression is the conscious and deliberate avoidance of disturbing matters. Unlike repression, suppression involves a conscious choice. One copes with emotional conflicts by deliberately substituting an alternative thought to avoid thinking about distressing problems, wishes, feelings, or experiences. In the vernacular, the expression "don't go there" exemplifies suppression.

Mercury/Virgo—Opening Quincunx

Repression of the Virgo variety consists of withholding from conscious awareness a distressing idea, feeling, impulse, or wish that is associated with matters pertaining to work, health, or competence. For example, one may repress awareness of making mistakes in a task. Or, a person may have an impulse to quit their job or go to the doctor, but represses these impulses due to fear of the consequences.

Somatization is an excessive preoccupation with physical symptoms in response to psychologically stressful situations. One's fixation on symptoms is disproportionate to any actual physical disturbance. For example, a boy becomes obsessed with a welt caused by a bee sting, exaggerating its significance and pain. His preoccupation with the sting could mask a fear of his father who is frequently angry with him.

Compulsion is not normally listed as a defense, but constitutes an attempt to ward off anxiety by engaging in a specific repetitive action. Common compulsions are washing and checking. The latter include checking text messages, making sure the door is locked, and similar acts that counter fears of unwanted experiences that could result from having made a mistake. Other compulsions include shopping, hoarding, eating, counting, and virtually any persistent, repetitive behavior that serves as a distraction or countermeasure to an unreasonable worry.

Venus/Libra—Opposition

Projection is the unconscious rejection of unacceptable thoughts, traits, or wishes by ascribing them to others. An impulse or idea is attributed to the external world, usually in a negative way. For example, people who struggle with their own hatred may develop a delusion that others are out to get them. This gives one an acceptable rationale for hating, and allows the self to avoid recognition of its own selfish or destructive impulses.

Compliance and *appeasement* are sufficiently similar to constitute a single defense. Compliance is the unconscious compulsion to comply with another's wishes in order to avoid their anger or threaten the relationship. Likewise, appeasement is the policy of granting concession to a person with whom one is in relationship in order to maintain peace. Couples who chronically utilize compliance and appeasement as a way of staying together are said to have a relationship characterized by pseudomutuality.

Pluto/Scorpio—Closing Quincunx

Repression of the Pluto variety consists of withholding from conscious awareness a distressing idea, feeling, impulse, or wish associated with death, sex, power, pain, or evil. For example, ideas and feelings associated with a traumatic event, along with the event itself, are likely to be repressed (amnesia or buried memories). Thoughts and feelings that might cause harm to another are subject to repression as well. For example, sexual attraction toward the spouse of a best friend may be repressed, or one may repress hatred for a person one would normally be expected to love, such as a sibling.

Projective Identification is a variant of projection but operates in a deeper, more evocative way in response to someone with whom the self has an actual relationship. It occurs when an aspect of the self that one does not wish to acknowledge is unconsciously projected into the other person.

Projective identification operates like a self-fulfilling prophecy in that it evokes feelings and behavior in the other that actually conform to the nature of the projection. For example, an individual may unconsciously be angry with someone; yet, rather than distancing oneself from this person, the self projects angry feelings into the other, who is now viewed as being angry at the self rather than vice versa. One may then provoke the other person to behave in a hostile manner, thus providing a reality basis for locating one's own anger as if it were in the other person.

Passive into Active entails doing to others what was done to oneself. In this regard, passive into active is a variant of projective identification except in reverse of what was explained above. The first variant is active into passive; one perceives the self as a passive (innocent) victim by imagining that the other is doing to the self what one denies doing to them. In passive into active, however, one defends against being weak and vulnerable by identifying with the more powerful role of the original perpetrator and projecting the weak position. Again, this is doing to the other what was done to you. Identification with the aggressor is one form of this defense.

Humor is the use of irony or amusing, incongruous, or absurd associations to reduce what otherwise might be unbearable tension or fear. Humor often reveals a grievance, which is the feeling of resentment stemming from an experience of having been violated, hurt, or wronged. Likewise, humor frequently deals with a taboo subject that is too anxiety provoking to discuss openly (sex, death, shame, pain, defecation, degradation, and so on—all Pluto ruled).

Reaction formation prevents the expression or experiencing of unacceptable feelings by developing opposite attitudes and behaviors to an exaggerated degree. If a warded-off impulse, idea or feeling is sufficiently threatening, it may be replaced by an unconsciously derived but consciously felt emphasis on its opposite. One of the most common examples of reaction formation is laughter when discussing a painful, disturbing topic (see *humor*). Another example: A woman covets the position of a superior at work and wishes the man would die. She realizes that having such a desire is "bad." Thus, she unconsciously replaces the wish to be rid of her superior with an exaggerated concern for his welfare. If the conflict is intense, she might have a compulsion to protect him from any stress or threats to his health. In Shakespeare's Hamlet, reaction formation is implied by Queen Gertrude's statement, "The lady doth protest too much," meaning the lady (to whom the Queen is referring) claims to feel one way while secretly feeling the opposite.

Jupiter/Sagittarius—Closing Trine

Generalization is the overuse of abstract thinking as a means to reduce psychic discomfort. The person avoids the emotional implications of a topic by dealing with it on a purely theoretical level. For example, sex addicts may argue about general social attitudes toward sexuality as a means of avoiding personal shame associated with their sexual compulsivity. With generalization, the person deals with the topic at an abstract, general level in order to avoid excessive or unwanted emotion. An incest victim, for example, is more comfortable talking about molestation in general rather than disclose the specific details of her own experience.

Rationalization is the self-serving use of plausible reasons to justify actions caused by repressed, unacceptable emotions or ideas. An astrologer, for instance, may claim that his exorbitantly high fee is necessary in order for the consultation to be meaningful to the client. In order to avoid stress or self-blame, rationalization consists of proclaiming logical, more acceptable reasons for actions actually performed for less honorable reasons. Rationalization may be used to justify avoiding unpleasant duties. A person claims she cannot stay to clean up after a party because she has to get up early for work the next day. Note that rationalization is justification, and justice is a Jupiterian theme. A funny example was illustrated in an episode of the television show, *Cheers,* when Norm Peterson asked his barroom buddy, Cliff Clavin, about the hazards of drinking. Cliff responded:

> "Well, ya see, Norm, it's like this…A herd of buffalo can only move as fast as the slowest buffalo. And when the herd is hunted, it is the slowest and weakest ones at the back that are killed first. This natural selection is good for the herd as a whole, because the general speed and health of the whole group keeps improving by the regular killing of the weakest members! In much the same way, the human brain can only operate as fast as the slowest brain cells. Excessive intake of alcohol, as we know, kills brain cells. But naturally, it attacks the slowest and weakest brain cells first. In this way, regular consumption of beer eliminates the weaker brain cells, making the brain a faster and more efficient machine! That's why you always feel smarter after a few beers."

Moralization is a close relative of rationalization. It entails seeking reasons to establish that it is one's moral duty or obligation to pursue a course that is actually done for other, less acceptable reasons. There is often a self-righteous, pseudo morality that functions as a mask for selfish or destructive behavior. Moralization provides false justification for doing or pursuing what one wants. It resolves, by recourse to principle, mixed feelings that the self has been unable to reconcile. Because it camouflages less admirable motives with moral justification, people that use this defense can be intractable. If one does not validate their position, they regard the person as deficient in virtue. A humorous example of moralization is provided by the famous baseball player, Babe Ruth, who when asked why he drank so much responded:

"Sometimes when I reflect on all the beer I drink, I feel ashamed. Then I look into the glass and think about the workers in the brewery and all of their hopes and dreams. If I didn't drink this beer, they might be out of work and their dreams would be shattered. I think, 'It is better to drink this beer and let their dreams come true than be selfish and worry about my liver.'"

Saturn/Capricorn—Closing Square

Repression of the Saturn variety consists of withholding from conscious awareness a distressing idea, feeling, impulse, or wish associated with duty, success/failure, inadequacy/inferiority, or loss of control. For example, a man may repress his guilt for not measuring up to a high standard or for failing to fulfill his responsibilities. Grim ideas such as "I'm not good enough [for a desired career]," or that one lacks required attributes for success in relationships, are likely to be repressed. *Procrastination* is a symptom of Capricornian repression, for it entails the avoidance of impulses toward fulfillment of responsibility.

Devaluation is the demeaning of another or oneself by the attribution of exaggerated negative qualities. In devaluation, one deals with internal conflicts by putting oneself or others down. For example, a man might negatively judge or ridicule his boss rather than face his fear that his boss's criticisms are valid. Self-devaluation can also fulfill a defensive purpose, as when a person avoids a fear of failure by exaggerating his negative qualities and claiming to be inferior, thus providing an excuse for not trying.

Uranus/Aquarius—Closing Sextile

Detachment or "emotional blunting" entails disconnecting from unsettling emotions related to behaviors, events, or memories that the individual does not want to face. Emotional detachment is a way of coping with people and experiences that are overwhelming. For example, a girl may say something hurtful about a classmate and when confronted, act cold as if the confrontation does not matter. A state of being distant, aloof, or emotionally numb may also occur in response to separation from loved ones, as occurs, for example, on the last day of school with friends one might not see again. Rather than cry, the person seems emotionally removed or preoccupied with trivial matters.

Minimization consists of undervaluing the significance of a topic as a maneuver to reduce stress. For example, the degree to which the self was to blame for an accident could be minimized to avoid shame and guilt. If told that his wife might be cheating on him with his boss since they were together the entire weekend, a man might say, "Oh, they're just good friends."

Disavowal is very similar to 'minimization' in that it can be used to avoid stressful news or its implications by asserting that the situation does not matter. Rather than simply minimize the significance of something, however, disavowal goes further by denying any knowledge of, involvement with, or responsibility for someone or something. For example, if a person is experiencing unwanted fears, wishes, or feelings, he may claim that the situation that might conceivably generate such emotions is not important to the self. In this regard, disavowal can be a sour grapes attitude. Rather than feel rejected for incompetence, a person fired from his job might say, "No big deal, I didn't want the job anyway." Thus he disavows wanting the job and any feelings of rejection, while also denying responsibility for getting fired since his alleged disinterest in the job and not his incompetence is what ended his employment.

Neptune/Pisces—Closing Semi-sextile

Denial is the avoidance of awareness of external realities that are too painful to acknowledge. It differs from repression, which is a denial of internal realty. Like repression, however, denial is an integral aspect of most defense mechanisms in that it refers to the reality-repudiating aspect of defensive operations in general. Denial is accomplished by withholding conscious understanding of the meaning and implications of what is perceived—especially by refusing to take in the extended significance of new information. Denial operates when a mother ignores the signs of her teenage son's drug use, or when a husband ignores evidence that his wife is having an affair. Magical thinking ("pay no attention and it will go away") can play a powerful role in denial. Within normal limits, denial is adaptive. It helps to slow down the response to bad news by allowing for a graded acceptance. However, denial is maladaptive to the extent that it interferes with rational action.

Altruism is dedication to the needs of others partly to fulfill one's own needs. For example, a girl protects her boyfriend from the consequences of his academic irresponsibility by doing schoolwork for him; yet, by making herself indispensable, she is unconsciously striving to keep him from ending the relationship. While altruism may partially fulfill some needs, other needs are sacrificed. The girl is so busy doing her boyfriend's schoolwork that she is unable to pursue her own interests. Altruism is the primary component of *co*-dependency.

Fantasy is the excessive retreat into daydreams and imagination to avoid conflicts or escape problems. Fantasy can be an important way of restoring morale during times of dismay. If a wife abandons her spouse for another man, the husband may restore his morale with fantasies of being with a new, desirable, even more attractive woman. With fantasy, the ideal is substituted for the real.

Regression is retreat to immature patterns of behavior and gratification in order to avoid the stress of adapting to a threatening event. For example, when an eight-year old learns that his parents are getting a divorce, he begins sucking his thumb and wetting the bed. In effect, regression consists of turning back the maturational clock and returning to earlier modes of dealing with the world. Falling apart, dissolving, giving up, or collapsing into helplessness are all forms of regression.

Undoing is the use of behavior or thoughts to cancel or eradicate the effect of a previous act or thought. Undoing is frequently used to absolve oneself of guilt for doing something that one imagines will be hurtful to others. A teenage boy quits the football team despite his success because he feels badly for his father who recently lost his job. In effect, the boy has to undo what he has done in order to not outshine his father. Sometimes undoing can express both an impulse and its opposite in rapid fashion, as in being very domineering one moment and then deferring obsequiously the next. Undoing can lead to indecisiveness, confusion, and, ultimately, self-castigation for the failure to actualize one's potential.

Turning against the self is when the person takes a hostile thought or impulse aimed at another and inappropriately redirects it inward. He or she experiences less distress by blaming, hurting, or even mutilating the self than by feeling guilty for being furious at the other person. Turning against the self is a way of acting out excessive, irrational guilt. It is a primary feature of masochistic personality disorder (also known as self-defeating personality disorder).

Dissociation is an extreme form of repression. It occurs by severely distancing oneself emotionally and perceptually from a threatening internal or external reality. Dissociation involves a temporary alteration in the integrative functions of consciousness or identity, as when a group of related psychological activities are separated into autonomously functioning units. A person might go into a dissociative state, for example, when experiencing anger and aggression. Since the dissociated function does not go away, however, dissociation can lead to the generation of multiple personalities.

Miscellaneous

Sublimation is the gratification of a repressed instinct or unacceptable feeling by socially acceptable means. Because sublimation entails the conversion of negative feelings into positive expression, it is less a defense than an example of a positive, successful resolution of intrapsychic conflict. An individual, for example, channels hateful feelings toward police into political work for promoting better police training. Thus sublimation entails replacing an unacceptable wish, "kill the racist pig," with a course of action that is similar to the wish but does not conflict with one's overall value system.

A BLENDING OF ARCHETYPAL DEFENSES

In analyzing defenses that correlate to a particular planetary aspect, the specific issues are going to result from a blend of the planets and signs involved. Consider the following scenario with a person that has an opening square between Mars in Aquarius and Saturn in Scorpio.

The opening square (Cancer angle) suggests potential repression of distressing ideas and feelings associated with themes of belonging, care, and protection. Imagine someone who is a financial controller that works for a major corporation. He experiences feelings of hostility (Mars) toward his superiors (Saturn), who are perceived as corrupt (Scorpio). He would like to initiate (Mars) radical changes (Aquarius) in the workplace that would allow him greater freedom from their control. Such changes, however, would clearly be in defiance of his superiors (Saturn), who direct the way money is managed (Scorpio). He knows that if he challenges the rules of the system, he could be accused of not being a 'company man'; his superiors would regard him as disloyal to the corporation "family." He may even be rejected (terminated). However, if he passively submits to company policy, he may end up hurting employees (stockholders) who have entrusted him with their savings. For the most part, the stress associated with this dilemma is repressed from awareness. However, when transiting Pluto conjuncts his natal Mars, the entire matter erupts into awareness, thus precipitating a crisis.

In this example, we see how the theme of the opening square is implicit in the conflict: fear of being rejected versus hurting people who depend on him. Clearly, this is a Cancerian (opening square) theme. However, the planets and signs that make up the square provide greater specificity to the conflict. Mars impulses for assertion and action are linked with Aquarian themes of change and reform. Likewise, Saturnian drives for authority, control, and career are linked to the Scorpionic domain of corruption, finance, and other people's money. In short, not only are Mars/Aquarius themes in conflict with Saturn/Scorpio themes, but the entire package is contained in a square that implicates Cancerian themes as well.

In response to this internal pressure, the man attempts to repress his angry feelings toward his superiors. This is only partially successful, however, as his resentment occasionally leaks out via passive aggressive behaviors. Sometimes he neglects his responsibilities in a manner that compromises company profits. Fights with his children entail a displacement of his hostility onto less threatening objects. When he talks about his work with friends, he devalues his boss in a manner that enhances his sense of personal strength. Finally, when transiting Pluto conjuncts his natal Mars, he acts out via an explosion of rage at his boss and the confrontation erupts into a vicious encounter. He accuses his superiors of selfish insensitivity to the employees that are in their care, and he is subsequently fired.

In the above scenario, a number of defenses come into play—repression and passive aggression associated with the opening square; Martian displacement and acting out; and Saturnian devaluation. Each defense is an element within the aspect as a whole. That is, each defense does not operate independent of the others, but rather in concert with the dominant themes and issues that are implicit in the total configuration.

In our overall listing of defenses, the first one, acting out, corresponds to a Mars/Aries/Conjunction trait. It is appropriate that this defense heads our list, for when feelings and impulses are not adequately regulated there is a tendency to act on impulse without forethought or regard for consequences. 'Acting out' might more properly be described as behavior that occurs in the absence of defense, for the essence of defense is control. As Horowitz (1988) put it, "One way to regulate emotion is to control the rate of processing of themes and to choose which topics to think about or communicate" (p. 196). At any given moment, there are several topics stored in active memory that await further information processing. Control systems inhibit and facilitate these options so that only some of them gain representation. In effect, defenses control what will be thought about, how it will be thought about, and the duration of the thought process. In the absence of such controls, one simply *acts,* which is what infants do (Aries stage of consciousness).

It cannot be overstated that defense mechanisms are normal and help to maintain personality organization. They are the glue that holds the psychic system together. Without them, human beings would be overwhelmed by inordinate and unmanageable amounts of guilt and anxiety. Just as conflict is unavoidable within a typical corporate board, so conflict is inherent within the psyche. The real question is not whether there is conflict, but how it is managed.

A defense mechanism can be described in three ways: purpose, process, and outcome. A defensive purpose is to avoid a dreaded state of mind; a defensive process is the way in which the dreaded state is avoided; and a defensive outcome constitutes the achievement of a substitute state that compensates for what is dreaded.

In regard to this last point, imagine that someone with Sun in Pisces in the 12th believes that he is an utterly worthless human being with no redeeming qualities. This deep, core belief, which is grim to say the least, is merely the hub of a network of associated schemas, memories and feelings. In order to inhibit such material from entering consciousness, other schemas and feelings must be created to take their place. To avoid feelings of worthlessness, he may substitute fantasies of being a rock star that is adored and admired. The same defense—fantasy (Neptune)—inhibits the dreaded state of mind and substitutes an antidote.

Defenses also determine when a distressing topic is allowed entrance into consciousness. Scarlet O'Hara's famous last line in *Gone With the Wind*, "Oh, I'll think about that tomorrow," illustrates this point. She was using the defense of suppression, which is the conscious and deliberate avoidance of disturbing matters—namely, that Rhett Butler was leaving her and may never return. If Scarlet was living in current times, she might say, "Oh, let's not go there" in response to anyone bringing up the subject of Rhett's departure.

Very often, people do not allow themselves to experience painful feelings until the distressing ideas that underlay them are disconfirmed. If there were a sequel to *Gone with the Wind* in which Rhett Butler returned to Scarlet, forgave her, and pledged his undying devotion, she might *then* cry, for the distressing idea that Rhett no longer cared for her would be disconfirmed. Her stored and suspended grief would now be safe to release.

Control systems determine whether words, images, and emotions will be experienced in isolation or with cross translation. Imagine, for instance, that an adolescent girl with a Moon/Uranus conjunction forming a closing square to Neptune suffers the shocking loss of her mother to suicide. Initially, she pretends that her mother is not really dead (Neptune/denial), and thus represses (square) her feelings of grief, loss, and despair. During the months following her loss, she acts out destructively with alcohol and drugs rather than contain and articulate her feelings. Acting out typifies the conjunction. When she finally is able to think about her mother's suicide, she conceives the event as evidence that her mother abandoned her. Her chosen schema is that of the "good" child whom the "bad" mother deserted. The defense of devaluation is consistent with the closing square and compensates the girl's unconscious thoughts of being "bad" and undeserving of love (Neptune/unconscious guilt).

Eventually, however, with the support of therapy, she is able to allow herself to admit that she feels guilty about her mother's suicide. She remembers how she sometimes upset her mother with typical adolescent rebelliousness. Also, she recalls that she resented her mother's efforts to restrict her and sometimes wished she could be free of her. In her mind, these actions and wishes contributed to her mother's depression and subsequent suicide. Acknowledgement of this guilt, however, occurs without full awareness of its accompanying sadness. The defense of detachment (Uranus) enables her to talk about her mother's suicide without being overwhelmed by feelings that are associated with the topic. Such feelings are split off and isolated from the thoughts to which they would normally be linked.

In this example, we see how a single aspect and a single event can involve the interplay of several different defenses—denial, repression, acting out, devaluation, and detachment, which are linked to their astrological correlates. These defenses regulated the processing of various dimensions associated with the suicide—memory of the event itself, schemas about her relationship with her mother, and diverse thoughts and feelings evoked by the experience.

Clearly, some controls are necessary, for otherwise we would be besieged by emotional topics and not be able to stop thinking about them. A given control process, such as inhibiting a theme, can be adaptive to the purpose of reducing emotional arousal. In fact, explicit or implicit denial is an integral aspect of all defense mechanisms. Although denial is primarily associated with Neptune, it refers less to a discrete defense mechanism and more to the reality-repudiating aspect of defensive operations in general. Some degree of transient denial is a normal reaction to stress, trauma, or loss.

A defense is adaptive when it enables a person to think about difficult and upsetting topics for usefully paced periods of time so as to not become overwhelmed. A defense becomes maladaptive, however, when it more or less completely blocks the processing of a particular theme. For example, denial can involve massive distortions of reality that culminate in a delusion. If our adolescent girl never allowed herself to admit that her mother is dead, her denial may eventually precipitate a psychotic break. Such avoidance of a conceptual area is called defensive regulation and is equivalent to the compensatory, overfunctioning of a planetary process, in this case Neptune. Eventually, defensive regulation is likely to give way to dysregulation, which constitutes a breakdown in the ability to regulate the inhibition of topics. When a conflict is dysregulated, the person may go into a daze, become confused, or experience a chaotic jumble of emotions associated with a particular archetypal configuration. In effect, the person decompensates in a sort of mutiny of the psyche.

Since control is essentially a yin process, hard aspects appear to be implicated in defenses more than soft aspects like the sextile and trine. Although yang planets like Mars, Sun, Jupiter, and Uranus can be involved in defensive functions, these planets would need to be under stress from hard aspects to manifest their more defensive properties. If Mars is under stress from Pluto, for example, the defense of omnipotent control might be utilized to ward off feelings of impotence. Likewise, yang aspects—the conjunction, opposition, sextile, and trine—can serve defensive functions, but again the planets involved in these aspects are likely to also be involved with hard aspects to bring out their defensive properties.

Consider, for example, a trine from Mars to Jupiter, with Mars squaring Pluto. Occasionally this individual loses control of his angry feelings and behaves in a hurtful, malicious way toward others (♂ □ ♇). His aggression, which is repressed (square), is periodically "acted out" in accordance with a defense that typifies Mars. However, when asked to account for his destructive behavior, he utilizes his trine to Jupiter to rationalize his actions. Rationalization is the self-serving use of plausible reasons to justify an action that is actually caused by repressed, unacceptable emotions or ideas. Rationalization is a Jupiter defense, even though Jupiter and the trine are not normally associated with intrapsychic conflict. In this case, however, one can readily see how a Jupiterian defense might come into play.

Certainly when you take a yang planet, like Uranus, and place it in stressful relationship to another planet, such as a square the Moon, the tendency toward the negative side of that planetary combination is more likely to manifest. Moon square Uranus may evidence a tendency toward isolation of affect, minimization, disavowal, and so forth. When working with actual charts, however, there is no way of knowing the extent to which the person might have integrated the conflict.

A hard aspect may entail a use of various defenses; yet, that does not make it neurotic. The decisive factor in how a square manifests is not merely the nature of the planets, signs, and angle, but their degree of integration. To assess this one must examine the actual life experience of the person. This is sometimes difficult for astrologers to grasp, for there is a temptation to presume that how one behaves (character), and what one experiences (fate) is solely the effect of the planetary configuration. Such a conception is deterministic in that it fails to recognize the self-regulating, growth-seeking properties of the psyche. To evaluate the degree to which a conflict has been managed, one must talk to the person.

INTEGRATING NEUROTIC CONFLICT

If a conflict remains unintegrated, the individual will utilize various defense mechanisms in maladaptive ways to prevent conscious recognition of internal conflicts. As Horowitz (1988) put it, "One finds a tendency to repetition of the same unrewarding patterns in interpersonal behavior and to an enduring avoidance of conscious knowledge of unpleasant aspects of the self" (p. 211).

For example, I have a client with Venus square Saturn who avoids thinking about her relational needs by telling herself that she is unattractive and that no one would want her. In truth, she is reasonably attractive, but the Saturnian defense of devaluation serves to keep her from risking rejection (opening square). Although she desires marriage, she cannot bring herself to take steps that would increase the probability of meeting a suitor. Whenever the subject of intimacy comes up, it is as if she makes an unconscious appraisal of where her conscious thought might go, and then gradually or suddenly moves away from the emotional heart and central meaning of the theme. She cannot stay with the issue of her loneliness and allow for the full experiencing of its emotional components.

Unresolved intrapsychic conflict of this sort generally involves two, mutually exclusive and equally negative schemas that are symbolized by the planets forming the aspect. Consider someone with Sun opposition Uranus, which is a classic conflict between the need for validation and the need for detachment. The person is likely to vacillate back and forth between contradictory ideas, both of which relate to the aspect. A client with this aspect, Bill, simultaneously wished to be important and to subordinate his will to the larger group. Instead of finding an adaptive way to satisfy both needs, he used either position as a defense against the dangers embedded in schemas for the opposite need.

On the one hand, Bill feared that if he became attached to preferred outcomes and competed for attention (Sun), he would be ignored. As an individual, he feared that he just didn't matter; thus, when threatened by the consequences of wanting approval, he switched to Uranian schemas involving the self as detached, "I'm just part of the passing parade," he might say. On the other hand, he also feared that if he disavowed his intentions and opted instead for a *que será será* existence, "Whatever happens, happens," then he would eventually lose all sense of individuality and self-volition. Hence when faced with the dreaded consequences of being completely unimportant, he switched to schemas of being very important, "I can change the world."

It was not just that Bill's wishes for approval conflicted with his wish to be detached. The problem was that being important and being detached both had feared consequences. As a result, Bill had no schema to be stabilized; thus, he continually switched back and forth between opposite schemas. Whichever schema was in control, the other was repressed. Before he could clearly think about either side of his Sun-Uranus conflict, he had already felt its emotional consequences in small affective signals. So he switched away the ideational routes to prevent more intense feeling. "The rapid switching between different subthemes of a topic limits conceptual progress to reach solutions to dilemmas and conflicts about any one subtheme," says Horowitz (1988, p. 220).

Bill's derailment of thought from a central, emotional focus was disguised by a defensive logic rather than reasoning through to the solution of a life problem. Rather than say, "I feel unimportant and inconsequential in the big picture," he would complain, "I hate the 'me-generation'; everybody is hung up on their own self-importance." In this remark, the Uranian defense of disavowal is used to undervalue the significance of his healthy, narcissistic (solar) needs, which he is projecting (opposition) onto the 'me-generation'. Minutes later, however, he would boast, "I'm an individual and don't want to be part of a society that worships technological progress. Our culture creates alienation and I'm going to enlighten the masses by writing a book about it." In this later remark, Bill is projecting his Uranian impulses onto "society" while exaggerating his importance in the grand scheme of things (solar defense).

The one thing Bill could not do is hold both sides in mutual awareness. To do so would mean not only that he has to find a single, stabilizing schema, but also allow for its emotional components. It would be painful for Bill to feel the uncertainty of his identity, his guilt about being an individual, and his fear of being subsumed by the collective; yet, if he is to create a stable, coherent sense of self in relation to a larger whole he must learn to tolerate the emotional tension that is inherent in his Sun-Uranus opposition.

COMORBIDITY

It is precisely the inability to reconcile intrapsychic conflict that leads to the employment of defenses designed to reduce pain, stress, or anxiety associated with the conflict. Again, intrapsychic conflict entails competing cognitions and associated unwanted feelings, impulses, and experiences. To manage conflict, defenses are utilized that derive from the nature of the aspect and the planets/signs that comprise it. Every specific defense belongs to a category of defenses that can be grouped under the heading of an astrological archetype, which itself has four variations: planet, sign, house, and aspect. Archetypal defenses that become rigid and excessive lead to mental disorders that constitute the extreme expression of that archetype. In other words, a mental disorder can be regarded as a chronic defense pattern that has metastasized into a full blown illness.

Unresolved intrapsychic conflict typically involves two (or more) mutually exclusive and equally negative schemas symbolized by the planets forming the aspect. The person tends to oscillate between contradictory ideas, each of which generates distress and impairment. This implies that mental illness cannot be reduced to a single archetype such as Uranus, for the over-functioning of Uranus is invariably related to one or more planets with which it is in conflict. It follows that actual mental illness will reflect archetypal compounds comprised of configurations made up of multiple planets, signs, and aspects. For my client, Bill (☉ ☍ ♅), this meant he had narcissistic (solar) traits as well as schizoid-like (Uranian) traits. While he was not wholly one or the other, he exhibited some symptomology of both.

The concept of comorbidity captures this situation precisely. Comorbidity is a psychological term indicating that different mental disorders can overlap and interact within the same person, just as archetypes do with planetary aspects. Accordingly, comorbidity refers to the presence of more than one diagnosis occurring in an individual at the same time. In psychiatric classification, however, comorbidity does not necessarily mean the definitive co-existence of multiple disorders, but instead reflects the current inability to supply a single diagnosis that accounts for all symptoms a patient has. For example, depression is a common comorbid condition in that it can coincide with a variety of symptoms that pertain to other disorders. Again, this is consistent with astrology. The difference is that astrology provides clear objective indicators that symbolize exactly the various components of a client's symptomology.

A closing square between Moon and Neptune, for example, may correlate with depressive symptoms while also involving some lunar (histrionic) and neptunian pathology (schizotypal). Picture a sad, lonely, and confused woman who dresses in an inordinately sexy way to capture the attention of men while simultaneously believing she is the reincarnation of Cleopatra. Is she histrionic? Yes, to a degree. Is she schizotypal? Yes, to a degree. Is she depressed? Yes, to a degree. The point is that no single diagnosis can possibly do justice to the unique compounding of archetypal factors that comprise this aspect (Moon square Neptune) of her character.

Because the comorbidity of personality disorders is excessively high, approaching 60% in some cases, the very concept of personality disorders has been challenged. Critics of the DSM argue that these categories of mental illness are too imprecisely distinguished to be usefully valid for diagnostic purposes and, thus, for determining how treatment should proceed. Moreover, alleged concomitance of two or more diagnoses may be incorrect because in most cases it is unclear whether the concomitant diagnoses actually reflect the presence of distinct clinical entities or multiple manifestations of a single clinical entity.

Astrology helps us to understand the nature of the problem. I have a friend with Moon conjunct Saturn in Virgo straddling his Ascendant. Having been depressed for the past five years, he is a textbook case of depressive personality disorder. In fact, he has virtually every symptom—gloomy, pessimistic, blaming, negative, guilty, and so on. Yet, he is also perfectionistic, exacting, miserly, fretting and anxious, overly focused on details, excessively devoted to work at the expense of play, preoccupied with cleanliness and health matters—in short, a textbook case of Obsessive Compulsive Disorder (OCD).

The question arises whether he is suffering from both depression and OCD, or merely depression with OCD features, or perhaps OCD with depressive features. As a product of mechanistic reasoning rooted in the medical model, the DSM framework tends to put people in boxes with clearly differentiated diagnostic labels. The implication is that for each disorder, one size fits all, even if in practice we know this to be untrue. Real people present clinical pictures as distinctive as a DNA signature—or, as the case may be, an astrological chart.

My friend with Saturn conjunct Moon in Virgo on the Ascendant cannot be easily diagnosed, for while a dominant Saturn on his Ascendant may symbolize depressive tendencies, he is depressed in a Virgonian way and for reasons that also involve his Moon. The Ascendant makes its own contribution to the mix (he can be very aggressive in his own depressed, obsessive fashion), so that in addition to the aforementioned symptoms he has many other traits as well, all of which contribute to a rich, complex clinical picture.

His condition is not merely the consequence of a univocal illness that can be explained away with a simple label, but emerges out of the interaction of multiple archetypal strands woven together in a singularly unique way, as is the case with every human being and as shown by every astrological chart.

From an astropsychological perspective, psychopathology is a synergistic process that shifts and evolves over time. It may seem to be focused on one or a few archetypes, such as solar pathology expressed in narcissistic traits, but even here there are variations contingent on the Sun's sign and house position, its aspects to other planets, and so on. Thinking about psychopathology in terms of singular diagnoses is inherently limiting, since an archetype is not likely to be pathological unless it is under stress and in conflict with some other archetype(s).

If the Sun is in hard aspect to Neptune, for example, then its most extreme, dysfunctional expression will likely be some combination of narcissistic and schizotypal traits—as, for example, in someone who claims to be a channel for divine beings from a higher spiritual dimension.[37] The claim to have transcendent, prophetic powers (thereby defining oneself as a being of superior evolutionary stature) is simultaneously narcissistic and schizotypal; thus, both disorders are present to varying degrees in the same person. Moreover, this same aspect may contribute both healthy and pathological traits thus forming a unique blend that resists easy categorization. And finally, a predisposition toward narcissistic/schizotypal vulnerability may be exacerbated by a transit of specific meaning and duration, which adds its own archetypal catalyst into the system.

By contrast, conventional approaches to psychopathology seem to operate on the presumption that psychopathology can be divided neatly into discrete categories that exist as actual entities, things rather than processes. The 'thing' approach is reductionistic in that it collapses a complex human being into a singular way of being. This is, in short, the classic disease model. A disease is associated with specific symptoms and signs that impair normal function and are the effect of antecedent causes of a physical nature—pathogenic microbial agents such as viruses, bacteria, and fungi. These infectious organisms produce a relatively precise set of symptoms. A patient suffering from malaria, or tuberculosis, or cholera will exhibit symptoms that are entirely consistent with the symptoms of other people that contracted the disease.

---

[37] See, for example, the chart of Elizabeth Clare Prophet (Sun conjunct Saturn with both planets quincunx Neptune), a self-proclaimed divine messenger who fraudulently claimed to be channeling some 200 different 'Ascended Masters' all of whom sounded suspiciously similar.

In some ways, the disease model can provide a useful analogy for psychological states and processes. However, it may also blind practitioners to ways that psychopathology is radically different from physical disease. Psychopathology is not the effect of antecedent causes such as infectious organisms that invade the system from the outside; rather, it is an emergent property of a person's distinctive, inborn character. We recognize this implicitly, of course, when we say that personality disorders are characterological. Note that character is plural, not singular; it is complex by its very nature, comprised of multiple, interacting parts in a state of continuous, dynamic flux and pulled, teleologically, toward higher, more integrated states of being.

While astrological archetypes may constitute discrete categories, the people that form from them do not. Just as a musical composition is made up of multiple instruments playing a spectrum of notes in coordinated orchestration, so a human being is made up of multiple functions expressed in diverse ways producing melody and harmony in proportion to their integration. All of this is to say that comorbidity is the norm rather than the exception. To reduce a human being to a single archetype in its most discordant form is analogous to an orchestrated score comprised of a single instrument playing loudly and obnoxiously. This, clearly, is not the natural order of things.

Due to its artifactual nature as a product of the DSM framework, the concept of comorbidity may be a Kuhnian anomaly leading the DSM into a scientific crisis. That is, the ubiquity of comorbidity in the psychopathology of everyday life is forcing the DSM to grapple with the unsettling realization that complex human beings cannot be reduced to mental diseases that are analogous to physical diseases. So long as psychopathology is not properly understood in terms of its archetypal and psychodynamic underpinnings, the complexities of which are so aptly symbolized in horoscopes, real people will be chopped and stretched to fit procrustean beds of falsely simplistic diagnostic categories.

STABILIZING SCHEMAS

The concept of a stabilizing schema refers to an integrative belief. It is essentially an adaptive compromise formation that bridges the conflict of two planets and allows for mutual satisfaction of relevant needs. Again, when there is enduring conflict, individuals tend to oscillate back and forth between contradictory schemas. Conversely, an integrative belief assumes mutual satisfaction of both functions.

When conflict is involved, it often can be difficult to follow clients' train of thought. First they say one thing, and then another, "Yes, but on the other hand." While this can be frustrating for the counselor, it is also maddening for clients. For they feel caught in damned-if-you-do and damned-if-you-don't dilemmas. Ideally, a new schema will eventually emerge that constitutes a stabilizing compromise for the aspect. The unconscious conflict embedded in contradictory schemas is thus modified by the development of the new schema. To achieve this, one has to change the competing beliefs that serve as defenses against dreaded feelings and experiences. Only by becoming conscious of heretofore unconscious ideas and negative feelings can one develop new, more positive and realistic schemas for managing the relevant needs.

For my client, Bill (☉ ☍ ♅), this meant saying something like, "I realize my power to change the world is limited. However, I can still feel good about my efforts to awaken others to new perspectives. We all have a role to play. I'm just a drop in the bucket, to be sure, but I can still make a difference." Such a statement feels better because it represents a stabilizing schema for integrating his Sun-Uranus opposition. The new schema does not constitute solar inflation at the expense of Uranian detachment; nor does it exaggerate his Uranian insignificance to the detriment of healthy, solar/egoic strivings.

As a person integrates a hard aspect, they can allow themselves to experience both planetary energies more fully, thus increasing their level of felt emotion. They can tolerate thinking about conflicting ideas without having to judge themselves or insist on immediate decisions. With this increase in tolerance for emotions, especially for sadness, fear, anger, and guilt, one can review his or her life patterns and see a repetitive story in them. Repressed memories are recalled from childhood, and one is able to get a clearer perspective on one's own life history and personal development. Memories once organized from a child's frame of reference can be reorganized by the new meanings available from adult contexts. Thus, irrational fears about current relationships can be better understood and eventually released.

DEVELOPMENTAL INTERFERENCES

In the proposed model, each sign symbolizes a specific developmental stage with an associated task. These stages and tasks will be more fully articulated in subsequent chapters. Suffice to say here that each house, like its corresponding sign, specifies certain kinds of experiences that occur during the developmental period to which it correlates. An individual's actual experience of that house/stage will be reflected by the planets that tenant that house. If the 2nd house signifies security and attachment needs—the task of attaining self and object constancy—then planets in the 2nd symbolize the actual experiences that highlight this stage, as well as the likelihood of self and object constancy having been mastered. For example, there may be an experience of loss, tragedy, or degradation of security between 2 and 5 years old if Neptune is in the 2nd. In other words, the impact of Neptune vis-à-vis issues of security, safety, and attachment will be most acute during this period.

Environmental events that prevent fulfillment of the child's developmentally appropriate needs constitute *developmental interferences*. For example, the tragic loss of an important attachment figure at 3 years would interfere with the development of self and object constancy. Such interferences are prototypical of internal conflicts, which take shape as the child interprets and internalizes his or her actual experiences.

With Uranus in the 4th, for example, the period of 9-14 years may be particularly difficult. This can be surmised from the fact that the archetypal relationship of Uranus to the 4th is quincunxial. That is, the signs that correspond to Uranus (Aquarius) and the 4th house (Cancer) are quincunx in the natural zodiac. The 4th house signifies a time of life when children are developing Cancerian attributes. These include the capacity to reflect upon, contain, and articulate feelings, which deepens their sense of belonging and connection with loved ones. With Uranus in this house, the child might have experienced significant change and instability during this period. Perhaps the family moved frequently, or the mother was schizoid, or the family was emotionally disengaged such that there was little modeling or support for appropriate expression of feelings.

The situation could be compounded if Uranus also forms a hard aspect to the Moon, thus repeating the message of Uranus in the 4th (Uranus in the Moon's house). Perhaps the Moon is in the 11th and forms a closing quincunx to Uranus in the 4th. Now we have a confluence of factors that in three different ways are repeating the same message. The Moon is in Uranus' house, Uranus is in the Moon's house, and the two planets are quincunx. If one considers that Uranus, as ruler of Aquarius, signifies the developmental period of 65-77 years, then its impingement upon the Moon suggests that the child of 9-14 is required to adapt to circumstances that would be appropriate for a 65 year-old. Moreover, these circumstances create a crisis (closing quincunx) that interferes with the development of age-appropriate (Cancerian) skills.

Uranus signifies a capacity for broad overview and emotional detachment that enables one to function in an altruistic, humanitarian way. The keynote is liberation from old, outmoded structures, and a revelation of how one has been conditioned by the past. Imagine, however, that a child's family is rendered unstable because of catastrophic events that create a shocking break-up in the family system. Perhaps the father loses his job because of company restructuring and the family suddenly has to move to a poor neighborhood. This is followed by a divorce, forcing the mother to find a job to support her family. Unable to cope with this upsetting development, she becomes so emotionally cut off that she is unable to respond in a sympathetic manner to her child's feelings of loss. The child senses this sudden drying up of support, identifies with his mother's emotional cut-off, and detaches from his own feelings.

One can see in this scenario how changes that might typify an adult in his 70's—retirement from career, a move to a smaller home in another town, new involvements in group activities—are utterly overwhelming to a child of 10 whose family is breaking apart like a ship in a storm. In this manner, an outer planet, like Uranus, signifies a developmental process that can impinge upon and conflict with processes that signify earlier developmental tasks. The child is forced to function in an altruistic, humanitarian manner by helping his parents adapt to their new surroundings and lifestyle; yet, such a task is utterly beyond the child's capacity and, additionally, interferes with what the child most needs during this period of her life: a tender, caring, intact, and emotionally stable family system. In the absence of such a family, the child's ability to fulfill the Cancerian task of this stage—the awakening of emotional intelligence, development of a capacity for reflection, and the ability to contain and articulate (rather than act out) feelings—is compromised. Thus, a developmental interference leads to an internalized conflict that may persist into adulthood.

This underscores how an adult's internal conflict is frequently the continuation of a developmental conflict from childhood that could not resolve itself properly at the appropriate time. Some conflicts persist throughout life, leading to various degrees of pathology. Of course, manifestations of pathology vary according to one's developmental level and the nature of the pathology. As an adult, our person with Moon quincunx Uranus may be emotionally unstable and will find it difficult to access feelings.

It is important to note, however, that developmental interferences do not always lead to enduring internal conflicts. Circumstances that might contribute to an internal conflict at one stage may give way to circumstances at a subsequent stage that can aid in the mastery of problems. Many conflicts are more or less resolved as development continues.

Recall that experiences in a given house are going to be most acute during the developmental stage that corresponds to that house. For example, our Uranus in the 4th child at 10 years old may appear to be in a state of shock, exhibiting signs of psychic numbing and emotional anesthesia in response to the break-up of her family. Imagine, however, that her Uranus in the 4th not only is quincunx the Moon, but also sextiles Mars in the 6th and trines Jupiter in the 8th. By the time she graduates from college and goes to work (20-27 yrs = Virgo/6th stage), her Mars in the 6th is predominant. Perhaps she utilizes a degree in social work (♃ 8th) to advocate (♃ ✶ ♂) for children of divorce (♃ ✶ ♂ ✶ ♅ 4th) and thus becomes a powerful ally to families that are undergoing stressful upheavals of the sort that she experienced as a child.

Such a 6th house job would reflect Mars' sextiles to Uranus and Jupiter. Moreover, her experiences at this stage might serve to repair some of the damage that occurred when she was 9-14. By identifying with the recipients of her own good 6th house works, she is helping herself master an earlier developmental trauma that originated in 4th house circumstances. Also, her higher education (♃) as a social worker (8th house of healing) may actually require her to heal some of the trauma that occurred earlier in her life. This is suggested by Jupiter's likely square to the Moon in the 11th and its trine to Uranus in the 4th. In order to help the families for whom she must advocate, she needs to teach (♃) them how to contain, reflect upon, and express feelings (☽) in an appropriate manner. If she cannot do this herself, she will need appropriate help, such as through supervision or therapy—thus making up for the deficit of support that she experienced at age 9-14. Again, this might enable her to recover lunar potentials that were compromised during that earlier stage.

SUMMARY AND CONCLUSION

Pathogenesis refers to those processes within an individual that produce and maintain psychopathology. Inherent factors refer to essential constituents of a disorder, such as a conflict between specific functions and needs. The consequences of a disorder, however, derive from an individual's capacity to integrate, manage, and express the conflicting functions that underlay the condition.

Whereas causes in astrology can be understood as facilitating and predisposing, they are neither necessary nor sufficient to bring about a particular condition. A given chart factor can symbolize a contributing dynamic to a mental disorder, but is never in itself a determining factor.

Intrapsychic conflict is at the heart of psychopathology. Conflict occurs when instinctual wishes come into contact with internal or external prohibitions. What is wished for vies with what is dreaded, and potential conflicts are negotiated by schemas that strive to find a compromise between satisfaction and frustration. External prohibitions generally derive from parental failures, either sins of omission or commission. These are metabolized into negative expectations and internal prohibitions. A wish for a desired state and a corollary fear of a dreaded outcome produces compromise formations: self-limiting beliefs and maladaptive schemas that generate self-defeating behavior.

Whereas conflict is inherent in the zodiac, the type, degree, and intensity of a conflict derives from the nature and exactitude of the angle between the respective planets. The specifics of a conflict depend upon the planets that make up the aspect, as well as the signs and houses involved. Typically, an intrapsychic conflict is comprised of bi-polar pathogenic beliefs. These are competing schemas that accrue to separate planets, each of which predicts a negative consequence if the other planet achieves its aims. One or the other schema influences behavior from an unconscious level; and there is a tendency for control to oscillate between them.

Defense mechanisms are designed to prevent the individual from becoming emotionally overwhelmed and psychologically disorganized in response to internal or external conflict. Each sign-planet system and its corollary aspect can be linked with a set of related defenses. A defense mechanism, in effect, is a behavioral process that has become rigid and excessive. To the extent that conflicts remain unintegrated, individuals will employ defense mechanisms in habitual, maladaptive ways to prevent conscious recognition of dreaded thoughts and feelings.

For healing to occur, the individual must integrate bi-polar beliefs into a single, stabilizing schema that allows for mutual satisfaction of respective wishes. In so doing, a greater capacity to tolerate intense emotion is realized. Feelings that derive from old, maladaptive schemas can then be released. Very often the origins of these schemas can be traced back to traumatic childhood experiences that are symbolized by difficult planetary placements in specific houses. Each house represents a developmental stage. Planets that tenant that house, along with their sign positions and aspects, suggest probable experiences that occurred during that period.

Chapter Nine

COMPLEXES IN THE BIRTHCHART

In Chapter Two, we explored how the individual psyche is rooted in the Universal Psyche, which fosters development of the human mind via archetypal nutrients that saturate the field of consciousness. Archetypes comprise the structure and dynamics of the Universal Mind. As such, they also comprise the structure and dynamics of the individual mind, the conscious part of which is but the budding of a vaster organism, the *Self*, which is deeply rooted in the divine ground.

For unknown, possibly karmic reasons, certain archetypal configurations function like a cramp in the soul, a kind of knot or contraction that causes psychic pain. This is Jung's concept of the *complex*—an emotionally charged psychic entity comprised of a group of related, often repressed ideas and impulses that compel distinctive patterns of thought, feeling, and behavior. Like a vortex in the field of consciousness, the complex draws attention to itself and represents a habitual sore spot.

At the center of the complex is an archetype, or cluster of archetypes. Because the complex by definition contains repressed material, it is at least partially unconscious. These emotionally sensitive areas reveal themselves by the emergence of an affect that upsets psychic balance and disturbs the customary function of the ego. A person may suddenly react in an extreme way that is disproportionate to the stimulus. He or she overreacts, is inexplicably angry, or "jumps the gun". When a complex is activated, something seems to "take over" that has its own autonomy, its own ideas about reality, and its own feelings that seem compacted and ready to explode.

Freud discovered that the complex could also communicate itself through an unconscious pun or word substitution, which came to be known as, "The

Freudian slip." Just as dreams can symbolize parts of the self, so also the complex can intrude into consciousness in disguised form, often through some silly but meaningful miscombination of words and images. Other times the complex reveals itself by a memory blockage. In the middle of a conversation, the individual may suddenly lose his flow of thought as if unexpectedly stumbling upon an inner image that is disturbing. The eyes glaze over; a startled expression comes over the face; the voice stammers. These are all signs that a complex has been encountered.

As a psychological concept, the complex had its origins in late 19th century France. Charcot theorized that mental disorders were characterized by isolated pockets of associated ideas that were disconnected from consciousness and seemed to have a life of their own. The French physician, Pierre Janet, later coined the phrase *idée fixe subconsciente* (subconscious fixed idea) to describe these split-off personality fragments that wielded such power. Janet's *idée fixe* eventually became Jung's concept of the complex, which he introduced into psychoanalytic thought in the early 20th century.

As a cognitive structure, the complex is characterized by an exaggerated or obsessive concern. Just as personality disorders entail chronic, maladaptive schemas, these "fixed ideas" are rigid and difficult to change despite the negative consequences they bring in their wake. The complex may attach itself to any number of things—a political or religious ideology, a scientific theory, a compelling topic of interest, a cause, or a personal crusade. Regardless of the manifest content of the complex, the energy around the objective is all consuming, as if the person is possessed. There is little tolerance for looking at alternative perspectives or for giving up the quest. The complex is so inextricably intertwined with the person's identity and *raison d'etre* that s/he couldn't conceive of being any other way.

While the complex may comprise a powerful force within the overall identity, it also has an identity of its own. Early researchers spoke in terms of "divided will," as if the complex had its own self-will and intentions. Jung called them "splinter psyches." Since a complex is only relatively modulated by the ego/Sun, it tends to be extreme and primitive in its manifestation. Once possessed by the complex, the mental and emotional attitude can be rather frightening because there seems to be little capacity for reason, objectivity, or balance. Something has taken over and the person is no longer his or her usual self. At such times, one cannot dialogue with the individual in ordinary ways.

LOCATING THE COMPLEX IN THE CHART

Astrologically, a complex can be depicted in the same ways that symbolize psychopathology in general—a hard aspect from either Saturn or an outer planet, a singleton, the focal planet of a T-square or Yod, planets in the 8th or 12th, a stellium, and other indicators that were covered in Chapter 6. The more a planet is characterized by the above factors, the more likely it will constitute at least part of a complex.

By way of example, I had a client, Sarah, with Moon conjunct Mars and Pluto in the 2nd, with all three planets squaring Uranus in the 11th. When it comes to any situation involving war (Mars), she becomes completely unreasonable. Her protective instincts (Moon) are activated, which, in turn, catalyzes her Pluto and Uranus. At such times she is aggressively protective, reactive, and emotional in her opposition to violence (no matter what the circumstances). Moreover, she is revolutionary in her attitude toward the United States government. To call her a pacifist would be missing the point, since she has been arrested on numerous occasions for her anti-war protests.

The Moon, of course, is the most personal of all planets, and is associated with patriotism and nationalism. Mars signifies war/aggression, and Pluto rules trauma and shadow issues. If these three planets were merely operating in a triple conjunction, Sarah might have been fervently, militantly nationalistic. But the fact that Uranus squares this three-planet combo adds a conflictual element of radicalism, globalism, and revolutionary sentiment to the mix.

By itself, Uranus is wholistic and thus more global and international in its perspective. Accordingly, the square from Uranus correlates to her rabidly anti-American stance. In effect, all four planets are bound up in her complex, which could be summarized as a radical conviction that: "Life must *always* be protected against aggression no matter what the circumstances." It never occurred to Sarah that the hatred, anger, aggression, and violence that she displayed in her protests (she would resist arrest and fight police) encapsulated the very thing she allegedly was fighting against. Note the Plutonic defense of reaction formation that is implicit in her behavior. It is others who are viciously warlike, not her, for she professes to be absolutely the antithesis of what she is fighting against. This is perhaps another example of, "The lady doth protest too much."

Timothy McVeigh, the expatriate/terrorist who in 1995 blew up the Federal Building in Oklahoma City and waged a one-man war against the U.S. government, had a similar configuration: Pluto conjunct Uranus in the 4th with both planets opposing Moon in the 10th. McVeigh's Moon also sextiled Mars in the 12th, which is trine Uranus and Pluto. So, the same four planets were involved as with Sarah. And like Sarah, McVeigh was utterly unrepentant, unreasonable, and extreme in his opposition to the U.S. government. McVeigh and Sarah both seemed relatively unconscious of their own aggression and violent attitudes—or, at least found a way to rationalize them. This suggests a shadow issue, which can be implicit in a complex.

In severe instances, the complex can gather so much energy and intensity that it forms a split-off personality dissociated from the ego. So-called "multiple personality disorder" is an extreme example of how the complex can germinate in a dark corner of the psyche inaccessible to the individual, and then suddenly "take over." It operates subversively and brings about various kinds of personality disorders. For example, the alleged Boston Strangler, Albert DeSalvo, who sexually assaulted then murdered 13 women in Boston over a period of two years, has a 4-planet stellium in Virgo involving Venus, Mercury, the Sun, and Neptune, all in the 10th house.[38] More importantly, his stellium makes no other aspects; thus, it functions alone, like a runaway train.

Whenever DeSalvo experienced a Venusian impulse, he went into a trance and acted out his desires without any apparent reflection, guilt, or regard for negative consequences. Unmediated by other planets, the stellium simply operated as a pure unconscious impulse to overpower women and force his will (Sun) upon them. Neptune's involvement in the stellium would appear to correlate with the trance-like, dissociated state that DeSalvo would fall into when he sexually assaulted his victims. DeSalvo's berserk behavior seems eerily captured by Jung's (1960) description of the complex:

> It [the complex] is the image of a certain psychic situation that is strongly accentuated emotionally and is, moreover, incompatible with the habitual attitude of consciousness. This image has a powerful inner coherence, it has its own wholeness and, in addition, a relatively high degree of autonomy, so that it is subject to the control of the conscious mind to only a limited extent, and therefore behaves like an animated foreign body in the sphere of consciousness. The complex can usually be suppressed with an effort of will, but not argued out of exis-

---

[38] DeSalvo's birth data is: 9/3/31, 11:58am, Chelsea, MA. Reported in Young and Rowland's (1995) *Destined for Murder*, published by Llewellyn.

tence, and at the first suitable opportunity it reappears in all its original strength. (p. 96)

Jung's description of the complex emphasizes two factors. First, there is a nuclear element, or archetypal core, which acts as a magnet. Second, there are myriad personal experiences replete with associated memories, meanings, and feelings, which are attracted by this magnet. Complexes can be understood, therefore, as containing archetypal cores that, when activated, draw personal experiences to them.

This conception effectively reverses conventional notions of causality. Rather than depicting psychological problems as the effect of externally originating causes, such as parents or society, Jung suggested that pre-existent problems actually draw to themselves corollary events. The outer events are not primary causes, but merely the outer, surface covering of a deeper, inborn dynamic, which is its own cause. This conception is clearly in accord with astrology and the doctrine of reincarnation.

The nuclear element of the complex is analogous to what is inherent to a disorder. Astrologically, this can be depicted by a planetary aspect, which is comprised of signs (needs/impulses), planets (functions), houses (contexts), and angle (type and degree of conflict). This constellation of archetypal elements comprises the core of the complex. Attracted to this structure, however, are characteristic experiences made up of people and events that synchronistically mirror the archetypal core. These outer experiences are the consequences of the complex; that is, they reflect the degree to which the complex has been integrated.

The external corollary to the internal wound (complex) may be a tragic or otherwise difficult fate that constitutes a source of chronic stress. Generally, there will be a prototypical childhood event that crystallizes and encapsulates the meaning of the complex. These are signature events in that they symbolize a core theme of the life story. Whereas the theme may be encapsulated in a singular event—a child is molested, a parent dies, a boy is humiliated by an older brother, a girl suffers a debilitating accident and almost dies—the event itself may merely be the most salient of an ongoing pattern. However insignificant an isolated incident might appear, it can be "the straw that broke the camel's back". As such, it leaves a deep, enduring scar on the psyche. James Hillman calls such events "initiation cuts," or marks of character, which constitute the defining features of one's life and soul.

A signature event might correlate to a major transit or progression during childhood. The experience fleshes out the archetypal core of the natal aspect and gives it a particular slant or meaning. The complex then becomes associated with these personal memories, which form around the complex like tissue on bone. The underlying structure of the natal aspect—the bone—may eventually attract any number of flesh and blood personal experiences. Ultimately, such experiences, beginning with the signature event, are internalized (introjected), assigned a meaning, and come to comprise the layering of personal associations that surround the archetypal core.

The life of the complex is an iterative cycle of projecting and introjecting the contents of which it is comprised. In childhood, the initial manifestation of the complex may be some situation or relationship that is frustrating, depriving, traumatizing, or otherwise painful. These early experiences constitute the prototypical event-pattern that characterizes that complex. Once experienced, they are taken in, metabolized, and assimilated into psychic structure. Subsequently, the individual puts out (projects) the state of his inner world; that is, his cast of characters or "internal objects," which inhabit him. He does not perceive the outer world objectively, for his complexes color his perceptions and shape his responses. Resultant experiences are once again introjected and added to an ever-changing inner-world reality—a story that builds and evolves over time.

Introjected objects are not totally accurate perceptions of an outer reality, for they are altered to some extent by the individual's pre-existing complexes. In other words, what is important is not so much the event itself, but what it symbolizes on an inner level. The signature event might be a molestation, the trauma of which dissipates over time; yet, subsequent recollections still disturb because of what it the original event means—that one is vulnerable to violation by an overwhelming destructive force. Later experiences that remind one of the original trauma are assigned a similar meaning and evoke a similar response. For example, a woman might react intensely when a man moves to kiss her at the end of a first date. He is expressing affection; she experiences violation in accord with her internal objects. Another woman without such a pre-existent trauma would regard the same event (kissing) as relatively benign or even desirable.

Exteriorization of archetypal contents is the usual and customary way a complex comes into view. Such externalizations initially constitute signature events that are wounding or disturbing. The early manifestation of the complex may seem like fate, or even a curse. Liz Greene (1997), for example, says:

Greek myth, with its vivid portrayals of the 'family curse' and the compulsions visited upon humans by gods, gives us our earliest models of how a complex operates....Not only family curses, but also family gifts could be inherited in this way. What is most psychologically relevant about these mythic portrayals is the compulsive nature of this 'something' which drives human beings into beliefs, actions and feelings over which they have no conscious control and which are often in violent opposition to their ethics and values. (p. 1-2)

While experience of the complex may initially manifest as a real event-pattern in childhood, subsequent outer events will be perceived as conforming to the complex. That is, external reality will be distorted to conform to the mind's own structures. The mind sees what it expects to see.

EVALUATING A COMPLEX

Jung thought of the complex primarily in terms of psychic energy. A complex was strong or weak according to the amount of psychic energy bound up with it. While there was no objective way to quantify the energy of a complex, its strength could be assessed by noting the degree to which it dominated consciousness. How intense were certain associated feelings, thoughts, and ideas? How preoccupied was the person with this area of life? To what extent did it usurp control and influence behavior?

When evaluating the nature and strength of a complex, objective indicators in the birth chart can supplement observations of actual behavior. We know that the more aspects a planet receives, the more likely that planet will be a central player in the life drama. Likewise, to the extent that a planet is under stress by hard aspects and/or difficult sign and house placements, that planetary archetype is likely to constitute a key component of a complex. All aspects involved with the planet would symbolize the complex as a whole. In this way, one can evaluate its strength and pervasiveness. A simple square involving two planets will bind less psychic energy than a T-Square involving four or five planets.

Yin aspects (squares and quincunxes) represent a concentration or pooling of psychic energy that builds up pressure. This is because planets are impulses to be expressed; yet, the counteracting, suppressing nature of the square or quincunx tends to hold them back. This is similar to what happens in any energy producing system. Planets under stress are like hydroelectric power plants. First, a damn is built that stores a large quantity of water. The water is then released in measured amounts and in such a way that a mechanism is driven by the power of the onrushing current, which can be captured and stored as energy. The same principle applies to hard aspects. Archetypal energy is pooled, or stored, by the natural inhibitory nature of yin angles. When this energy is released, it generates power. The key is containment and control. To the extent that psychic energy can be regulated and released in a measured way, work can be done and goals accomplished.

Although conjunctions and oppositions can present problems, too, there is not really a suppression of energy; thus, these aspects are less likely to work in the slow, methodical way of the yin angles. Yang aspects are more impulsive and spontaneous. Rather than energy building up, it is quickly released. Whereas the opposition requires coordination and balancing of the respective planetary energies, the conjunction (or stellium) has no restraints whatsoever. Unless balanced by at least some yin aspects, a stellium is apt to function in a primal, impulsive, and egocentric manner. Even stelliums, however, can be projected. I have witnessed cases in which a person's stellium seems relatively quiescent. Invariably in such instances it is embodied by someone with whom the individual is in a close relationship, who acts it out for the person often at their own expense.

FRANK'S COMPLEX

As an example of a complex, a former client, Frank, had four planets in Aries in the 10th house opposing three planets in Libra in the 4th (see Figure 23, page 297). His Aries planets, which included his Sun, Jupiter, Mercury, and Venus, were clearly represented by his father (10th house), who was a brilliant narcissist (Sun), a publisher of educational materials (Jupiter and Mercury), and a consummate know-it-all with a rather nasty aggressive streak (Aries). Conversely, his 4th house Libra planets, which included Saturn and the Moon conjunct Neptune, clearly symbolized his beautiful, kind, ultra-sensitive, suffering, and depressed mother, whom the father would periodically eviscerate with his intellect.

What was traumatic for Frank was that he had to witness this devaluation of his mother over his entire childhood. He could feel his mother's pain, but was helpless to protect her. Although Frank would challenge his father in his mother's defense, this only succeeded in bringing the father's wrath upon Frank. Without mercy, Frank's father physically abused him for siding with his mother. When Frank's mother eventually left her husband, he was so embittered that he refused to speak with her for 24 years. Frank's failure to rescue his mother, sensitize his father, or save his parent's marriage, all resulted in a heap of guilt.

Again, this is symbolized by the aforementioned Aries and Libra planets, two of which—Mercury and Saturn—are involved in a T-square to Uranus. This three-planet combo seems to parallel Frank's triangulation into his parent's unstable marriage. Most important, however, is the Sun-Jupiter opposition to Moon-Neptune, which symbolizes the father's lack of empathy, the mother's victimization, and Frank's guilt over not being able to relieve the suffering of all concerned. Taken together, this astrological configuration symbolizes a complex that states: women (and underlings) are forced to endure male dominance and devaluation.

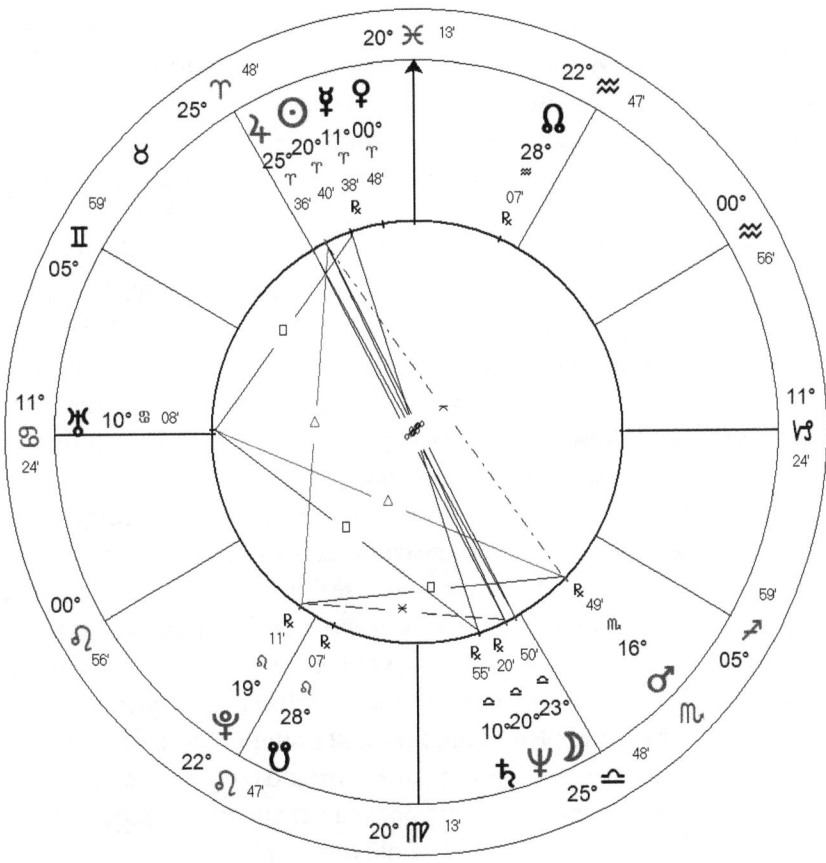

Figure 23: Birthchart of Frank

By the time Frank was an adult, he settled into a relationship pattern that recapitulated his childhood predicament. He would become compulsively attracted to the wives of his associates and superiors. Invariably, these marriages were unstable, which no doubt accounts for why the women were willing to sleep with Frank. It was not the sex or romance, however, that motivated Frank, but the need to re-educate the wife and make her more assertive in relation to her husband. This was his real compulsion. His affairs would typically devolve into a type of counseling relationship in which Frank would offer free and endless advice as to how the wife could save her marriage by being more assertive and confrontational—or, if that didn't work, why she should leave her husband for him.

Without realizing it, however, the years were passing by. Frank was nearly fifty and had never married—though marriage and children were things he thought he always wanted. Despite his behavior in these unfortunate affairs, Frank was otherwise honest, kind, and deeply spiritual. The tragedy was that he had sacrificed his best years for reasons that were more or less completely unconscious. With his realization of this sacrifice came a deep sense of sadness and loss, which motivated him to seek therapy.

Eventually it became clear that Frank avoided real relationship for two interrelated reasons: (1) he didn't feel deserving of having a better relationship than either of his parents, since he unconsciously felt responsible for their pain; and (2) he feared being domineering toward woman in the same way that his father dominated his mother. To compensate for this latter fear, he projected domineering traits onto the husbands of the women that he seduced, and elected himself as their savior.

During the course of therapy, his fears about relationship became manifest in relation to me. As always, the complex has to be projected for it to become conscious. It was difficult to get close to Frank because although he yearned for connection, unconsciously he was afraid of it. His direct transference (projection) was that I was like his father—egocentric, nonempathic, demeaning, rigid, impatient, domineering, and the like. In other words, he was projecting his Aries planets onto me and assuming the role of Moon/Neptune in Libra. At such times he was evasive and tangential, as if he were trying to avoid being a target. He did not want to submit, or depend, or be vulnerable in any way, for fear that I would run over him like a train. In fact, it was often just the opposite. Utilizing the strategy that the best defense is a good offense, Frank would aggressively filibuster during sessions in order to keep me at bay. I simply couldn't get a word in edgewise. In this sense, Frank was "acting out" his Aries planets in a defensive manner.

At other times, he would switch "passive into active" and treat me the way his father treated him.[39] Now he would act out his Aries planets in a more direct, conscious manner by being competitive, angry, demeaning, and devaluing of the therapy. What was evoked in me was the Moon-Neptune experience of being run over, misunderstood, and hurt by an aggressive, obnoxious man.

Of course, I did my best not to identify with and act out his Moon-Neptune projection. As his therapist, my job was to contain the experience and talk about it in a way that provided Frank with a positive model. Until Frank's "transference" was interpreted and resolved, his progress in therapy was minimal. Frank's tendency to switch back and forth between direct and passive-into-active transference illustrates the phenomenon of oscillating bi-polar beliefs. First one belief is in control, and then the other.

While a full analysis of Frank's complex is beyond the scope of this chapter, we can summarize it briefly. First, it consisted of a group of archetypes symbolized by his planets in Aries and Libra, along with the T-square to Uranus. This was the nuclear element of the complex. Second, Frank's initial experience with his parents was the first manifestation of his complex, the difficult fate that immersed him in their pain. Note how the strong, outgoing, yang planets—Sun conjunct Jupiter in Aries—which symbolized his father (10th house), were opposed to the more passive, sensitive, yin planets—Moon conjunct Neptune in Libra, which symbolized his mother (4th house).

The unintegrated version of this configuration is expressed in the prototypical manifestation of his parent's marriage: an irrepressible, domineering father who projected his sensitive, spiritual side onto his wife, and a suffering, vulnerable mother who projected her strong, aggressive side onto her husband. Yet, both sides were in Frank, though he was more consciously identified with his mother. It is worth noting that since Frank is male, one might expect him to be more identified with his father; however, if a father is too frightening, abusive, or rejecting, the child is more likely to consciously identify with the other parent. On an unconscious level, however, Frank would still carry an inner image of his father as a complex that could unconsciously be acted out at any time. In other words, Frank's Aries planets, which, like his mother, he projected, symbolized the more problematic aspect of the

---

[39] Passive into active transference occurs when the client treats the therapist the way that he was treated as a child. This is in contrast to "direct" transference in which the client perceives the therapist as like a significant person (usually a parent) from childhood. Clients can switch back and forth between *direct* and *passive into active* transferences.

complex. This is what he feared and reviled in other people—aggression, dogmatism, and selfishness.

The prototypical situation of his family later repeated itself via habitual affairs with the spouses of his friends. By recreating his childhood predicament, Frank attempted to work out unfinished business from his past. To the extent that he felt guilty for not saving his parent's marriage, he was compelled to recapitulate his childhood scenario. With each affair, he hoped it would come out differently. That is, the woman would feel empowered, stand up to her husband, and reform (or leave) him.

Frank projected his complex by assuming that the primary problem in troubled marriages was a dominant man and a passive woman. Having infiltrated the marriage, he would once again perform his customary role of advising/helping by playing the wise, know-it-all counselor (Sun-Jupiter in Aries). That he was also manifesting some of his father's negative attributes escaped his recognition. Intruding into a colleague's marriage and appropriating the wife's love was selfish and aggressive, just like his father. At the same time, he would set himself up to conform to his mother's role. For when the women would not leave their marriages, Frank would end up feeling used, unloved, and victimized, just as his mother felt victimized.

On a conscious level, Frank's intentions were good. He wanted to help. Yet, so long as he was the object of the wife's attention, Frank became the problem rather than the solution to the couple's marital woes, thus further entrenching the guilt that stemmed from his childhood failure to help his mother. It was a vicious cycle, a kind of curse, which compelled him to behave in ways that contradicted his own moral values. Recall that complexes have this quality of redundancy and compulsivity, a repetitive layering of similar experiences over an archetypal core.[40]

Transference is repetition compulsion within the therapeutic relationship. Thus whenever Frank perceived me as acting like his father, the complex came into view. He would often react with fear or anger whenever I offered an opinion or made an interpretation. Despite my pains to approach him in an empathic, patient, and caring fashion, his *idée fixe* was that all men in positions of authority were like his father. A primary defense was to do onto me what had been done onto him (passive into active), a kind of perversion of the golden rule.[41] By demeaning and devaluing the therapy (and

---

[40] This exemplifies *repetition compulsion*, which is the compulsion to repeat earlier, traumatic experiences in an attempt to gain mastery over them.

[41] Passive into active transference is linked to the solar defense of *identification*, one form of

the therapist), he could change a passive experience into an active one, thus distancing himself from the role of the victim.

COMPLEXES, KARMA, AND REINCARNATION

From a karmic perspective, complexes are not simply inborn pathological entities that wreak havoc in the lives of mortals. More likely, they represent an inherited psychic tendency that derives from past life actions and experiences. This implies that they are purposive; that is, they provide a lesson. Liz Greene (1997) writes,

> Complexes are what we really mean by fate....If one is sympathetic to the idea of reincarnation, one will probably view the various issues that one grapples with in one's present life as the continuing unfoldment of the efforts, failures, successes, and conflicts carried over from other lifetimes....Thus the complex may be seen as an encoded energetic container of past life patterns, in the same way that DNA is an encoded container of heredity. (p. 6-7)

If complexes are purposive, what might be the purpose of Frank's complex? Although there is no way of knowing with certainty, and one must be wary of oversimplification, it is useful to think in terms of karmic lessons. Painful experiences can be purposive in that they teach us how not to be—or, stated in the reverse, how *to* be. For the lesson to be fully learned, however, we must develop compassion for the victim—in this case, ourselves. This underscores the importance of allowing the full emotional impact of one's experiences to penetrate conscious awareness. Given our own experience, we are less likely to treat others in ways that we know can be hurtful. If the pain of a traumatic experience remains repressed, however, then it will be acted out unconsciously in one of two ways: (1) We will project hurtful behavior onto others and reassume the role of victim, or (2) we will distance ourselves from the victim role by doing to others what has been done to us.

Initially, the complex manifests as a childhood event-pattern that is painful physically, emotionally, or both. Typically, the child defends against this pain through repression and projection, as if to say, "That type of behavior is what's bad in other people, not me." Yet, unconsciously there is a fear,

---

which is identification with the aggressor. The "aggressor" is an internal negative component of the self with which the individual temporarily becomes fused; in effect, being possessed by it.

and an intuition, that *this is what I deserve; this is who I really am.* At an unconscious level, the child identifies with the experience; bad experience equals bad child. On a conscious level, however, the personality may defend against such negative self-perceptions by compensating in the opposite direction. This can be accomplished through a variety of defenses. Omnipotent control, exaggeration, idealization, projective identification, passive into active, reaction formation, splitting, devaluation, disavowal, fantasy, and undoing all constitute compensatory maneuvers to defend against distressing self-perceptions. In each instance, a painful idea or feeling is replaced in conscious awareness by its opposite. Recall that Jung emphasized the compensatory nature of conscious and unconscious. Whatever extreme was true on a conscious level, thought Jung, the opposite was equally true in the unconscious.

While such defensive maneuvers help to maintain self-esteem, they also impede learning the lesson that the complex potentiates. In Frank's case, he reacted to his father's aggression by identifying with the opposite characteristics; thus, he resonated with his mother's suffering and saw himself as rescuer (Moon-Neptune Libra) rather than perpetrator (Sun-Jupiter Aries). In so doing, however, he lost conscious awareness of his own selfish, aggressive tendencies.

As long as negative ideas—pathogenic beliefs—remain unconscious, they continue to generate experiences that recapitulate childhood prototypes. Repetition compulsion may partially be in the service of atonement. Again, children tend to believe they deserve whatever happens to them. Actually, the natural egocentricity of childhood may be close to a karmic truth—that we are responsible for our experiences. Conversely, from the perspective of a single lifetime, the child is clearly not responsible. We cannot blame the child for a parent's abusive behavior or for a tragic twist of fate. Yet, the parent, or what we call "fate", may merely be the instrument of the child's karma—what Whitmont calls a 'destiny factor'. Once a complex is activated by lived experience, guilt is the inevitable accompaniment. The child assumes, "this must be what I deserve." And when that idea takes root, the native continues to make choices that attract painful experiences of a similar nature in hopes of disconfirming the underlying pathogenic belief.

It may be that self-defeating, self-depriving behavior persists until the individual feels that he or she has paid their debt and atonement has been completed. This, in effect, is how karma operates, which is also known as the law of compensation. What we once did to others is now being done to us. Edgar Cayce's biographer, Gina Cerminara (1950), notes that Cayce indicated that some karmic experiences are due not to sins of commission, but to sins of omission. In other words, certain experiences are designed to help individuals become more compassionate, courageous, or caring, not because of what they did in past incarnations, but because of what they did not do but should have. In either case, the karmic lesson is contained in the specifics of the negative, painful experience. With each new incident, there is an opportunity to allow the full impact of the karma into conscious awareness, and with the pain, the lesson.

In Frank's case, he kept encountering men that he perceived as powerful, egocentric, and insensitive (like his father), and woman who were their victims. He set himself up again and again to re-experience his childhood predicament of failing to save female victims of an abusive male authority, while not recognizing that his affairs were evidence of his own narcissistic sense of entitlement. When the women would remain with their husbands, Frank would feel impotent and defeated, just as he did in his family. Unconsciously, this is what he felt he deserved. We can speculate that Frank's karma had something to do with aggressive righteousness and narcissistic entitlement (Sun conjunct Jupiter in Aries), qualities that other men seemed to embody at his expense.

ATONEMENT AND FORGIVENESS

The next stage of the process has to do with resolution and forgiveness. For this to come about the individual has to open to the pain of his or her unmet needs, become conscious of pathogenic beliefs, and see how these, in turn, perpetuate psychological problems and attendant suffering. At each point, there is an opportunity for forgiveness, first for oneself, and then for one's perpetrators. Self-forgiveness is primary because on some deep, soul level there is indeed sorrow for having to endure the suffering. Forgiveness entails "letting oneself off the hook" and allowing that one is not interminably responsible for a parent's actions or distress. And if one is not responsible, one can stop seeking parental surrogates with whom to re-enact the struggle.

For Frank, it meant disconfirming twin pathogenic beliefs that he was guilty for (1) not being able to protect his mother, and (2) not being able to win his father's love and approval. To the extent that Frank could release these fixed ideas, he was able to experience the tragedy of his childhood on an emotional level. Once a negative idea is disconfirmed, all the pain attached to that idea surfaces into awareness. Old, pent-up feelings are finally released; the floodgates open, tears flow, grief spills out, and one is awash in a healing flood of emotion that arises from the depths of one's soul. Self-forgiveness would enable Frank to stop projecting selfishness and insensitivity onto other men, for he would no longer need to re-create his childhood experience. Also, it would mean allowing himself to have a better experience in relationship than his parent's had.

Resolution of the complex constitutes a paradox. For on a psychological level, recovery requires disconfirmation of pathogenic beliefs rooted in childhood guilt and trauma. Again, this is letting oneself off the hook and accepting that one is not the cause of childhood miseries, failures, and frustrations; that one is, in fact, deserving of a better life. The individual is henceforth free to make new decisions and create more fulfilling experiences. Disconfirmation and release of childhood guilt, however, would appear to contradict the operation of karmic law, which implies that the soul is responsible for its childhood experiences. How can this apparent contradiction be resolved?

I believe the answer requires a subtle shift in perspective, a kind of seeing in stereo (seeing double). With the realization that one is not responsible for a parent's behavior comes the recognition that one's karmic debt has been fulfilled; that is, one is no longer required to endure a pattern of suffering that originated in the mistakes of a previous incarnation. The soul has evolved sufficiently that one is no longer the person that committed those errors. A change has occurred. Something in the soul accepts that there has been adequate atonement for past sins; one's guilt has been expiated, one's lesson learned, enough suffering! This entail's "waking up" and realizing that one has a choice; there are other options, other stories, and other ways to be. One is not doomed to keep making the same choices and experiencing the same pattern, over and over.

This process of self-forgiveness is mysterious, for it cannot be predicted or forced. I imagine that only the soul knows when it is ready, although that readiness is often indicated by transits and progressions to the relevant planetary configurations. Forgiveness is inextricably bound to recovery. Again, the critical factor involves allowing the full depths of one's pain and guilt into awareness without becoming identified with it—that is, by releasing it. This is the key to both healing and resolution of karmic debt.

Frank, for example, needed to feel the pain of not being able to relieve his mother's suffering or gain his father's approval. Often the bridge to the past is the pain of a present relationship that relates to the past in an analogous way; it is, in effect, an extension of the karmic pattern. Frank's painful affairs were simply an extension of the triangulation he experienced in his family of origin. Whether one grieves the present or the past or both doesn't really matter, so long as one feels deeply into the experience. It is through surrender to suffering that karmic lessons are learned.

The purpose of karma is not simply retribution. For a certain amount of ignorance and selfishness is inherent to being human; it is our "thrown condition", as existentialists like to say. Karma, therefore, should not be conceptualized as punishment, but as a set of experiences that are perfectly designed to release the soul's potential; that is, to activate healing and growth in specific ways for each person. In this regard, suffering is the medicine that provides an antidote to the soul's ills. The poet, Kahlil Gibran, describes it thusly:

> Much of your pain is self-chosen. It is the bitter potion by which the physician within heals your sick self. Therefore trust the physician, and drink his remedy in silence and tranquility. For his hand, though heavy and hard, is guided by the tender hand of the Unseen. And the cup he brings, has been fashioned of the clay which the Potter has moistened with His own sacred tears.

Gibran is saying that although medicine for the soul's ills can be difficult to swallow, it is never-the-less intelligently and compassionately formulated; therefore, one must strive to trust the process. However painful it was for Frank to feel devalued by his father, or to witness his mother's devaluation, the requirement is to feel deeply into that experience and to identify exactly what was hurtful. What was it like to have that experience? How does it feel to see one's mother suffer and not be able to stop it? What can one learn from that?

This kind of suffering is inseparable from self-love, for it entails embracing one's pain with the most exquisite compassion. At the bottom of self-caring (Moon) one discovers universal compassion (Neptune), which can now be extended to one's perpetrators, whether this is father, mother, sibling, spouse, boss, or whoever the instrument of one's karma might be. Forgiveness, of course, is not moral endorsement; it does not mean that the victim exonerates the perpetrator from responsibility for wrongdoing or that one should subsequently renew a relationship with that person. Rather, forgiveness entails the simple recognition that the perpetrator is human, flawed, limited, and vulnerable to error like oneself. As such, he or she is more than the cause of suffering; s/he is the instrument of one's redemption.

Forgiveness moves the individual to a level of soul in which relationships are experienced on a transpersonal level. They are no longer merely personal, for now one can now feel, "There but for the grace of God go I." This is why Neptune as an outer, transpersonal planet symbolizes our capacity for compassion and forgiveness.

RECOVERY

Empathy for the perpetrator allows for recovery of one's own split-off potentials. Recall that the usual and typical response to painful early experience is reactive, or compensatory. On a conscious level, we polarize to the karmic experience. We cannot empathize with it. Yet, this process of disidentification necessarily entails the repudiation of certain archetypal parts—the very ones that are embodied in a hurtful way by those we love. Frank, for example, could not identify with his father's selfishness, righteousness, or arrogance—traits symbolized by his Sun conjunct Jupiter in Aries. To heal the complex, however, the reactive organization of the personality has to soften and break down in order to re-assimilate its repudiated parts.

In forgiving the perpetrator, we are really forgiving ourselves; and in forgiving ourselves, we are forgiving the perpetrator. The two processes are inseparable. For what hurt us in this life may be the very thing we did to others in a prior life, even though the crime is buried in the dark recesses of the soul's memory. It may be the thing we are still doing, albeit unconsciously. This is what karma—the habitual reenactment of past behavior and experience—implies. When the individual can find something of himself in the perpetrator, then healing and integration has begun. The very traits that were most problematic in Frank's father were symbolized by Frank's chart; thus, they were in him, not just in his father.

Healing the complex requires consciously identifying with the experience that was initially wounding, for at the heart of the wound is an archetypal entity that contains both light and dark potentials. To recover the light, one must face the dark. Whereas psychological defense mechanisms cause the conscious personality to swing toward the opposite extreme and away from the (unconscious) complex, recovery requires moving back toward the dark side and reintegrating it, yet with new awareness of its destructive potentials. In lieu of this, the ego polarizes to the complex and forfeits the complex's positive potentials. The baby is thrown out with the bathwater. Only by surrendering the compensatory, defensive organization of the ego can one gain conscious access to the archetypal structure that constitutes the complex. Otherwise, it will compel one to extremes. The person will either project the negative features of the complex onto others and assume the role of victim (again), or unconsciously identify with the complex and act it out by victimizing others (again).

If Frank is to stop projecting aggression, dominance, and insensitivity onto other men, he must first identify his own tendencies in this regard, as if to say, "I, too, can be devaluing, impatient, selfish, dogmatic, insensitive," and so on. It is tempting to speculate that these very traits might have dominated Frank's consciousness in a previous embodiment. We can never know. Yet, the law of karma suggests that it was precisely these tendencies deriving from a prior incarnation that generated the karma of which his father was the prime instrument in this life.[42]

Like any other part of the chart, the complex has inherent positive potentials. For Frank to recover his lost potentials, he needs to identify with his stellium in Aries and bring it into balance with his overly developed Moon-Neptune side. This process of healing and integration will be more fully explored in later chapters. Suffice to say that integration is about restoring balance to the soul so that both sides of the psyche are enriched and moderated by a union of opposites.

Frank's karmic lesson has to do with balancing strength with grace (♈ ☍ ♎), autonomy with intimacy (♈ ☍ ♎), individuality with belonging (☉ ☍ ☽), intention with surrender (☉ ☍ ♆), teaching with listening (♃ ☍ ☽), righteousness and judgment with humility and compassion (♃ ☍ ♆), and a host of other related dichotomies that are contained in the opposition between his Aries and Libra planets. With resolution of these archetypal conflicts, emergent properties are released. New traits and capacities are born that are more adaptive than those symbolized by the respective planets or signs alone.

SUMMARY AND CONCLUSION

Psychopathology in the birthchart can be understood via Jung's concept of the complex. These are emotionally charged psychic entities comprised of repressed ideas and impulses. Like psychic magnets, complexes attract experiences to themselves that are consonant with the fixed ideas that are embedded within them.

---

[42] Past life Jungian analyst, Roger Woolger, has observed that it is common for souls to alternate opposite roles from life to life. In one life a man is a brutal warrior who hates pacifists; in the next a sensitive priest who abhors violence. A woman is a rape victim in one life, and a rapist in the next. These complementary lives are consistent with Jung's notion of the compensatory nature of the conscious and unconscious. Always, it seems, the soul strives for balance.

From a reincarnational perspective, complexes may be inherited psychic tendencies that stem from past life actions and experiences. Such karmic patterns appear to be purposive. By generating experiences consistent with themselves, complexes further the growth and evolution of the soul. The individual continually meets himself in the guise of outer events and relationships. Healing the complex requires that painful experiences be allowed maximum impact upon consciousness, followed by forgiveness of self and perpetrator, and integration of split-off parts.

Chapter Ten

PSYCHOPATHOLOGY AND CHARACTER

In Chapter nine, we explored how psychopathology is a consequence of intrapsychic conflict. When basic needs clash with internal prohibitions, or when differing needs seem mutually exclusive, the psyche adapts by producing compromise formations—cognitive structures with attendant behavioral patterns that strive to find a viable balance between what is wished for and what is dreaded. In this chapter, we will examine how maladaptive schemas give rise to specific character types and associated defenses that constitute personality disorders. We will also continue exploring how these character types can be correlated with specific sign-planet systems, aspects, and house placements.

Once again, Maslow (1968) reminds us that human behavior is governed by basic needs—for survival, security, belonging, and self-esteem. Basic needs motivate the individual to behave in ways that provide for their satisfaction. If such needs are not satisfied, says Maslow, sickness results. We can apply this model to astrology. The signs of the zodiac are reflective not only of twelve basic psychological needs but also of psychological issues that may arise when these needs are chronically frustrated.

To be specific, when a sign-planet system[43] is under stress as a consequence of intrapsychic conflict, it can mutate into a specific defensive style that is characterized by the hypertrophy of associated modes of behavior. If the Moon is under stress, for example, the individual may be inordinately emotional, oversensitive, and exaggeratedly childlike. This is similar to what happens

---

[43] When I speak of sign-planet systems, not only am I referring to the general principle of the sign as a motivational need and of its ruling planet as a set of functions geared toward satisfying this need, but also of its corollary aspect and house. In other words, if Aries-Mars correlates to the defense of "acting out," then so, also, do the conjunction and the 1st house.

in body building when, for instance, the abnormally large development of a specific muscle is brought about by means of continuous exercise. The stress placed upon the muscle from strenuous lifting of heavy weights causes it to grow unusually big—that is, to *hypertrophy*.

There is nothing particularly unusual about this if the body-builder develops his other muscle areas to proportionate size and strength. However, imagine an individual who is compelled by circumstances to exercise only one muscle area at the expense of the rest of his body. He may, for instance, have abnormally large biceps and yet be comparatively underdeveloped in every other area. This, in effect, is what happens in psychopathology, which is characterized by the compensatory overdevelopment and overfunctioning of a single way of being.

These ways of being, or modes of behavior, can be correlated with sign-planet systems. For example, if the Leo-Sun system is overfunctioning, the individual may be characterized by narcissistic traits—a grandiose sense of self-importance, feelings of entitlement, lack of empathy for others, and an exhibitionistic need for constant attention and admiration. Such traits operate defensively, for they forestall awareness of other drives and needs that are threatening to the Sun's purpose, which is to maintain identity and self-esteem.

By definition, intrapsychic conflict involving the Sun places stress upon the Leo-Sun system. When planetary impulses impinge upon the solar function, this can lead to actual or potential frustration of the Leonian need for validation; hence, defensive measures are triggered. By exaggerating the expression of solar impulses, awareness of other impulses can be blocked. For example, if the Sun is in hard aspect to Pluto, which symbolizes the need for transformation, the individual may react to this impulse by amplifying solar functions so that they become bloated and extreme. In effect, narcissistic traits operate in a compensatory way as a defense against the plutonic pressure to transform, which is perceived as a threat to identity and self-esteem.

In subsequent sections, we will examine this process more closely by showing how sign-planet systems can be correlated with personality disorders, which, in turn, are related to specific character styles and associated defenses. The dynamics of psychopathology, in other words, can be anticipated and clarified within the context of relevant astrological configurations.

LOSS OF AGENCY AND VOLITION

In chapter six, a mental disorder was defined as a clinically significant behavioral or psychological syndrome that is associated with a painful symptom (distress), and impairment in one or more important areas of functioning (disability).[44] On a yet more fundamental level, notes Shapiro (2000), psychopathology is marked by self-estrangement and the loss of personal agency and volition. Hence patients in psychotherapy regularly say such things as, "I don't know why I did that," or "It just happened, I didn't mean to hurt her," or, "I know he's dangerous, but I can't stop myself from going out with him; it's like an addiction." Such statements reflect loss of a clear sense of what one actually feels, wants, or intends. The person behaves in ways that reflect the operation of impulses that are occurring outside of awareness.

Psychologists refer to this as a diminished sense of agency, or personal responsibility, or self-direction (Kaiser, 1965; Schafer, 1976). It is characterized by a disavowal of intention and an impairment of volitional action, as if the individual were compelled to behave in ways that are not consciously chosen. In astrology, this clearly implicates the Sun, which symbolizes will, volition, or intentionality. The Sun is the decider subsystem, the part of the psyche that decides one course of action over another. In mythological terms, it is the ruler, or king, which is an apt metaphor since a king must hold dominion over his subjects. Astrologically speaking, "subjects" refers to the planets and their respective functions that make up our inner kingdoms.

It is not difficult to see how dilution of a sense of personal agency can lead to distress and disability. If an individual is not able to consciously utilize his capacity for assertion (Mars), or discipline (Saturn), or cooperation (Venus), this can lead to suffering and impairment in those areas of life that require such abilities. In other words, if a planetary process operates more-or-less outside the province of the will (Sun), so that its expression is either resisted or ignored, it is apt to function in ways that are problematic. This would be analogous to a rogue knight operating in ways that contradict the edict of the king.

I do not mean to imply that all pathology is necessarily solar pathology. The Sun, in fact, may be relatively functional despite one or more planetary processes being dysfunctional. For example, a client of mine has high self-esteem even though she laments her inability to choose a career. She

---

[44] Like movies, planets can be rated, too. If a planet's functioning entails both distress and disability, perhaps we should rate it "DD." This might be the equivalent of an "XX" rating since one's experience of the planet is that it's relatively dangerous and forbidden. It may also be eroticized!

procrastinates when it comes to obtaining vocational guidance despite her wish to succeed at something. Her Sun is not in aspect to Saturn, which, however, is under stress from several other planets in addition to being in Cancer in the 12th house. While she is quite serious in her devotion to what she calls her spiritual family—a woman's group that practices meditation and other spiritual disciplines—she cannot seem to utilize her Saturn in a conscious, self-directed way for the sake of realizing a career goal. In effect, her Saturn is not under control of her will (Sun).

This example underscores a general rule: while not all psychopathology is solar, all psychopathology involves the Sun. It involves the Sun in the sense that if we cannot access a given planetary function, and thus cannot direct that function in a conscious, intentional way, then it is not apt to provide for maximum satisfaction of its relevant need. For example, my client has little or no sense of authority, mastery, or achievement in her life—needs symbolized by Capricorn, which it is Saturn's job to fulfill.

That she is out of touch with her Saturn is not necessarily a consequence of the fact that it makes no aspect to the Sun. If Saturn were in hard aspect to the solar principle, this might trigger narcissistic issues and/or correlate to difficulties integrating Saturn. If Saturn is well integrated, it could simply indicate that Saturn is strong in her nature. One would have to talk to her to find out. She might report that she feels driven to succeed, assumes responsibility compulsively, and is extremely disciplined and organized—all of which point to an excess of Saturn. If Saturn were in soft aspect to the Sun, these qualities would probably operate in a balanced way and be more effortlessly expressed.

Her actual problem, however, seems related to the way that Saturn is configured in her chart as a whole. Since it is under stress from hard aspects, occupies a sign to which it naturally opposes (Cancer), and tenants a house that correlates to a domain of experience that is outside of conscious awareness (the 12th), one could infer from all these factors that her Saturn is relatively unconscious. Even so, this does not in itself preclude her becoming conscious of Saturnian impulses and bringing them under control of her will (Sun). Ideally, every planetary impulse must ultimately be subordinated to solar intentions. Even the outer planets can be integrated in the sense that one has a choice to willingly cooperate with transpersonal energies. For example, one can choose to accept or resist one's grief in the face of irretrievable loss (Neptune).

A fundamental aim of psychotherapy is enlargement of the client's self-awareness and sense of personal agency. This means an increased clarity of his feelings, wants, and intentions, and of his having chosen to do what he has done. To put it in the reverse, psychotherapy aims to dissolve the self-estrangement that is central to psychopathology. I submit that this aim is also relevant to the astrological counselor, who invariably must deal with the same questions that are posed to psychotherapists: "I don't know what career I should have," or, "I don't know if I should marry Bob."

One question that psychotherapists do not have to answer that is nearly unavoidable in astrological counseling is, "What does the chart say?" If the astrologer answers this question directly and allows her self to be used in a way that reinforces the client's diminished sense of personal agency, she will have done her client a grave disservice. As May (1967) pointed out, neurotic persons have a tendency to externalize responsibility for problems and, therefore, to look for solutions in conditions outside themselves. When clients look to astrologers for answers, rather than using astrology as a means for deepening self-awareness and volitional control, this is itself symptomatic of their neurosis. The astrologer must not be seduced into colluding with the client's pathology by offering glib advice derived from the astrological chart.[45]

The zodiac in general and the astrological chart in particular depicts what Joseph Campbell famously called 'the hero's journey'. As the hero archetype, the Sun (ego/self), must recognize that every planetary archetype—warrior, messenger, master, monster, victim, trickster, lover, friend, and foe—is but a facet of the hero's own personality. Just as the Sun must hold all the planets within its gravitational field and thus incorporate them into one solar system, so the individual must hold all planetary functions within his field of awareness and integrate them into a self-system. In so doing, he enlarges his self-awareness, expands his identity, and increases his sense of personal agency. In short, he becomes whole. The hero's journey is the process of integrating the astrological chart. This is precisely what Jung meant by the path of individuation leading to Self-realization.

DISORDER AS CHARACTER BASED

In his classic book *Neurotic Styles,* Shapiro (1965) explained that pathological behavior is rooted in certain "neurotic styles," of which there are a limited number. He defined "style" as a mode of functioning that is identifiable through a range of specific acts. These include ways of thinking and perceiving, ways of experiencing emotion, forms of subjective experience in

---

[45] Use of the astrological chart in counseling will be the subject of a separate text. Suffice to say here that the typical "reading" involving description of character traits, the dispensing of advice, and predictions of concrete events are not necessarily in the client's best interest.

general, and modes of activity that are associated with various pathologies. In other words, every mental disorder is characterized by a specific pattern of thinking, feeling, and behavior.

Neurotic styles, says Shapiro, "must in themselves represent psychological structures of importance, and these structures might be of a more general type than the specific traits or mechanisms that could be inferred from them" (p. 2). Included in such neurotic styles are adaptive features and traits as well, such that a general style "may be considered a matrix from which various traits, symptoms, and defense mechanisms crystallize."

The above is important in that it states that a general style of functioning comprises a matrix for specific symptoms and traits. In astrology, planets symbolize such matrixes. Mars, for example, is a general style of functioning in that it represents traits and symptoms related to the warrior archetype—vitality, spontaneity, independence, courage, aggression, impulsiveness, recklessness, and the like. It is significant that these same qualities are also consonant with antisocial personality disorder. This is not to suggest that Mars is equivalent to psychopathy, only that when taken to an extreme and expressed in a rigid way Martian traits are consistent with that disorder.

Shapiro (1965) points out that a neurotic symptom regularly appears in the context of attitudes, interests, intellectual inclinations, and even vocational aptitudes with which the given symptom seems to have an affinity. It would not be surprising, for instance, if an accountant with a penchant for numbers develops an obsessional neurosis, since the nature of the symptom fits the nature of the activities and inclinations that make up its background.

Such consistencies of functioning are broad and extensive in that they constitute formal patterns or "styles" that are capable of describing general aspects of function such as cognition, emotional experience, and behavioral tendencies, all of which are related and organized in a self-consistent way. Again, this is virtually identical to how planetary archetypes operate. Any astrologer would recognize the aforementioned example of the obsessional accountant as a Virgo-Mercury phenomenon.

The view of general forms of functioning as a matrix for specific traits or symptoms underscores that psychopathology is essentially a problem of character. In other words, there are particular character types or "styles" that consist of general and relatively stable forms of functioning. Within these types are included those traits and symptoms that characterize mental disorders.

This is significant in that it contradicts the claim of early psychoanalytic theory that neurosis is reducible to drive conflict. As discussed in Chapter two, early theorists asserted that the psyche was animated by instinctual drives, namely sex and aggression, which were capable of manifesting in a variety of ways. Freud theorized that these instinctual drives were thought to have originated in specific developmental stages, which he called oral, anal, oedipal, latency, and phallic. If trauma or chronic frustration occurred during a particular stage, then the drive associated with that stage would have to be defended against, thus giving rise to a "drive conflict."

For example, if during the anal (Taurus) stage, which is associated with development of a capacity for retention and control, an infant was unduly shamed for soiling himself, this could lead to the erection of defenses against the impulse to defecate. On the one hand, the child wishes to "go". On the other, he fears further shaming and loss of his parent's love. To the extent that this conflict remains unresolved, the child is "fixated" at the anal phase. According to Freudian theory, developmental arrest at this stage is thought to underlay obsessive-compulsive disorder (OCD). A person suffering from this condition utilizes reaction-formation as a defense against anal impulses; that is, his personality style is exaggeratedly "prim and proper." Behaviors such as compulsive hand-washing, overconcern with cleanliness, and fear of making a mistake, are all seen as adult manifestations of the earlier, unresolved conflict. In effect, preoccupation with issues of control is at the expense of the obsessives' capacity to enjoy and feel his body.

While such psychoanalytic formulations have a certain intuitive appeal and have comprised the heart of attempts to explain neurosis over the past century, they fail to account for an enormous variety of psychological phenomena associated with such conditions. The obsessive (Virgo) character, for instance, with its excessive devotion to work and productivity, its scrupulous attention to detail, its perfectionism and narrowness of focus, is not easily explained from the specific content of the alleged drive conflict as merely the derivative of a fear of inadequate bowel control.

What such a formulation lacks is a deeper appreciation of how generalized forms of functioning—what astrologers call planetary archetypes—are implicated in neurotic symptomology. Instead, character is reduced to drive derivatives (sublimations of instinctual drives or reaction-formations against them) that result from drive conflicts. From an astrological perspective, OCD is not merely the consequence of a conflict involving Virgo as a motivational drive, but of Virgo-Mercury as a character *style*. If the Virgo archetype is sufficiently stressed, it can manifest in the particular kind of thoughts, feelings, and actions that characterize obsessive-compulsive pathology. The point here is that this style of functioning is innate and exists independent of instinctual conflict and developmental fixation. This underscores that choice of neurosis is a matter of character, not merely of conflict.

A glaring deficiency in psychoanalytic theory is lack of an adequate terminology for naming psychological structures that comprise what we call character. Such terms as ego, id, superego, and internal object are burdened with responsibility for articulating the enormous complexity of parts and functions that comprise psychic structure. Their supposed products—mental disorders—are mere clusters of traits that presumably result from deeper, underlying conflicts involving the aforementioned structures. The problem, however, is that the structures allegedly responsible for these conflicts are woefully inadequate as explanatory constructs.

Significantly, what psychoanalytic theory regards as a diagnostic entity is actually closer to being an archetype despite covering only the archetype's negative, pathological expression. A planetary archetype, however, is not the epiphenomenon of a deeper, more fundamental drive conflict. Rather, the archetype—the fundamental form—was present from the beginning. Archetypes are the primary, irreducible matrices out of which all psychological phenomena emerge. While an archetype includes a need/drive, it cannot be reduced to a need. It is too broad and extensive for that. Drive (sign) and function (planet) are two sides of the same archetypal coin. This is why astrological archetypes are referred to as sign-planet *systems*.

Shapiro (2000) seems to anticipate the existence of such archetypal structures even if he cannot name them. He refers, instead, to innate "organizing and regulatory systems" (p. 13). Such systems, he claims, assure that there will not be an unlimited diversity of pathology.

> Rather the development of psychopathology will be limited to those general directions offered by the structural fault lines of the mind, so to speak. I believe that clinical experience confirms this. Of course, there is no limit to individual variation. But there seem to be comparatively few fundamental forms of psychopathology. (p. 13)

What Shapiro calls "structural fault lines of the mind" is a pretty could description of zodiacal archetypes and their angular relations—that is, the structure of the zodiac, which, along with planetary rulers, symbolizes the generic structure of the human psyche. Recall that Jung described archetypes as structural elements of the psyche that manifest in common patterns of emotional and mental behavior. When expressed in an extreme, unbalanced way, planetary archetypes not only conform to the basic forms of psychopathology, they also allow for individual variations in accord with their sign and house placements and the aspects they form to one another.

THE TWIN TOWERS OF DETERMINISM

In psychoanalysis there is no theory of general ways of functioning, no characteristic forms or styles that would comprise what we call character. Instead, there is the assumption that behavior is more or less the effect of unconscious forces, whether these forces are instinctual drives or internal objects that have been introjected from relations with caretakers.

In this view, character is presumed to arise solely out of infantile instinctual conflict or via the introjection of external objects that come to determine one's thoughts and feelings. In either case, the individual is conceived not as a responsible, self-determining agent capable of self-governance, but as a hapless marionette jerked about by unconscious forces and experiences that derive from the past.

Although cognitive behavioral psychology has, to some extent, remedied this one-sided view with its emphasis upon self-organizing mental habits that construct a self and a world, there is still the presumption that these habits have been conditioned by external circumstances for which the individual bears little or no responsibility.

The fact remains that the two most influential models of the past century, psychoanalysis and behaviorism, were both founded upon mechanistic principles and both equally denied the possibility of genuine human freedom. The marionette view of both camps suggests that pieces of history insert themselves into the mind of the individual, bypassing innate modes of functioning, and leaving him as a passive witness of his own behavior and the victim of his history.

Neither is the problem solved by postulating a teleological, self-actualization motive, as has been advanced by personality theories over the past twenty years. Humanistic psychology, cognitive behaviorism, and object-relations theory[46] have all emphasized in their own way the growth seeking tendencies of the human organism. While this is an important theoretical development, it is not the same thing as delineating the fundamental structures of the mind that underlay character in general and psychopathology in particular. The issue is not merely one of self-determination, but of self-determination in

---

[46] Object relations theory is a contemporary offshoot of psychoanalysis.

conjunction with innate, self-organizing modes of behavior (archetypes, or general styles of character).

Conventional attempts to explain the origination of behavioral traits rely invariably upon mechanistic reasoning. Either personality is genetically determined or the cognitive structures that generate behavior are conceived as having been conditioned by the random nature of external experience. If cognitive structures are maladaptive, it is presumed that the individual was overwhelmed by excessive stress caused by a faulty and impinging environment. That the individual might have a limited capacity to cope with certain kinds of stress because of inherent weaknesses or flaws in his character is generally not considered a viable explanation of psychopathology. Yet, astrology suggests that these structures are innate; they exist before lived experience and they influence both what is perceived and how it is responded to. Planetary archetypes, in other words, symbolize general forms of functioning that shape character and have a stable existence apart from the defensive requirements of instinctual conflict or of adaptations induced by environmental stress.

CHARACTER IS PRIMARY

Psychoanalytic theory is rooted in the assumption that there are certain basic needs that underlay psychic functioning. Whether these are described as instinctual drives for sex and aggression (drive theory), or needs for relatedness to external objects/caretakers (object relations theory), the underlying assumption remains the same: character traits are derivatives of how these basic needs are responded to by others, especially in childhood. There is no psychoanalytic concept of innate, pre-existing forms of character that distinguish one person from another and that originate independent of lived experience. As stated, a consequence of this lack of appreciation for innate modes and styles of functioning is the more or less complete lack of a psychoanalytic psychology of character.

Whereas psychoanalytic theory is deficient in its ability to provide an adequate terminology for the organizing matrices (archetypes) that underlay mental disorders, it is noteworthy that traditional astrology had the opposite deficiency: there was no theory of fundamental drives/needs. Instead, signs were invariably described in terms of broad personality "types" with distinguishing attributes, traits, and characteristics. Planets, too, were correlated with parts of the personality such that each planet symbolized a range of psychological functions. Saturn symbolizes our capacity for achievement and control; Neptune our capacity for imagination and charity; Venus our capacity for love and relatedness, and so on.

Not only does each planet symbolize a set of interrelated functions, it also constitutes a type of subpersonality with its own cognitive mode, affect states, and behavioral traits. Jupiter, for instance, is a cognitive style (abstract, theoretical), an emotional propensity (optimistic, enthusiastic), and a behavioral pattern with an extensive range of self-consistent attributes—expansive, philosophical, hopeful, moralizing, truthful, direct, bombastic, preachy, and so on. In short, both signs and planets are depicted as broad, general styles of functioning. While there is nothing wrong with this formulation, it fails to establish the core, underlying motives that activate psychological processes.

An unfortunate consequence of this deficiency is the assumption perpetrated by astrologers that human behavior is somehow determined by the positions of the planets at birth. Since the signs are not understood to symbolize basic drives intrinsic to human beings, the inescapable implication is that people are marionettes jerked about by cosmic forces. This is not much different than the classical psychoanalytic view of people being passive agents of unconscious, libidinal forces.

The view offered here is that signs symbolize two primary functions: (1) the underlying needs that motivate the expression of the planets that rule them, and (2) behavioral styles that modify the more fundamental expression of planets that tenant them. In regard to the first function, the need of a sign can be inferred from its behavioral attributes. Aries, for example, is associated with an assortment of interrelated traits—impulsive, aggressive, fierce, bold, impatient, and egocentric. From these and other Aries behaviors can be inferred the psychological need for survival. All Arian characteristics can be understood in the context of the need to assure one's continued existence.

It would actually be more accurate to say that a sign symbolizes a *set* of interrelated needs. There is probably no one word that best describes a sign motive. Aries symbolizes not only the need for survival, but also the need for freedom and autonomy. Given that such a need-set exists, there must be a part of the psyche that is dedicated to fulfilling this need(s). In astrology, this would be symbolized by the planet Mars, which rules Aries. Again, signs and their ruling planets are interdependent sign-planet systems. As psychological functions, planets are not independent of instinctual drives; rather, the drive (sign) is the root of the more general function. A sign is the spark that sets into motion the engine of its ruling planet. Planets, therefore, are psychological functions geared toward satisfying the needs of the signs they rule.

In regard to signs as planetary qualifiers, the behavioral style of the sign remains more or less constant regardless of the planet that resides in that sign. Sun in Aries expresses itself in a bold way; Moon in Aries is fiercely protective; Venus loves impulsively; and Jupiter concludes impatiently (as in a "hasty conclusion"). It is not difficult to see that the behavioral attributes of Aries—bold, fierce, impulsive, and impatient—operate independently of the planet that resides in that sign.

This has an important implication in regard to character style and potential pathology. When considering diagnosis, there is generally a predominant style with one or more sub-styles. An individual, for instance, may be mainly narcissistic with some paranoid and obsessive traits. Signs and planets both have a role to play as reflections of character. However, whereas there can only be one Sun, Moon, or Mercury in a birthchart, a single sign can appear multiple times by virtue of planetary placements. If there are three or more planets in Virgo, for example, then Virgo is likely to be a predominant characterological theme for that individual.

Of course, there are ways that planets can show dominance, too. They can reside on angles, be focal planets of a T-Square or Yod, occupy the sign or house they rule, or receive multiple aspects. The more of these strengthening factors occur, the more dominant the planet. In the end, a client's predominant characterological style can only be assessed by looking at multiple, overlapping factors in the birthchart.

Sign preponderance in a birthchart is an especially important signature of character. The more planets in a given sign, the stronger the ruler of that sign. A planet that disposes of several other planets is like a landlord with multiple property holdings. Since characterological style is reflected by planetary strength, the strength of a style is proportionate to the number of planets disposed; thus, someone with four planets in Scorpio would have a strongly Plutonic character.

How a planet is affected by its sign position is also significant. We normally think of signs as descriptive of planetary expression; however, before a planet expresses itself, its activating drive must be processed. A planet's sign placement affects the way that planet's motivating impulse (ruled sign) is responded to and managed at a subjective level.

For example, the Moon's motivating impulse is always Cancer. However, if the Moon is in Capricorn, then whenever a situation arises that calls for a lunar response it will be filtered through Capricorn. Since Capricorn naturally opposes Cancer, this sign position contradicts the Moon's natural tendency toward warmth and softness. Capricorn will inhibit the impulse to express tenderness because hardness and restraint is the essence of Capricorn. As one of my students jokingly put it, "crying is useless" when complaining to a Moon Capricorn. Cognitively, the person is apt to be thinking, "Don't lose control of your feelings," which relates both to their own feelings as well as to the feelings of anyone with whom they are interacting. Emotionally, the individual is apt to feel cold, stern, or callous in situations that evoke lunar needs and responses. All of this is happening internally before any actual behavior is expressed!

This illustrates how character style (sign) can actually affect the influence that a motive exerts. The motivational impulse of any planet in Capricorn is going to be damped and its subsequent behavior rendered more cautious and controlled. The general principle here is that any planet in a sign other than the one it rules is analogous to an individual entering a foreign culture; the nature of the culture is going to influence how the person thinks, feels, and behaves. A planet is like a temporary visitor in a foreign land (sign); thus; the sign is going to influence the action of the planet.

The old adage, "When in Rome, do as the Romans do," applies here. To a certain extent, a planet is forced to adapt to the demands of the sign it occupies. If Mars is in Aries, then it operates in a pure way. However, if Mars occupies Capricorn, then it is in Capricorn's domain and will feel the nature of Capricorn's influence. If Capricorn could speak, it might respond to a Mars impulse by saying, "Are you sure you want to do that? Have you thought about the consequences? If you're going to do it, you better do it perfectly."

Capricorn not only determines the way the planetary impulse is managed, it also influences perceptions and meaning attributions relative to that planet. Someone with Moon in Capricorn, for example, is likely to perceive a permissive childrearing environment as seriously deficient in rules and order. It is only a short step from here to character pathology. If a Capricorn style is taken to an extreme, there can be a tendency to feel that one's own impulses are seriously deficient, inadequately controlled, and out of order. Planetary impulses may become over controlled, resulting in depression. Capricorn is saying to the planet, "If you do that, you're going to fail. Why bother?" Here we see how a specific pathological symptom—depression—can be related to a sign configuration that reflects a character-type.

UNDERLYING DYNAMICS & EXTERIOR STYLE

The forgoing underscores that it is important to differentiate signs as character styles from underlying dynamics and intrapsychic conflict. Planetary processes and aspects reflect psychodynamics. By itself, however, psychodynamics cannot account for style, for style is a product of the planet-sign combination. Solar dynamics, for example, entail a continuous striving to meet the Leonian need for creativity and self-esteem via specific actions—to identify, to express, to create a preferred outcome. This dynamic understanding, however, no matter how correct in itself, cannot explain the particular form that the solar behavior takes. Sun in Virgo is going to be characterized by relatively consistent ways of thinking, certain entrenched attitudes, and so on, all of which reflect Virgonian preoccupations. These ways of functioning not only describe how solar energies are discharged, but also constitute ways of experiencing solar impulses, needs, and affects before any actual behavior takes place.

For example, efficiency and compulsivity are not simply expressions of Virgonian attributes; they are also how the person responds to the solar stimulus for self-expression. If the Sun is in Virgo, then Virgo characterizes how the individual converts the instinctual impulse behind the Sun into conscious subjective experience, manifest behavior, or overt symptom. Thus, the person may need to make a decision (Sun) and immediately begin to experience doubt and worry, question whether the impulse is a proper one under the current circumstances, and inhibit any immediate urge for self-expression so that the eventual behavior is, hopefully, more efficient in accomplishing the desired outcome.

Alternatively, if the Sun is in Sagittarius, then the solar impulse is expressed through a Sagittarian filter. Again, however, self-expression is not only characterized by a Sagittarian behavioral style, but the solar impulse is processed in a Sagittarian way. As a fire sign that naturally trines Leo, the Sun finds a friendly host in Sagittarius, which is apt to regard any impulse for creative self-expression as right and just. If the person has to make a decision, Sagittarius affirms and encourages the decision-making process, "Surely you will make the right decision (one tells oneself); I trust you implicitly in such matters!" Sagittarius will tend to imbue faith in all impulses connected to the Sun. The urge to play, for instance, evokes feelings of hope, optimism, and enthusiasm. Taken to an extreme, however, this very same process can lead to manic behavior—overextension, elevated mood, inflated self-esteem, flight of ideas, and grandiose delusions.

The above implies that different signs will respond differently to the same underlying dynamics. For example, the essential needs of Venus are for attachment (Taurus) and companionship (Libra), both of which Venus rules. As a psychological dynamic, Venus thus signifies processes such as *to secure, to attract,* and *to relate*. If Venus is in Aries, the style of attachment and relatedness will be characterized by directness, forwardness, aggressive pursuit of pleasure, and reckless abandon. The same underlying dynamic in Scorpio, however, will function in a radically different style. Now Venus will pursue pleasure in a controlled, strategic way, and will relate to others in a deeper, more intense, and possibly guarded manner. Scorpio processes the Venusian impulse for attachment by warning of dire outcomes if the individual is not sufficiently wary.

The negative, more pathological features of a sign tend to be evoked by hard aspects, which cause the planet to over- or under function within that sign. For example, if the Sun is underfunctioning in Taurus, the person may have difficulty feeling entitled to prosperity and, consequently, he may avoid making and saving money. This results in both a loss of security (Taurus) and self-esteem (Sun). If the Sun is overfunctioning in Taurus, the person may try too hard to make money, hence becoming miserly, grasping, and materialistic. Accumulation of wealth may produce a compensatory self-esteem; however, if self-esteem is overly dependent upon prosperity, it will rise and fall with one's financial status.

This illustrates how thinking and behavior—a symptom of insecurity, for instance—not only reflects the content of a planetary impulse, but also is a product of the sign's characterological style. The ultimate result of planet-sign combinations is a complex layering of psychological meaning. At the root is the impulse of a sign that triggers the expression of its ruling planet, which is then filtered through the sign it tenants. While psychopathology must be considered in the context of the underlying need and overall function of the relevant planet, the overt symptomology will invariably be colored by the character style of the planetary sign position.

ASPECTS AND CHARACTER STYLES

The foregoing principle also holds true when considering planetary aspects, which add yet another layer of complexity. The planets and angle will symbolize the underlying dynamics, but the characterological style will be a hybrid of the respective sign positions. Someone with Sun Square Saturn, for example, may have a fear of inadequacy and thus a vulnerability to depression, but how will this be expressed? If the Sun is in Pisces and Saturn in Sagittarius, there may be a tendency toward masochism (Pisces) along with an anxious concern that one is ignorant rather than wise (Sagittarius).

A client with this aspect chronically complained that he was passed up for promotions at work due to his lack of a college education. However, he was reluctant to do anything about the problem, preferring, instead, to grumble and act victimized. The aspect's underlying dynamics activated potential features and themes of the respective signs. Self-defeating, masochistic behavior is characteristic of Pisces, and concern about higher education is Sagittarian. He was depressed, to be sure, but he was depressed in ways and for reasons that relate to the natural square between Pisces and Sagittarius.

Another possibility with this configuration is what Chogyam Trungpa called "spiritual narcissism". Feelings of inferiority are compensated by a false-self bravado that masquerades as a Sagittarian know-it-all with superior mystical (Piscean) understanding (an affliction that is epidemic among new-agers). In this version, the Sun defends itself against Saturnian pressure via the defense of reaction-formation, as if to say, "I'm not inferior, I'm superior!" Although concerns about inferiority versus superiority are characteristic of any Sun-Saturn Square, the dynamics of the aspect take their form via the character-styles of Pisces and Sagittarius—mystical wisdom and scholarly insight.

The same aspect in different signs will produce different pathological symptoms. Another client, this one with Sun in Virgo squaring Saturn in Sagittarius, had a similar vulnerability to depression, yet her style was completely different. She reacted to Saturnian pressures by developing obsessive-compulsive traits, characteristic of Virgo. Worried that her education was insufficient to guarantee career success, she jumped from one academic program to another. No matter how many degrees she obtained, however, it was never enough. By the time she finished school she was so old and hopelessly in debt that her failure was virtually assured. Again, she was depressed, but she was depressed about her inability to work (Virgo) and the fact that she wasted so many years in college (Sagittarius).

Yet another variation on the Sun-Saturn theme can be seen with Charles Manson, who has Sun in Scorpio square Saturn in Aquarius. One could easily infer from Manson's history that he suffers from feelings of inferiority and underlying depression. However, his overt symptoms manifest as paranoid tendencies (Scorpio) with schizoid (Aquarian) traits. His frightful intention of instigating a race war via the murderous rampages of his revolutionary cult—the Manson Family—expressed a combination of Scorpio and Aquarian themes. Fear and hostility are characteristic of Scorpio, whereas detachment and radicalism typify Aquarius. The so-called Manson Family was an evil, terrorist (Scorpio) group that isolated itself on the fringes of society with the intent of activating a cultural revolution (Aquarius).

The point is we are all motivated by the same fundamental drives. We all have twelve sign-needs along with ten planets that represent a cadre of psychological functions designed to fulfill those needs. While instinctual drives can be repressed, distorted or redirected, depending upon aspects, they are nevertheless always present in whatever form our behavior takes. However, as the above examples demonstrate, the underlying dynamics of an aspect manifest through an exterior theme, which is a kind of covering or surface manifestation of the intrapsychic conflict. The planets and angle constitute the psychic infrastructure, whereas the occupied signs are the outer expression or style.

A CONSTRUCTIVIST VIEW

A neurotic person's conscious attitudes and the way he sees things are essential parts of his disorder. Again, psychopathology is not solely a product of repressed impulses and intrapsychic conflict, although these, too, are fundamental constituents. Rather, a person's intrinsic character—about which he has no choice—moves him to feel, think, and do things that perpetuate the neurotic experience and are indispensable to it.

For example, an extreme version of Aries-Mars behavior correlates to psychopathy (antisocial personality). If a robustly Aries-Mars man perceives the world as a Darwinian jungle "red in tooth and claw" in which only the strong survive, then he is apt to feel aggressive, think in terms of competition, and behave in a ruthlessly selfish way—all of which are central to psychopathy (antisocial personality disorder). Likewise, an extreme version of Cancer-Moon correlates to hysteria (histrionic personality disorder). If a Cancer-Moon dynamic is excessive in a woman's makeup, she will tend to perceive the world as potentially rejecting and devaluing, feel small and vulnerable, think predominantly in terms of attracting love, and behave in a seductive, dependent manner—all of which is typical of hysteria.

In other words, neurotic behavior is a feed-forward, proactive, self-sustaining process that actively seeks information to confirm the general predisposition. The neurotic does not simply suffer from a neurosis, but constructs it and actively participates in it with his every perception and action. Again, this view contradicts the determinism of 20th century psychology, which cast human beings as passive marionettes in the grip of unconscious, libidinal forces. In that view, the neurotic was not a conscious, active participant in that which ails him, but a helpless victim of forces beyond his control.

RESTORING PERSONAL AGENCY

Since astrology reveals that character structure is innate, types of pathology cannot be said to derive solely from instinctual conflict or the internalization of a faulty environment, but also from an innate, pre-existent psychic structure that generates lived experience and responds to that experience in a manner that is consistent with its own nature. From this point of view, the neurotic person is no longer merely a victim of historical events; rather, his way of thinking and his attitudes—his style, in other words—having shaped and been shaped by that history, are now integral parts of his neurotic functioning and move him to think, feel, and act in ways that are indispensable to it.

Earlier I stated that psychopathology is marked by self-estrangement and the loss of personal agency and volition. When astrologers convey a picture of the client's passivity before cosmic forces by making interpretations such as, "Pluto square the Sun tends to cause paranoia," they are unwittingly entering into collusion with the client's own disclaimers of intention. If the client discloses that, indeed, he can't help feeling distrustful and suspicious of others, he is not going to be helped by locating the source of his neurotic suspiciousness in forces outside his own psyche.

An alternative approach is to focus on the client's character and the way in which he or she constructs reality. In this regard, it is critically important that the astrologer interpret the chart in terms of purposeful action, or "action language," such as:

> Sun square Pluto indicates a dynamic tension between the part of you that is self-expressive and the part of you that seeks transformation, or healing. This suggests early experiences that might have been wounding to your sense of self—that is, experiences that you might have interpreted as implying that you were bad, impotent, or unworthy.
>
> To the extent that you remain unconscious of these wounds and resultant negative ideas, you will behave in ways that are based on an expectation of further harm. For example, you could be overly fearful, suspicious, or needlessly hostile, all of which can be self-defeating.
>
> Your task, therefore, is to heal these wounds and transform your identity so that you are no longer so fearful of being hurt or shamed. Ultimately, this is an act of self-empowerment; yet, it requires the courage to face irrational fears and beliefs that may be left over from hurtful childhood experiences. Once you do this, then your Sun and Pluto will combine in ways that enable you to be a positive, regenerative, and transformational agent in life.

Such an interpretation does not portray the client as the passive marionette of unconscious forces that rule from below, or of cosmic energies impinging from above. Rather, a description is provided that highlights the client's responsibility in constructing meanings from early events. More importantly, it emphasizes that the client is an active agent in both that which ails him and that which is potentially healing. In other words, if the higher, more positive potential of Sun square Pluto is to be realized, then the client must make this happen of his own volition.

The conception of adult pathology as the unconscious living out of the family dynamics of childhood is an important truth, but it is a partial truth. It is partial because it leaves out the equally important contribution of one's innate character style. In the preceding interpretation of Sun square Pluto, the client is invited to take responsibility for how he constructs a world and a self. Astrological symbols depict a language of action. Sun square Pluto means that specific actions, or purposes, which are intrinsic to the psyche, are in conflict; actions *to express* (Sun) and *to transform* (Pluto) are in dynamic tension.

Such processes constitute an innate striving to meet clashing needs that ultimately must be integrated, managed, and consciously directed. Generally with the square, one process will be repressed and thus unconsciously expressed, while the other will be accepted and thus consciously expressed. For example, if he represses his plutonian need for transformation and accepts his solar impulses, plutonian processes will influence his Sun in ways that appear to originate in conditions outside the self. For example, he will consciously attend (solar process) to an external threat (Pluto) that appears autonomous. The person thinks, "They're out to get me." At some point, however, he is likely to behave in a way that apes the very threat he is resisting. Then, either he will 1) deny his own bad behavior, 2) blame someone else for his actions, and/or 3) claim that he never meant to do what he did. In each instance, plutonic processes will be operating apart from his conscious volition.

The restoration of the client's sense of agency is, in many respects, equivalent to therapeutic cure, for the opposite—self-estrangement and the sense of being controlled by forces outside of awareness—is by definition neurotic. Astrologers can enlarge the client's sense of agency by pointing out the most immediate and general ways in which she avoids that experience. By calling attention to ways in which the client fails to express her genuine feelings, wishes, and intentions, the astrologer can assist the individual in becoming aware of psychological processes that have heretofore been unconscious.

In regard to Sun square Pluto, this might entail assisting the client in recognizing his need for growth and healing. Rather than siding with the client's perception that the outside world is aligned against him, the astrologer helps the client recognize his own self-rejection, self-destructive attitudes, shame, fear of self-expression, repressed creativity, and other such processes that are symbolized by the aspect. In other words, needs for growth and change are being denied and rendered evil, and then they are projected outwards. As he grapples with these issues, he can restore a sense of agency to the extent that Plutonic processes of transformation are brought into alignment with his will (Sun). He must, in effect, choose to die to his old identity as a persecuted victim. By eliminating toxic attitudes and pathogenic beliefs, he can be reborn in a new, more integrated version of his former self.

IS IT MEMORY OR IS IT CHARACTER?

The notion of active, though unconscious, anachronistic childhood conflicts and anxieties impinging on the present is central to a dynamic understanding of adult psychopathology. Such conflicts are presumed to have a source in early experiences that were traumatic. Freud (1937) said, "The adult's ego continues to defend itself against dangers which no longer exist" (p. 238). While the content of an obsessive idea or irrational fear may, in fact, be an expression of a particular childhood anxiety, it is another matter entirely to explain general attitudes and characteristic ways of living. The re-enactment of early childhood experience is not an adequate explanation for the general, characteristic, adult form of symptoms.

Shapiro (2000) reasons that if early memories and anxieties are still vital in the adult, it is probably "because they have been endowed with significance by, or in some way embody, more general dynamics of the adult character" (p. 22). In other words, an individual's character organization, which regulates and stabilizes the personality, can itself be a source of anxiety.

This formulation is entirely consistent with astrology, for the chart symbolizes an innate character that generates lived experience—including and especially the apparently formative experiences of childhood. Astrologers would argue that childhood experiences are not the cause of neurotic symptoms; rather, such experiences are synchronistic reflections of a pre-existent character that will ultimately generate analogous adult experiences and possibly symptoms consistent with that characterological structure.

Consider, for example, an individual with a Yod involving Mars in quincunx to Neptune and Saturn. Since Mars is the focal planet, this configuration suggests there will be some problem and/or crisis related to his capacity for assertion and autonomy. The specific content and quality of the problem/crisis will necessarily involve functions and experiences that are ruled by Neptune and Saturn. Although there will undoubtedly be some pattern of childhood experience that conforms to this aspect, any analogous adult experience derives not from the childhood experience itself, but from the structure of the personality configuration.

One client with this aspect experienced a traumatic loss (Neptune) of his capacity for competitive striving (Mars) because of an injury to his spinal column (Saturn) during gym class in the 5th grade. He underwent an operation that required several vertebrae to be permanently fused. Subsequently, he felt weak (Neptune) and stiff (Saturn) in any situation that required a Mars response of strength, vitality, and combativeness. Whenever his Mars function was activated thereafter, he experienced distress.

One could argue that his anxiety in Mars situations derived from the beliefs he developed about himself subsequent to his childhood injury. As an adult, his anxiety functions as an inhibitory signal that warns of danger in the face of any competitive/Mars situation. However, a closer examination reveals that there are other experiences, ideas, and habits of functioning that conform to the nature of his Mars Yod to Neptune and Saturn. For example, my client is a homosexual who feels inferior to other men; his sexual desires are a source of pain to his family, so he hides what he really wants and does; he feels guilty in any situation that involves putting himself ahead of others; any display of boldness or strength arouses a fear that he will hurt people and suffer retaliation; he is especially intimidated by authority figures; the suffering of victims galvanizes his ability to assert on their behalf; his work entails adjustments that restore fluidity to rigidified structures; and his spiritual practice entails movement exercises such as Tai Chi and Yoga, which are designed to promote optimal health and well-being.

When one considers the many and varied manifestations of his Saturn/Neptune Yod to Mars, it is easy to appreciate that his distress in Mars situations derives not from any singular childhood experience, but from the pathological workings of his character. In fact, one could argue that his spinal injury was not the cause of his distress, but rather was symptomatic of a general pattern of experience. If he endows his injury with great significance, it is because it embodies the more general dynamics of his character. Clearly, however, these dynamics are not merely by-products of early childhood experiences. Rather, quite the opposite may be true: his childhood injury is but one of several interrelated experiential themes that derive from the dynamics of the characterological pattern symbolized by the Mars Yod.

His personality is organized in such a way that certain attitudes have developed that are, for the most part, intolerant of his Martian propensities except under specific circumstances—acting on behalf of victims (Neptune) or working to restore ailing structures (Saturn). Otherwise, his Martian impulses are defended against, as they are inimical to the dominant values and attitudes symbolized by Saturn (restraint, control, rigidity) and Neptune (guilt, sacrifice, surrender). When Martian impulses are activated and become conscious as specific intentions—to assert, to fight, to compete—they trigger anxiety. This anxiety is not merely based on anticipation of external danger that derives from memory of his prior injury; rather, his anxiety is a response to an internal structural threat that derives from the way his personality is organized. That is, it is a direct sensation of threat to his existing character.

This suggests that the particular quality and content of pathological anxiety will depend upon the nature of the individual character and its attitudes. These, in turn, will be reflected in hard aspects. Accordingly, anxiety has as many qualities and contents as there are aspects between signs and planets. Anxiety of the sort mentioned above could be summarized as a fear that spontaneous action is likely to be hurtful to others, shameful to the self, and blocked by authority except and unless it helps to restore order and relieve the suffering of the innocent. Needless to say, this is a rather precise and narrow framework within which his Mars is allowed to work; yet, it may well be that for this individual at least, it provides exactly the right set of restraints for Mars to function in accord with his characterological imperative. My client ultimately became a chiropractor in which all of the above found a ready expression.

Although pathogenic ideas can be embedded in the structures of character, character itself constitutes a level of personality organization that transcends any particular belief. In fact, one could even say that character generates ideas consistent with itself. While these ideas will often appear to derive from earlier experiences, such that the idea appears to be the effect of an experiential cause, this line of reasoning fails to recognize that the meaning the person gives to his experience helps to determine its shape and impact. In other words, pre-existing tendencies to interpret events a certain way can have as much influence on the quality and content of our experience as the event itself.

Self-regulatory dynamics of innate character function as a kind of template imposed on outer experience, thus permitting the individual to see only those dimensions, qualities, and meanings that conform to the nature of the template. Since both childhood and adult experiences will be filtered through this template, one may mistakenly assume that the earlier experience is a progenitor of the later. In fact, however, all such experiences conform to the general pattern, which we might call fate, so long as we remember that fate and character are mirror images of one another.

Self-regulatory dynamics have previously been described as processes of defense symbolized by astrological configurations. Such defenses do not require ideation; rather, they operate in accord with thresholds of sensitivity. Whenever a situation occurs that crosses a threshold of sensitivity, the psyche responds with a corrective action to restore homeostasis. For example, if someone has Venus in the 10th opposing Pluto, she may be calibrated to tolerate only minimal relatedness with anyone in a position of authority, such as a father, boss, or a governmental agent (all 10th house figures). If she begins to feel too close, either because of her own attraction or because of the other's attraction to her, she will be compelled to perform an evasive maneuver in order to prevent an unwanted seduction. At such times, she is apt to feel anxious and behave in a guarded, highly vigilant manner.

Her anxiety signals a threat (Pluto) to her need for affection, attachment, and intimacy (Venus). Although her anxiety may be accompanied by certain thoughts such as, "He is charming and attractive, but I don't trust him," such thoughts are secondary to her gut reaction. Again, the defensive process does not require ideational content, which, if it does occur, may be vague and fleeting. Her boss may remind her of an uncle, or older brother, or babysitter who molested her; yet, the previous experience is not necessarily the cause of her current fear. The nature of her pathological anxiety is determined not merely by her memories or thoughts, but by her character.

Alternatively, this same configuration may predispose her to sexualize all hierarchical relationships so that she unconsciously behaves in a seductive, manipulative manner toward superiors. Often, this type of behavior entails the re-enactment of an earlier seduction, except this time the roles are reversed. The person is, in effect, beating fate to the punch by evoking the feared experience. Equally likely, if she is in a superior position, she may strive to seduce and sexually dominate subordinates.

Venus in the 10th opposing Pluto in the 4th will not only signify her "fatal attraction" to men in positions of power, but also the quality and content of her career achievements (10th house). For example, if she works as a purchasing agent for an import company that specializes in the sale of primitive art, this can hardly be said to derive from childhood experiences of being molested. Venus in the 10th (a career that involves acquisitions and art) and Pluto in the 4th (the mining of the past for objects of hidden value), combine to create her career position and achievements. This same configuration, however, can also symbolize her experience of being molested by a childhood caretaker and her current sexual ambivalence toward her boss. The point is all these experiences conform to the same archetypal pattern; they are all manifestations of a fate that reflects the structure of her character. Why this is so is a mystery of profound significance.

SIGNIFICANCE OF ENVIRONMENT

When I say that pathological anxiety is determined not by the adult's memories but by his character, I do not mean to imply that the original source of that anxiety—a prototypical childhood event—has no etiological significance. Recall from Chapter 8 that etiology of a mental disorder includes both a predisposition as a primary cause, and an initiating factor as a secondary cause. Whereas a predisposition is inherent in the birthchart and constitutes innate character structure, initiating factors entail actual experiences that were particularly intense or traumatic and can have a lasting pathogenic effect. Subsequent experiences of anxiety may, in fact, be in anticipation of some external danger that previously occurred. However, what ultimately becomes pathogenic is not the memory itself, but its influence on the developing personality. These influences may entail the formation of certain anxiety-forestalling attitudes, such as timidity, guardedness, or seductiveness.

Once these inhibitory, restrictive attitudes are in place, the person is no longer the same, for she has generalized from the original experience. Rather than merely being frightened by a particular danger or a reminder of it, she is threatened by any impulse that runs counter to the restrictive attitudes that have formed. If, for example, she has Mars square Saturn, she may have learned that acts of initiative will arouse punitive responses from an external authority initially embodied by her father. If, in response, she has become dutiful and obedient, then an inconsequential act of assertion will now feel audacious and impudent; it will arouse anxiety. The infraction, perhaps even the intended infraction, will arouse anxiety not because it revives the memory of a punitive father, but because it embodies an attitude that is inimical to the dutiful and obedient character that has formed.

The general attitude thus becomes a perpetuating factor in the etiology of the disorder. In this manner, a pathologically restrictive character will be threatened not merely by particular actions or motivations or circumstances, but by general categories of actions, motivations, or circumstances. Astrologically, these general categories are symbolized by astrological configurations such as a planet in a sign, house, and aspect. Such configurations are predisposing factors that are initially activated and fleshed out by early formative experiences, memories of which become metaphors of the general pattern.

In effect, the astrological chart not only symbolizes one's character structure, but also the developmental processes that have contributed to the formation of that character—again, like tissue on bone. One could say that in childhood the horoscope symbolizes a proto-character structure, a kind of abstract pattern and primitive forerunner of its later, full-bodied adult form. In this sense, the chart never signifies a fixed character, but a character in a process of continuous unfoldment. Early traumatic experiences that contribute to the development of character can be symbolized by the same astrological configuration that later signifies a more integrated, higher level awareness that constitutes a functional skill.

JUNG'S RELIGIOUS WOUND

A case in point is the development of Jung's religious sensibility. Jung had Jupiter in Libra in the 8th forming an opening quincunx to Pluto in Taurus in the 3rd (see Figure 24, page 334). Jupiter, of course, signifies religion and religious figures, whereas the 8th house represents an area of wounding. Planets in the 8th represent psychological functions that require transformation. Pluto, as the god of the underworld and natural ruler of the 8th, signifies that which is wounding and, also, that which is ultimately healing. Any planet connected to Pluto by hard aspect may become associated with images and memories of danger, pain, death and rebirth (renewal, healing).

A hard aspect from Pluto to Jupiter in the 8th constitutes a repeating theme: Jupiter is both in Pluto's house and forming a hard aspect to Pluto. Almost certainly, therefore, Jung's religious instinct is initially going to be wounded and buried in the underworld (unconscious). Thus, it will be a source of significant anxiety until and unless he can transform it, at which point it will become a powerful resource to be utilized for purposes of healing. The opening quincunx between these two planets suggests that Jung's religious wound is also a dilemma or problem to be solved; that is, something that he will tend to obsess about until he acquires the requisite skill to utilize his capacity for faith in a manner that is regenerative for both himself and also others.

There are many accounts in Jung's (1961) autobiography that provide testimony to his religious wound. For example, at age 3, Jung was taught to say a prayer about Jesus that he found deeply disturbing. One part of this prayer, "take to thee thy chick, thy child" (*nimm dein Küchlein ein*), was

334 • DEPTH ANALYSIS OF THE NATAL CHART

misinterpreted by Jung to mean that just as one "takes" medicine, so Jesus would "take" (devour) little children.

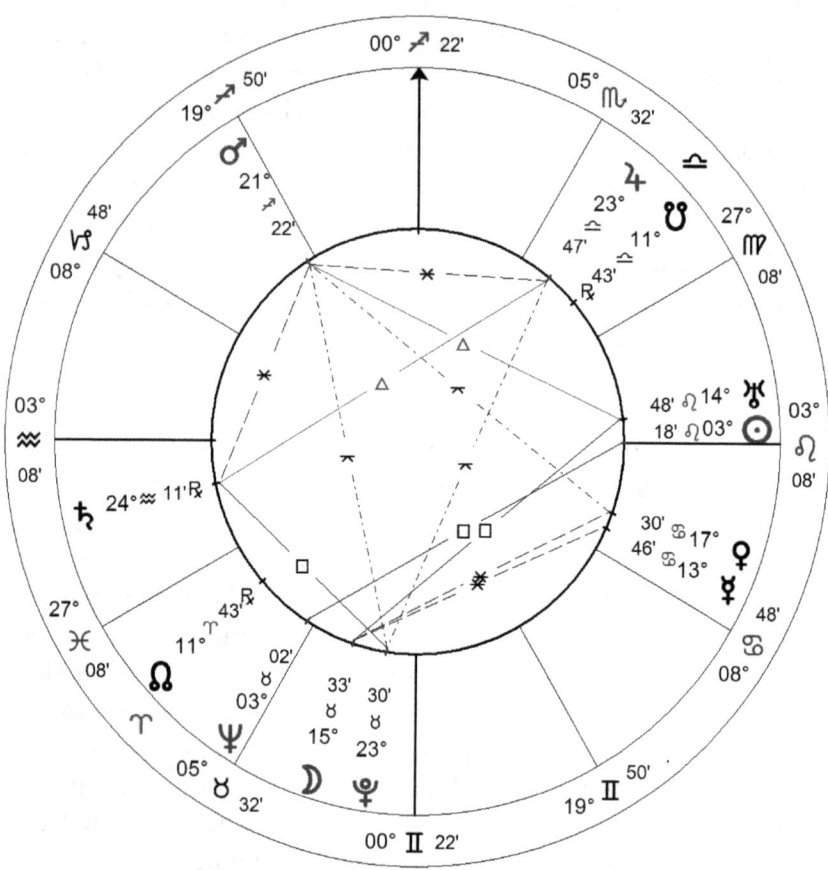

Figure 24: Birthchart of Carl Jung, July 26, 1875, 7:20pm, Zurich, Switzerland

The ominous connotation of the word "take" in this connection was reinforced by Jung's childhood observations of funerals of young men who drowned in a nearby river. His father, who was a cleric, presided over burials in which sinister appearing older men dressed in black frock coats, top hats, and shiny black boots—all parsons—gathered about a hole in the ground into which was lowered a mysterious black box. As women wept, Jung was told that the young men were being buried and that "Lord Jesus had taken them to himself" (p. 9). Jung reports that he was terrified by these experiences.

This image of parsons dressed in black and gathered about a hole in the ground, into which was lowered a black box containing a dead youth, re-activated Jung's childhood association of Jesus as a devouring figure that "takes" little boys. Here we see Jung's early association of religion (Jupiter) with death (Pluto). He had been taught to think of Jesus as a wonderfully kind figure seated on high, a god-man toward whom he could be entirely trusting and positive. However, over time, Jesus gradually became associated with a dark, negative image: a menacing, devouring god of death who resided in the underworld—an apt figure for Jung's 8th house Jupiter quincunx Pluto. The benevolent, sustaining, and life-giving attributes of the heavenly Jesus were in stark contrast to the terrifying and devouring qualities of His negative counterpart.

This same split was also evident in Jung's father, whom, according to Jung, suffered grievously from religious doubt. Recall that the opening quincunx represents a dilemma or conundrum and is associated with Virgonian doubt. Since Jupiter is the ruler of the 10th house, and thus a significator of father, it is significant that Jung's father, a cleric, suffered from a secret religious mistrust. Such a paradox is a perfect illustration of a Jupiter-Pluto quincunx.

In short, Jung's Jupiter complex residing in his own personal underworld was religion itself. Accordingly, his first conscious trauma involved the sighting of a Jesuit priest whom he imagined was coming to kill and devour him (1961, p. 10). At first, Jung thought the priest was disguised in woman's clothes, but then realized the man was wearing a long black robe that reached to his feet, just like the robes of the clerics at the burials. Jung was terrified and assumed the priest had "evil intentions." For weeks afterward he was "hellishly frightened" that the Jesuit might return.

At about the same time, Jung had a terrifying dream in which he descended down a hole in the ground and saw, at the end of a long chamber, a huge, 15-foot tall erect penis upon a magnificent throne. Then Jung heard his mother's voice, "Yes, just look at him. That is the man-eater!" (p. 12). Jung awoke, "sweating and scared to death." The dream haunted him for years. "In my childish imagination," wrote Jung, "Lord Jesus, the Jesuit, and the phallus were identical." They were all symbolic of a frightening, subterranean god of death. The terrifying image of the enthroned phallus would reappear in Jung's mind whenever someone spoke too emphatically about Jesus.[47] These early experiences and dreams left in Jung a residue of

---

[47] This momentous dream singularly captures many elements of Jupiter-Pluto. It's a Jupiter (religious) dream in that it contains images of a church—the long chamber, at the end of which was a throne, or shrine, supporting a god. That the church was down a deep hole and that Lord Jesus was a phallic, devouring god of death is testimonial to Pluto's involvement with Jupiter.

suspicion, distrust, and a deeply troubling religious doubt that would occupy him much of his life.

Note, however, that while the religious dreams and events of Jung's childhood constitute specific memories that are consistent with his 8th house Jupiter quincunx Pluto, they are subordinate to the more general category of action, motivation, and circumstance symbolized by this aspect. Jung's early experiences may have activated that characterological structure; however, once activated, it would continue to attract experiences in accord with the meaning of the aspect. Sagittarian impulses involving the search for truth would necessarily stimulate Jupiter, thus evoking the anxiety, distrust, and doubt contained in its quincunx to Pluto. Likewise, any truth claim made by a supposed authority (10th house), especially those representing a conventional religious attitude, would stimulate similar feelings of unease and disbelief.

Again, Jupiterian impulses and experiences aroused anxiety not because they revived memories of early religious traumas, but because they constituted a desire to have faith that was inimical to the distrusting and doubting nature of his Jupiter-Pluto cognitive structure.[48] For this anxiety to be relieved, Jung must strive to resolve his religious anxieties and, ultimately, utilize his capacity to make meaning in a manner that solves problems related to religious uncertainty.

Evidence of Jung's success in this regard can be found throughout his writings. For example, in his autobiography he writes, "The majority of my patients consisted not of believers but of those who had lost their faith" (p. 140). Coincident with a need to integrate his own Jupiter-Pluto quincunx, his work entailed treating those who embodied its problematic, unintegrated version. As always, fate reflects character. Jung still had to deal with the aspect despite having at least partially resolved the problem it previously represented. Accordingly, he described many cases in which therapeutic cure of his patients simply involved the restoration of their faith; that is, their capacity to believe in something beyond reason. The action *to restore* is, of course, Plutonic.

Jung laments how an overly scientific attitude underlies much of psychology and thus prejudices us against the spiritual. Although he admits that the existence of a Supreme Being cannot be proven, he asks, "Why...should we deprive ourselves of views that would prove helpful in crises and would give

---

[48] I am not saying that Jung's entire character can be reduced to his Jupiter-Pluto quincunx. Sun square Neptune, among other aspects, is also a critically important factor. I am saying that the Jupiter-Pluto quincunx is a significant *facet* of his character. It is, in effect, a structure within a larger structure.

meaning to our existence?" (1964, p. 87). In this single sentence, the entire aspect is represented: Views (Jupiter) that would prove helpful (quincunx) in crises (Pluto). He continues:

> In our time, there are millions of people who have lost faith in any kind of religion. While life runs smoothly without religion, the loss remains as good as unnoticed. But when suffering comes, it is another matter. That is when people begin to seek a way out and to reflect about the meaning of life. (1964, p. 87)

As Jung famously said, neurosis is suffering yet to find its meaning. A person can endure just about anything so long as his suffering had meaning. Thus, Jung asserts that human beings "positively need general ideas and convictions" that will enable them to discern the purpose of their challenges and hardships (p. 89). Jung's emphasis upon "meaning" and "general ideas and convictions" is Jupiterian, while healing and regenerative power is Plutonic. In his words:

> Modern man does not understand how much "his rationalism" has put him at the mercy of the psychic "underworld." He has freed himself from "superstition" (or so he believes), but in the process he has lost his spiritual values to a positively dangerous degree. His moral and spiritual tradition has disintegrated, and he is now paying the price for this break-up in world-wide disorientation and dissociation. (1964, p. 94)

It is ironic that the preceding passage, written by Jung near the end of his life, is an apt description of an unintegrated Jupiter-Pluto quincunx. Again, it is precisely because Jung had integrated this aspect that he was sensitive to the destructive consequences of its non-integration in modern culture.

There is not space here to explore the full significance of Jung's Jupiter-Pluto quincunx, especially Pluto in the 3rd, which I believe relates to his battles with the hyper-scientific rationalism of his day. Suffice to say that Jung's childhood traumas involving religion were but an early manifestation of a wound symbolized by his Jupiter-Pluto configuration.

In effect, these initial experiences were necessary forerunners of what was ultimately to become a profound transformational power within Jung's therapeutic arsenal. Jupiter quincunx Pluto symbolized not only his early religious traumas, but also its later form in the mature, regenerative power of his faith. Indeed, Jung's obsessive childhood ruminations prefigured a later work, *Answer to Job* (1952), in which he was able to reconcile the dark and light aspects of the Judeo-Christian God in a brilliant *tour de force*.

THE ACORN THEORY

Jung's accomplishments provide a good example of Hillman's (1996) "acorn theory," which proposes that each life is formed by a particular pattern—a destiny image—that represents the soul's code of fate. Just as the mighty oak's destiny is written in the tiny acorn, so each individual soul has a blueprint of destiny that operates from birth. Hillman's view is in remarkable correspondence with astrology, for the horoscope *is* a code of fate that operates from the first breath. As a symbolic portrait of the soul's essential structure, the astrological chart presents a core image that symbolizes both character and fate.

According to Hillman, "Each person bears a uniqueness that asks to be lived and that is already present before it can be lived" (p. 6). Each person is born with a given character, which is also his calling or *daimon*. Fate is the unfoldment of that character. Early experiences provide a preliminary glimpse of the daimon in action, such that a person's ultimate accomplishments are prefigured in the challenges and hardships of childhood. "One must realize," says Hillman, "that accidents, including the heartache and natural shocks the flesh is heir to, belong to the pattern of the image, are necessary to it, and help fulfill it" (p. 8). In other words, what children go through—their sufferings, traumas, and struggles—can be viewed not as undeserved calamities that wrongly shaped them, but as necessary preparations for a specific calling.

Hillman argues that neurotic issues belong in some way to the unique destiny of the child. A certain amount of psychopathology may be inescapable and even necessary for a child's gifts to be fully realized, for it is only in the furnace of suffering that a steely resolve and ironclad determination can be forged. By discerning the purpose of one's pathology, we discover what the daimon is wanting, and what destiny it may be calling forth.

Jung's secret religious anxieties of childhood, and his experience of his father as suffering from a religious wound, exemplify Hillman's contention that the daimon first makes its presence known in the challenges of childhood. Jung's autobiography reveals that his father was tormented with religious doubts, yet unable to break free from the stifling dogma of his profession. Nor was he able to provide his son with meaningful answers to deeper questions involving the nature of God and the devil or the struggle between good and evil, questions which haunted Jung from his earliest years. To say that Jung was disappointed in his father would be an understatement. In recalling his father's apparent endorsement of certain protestant tenets, Jung writes: "I was disillusioned and even indignant, and once more filled with pity for my father, who had fallen victim to this mumbojumbo" (1961, p. 59).

Jung makes clear the anguish and torment he felt regarding his own religious training. At age 14, after receiving his first Communion at his father's hands, which was supposed to be "the pinnacle of religious initiation," Jung was so disheartened at its utter lack of significance that he regarded it as "a fatal experience for me." He thought to himself, "The church is a place I should not go to. It is not life which is there, but death," (p. 55), echoing Jupiter's tenancy of the 8th.

At the same time, he was "seized with the most vehement pity" for his father, and at once understood "the tragedy of his profession and his life" (p. 55). Following his first Communion, Jung's sense of union with the Church and with the human world was shattered. He felt utterly defeated, and the religious outlook that constituted his sole meaningful relationship with the universe had "disintegrated" (p. 56). Determined to find God on his own terms, he found himself cut off from the Church and from his father's and everybody else's faith. "In so far as they all represented the Christian religion," Jung said, "I was an outsider. This knowledge filled me with a sadness which was to overshadow all the years until the time I entered the university" (p. 56).

Clearly, both Jung and his father suffered from a religious wound, a condition that is aptly symbolized by Jupiter's placement in Jung's chart. It rules the 10th, thus signifies the father, tenants the house of wounds (8th), and forms a difficult opening quincunx to Pluto, which seems to symbolize Christianity's failure to reconcile good and evil in a way that is psychologically meaningful. As significator of the 10th, Jupiter also signifies Jung's career path. The message of his chart is clear: to become a success, Jung must achieve in his own life what his father could not; he must heal his religious wound by transforming his Jupiter-Pluto quincunx into a powerful, therapeutic faith and employ that faith in his profession.

Hillman's acorn theory holds that childhood anxieties provide the fertile soil out of which will sprout the mature form of the *daimon*—the fulfillment of one's character and destiny. Jung's achievement as the founder of analytical psychology—a psychology that holds at its core the relationship of human to divine—was born out of the painful struggles of his childhood and, particularly, his relationship with his father. In effect, Jung completed a task that his father had begun but left unfinished. Here again, the astrological chart not only symbolizes the structure of character, but also the developmental process by which that character is realized.

Included in this developmental process, and central to it, is the child's experience of his or her parents. In a very real sense, the astrological chart signifies the parent's psychological legacy, their gifts as well as their unactualized potentials. Whereas the gifts are internalized as psychological resources, the unactualized potentials are inherited as a mandate for a mission to be completed. Jung (1961) put it this way:

> I feel very strongly that I am under the influence of things or questions that were left incomplete and unanswered by my parents and grandparents and more distant ancestors. It often seems as if there were an impersonal karma within a family that is passed on from parents to children. It has always seemed to me that I had to answer questions which fate had posed to my forefathers, and which had not yet been answered, or as if I had to complete, or perhaps continue, things which previous ages had left unfinished. (p. 233).

SUMMARY

When a sign-planet system is under stress as a consequence of intrapsychic conflict, it can mutate into a specific defensive style that is characterized by the hypertrophy of associated modes of behavior. Hypertrophication means the compensatory overdevelopment and overfunctioning of a single way of a being; that is, the planet expresses itself in an unbalanced, extreme, and problematic way. If two planets are in hard aspect, the overfunctioning of one planet generally correlates with the underfunctioning of the other.

Loss of personal agency and volition is a primary symptom of psychopathology. Individuals engage in self-defeating behaviors for reasons that are outside of conscious awareness and control. A fundamental aim of treatment, therefore, is to enlarge the client's self-awareness and sense of personal agency. This means assisting the individual toward conscious recognition of his wants, feelings, and beliefs rather than directing him toward particular choices that the astrologer regards as desirable. If astrologers fall into the trap of being directive with clients—that is, advising them on the basis of the chart—they may merely reinforce the client's pathology.

A neurotic style is defined as a way of thinking, feeling, and perceiving that is associated with a specific mental disorder. Neurotic styles, however, may simply be extreme expressions of general archetypal propensities as reflected in sign-planet systems. What psychoanalytic theory regards as a diagnostic entity is similar to what astrologers call a planetary archetype, except psychiatric labels cover only the archetype's negative expression.

Conventional explanations of psychopathology are deterministic in that they regard psychopathology as an effect of causes originating outside of the individual's psyche, either genetic or environmental. Astrology, however, suggests that psychopathology is a consequence of innate (inborn) intrapsychic conflicts that challenge the individual's capacity to deal with certain kinds of stress that are an inevitable consequence of the conflict.

Not only are signs descriptive of planetary expression, they also suggest how the motivating impulse of a planet is responded to and managed at a subjective level. Different signs will respond differently to the same planetary impulse; thus, a planet is required to adapt to the demands of the sign it occupies. The pathological expression of a planet under stress will evidence a blending of planet and sign; that is, the planet may be dysfunctional but in a way and in a domain that is symbolized by its sign position.

Repressed impulses and intrapsychic conflict are neither the sole nor primary causes of psychopathology, although certainly it is a factor. More importantly, neurotic behavior is a feed-forward, proactive, self-sustaining process that derives from an innate, pre-existent psychic structure symbolized by the horoscope. This implies that pathological anxiety is not determined merely by repressed memories of earlier traumatic experiences, but by characterological predispositions that manifest outwardly as exactly those circumstances and relations that come to be seen as traumatic. In effect, psychopathology and pathogenic events co-determine one another.

The same astrological configuration that symbolizes earlier frustrations and subsequent defenses may later symbolize the emergence of powerful attributes, or talents, which result from working through the original difficulty. Hillman's acorn theory is consistent with astrology, for a chart symbolizes both the character of one's fate and the fate of one's character. In the end, they are mirror images of one another. This underscores that pathology is a consequence of character, not merely the unfortunate by-product of random experience. Moreover, early experiences that are wounding can also be purposive in that they serve as catalysts to the fulfillment of the child's unique destiny.

Chapter Eleven

A ZODIACAL DEVELOPMENTAL MODEL

In the previous chapter, we explored how psychopathology is a problem of character rather than of antecedent childhood experiences. Again, however, this should not imply that developmental processes have no bearing on the subject in question. In this chapter, we will explore whether certain kinds of formative experiences at critical periods of development might activate innate characterological patterns and how such developmental processes might be prefigured in the astrological chart.

DEVELOPMENTAL STAGES & PSYCHOPATHOLOGY

A central conviction of psychoanalytic theory is that current psychological preoccupations reflect infantile precursors. Interactions in our earliest years set up the template for how we assimilate later experience. In other words, adult experience becomes comprehensible according to meanings that were initially constructed in childhood, even though these meanings may be unconscious. A genetic, or more accurately, *psychogenetic* view of the personality is based on ways in which an individual's past is thought to influence his current functioning at an unconscious level.

This perspective has been part of psychoanalytic theory since Freud's clinical work led him to investigate psychic conflict. Early in his thinking he conjectured that certain kinds of childhood experiences were antecedents to adult neurosis. The genetic view emphasized drive development, internal conflict, and traumatic experiences. That is, it emphasized the developmental impact of childhood experiences at specific stages of life. These experiences were presumed to underly the particular difficulties that brought the person to treatment. If trauma or chronic frustration occurred during a particular stage, then the drive associated with that stage might not develop properly. So called "drive conflict" results from defending oneself against the pain and fear associated with specific impulses (drives).

Freud's observations led him to formulate a developmental theory that articulated five stages of psychosexual maturation—oral, anal, genital, latency, and adolescence. Subsequently, these initial formulations were elaborated upon and supplemented by other theorists—most notably, Erik Erikson (1959; 1968).

In addition to psychogenetic theories, carefully designed experiments and observational research of children in clinical settings have converged to produce an ever-expanding understanding of childhood and adult development. Theories that are based on actual observation rather than reconstructions of the client's past are called *developmental* (as opposed to psychogenetic) theories.

The relation between psychogenetic and developmental points of view is a complementary one. The psychogenetic point of view looks from the present to the past and is particularly concerned with psychopathology. It recognizes that all earlier aspects of psychic life are potentially active and can influence current functioning. Conversely, the developmental perspective looks forward with a focus on the process of psychic structure formation. It considers how psychic structures and functions come about from the combined influence of a) innate givens (inborn propensities); b) maturational sequences; and c) individual experiences. Together, these three factors combine to create the ever more complicated labyrinth of intrapsychic life.

The underlying presumption of both psychogenetic and developmental theories is that psychological problems originate in traumatic experiences that impair the development of specific psychological functions at their appropriate stage of development. In other words, certain kinds of functions have a critical time of emergence and danger of defect. If these psychic systems or structures[49] do not develop properly at their designated time during the life cycle, then the entire subsequent development of the individual is com-

---

[49] I use the terms *system* and *structure* interchangeably. A psychological structure is a relatively stable yet slowing evolving system that involves a set of interrelated functions. For example, Cancer-Moon is a sign-planet system that symbolizes functions of nurturance, caring, and listening. These functions evolve and become progressively more differentiated and integrated over time. Because terms like *system* and *structure* utilize a metaphor of spatialization that conveys a static object, I will sometimes substitute terms like *process-structure* or *dynamism*, which convey active processes. One needs to be mindful that a metaphor of spatialization is limited and not to be taken literally. Sign-planet systems are not inert things. It is more accurate to think of them as dynamic configurations characterized by a slow rate of change.

promised. Presumably, defects at any one stage give rise to mental disorders associated with that stage. That is, an "arrest" or crisis at a particular stage is thought to produce certain types of psychopathology.

If there were a way to identify these stages, experiences, and disorders in the astrological chart, such information would have important diagnostic and prognostic implications. Chapter Three touched on this possibility. A 12-stage developmental model was presented in which each sign of the zodiac represents a period of the life cycle. In Chapter Seven it was subsequently postulated that houses may correlate to the same stages as their associated signs—Aries and the 1st house represents birth to 2 years, Taurus and the second house 2 through 5 years, and so on. Planetary configurations in specific houses may symbolize the person's general experience during that stage.

If planets in a house are under stress from difficult aspects, two related hypotheses emerge: (1) psychopathology associated with that planetary configuration may originate or peak during the developmental period signified by that house; and/or (2) psychopathology associated with that developmental stage/house may be triggered by the nature of the planetary processes that reside and impinge on that house. For example, if Saturn is under stress in the 3rd house, a child may be particularly vulnerable to depression (Saturn pathology) during the ages of 5 through 9 years, which is the 3rd house period. However, he may also be subject to a learning disorder or the development of obsessive symptomology (3rd house pathology) as a consequence of stresses and pressures symbolized by Saturn. In fact, one type of pathology may be related to another. He may be depressed because of his learning disorder and his learning disorder may be exacerbated because he is depressed. In subsequent sections, we will be exploring this idea further.

ASTRO-PSYCHOLOGICAL EPIGENESIS

To more fully understand the interface of astrology, human development, and psychopathology, we need to examine the topic of maturational stages more closely. While different researchers tend to emphasize different lines of development such as the evolution of cognitive functions or moral perspectives, there is substantial agreement as to how and when development occurs. The consensus view is that human beings are born with a blueprint of psychic development that is determined in part by a maturational timetable.

Erik Erikson (1968), one of the leading figures in human development, coined the phrase "psychological epigenisis" to describe stages of psychosocial maturation. The term *epigenisis* is derived from *epi,* which means "upon" and *genesis,* which means "emergence." Psychological epigenisis implies that each stage of development is built upon previous stages and constitutes the emergence of a new emotional, cognitive, and behavioral capacity. Thus, there is a gradual differentiation of parts in the maturing individual. Human beings obey inner laws of development that create a succession of potentialities for interaction within a variety of new contexts—play, school, work, intimacy, and the like. Such processes of unfoldment conform to a precise rate and sequence. The psyche becomes increasingly differentiated and hierarchically organized as it interacts with its environment over time. In general, the psyche evolves from simple to more complex forms of organization and function, and new structures constitute advances in self-regulatory and adaptive capacities.

Erikson described the progressive unfolding of general modes of functioning as patterns of going at things and ways of seeking relationships. His descriptions presented a model of the dominant instinctual mode of successive periods. Each stage characterized the emergence of a specific maturational capacity and tendency. The crowning achievement of a developmental phase is a new way of functioning, an attitude, and a frame of mind, that did not previously exist in a mature way.

For example, we can see this in the developmental period of adolescence, during which Leonine behavior assumes prominence. Adolescents are characterized by classic Leonian traits—creativity, prideful self-expression, concerns about identity and self-esteem, counterdependent behavior (compensatory to the preceding Cancerian stage of development), heroic attempts to triumph in sports, playful interest in the opposite sex, and the awakening of romantic love—all qualities, it should be noted, that existed in only rudimentary form in previous stages.

The general forms of functioning in Erikson's scheme have three roots: 1) instinctual development, 2) the unfolding of maturational capacities and tendencies, and 3) the external social forms that society provides at each developmental phase. Astrologically, we can describe these general roots in terms of associated signs, planets, and houses. As stated, during adolescence the instinct for identity and self-esteem comes into ascendancy, which is symbolized by Leo. Coincident with this emergence is the unfolding of a maturational capacity for dating, competitive sports, socializing, and creative self-expression, capacities which are symbolized by the Sun. Finally, the external social form that corresponds to this period is depicted by the 5th house, which symbolizes institutions and activities that provide an outlet for solar functions—the performing arts, sports competitions, cheerleading, theatrical productions, courtship and romance, parties, balls and proms, playtime with best friends, recreational activities, and so on.

While general forms of functioning come into ascendancy during their appropriate stage, immature forms exist in earlier stages, and the form itself may continue to develop and evolve in later stages. For example, the ability for efficient service (Virgo) may exist in rudimentary form in childhood, come into full bloom in one's early twenties, and evolve into yet more perfect forms as one continues to age.

Each successive stage constitutes a potential "psychosocial crisis" because of a radical change in perspective. Crisis implies a turning point, a crucial period of vulnerability and heightened awareness of new capacities. Every developmental period has its own salient theme with specific types of behavior, affects, and concerns reaching a point of ascendancy. Ideally, with the resolution of each crisis, there is an increased sense of inner unity and overall capacity, and an expansion of the individual's radius of significant relations.

This latter point is significant in that it underscores that development requires relationships with significant others. Not only does the person develop a new perspective of his own emergent capacities, he also learns how others are likely to respond to the expression of these potentials. Implicit in developmental models is the notion of self-environment relations. The human being does not develop his capacities in a vacuum but in relationship to specific kinds of environments that apply to each stage.

For example, how the environment responds to the infant's need for attachment (Taurus-Venus) is going to be internalized as a model or template for all future attempts at attachment. If a child's immature, party-girl mother is erratic or neglectful in response to her infant's attachment needs (☽ 5ᵗʰ □ ♅ in 2ⁿᵈ), then this can become an expectation that undermines the child's emerging capacity for self and object constancy. Such an internalized model constitutes an unconscious belief, "People I depend on will neglect me in favor of pursuing their own needs for fun and attention," which may persist into adulthood and have implications for how that person deals with money, possessions, and any figures that embody attachment needs. For example, a bank manager may not be trusted to adequately secure one's savings.

REVISITING ASTROLOGICAL STAGES

As outlined in Chapter Three, stages of development delineated by Freud, Erikson, Piaget and other pioneers are in remarkable correspondence with the sequence of astrological signs. The zodiac presents a natural developmental sequence with each sign building upon the contributions of the previous sign while adding something new. Just as in Erikson's scheme, each sign represents a specific psychological need, or instinct, while also signifying a stage for the unfolding of an associated maturational capacity. For example, Virgo signifies the need for efficient functioning and the period of 20-27, during which the capacity for productive service becomes preemptory (see Figure 25).

STAGE	BASIC NEED/MATURATIONAL CAPACITY	AGE	DURATION
Pisces/12th	Transcendence, unity/Capacity for compassion, surrender	77–90	13 yrs. +
Aquarius/11th	Awakening, liberation/Capacity for altruism, change, progress	65–77	12 yrs.
Capricorn/3rd	Success, structure, mastery/Capacity for authority, expertise	54–65	11 yrs.
Sagittarius/9th	Truth, meaning, justice/Capacity for faith, expansion	44–54	10 yrs.
Scorpio/8th	Transformation, renewal/Capacity to integrate, regenerate	35–44	9 yrs.
Libra/7th	Partnership, harmony/Capacity to relate, cooperate, balance	27–35	8 yrs.
Virgo/6th	Efficiency, competence/Capacity to work, serve	20–27	7 yrs.
Leo/5th	Identity, self-esteem/Capacity to play, create, express	14–20	6 yrs.
Cancer/4th	Nurturing, belonging, closeness/Capacity to feel, reflect, care	9–14	5 yrs.
Gemini/3rd	Information, knowledge/Capacity to learn, communicate	5–9	4 yrs.
Taurus/2nd	Constancy, safety, stability/Capacity to have, pleasure	2–5	3 yrs.
Aries/1st	Survival, freedom/Capacity to move, do, assert	0–2	2 yrs.

© Glenn Perry, Ph.D.

Figure 25: A Sign/House Developmental Stage Model

Every sign/house signifies a developmental stage with the task of awakening the associated maturational capacity (planetary faculty) for fulfilling a particular need. New emotional, cognitive, and behavioral abilities emerge at each phase, which mark a logical progression from relatively simple functions to more complex ones. Each stage is progressively wider in its perspective and one year longer than the prior stage. Yet, because there is a natural acceleration of subjective time as we age, each stage is experienced as constituting equal time. Just as each sign astronomically corresponds to a specific time-space phase of the earth's orbit about the Sun, so each sign-stage experiences time and space differently as reflected in that sign's psychology. At earlier stages, vision is relatively narrow and time moves slowly. At later stages, time seems to have accelerated, and concomitantly, vision has broadened. As consciousness expands, our subjective perception of time and space changes with it: we see more broadly and more quickly. Simply put, vision broadens as time accelerates with age.

As one proceeds through the 12-stage zodiacal life cycle, new emotional, cognitive, and behavioral capacities emerge at each phase. These capacities mark a clear, logical progression from relatively simple functions to more complex ones. And because signs become increasingly complex as we move through personal (♈-♋), social (♌-♏), and collective (♐-♓) perspectives, there is a natural hierarchical structure to the zodiac; each sign is progressively wider and more inclusive in its perspective. All of this is consistent with the discoveries of developmental psychology.

Actual experiences at each stage appear to be symbolized in a general way by planet-house combinations. A house signifies a certain type of environment that is associated with a specific developmental task; thus, houses represent the external social forms that society provides at each developmental phase, just as in Erikson's model. Moreover, planets in houses symbolize particular types of experience associated with that environment, as well as the kind of characters that one may encounter there.

In the preceding example of the erratic mother, we might find Uranus in the 2nd house under stress from hard aspects. Uranus, which can be erratic and unpredictable, is archetypally square the 2nd house. This is because Aquarius, which Uranus rules, is square Taurus, which corresponds to the 2nd house; thus, on an archetypal level, Uranus and the 2nd house have a square relationship. The 2nd house signifies the developmental period of 2 through 4 years, during which time the child's need for a secure, stable attachment is primary. The 2nd house also signifies attachment figures, which in childhood is generally the mother or some other primary caretaker.[50] Uranus in the 2nd signifies a potentially disruptive and unstable quality to this period. We can

---

[50] A mother can be associated with a variety of tasks and roles. Accordingly, mothers are implicated in every house of childhood (one through four), even though they are predominantly associated with the 4th house function of nurturing and protecting.

hypothesize, therefore, that the main task of the 2nd house—the attainment of self and object constancy—could be compromised by an inconstant, unpredictable pattern of experience with an unstable attachment figure.

Note that houses 1-6 correspond to the signs Aries through Virgo and the inner planets, Sun through Mars. These are the signs, planets, and houses of childhood through adolescence, with the 6th house signifying a transitional stage into adulthood.

ZODIAC AS INTEGRATIVE MODEL

Because different theorists have focused on different dimensions of the psyche, a variety of stage models have emerged that not only emphasize different developmental achievements, but also different time periods and numbers of stages for various lines of development. Freud's model had five stages, covering birth to adolescence, and stressed sequential organization in psychosexual drive development. Piaget's (1937) model had four stages and covers the same period, but focused on cognitive integration and predominant modes of thinking at different ages. Erikson (1968) studied identity and the emergence of psycho-social capacities, which he covered in eight stages that encompassed the whole life span. And Kohlberg's (1976) six-stage model demonstrated the evolution of moral reasoning from childhood through old age. In short, each model provides a wealth of information and detail on the evolution of a specific line of development, all of which can be described by varying stages of differing lengths.

It would seem that an integration of theories and models is essential for a comprehensive view of personality formation. Yet, it is widely acknowledged that there have been few attempts to do so (Miller, 1983; Tyson and Tyson, 1990). Reasons for this are threefold: First, developmental theorists have struggled to demarcate a temporal structure of stages for which there is no objective corollary; hence, they are forced to make up life-stages of varying number—4, 5, 6, 8, and so on. Second, each theorist focused on a different line of development rather than on the psyche as a whole; thus, stages are described according to the idiosyncratic focus, framework and terminology of the investigator. And third, each model postulates different time periods for the emergence of new capacities.

It is significant that despite differences in numbers and lengths of postulated stages, there is some agreement as to when major shifts of development occur. Regardless of the dimension in question—drive, cognition, or psychosocial capacity—everyone agrees that important changes seem to take place during the transition from roughly: one to two, four to five, eight to nine, thirteen to fourteen, and nineteen to twenty (Tyson & Tyson, 1990, p. 19). In a zodiacal model, these transitions roughly correspond to the start of the Taurus, Gemini, Cancer, Leo, and Virgo stages. Aries would constitute birth to the end of age one (first two years of life).

This correlation underscores that the zodiac is a meta-model uniquely capable of synthesizing the various theories into a single, coherent system. A zodiacal model solves each of the three aforementioned problems. First, it provides an objective temporal structure to stages of human development based on the sequence of signs in the zodiac. The earth's revolution about the Sun, which produces the annual cycle divisible into twelve stages, provides an objective corollary to the human life cycle, even though the human life span extends more than one year. A year is simply how long it takes the earth to revolve about the sun. Other planets take varying lengths of time, culminating in Pluto, which can take as long as 230 years for a single revolution. The point here is that revolution about the Sun is a 12-stage evolution in time independent of any particular planetary period; thus, the zodiacal cycle is a kind of meta-cycle that can serve as a metaphor of development in general.

It has been well established that human biological cycles are isomorphic with astronomical ones. Temporally, we incorporate celestial rhythms and cycles as internal cycles and periodicities, or 'biological clocks' (Watson, 1973). "The capacity to create physiological clocks in response to environmental rhythms appears to be a necessary feature of all life forms," says Fraser (1975, p. 180). In other words, the physical structure and internal periodicities of human beings are an embodiment of the environment—both terrestrial and celestial—within which the human bio-system evolves. It would not be stretching the point to propose that psychological structure and periodicities likewise reflect astronomical cycles. If human biological cycles mirror astronomical ones, then psyche and cosmos mirror one another as well. This provides at least some basis for the claim that the human life cycle is synchronous with the sequence of zodiacal signs.

A zodiacal developmental model also resolves the second problem that plagues integration of the various theories—namely, that each theorist focused on a different line of development rather than on the psyche as a whole. In a zodiacal model, each sign embodies every dimension; that is, each sign signifies a specific drive, affect state, cognitive style, psychosocial orientation, and moral perspective. Rather than attempting to delineate different models, stages, and periods for each line of development, the zodiac enables us to see that there are twelve fundamental stages for every dimension. Cancer, for instance, symbolizes a drive for belonging, a capacity for affective containment and reflection, cognitive abilities that correspond to Piaget's concrete operations, the awakening of emotional sensitivity to others, and a moral sense rooted in the need to belong.

Finally, a zodiacal model solves the third problem that impedes integration of developmental theories: different time periods for the emergence of new capacities. Like Erikson and Kohlberg's models, a zodiacal theory encompasses the entire life cycle. Stages are clearly delineated for both child and adult development. Moreover, zodiacal signs easily subsume the differing periods of other developmental models. Kohlberg's six stages of moral reasoning are paralleled by Aries/Taurus (stage 1), Gemini/Cancer (stage 2), Leo/Virgo (stage 3), Libra/Scorpio (stage 4), Sagittarius/Capricorn (Stage 5), and Aquarius/Pisces (stage 6).[51] Similar correlations occur with Freud's, Erikson's, and Piaget's models.

Because each sign corresponds to a different sector of the earth's revolution about the Sun, it follows that each sign signifies a specific period of development within the yearly cycle of nature. Capricorn, for instance, corresponds to the time when the earth's axis is tilted at its maximum degree away from the ecliptic; thus, days are shortest and nights are longest in the northern hemisphere (winter solstice). It follows that each sign constitutes its own temporal-spatial orientation or developmental perspective within the annual cycle. Astronomically, time and space are literally different for each sign of the zodiac. This means, correspondingly, that each sign-stage signifies a different time-space orientation for the developing human.

The general rule is that consciousness expands and time accelerates as one moves through the twelve sign-stages. Accordingly, a rationale for the lengths of the various sign-stages is provided by the formula: *consciousness expands as time accelerates*. During the Aries stage of consciousness (first 2 years), time and space are experienced as "Me, here, now," whereas Pisces consciousness (after 80) could be characterized as, "Not-me, not-here, not-now" (or, stated in the positive, "Everyone, everywhere, forever"). This distinction between Aries and Pisces makes the point. At earlier phases of development, our vision is relatively narrow and time moves slowly. Time for the infant is extraordinarily slow—a year seems like an eternity—while perception in space is limited to the infant's immediate surroundings. At later stages, time seems to have accelerated, and, concomitantly, vision has tremendously broadened. As consciousness expands with age, our subjec-

---

[51] For a fuller discussion of correlations between Kohlberg's theory and astrology, see Chapter 4 in *Mapping the Landscape of the Soul* (Perry 2021).

tive perception of time and space changes with it: we see more in a shorter space of time—or, put simply, vision broadens as time accelerates. Later signs naturally perceive life in terms of longer periods of time. This is why each sign-stage is progressively longer in real time than the sign-stage that precedes it. While longer in real time, subjectively each stage is experienced as constituting equal time.

By defining astrological signs as stages of a more encompassing whole (360 degree) life cycle, an important principle is revealed: Psychic structures (sign-planets) are inseparably related to developmental processes. And because developmental processes are characterized by different temporal-spatial orientations, the modes of functioning symbolized by sign-planet systems cannot be fully understood without situating them within these time-space orientations. Each developmental stage provides a framework for understanding the psychology of its affiliated sign-planet system; that is, the function of each planet is inseparably related to a particular stage of life. As we will see, this has important implications for an astrological theory of psychopathology.

There is one additional correlation between the zodiac and developmental psychology. Psychological development is characterized by both continuity and discontinuity. Development is continuous in that progression proceeds along an array of pathways—emotional, cognitive, and behavioral. It is also discontinuous in that each stage has a unique organization with certain dominant characteristics that cannot be predicted from the preceding stage. That is, progression along the various pathways is not smooth; rather, it is characterized by major shifts. Forward movement is followed by periods of integration and consolidation before preparation for the next jump forward (major shift) begins.

This same pattern of continuity and discontinuity is implicit in the organization of the zodiac. As a model of developmental progression, it symbolizes a continuous unfoldment of innate capacities as symbolized by the twelve signs. Each sign, however, is discontinuous from the previous sign in that it constitutes a different polarity, modality, and element. Semi-sextile signs have a natural compensatory relationship; each sign defines itself, in effect, by being totally unlike the previous sign. Taurus, for example, is yin, fixed, and earth, whereas Aries is yang, cardinal, and fire. Taurus signifies a major shift in development in that it represents a movement from a predominantly impulsive (Aries) mode of behavior to one characterized by a capacity for restraint, from "going" to "holding," from "doing" to "having," from the archetype of "pioneer" to that of "settler." This can be graphically illustrated in the following table:

Aries	Taurus
Impulsive	Restrained
Spontaneous	Inhibited
Fast	Slow
Going	Staying
Doing	Holding
Pioneer	Settler

Similar distinctions can be observed in all adjacent signs. Each sign signifies the emergence of a new capacity, or major shift, which is radically discontinuous with the psychology of the previous sign.

INTEGRATION AND DEVELOPMENT OF PLANETARY FUNCTIONS

Thus far, we have seen that development entails the evolution of a number of functions that come to be linked and associated with other functions. These various systems, symbolized by signs and their ruling planets, eventually coalesce to form the relatively stable organizing structural units of the psyche that maintain a dynamic equilibrium with each other and with the external world. Tyson and Tyson (1990) describe it thusly:

> The coupling or organizing of a variety of functions into a coherent system is the essence of ego structuralization. The nodal points (transitional ages) at which various functions come to be linked, marking stages in ego formation, are characterized by notable advances in child's self-regulatory and adaptive capacities and, therefore, by notable changes in behavior. (p. 29)

Astrologically, the psyche can be viewed as an open system characterized by a continuous exchange with the environment and by a dynamic order among its component sign-planet systems. Development takes place through the increasing elaboration, differentiation, organization, and reorganization of these interrelated systems.

For example, the transition from Aries to Taurus consciousness, which occurs toward the end of the second year, means that the Aries function is changed by virtue of a new capacity for self-regulation (Taurus).[52] The capacity

---

[52] Self-regulation in a Taurus sense refers to behaviors designed to maintain physiological

for spontaneous assertion can now be regulated so that it is directed more effectively toward objects that one wishes to have and possess for reasons of comfort, pleasure, and security. Prior to this, the capacity for ownership, the notion that a specific object could be possessed, simply did not exist.

In every sign-planet system, the form taken at each stage is affected by the development of all the other systems in interaction with the environment. As psychic functions come to be associated and interdependent, a more integrated organization among the systems emerges. This implies that no one system is ever a fixed and final attainment; new additions or modifications may be made throughout life.

Each nodal point (transition from one stage to another) is characteristically followed by a period of regression and developmental consolidation. This is because a forward movement in one psychic system creates an imbalance among the other systems that disturbs the prior equilibrium. A crisis ensues, which is resolved by a temporary regression, followed by a shift to a new and higher level of development that is eventually consolidated. Each successful reworking brings a higher level of functioning within each psychic system as well as a higher level of integration among the various systems as the psyche matures.

A typical example occurs at age fourteen when children are heading into adolescence, or the Leo period of development. Differentiation from one's family necessarily triggers a temporary regression into Cancerian dependency. In other words, early adolescence is characterized by a wish to be independent and dependent at the same time. This is eventually followed by a shift into a new, higher level of self-differentiation and rebellion against childhood dependence. For example, adolescents want to be treated as unique, semi-autonomous individuals capable of making their own decisions.

Again, it must be emphasized that all processes of all stages are evident from the beginning of life in rudimentary form. Infant studies reveal that a baby will display a capacity for compassion and altruism (Pisces-stage) even in the first few months of life (Friedman, 1985). Just so, every function operates in an incipient, albeit unconscious form before its decisive stage of emergence. For example, children have feelings at every stage of development, not just during the Cancer period of 9-14. Prior to the Cancer stage, however, children are not able to fully contain, reflect upon, and articulate their subjective states. Feelings and the associated need for belonging acquire

homeostasis (comfort, pleasure, body temperature, hunger satiation, and the like). Comfort and pleasure are necessarily associated with the capacity for possessing things and people, e.g., my teddy bear, *my* mother, *my* food.

a **dominating significance** during the Cancer period of development, even though feelings and the need for belonging were evident in preceding stages.

Development does not occur like a series of building blocks in which each piece of developmental experience is built solidly on top of the preceding piece. Rather, maturity occurs because of developmental integrations. In other words, it's not simply that new intrapsychic structures form one on top of the other. Various independently emerging components and functions come to be linked and to work in relation to one another, forming a new, coherently functioning organization. This new organization is more complex than any one of its contributing elements.

In this way, the shape of the whole is never predictable, although there is predictability to the pattern; that is, the whole is affected by the development of the part, such that the whole is never static. It is continually evolving. Accordingly, if we consider the complexity of all the elements cascading together in the developmental process, a large measure of unpredictability is characteristic. Yet, there is a predictability and stability to the process itself.

For instance, under optimal conditions, the personality of a 10 year-old girl is going to reflect the emergence of a capacity for containment and articulation of feelings (Cancer stage). Her overall psychological organization, as symbolized by her chart, is going to reflect this development; yet, she will continue to evolve as new capacities emerge over time as she moves through the various stages of life. The expression of her chart will change accordingly. It is always the same chart, always the same pattern, but her expression of it is not predictable in an absolute way because every part will be affected by the emergence of new capacities in ways that are too complex to be predicted.

If she has Neptune in the 4th squaring her Moon, for instance, the Cancerian phase of development is likely to be problematic. A counselor cannot know exactly how she handled the challenge or how it affected her development until he or she talks to her. Moreover, it will make a difference if the interview occurs when she is age 40 rather than 20, for significant opportunities for integration and development would have occurred during the intervening twenty-years. The point is that people change and evolve in ways that are not entirely predictable.

HOLONOMIC DEVELOPMENT

This process of part-whole interaction can be understood in accordance with the systems principle of *holonomy*. Holonomy refers to a structural property of systems in which the whole (system) is contained in the part. While a system can be analyzed into component parts, and each part appears to have a certain autonomy, in the final analysis the structure and behavior of every part is reflective of the more comprehensive order of the whole in which it resides; that is, the whole is contained in the part—or, put temporally, the whole life cycle is contained in every stage.

This point deserves further emphasis. I have noted that each function comes to its ascendance, meets its crisis, and finds its lasting solution during a specific developmental epoch. But each function must exist from the beginning in some form, for every act calls for an integration of all functions. The Geminian need for learning (3rd stage), for example, is implicit in the baby's active efforts to explore its environment and develop autonomy (Aries/1st stage). Yet, learning is not the primary need of the 1st stage. Every psychic function exists in some form before its decisive and critical time of emergence. And because each part of the personality always (albeit unconsciously) exists in some form, any one stage reflects the whole cycle of development; that is, every part of the personality interpenetrates every other part. This is the core idea in holonomy.

Functions that assume a dominating significance in earlier stages continue to evolve throughout development. Yet, these functions become increasingly subordinate to the concerns of later phases. For example, while a capacity for assertion (Aries) is the dominant concern of the first 2 years of life, it is elaborated on in later stages and gradually becomes integrated with other sign-planet systems. By the time we reach the ripe old age of 70 (Aquarius stage), we may feel compelled to assert for changes that improve the quality of life for succeeding generations. At this stage, we are no longer asserting merely in our own self-interest; we are asserting for humanity as a whole and for the future of the race.

This point becomes even clearer when we consider how identity evolves. Concerns about identity and self-esteem reach a pinnacle during adolescence (Leo stage). Subsequently, the ego continues to evolve, but preoccupations with it gradually diminish and are replaced by higher social and transpersonal concerns—work (Virgo), cooperation with others (Libra), healing and integrity (Scorpio), universal justice (Sagittarius), public responsibility (Capricorn), and so on. Again, once the attributes of a given stage are realized, they become subordinate to and utilized in the service of the predominant concerns of later stages. At age 60, for example, one does not want to become a Leonian hero for its own sake, but for the sake of building something of lasting public value (Capricorn stage).

This implies that even though a psychic system reaches its preemptory phase at a given age, there is a developmental line for that system that traverses the entire life cycle. In building a model of this sort, one should be able to delineate the developmental trajectory of any one system, such as ego identity (Leo stage), and view that system in relation to the others. That is, even though there is predictable pattern to the order of acquiring certain functions, there is also a pattern to achieving levels of integration among those functions. Each stage, therefore, represents a nodal point along the developmental continuum where a certain level of functional integrity to the whole psyche can be postulated.

A further implication of a zodiacal model is that functions of later stages, which exist in rudimentary form from the beginning, will slowly evolve *before* they reach their decisive period of emergence. This means that certain functions associated with later sign-stages will not reach their preemptory phase until relatively late in life. A moral capacity, for instance, which is generally associated with the super-ego, goes through many stages of development and can be said to begin as early as two years (Kohlberg, 1976). Symbolized predominantly by Sagittarius, one's moral sense is progressively differentiated and integrated as each succeeding stage is traversed. However, it is not until one reaches the Sagittarian stage of life (44-54) that one's concern with ethics, truth, and justice reaches full maturity and predominates over all other concerns.

Astrologically, this process of development can be graphically depicted as a hierarchically organized sphere made up of twelve concentric smaller spheres. Each sphere represents a developmental stage/level and is exponentially wider and deeper than the one it encompasses. At birth, the entire structure is only dimly lit, though the first and densest level (Aries) gains in brightness through the first two years until, at the end of this period, it is completely illumined. In a series of ascending stages, each level is thus lit up, one at a time, though no level is ever completely dark. As each new level is fully illuminated, so every other level gains some measure of brightness, too. Even those levels already lit become progressively brighter. Thus the sphere expands and grows more brilliant over time as its various levels are awakened. As light swells outwards through successive stages, there is a progressive expansion and deepening of consciousness. Put simply: consciousness/awareness expands as complexity/integrity increases.

PROPENSITIES & PATHOLOGIES OF CHILDHOOD

I have mentioned there are three interacting factors that contribute to the development of personality: innate propensities, maturational influences, and actual experiences. In this section, we're going to focus on innate (or archetypal) propensities. These are inborn cognitive, emotional, and behavioral functions. Each sign-planet system, in effect, constitutes an instinctive way of being in the world. Infants have an inborn capacity for initiating (Aries), for attachment (Taurus), for learning (Gemini), for dependency (Cancer), for play (Leo), and for additional capacities symbolized by the remaining sign-planet systems. Of course, the most salient capacities of childhood are those depicted by the first four sign-stages.

McWilliams (1994) notes that, "regardless of revision, the same three phases of infantile psychological organization keep reappearing in psychoanalytic developmental theory" (p. 41).[53] These include: 1) the first 2 years (Aries, or Freud's oral phase); 2) the period from 2 through 4 (Taurus, or Freud's anal phase), and 3) the time between 5 and about 9 (Gemini, or Freud's Oedipal period). To these, we might add Freud's latency phase, or 9 through 13, which astrologically corresponds to the Cancer period of development.

Aries-Mars symbolizes the infant's innate propensity for activity and assertion. "Far from being a *tabula rasa*, opening and flowering by virtue of environmental input or genetically determined plan, the infant actively participates in and shapes his development, utilizing his own special array of constitutional factors" (Tyson & Tyson, p. 23). This view contrasts sharply with the early idea that the infant is a helpless and passive recipient of developmental forces. Studies confirm that infants spontaneously and actively engage in human interactions. Aries impulsivity is apparent in the infant's inability to regulate or control its impulse "to go and to do." If all goes well during this stage, the child develops a "can do" attitude and a basic trust in its capacity for autonomy. Conversely, difficulties or trauma during this period can produce a developmental arrest, causing a hypertrophy (exaggerated development) of the innate aggressiveness and egocentricity of infants. Psychopathy (antisocial personality disorder) clearly correlates with the consciousness of this period.

The infant also comes into the world predisposed for attachment and self-regulation (Bowlby, 1969). Self-regulation refers to behaviors designed to maintain physiological homeostasis—stability with regard to personal comfort, pleasure, body temperature, hunger satiation, and the like. Infants have an innate capacity to distinguish between what is pleasurable and what

---

[53] Here the word "infantile" refers to the whole preschool period of childhood emotional, cognitive, behavioral, and sensory maturation, or roughly the first five years of life. Although the sign of Cancer (9-14) is definitely associated with childhood, it is not technically a sign of infancy. Perhaps this is reflected in the fact that Cancer initiates a new cycle of Cardinal, Fixed, and Mutable signs; thus, it's a personal sign while also being the *second* Cardinal sign.

is unpleasurable and to prefer the former. Clearly, this capacity relates to the **Taurus-Venus** system. And while it is evident from birth, it becomes predominant in the 2nd stage of life—two through four years. Taurean rigidity is most evident in the toddler's tendency to persist and cling to that which is familiar and therefore comfortable. A child may prefer, for example, to have the same bedtime story read every night during this period.

Successful negotiation of the Taurus stage confers the capacity to inhibit impulses, accept the limitations of the real world, and soothe oneself in the face of frustration or anxiety. Conversely, a developmental arrest here can produce a hypertrophy of Taurean traits—pathological (rigid) attachments, frantic efforts to avoid actual or anticipated loss of attachment, and compulsive spending and hoarding in a desperate attempt to attain security. Failure to develop self and object constancy results in a tendency toward "splitting" with resultant instability of behavior, mood, and identity.[54] Such symptoms are typical of borderline personality disorder, which is the predominant pathology of this sign-stage.

The **Gemini-Mercury** system is also operative from birth. Research in infant development reveals that babies have a powerful capacity to acquire knowledge. They form hypotheses, solve problems, and arrive at conclusions in a manner that resembles practicing scientists (Gopnik et. al., 1999). Although the Gemini stage is preemptory from five to nine, infants are curious, resilient, and adaptive from the beginning of life. Piaget (1926, 1937) notes that babies not only have the capacity to accommodate to their environment, but also to assimilate the environment by making inner psychic modifications in response to new perceptions—in other words, they learn. According to Gopnik et. al., (1999), "what we see in the crib is the greatest mind that has ever existed, the most powerful learning machine in the universe" (p. 3).

The obsessive need to differentiate one thing from another; that is, to question, label, classify, and report, which is a marked Gemini trait, is most apparent in the developmental period of 5 through 8. This is the challenge of moving from Taurean twoness (me and my object) to Gemini threeness (me and my others who may have a relationship with each other that does not include me). Geminian objectivity requires giving up a Taurean attachment to mother ("mine") in order to make room for the other parent ("mine and

---

[54] Splitting entails an inability to see more than one dimension of a situation and is typical of infants in the Aries stage. Thus, rather than seeing the self, other people, or situations as a combination of good and bad parts, the person splits experience into "all good" or "all bad." Continuation of splitting in the Taurus stage prevents the individual from attaining and maintaining stability with regard to mood, identity, or behavior.

his/hers, too"). Gemini is the sign, therefore, of the famed Oedipal conflict that occurs at this juncture.

This requires reality testing and implies a capacity for compromise or at least delay of gratification, which presupposes that the Taurean stage has been successfully negotiated (Taurus symbolizes our capacity for self-restraint, frustration tolerance, and the ability to inhibit impulses for immediate gratification). Difficulties in the Gemini stage may result in qualities that are exaggeratedly Geminian—obsessiveness (hypermentation), scatteredness, inability to focus (excessive mutability), and subsequent learning disorders.

The **Cancer-Moon** system is evident in a baby's innate capacity to engage its mother in experiences of nurturing. There is an inborn recognition of the breast, for example. And the infant's ability to evoke feelings of love and tenderness in caretakers is frequently noted. Research indicates that infants are not simply passive recipients of maternal caring but have profound effects on mothers as well. Many authors have emphasized that mother-infant reciprocity influences the feelings of both mother and infant.

Chess and Thomas (1986) point out that the quality of fit between caregiver and infant is a significant contributor to the infant's development. In fact, it may be more significant that either the infant's innate personality or the mother's inherent ability to parent. Mother and infant form an interactional system in which each person's behavior continually affects and reinforces the behavior of the other. Accordingly, the child's effect on the parent can, in turn, influence the mother's response to the child and thus impact the child's subsequent development. The mother of an infant with a difficult temperament may become turned off to that child in some way, and as a consequence does not provide the stimulation and caretaking that would optimize her child's development.

Because mother and child constitute a circular infant-mother system, a complex interactional pattern develops such that eventual pathology cannot be attributed to either partner; that is, the child can just as easily induce pathological responses in the parent as vice versa. Astrologically, this can be depicted by the Moon's sign, house, and aspects, which symbolize not only the child's experience of the mother, but also the mother's experience of the child.

The dependency, vulnerability, and labile reactiveness of all children are clear parallels to Cancerian traits. It is not until children reach age 9-13, however, that they develop the ability to contain and articulate their subjective states. Difficulties at this stage may impair development of a capacity for self-reflection, resulting in the emotionally reactive, dependent, shallow, frivolous, seductive, childlike, and exaggeratedly feminine quality that is associated with histrionic personality disorder.

CHILDHOOD STYLES AND PSYCHOPATHOLOGY

Cognition, affect, and motivation undergo significant development during childhood. In general, motivational experience becomes increasingly planful and action becomes increasingly deliberate. By the time puberty is reached (Leo stage), volitional action, accompanied by a sense of agency and self-awareness, should supercede earlier, pre-volitional forms of behavior that were characterized by more impulsive (Aries), rigid (Taurus), obsessional (Gemini), and reactive (Cancer) modes of functioning.

Even in the adult, however, by no means is all action fully volitional—that is, guided by clear, conscious aims. Developmental derivatives of earlier modes of action remain operative within every adult's repertoire. These modes of action, being less volitional, entail a diminished self-awareness and, particularly, a diminished sense of agency. It is especially significant, therefore, that psychopathology is characterized by defensive styles that limit and distort self-awareness and the experience of agency.

Defensive styles forestall anxiety by obstructing awareness of one's impulses, decisions, and actions. And if one lacks awareness, one cannot feel responsible for what one does. Just as infants are excused from full responsibility for their actions (if a toddler hits a playmate for taking his toy, we don't hold him to the same moral standard as an adult), so certain psychological defenses tend to enable behavior that is rightfully considered childish.

Shapiro (2000) asserts, "These defensive styles are characterized by the hypertrophy of developmentally early modes, or derivatives of such modes, of diminished self-awareness and sense of agency" (p. 32). In other words, diverse forms of psychopathology can be understood as instances of hypertrophy of modes of diminished agency that characterize childhood stages of development. This implicates childhood modes of functioning in many forms of psychopathology; that is, some element of childishness, or lack of awareness and a diminished sense of self-control, is implicit in most mental disorders.

By extension, this also implicates the first four signs of the zodiac, which are the signs of childhood: Aries, Taurus, Gemini, and Cancer. Likewise, their planetary representatives—Mars, Venus, Mercury, and the Moon—are also implicated in many forms of adult pathology. It is not that these signs are more neurotic than any other sign, but that they are characterized by less awareness and control. The real question is: what contributes to the hypertrophy of childhood modes of functioning?

THE INEVITABILITY OF DEVELOPMENTAL CONFLICT

I have stated that there are three interacting factors that contribute to the development of personality: innate propensities, maturational influences, and individual experiences. Innate factors are inborn capacities, whereas maturational influences are the timetable of development in which these various capacities generically unfold. A capacity for self-regulation, for example, is an innate propensity that comes to fruition during the Taurean phase of development. Although human beings are born with a blueprint of psychic development determined in part by a maturational timetable, emphasis needs to be placed on "in part". This is because a critical third factor intersects with the first two: *experience*. Interactions with others in combination with innate propensities and maturational influences ideally lead to the formation of an underlying stable organization of psychic structures that characterize personality.

Psychic structures coalesce gradually through a series of individual experiences with the environment. Mother-infant reciprocal interactions provide the early context. Through affectively invested relations, and memories of these, the infant builds mental representations of himself, the other, and their interaction. Psychic structures emerge through various processes of internalization (introjection and identification). In this manner, innate and experiential elements combine to form an underlying organization of psychic structures, a process sometimes referred to as "psychic organization" or "structuralization."

Interactions with others at times lead to conflict, which plays an important role in psychic structure formation. Conflict is a ubiquitous, inevitable and essential aspect of psychic development. It would not be overstating the matter to say that challenge and frustration characterize the developmental process. Human beings are continually challenged by dissonance between competing needs, which initially manifest as particular types of conflict with the environment. It is precisely our attempts to resolve conflict that spurs psychic development.

This process of conflict and resolution is apparent in the structure of the zodiac. Not only are adjacent signs compensatory and thus conflictual, but a host of other tensions also exist between signs that square, quincunx, and oppose one another. A given sign is unequivocally harmonious with only four others—those to which it is sextile or trine, but it clashes with the remaining seven. For example, Aries sextiles Gemini and Aquarius and trines Leo and Sagittarius, but it semi sextiles Taurus and Pisces, squares Cancer and Capricorn, quincunxes Virgo and Scorpio, and opposes Libra; thus, there is nearly twice as much dissonance as consonance between signs. The human psyche and developmental process is inherently conflictual.

As stated, conflicts are first externalized between self and other, and are subsequently taken back inside to be re-worked. Conflicts are ideally resolved via emergent, adaptive behaviors. These are internal compromises mediated by ego functioning. In Chapter Five this process was discussed in reference to the Sun as a set of ego functions that include: 1) Conscious awareness of the various drives and impulses that make up psychic structure, 2) deciding what to express and what to suppress, and 3) performing some act of self-expression that constitutes a viable compromise between competing drives. In this way, psychic structure continually develops and is modified. The ultimate goal is to integrate the panoply of psychic impulses into a functional and harmonious whole. In effect, this is the hero's journey.

Throughout the life cycle, various types of conflicts inevitably arise. Developmental conflict is normal, predictable, and usually transitory. Everyone experiences conflict to a greater or lesser degree at each developmental stage when, for example, a mother makes specific, phase-appropriate demands (such as toilet training) that clash with wishes and impulses that continue from the previous stage. Toilet training occurs at about two to three years old when the infant is transitioning from the "just do it" Aries stage of consciousness to the "hold it" stage of Taurus consciousness. The environment makes a demand in the form of a parental injunction, "hold it," which conflicts with the infant's habitual behavior of "going and doing" whenever it feels the urge (Aries impulsivity). Gradually, the child resolves the conflict by internalizing the parental prohibition against soiling, thus developing a new capacity for restraint, control, retention, possession, and holding—all obvious Taurean attributes.

Environmental influences are sometimes so grossly out of harmony with the child's needs and capacities that the resulting distress interferes with forward development. Such developmental interference may lead to a variety of pathological deviations, depending upon the child's age and the developmental level at which they occur. Early interferences tend to have a more profound impact that may or may not be reversible. For example, severe neglect in earliest infancy (Aries stage) jeopardizes the infant's survival and is inevitably traumatic to some degree. Likewise, surgical intervention during the Taurus phase may be so overwhelming as to undermine the child's sense of body integrity and, hence, his capacity for self-regulation (Greenacre, 1952).

An example of developmental interference during the Gemini stage can be described in the following actual case history. A female client of mine had natal Saturn in Scorpio on the Ascendant squaring Moon Aquarius in the 3rd house. When she was approximately 7 years old and transiting Saturn conjuncted her Moon and squared its natal position, her mother suddenly died. Note that the 3rd house correlates to the Gemini stage of 5-9 years. Her Moon position precisely marked her 7th year. She was subsequently raised by her alcoholic, abusive father who completely denied the emotional impact of their mutual loss. Moon square Saturn is often associated with a deprivation of maternal love and/or a father who is emotionally cold.

Unable to understand or grieve her mother's passing, she developed a childhood depression that interfered with her schooling (3rd house). It also impaired her capacity to experience and articulate her feelings (Saturn square Moon). Her failure in school during this stage, and the chronic depression that followed the loss of her mother, left a profound impression upon her psyche. During this same 3rd house period, she witnessed her father's ongoing physical abuse of her older sister (3rd house/siblings), which left her with survivor guilt and a deep fear of authority. This subsequently impaired her capacity to assert her own authority (♄ 1st) and set limits with an abusive man whom she later married. In short, 3rd and 1st house pathologies were both catalyzed by a Saturn-Moon event that occurred during the 3rd house period of development.

DEVELOPMENTAL FIXATION AT SIGN-STAGES

What begins as a conflict between external demands and inner wishes eventually becomes a conflict between inner demands and inner wishes. We then speak of *internalized, or neurotic conflicts*. The first steps in conflict internalization are evident as early as the second half of the second year (Mahler, 1975b), or toward the beginning of the Taurean stage. The toddler wishes for a secure attachment to his mother, which begins to have conditions, while simultaneously wishing for the unrestricted gratification that typifies the Aries stage from which he is just emerging. An optimal outcome is that internal modifications are made between competing wishes (compromise formation). For example, instead of pursuing and enjoying unrestricted anal pleasures and "going" whenever he feels like it, reaction formations interfere and he begins to practice self-control in identification with his mother's wishes.[55] This is the prototypical conflict that occurs at the Aries-Taurus transition, which ideally is resolved over the next two years.

Once an external conflict is internalized, it may or may not get resolved. If a developmental interference is sufficiently traumatizing and overwhelms the child's capacity to adapt, a developmental fixation may occur. The child becomes arrested at a certain maturational level. Arrestation of development means that a substantial portion of a person's character remains stuck at the level the trauma occurs. If a trauma occurs during the Aries stage, for example, the adult may continue to experience fears around survival and have issues of entitlement, "I'm entitled to do whatever I want whenever I want." If a trauma occurs during the Taurean period, this may presage a lifelong difficulty with issues of security, stability, attachment, and self and object constancy.

Insufficiently resolved conflicts distort the subsequent developmental course. Rather than growing out of older adaptations, the child grows around them as if they were a tumor or wound that has been segregated within the psyche. These earlier styles of behavior tend to function autonomously, especially when activated by stressful situations. Although superceded by later forms, the more primitive form remains potentially active as an unconscious, split-off, independently operating unit. It is, in effect, a complex. Given sufficient stress, a functional regression may take place. The individual collapses into a behavioral style reminiscent of the earlier developmental period.

If someone is developmentally arrested at the Taurean period, for example, he may become overwhelmed with stress when facing an impending separation from a loved one. If his girlfriend withdraws or his wife threatens to divorce him, he is likely to regress to a Taurean level of development and refuse to relinquish the attachment. He may exhibit simplistic either/or, "black or white" thinking (splitting), become possessive and clinging, or stubborn and resistant. Such behaviors appear childlike and inappropriate from an adult perspective. Astrologically we might expect to see this symbolized by significant stress involving the 2nd house, or by a hard aspect from Pluto to Venus.

A rather dramatic case in point is Phil Spector, the infamous record producer who was incarcerated for murdering a woman in his home that spurned his sexual advances and merely wished to go home. Spector had a history of threatening women with a gun on such occasions. This time,

---

[55] In reaction formation, an unacceptable impulse is defended against by developing an opposite attitude and behavior. In effect, every sign-stage is a reaction formation to the sign-stage that comes before it.

however, he actually followed through, killing actress Lana Clarkson with a single shot through her mouth. Spector has Sun Capricorn 8th opposed Moon Cancer 2nd. He also has a tight Venus-Pluto opposition; thus, in two different ways, his chart repeats the theme of *difficulty with relinquishing attachments*.

As previously stated, maladaptive responses of the Venus/Taurean variety correspond to borderline personality disorder, which underscores that developmental stages bear some relation to the mental disorder(s) associated with the sign that rules that stage. For example, the mental deterioration/ego dissolution of old age and the delusions of schizophrenia are characteristic of Pisces as a developmental stage and mental disorder respectively. Likewise, the "mid-life crisis," wherein one recognizes one's own mortality, and paranoia wherein one lives in fear of annihilation, are equally representative of Scorpio. Each sign of the zodiac appears to (1) constitute a developmental stage with associated tasks, and (2) can be correlated with one or more mental disorders if these tasks, or those of earlier stages, are mismanaged.

Erikson (1968) believed that the origin of psychological problems could be understood through an analogy with physiological development *in utero*. During fetal development, each part of the organism has its critical time of ascendance or danger of defect. If an organ does not develop properly at its designated time during the intrauterine cycle, then the entire subsequent development of the organism is compromised. For example, if the eye does not arise at the appointed time, it will never be able to express itself fully, since the moment for the rapid outgrowth of some other part will have arrived, and this will tend to dominate the less active region and suppress the belated tendency for eye expression. The organ that misses its time of ascendancy is not only doomed as an entity; it endangers at the same time the whole hierarchy of organs.

Just as damage can occur to bodily organs at any stage of the intrauterine cycle, so damage can occur to psychological organs at any stage of the life cycle. Erikson described each developmental stage in terms of its potential for both positive and negative outcomes. For example, "autonomy" versus "shame and doubt" are the positive and negative poles of Erikson's 2nd stage. Ideally, the child develops a favorable ratio in which the positive pole dominates the negative. If, however, the child's inner resources do not enable him/her to successfully meet the challenges of a given developmental epoch, a derailment (fixation) occurs. Personality disorders are thought to be frozen adaptations to overwhelming stressors that occurred during early stages of development. The solution to the stressor was to keep doing the behavior that has now become the disorder. What was adaptive is now maladaptive to current reality. In effect, the solution becomes the problem—or, to use a common metaphor, "He's a broken record," repeating the same sad refrain, over and over.

THE PSYCHOGENETIC FALLACY

Explaining puzzling behavioral phenomena as residues of childhood trauma has a certain intuitive appeal. However, various authors have pointed out that the fixation-regression hypothesis in accounting for type of character structure is problematic (Hillman, 1996; McWilliams, 1994; Shapiro, 2000; Tyson & Tyson, 1990). Attempts to trace various personality disorders to childhood antecedents have yielded conflicting theories as to what stage corresponds to what disorder, which early phase is the fixation point, and what might have happened to cause a person to become frozen during that period. Speculations about what kinds of rearing, for instance, might influence youngsters in a schizoid direction have produced wildly different reconstructions of hypothesized pasts.

Shapiro (2000) asserts that there is no reliable evidence to support the assumption that deficiencies in early development cause particular disorders. "It may well be that the conception of adult pathology has sometimes been prejudiced by premature assumptions of one or another developmental or biological cause" (p. 15).

It cannot be overemphasized that the fixation-regression hypothesis, or what has become known as the psychogenetic fallacy, is rooted in the deterministic presupposition that character is primarily if not wholly a consequence of environmental influences. Freud was perhaps the first clinician to assert that parental failures were causative of adult psychopathology. According to Freud, these failures involved either the excessive gratification of drives or unwarranted deprivation of them. If drives were over gratified, then nothing impelled the child to move on developmentally; thus, s/he would become "spoiled" (demanding, infantile, egocentric). However, if drives were excessively deprived, then the child's capacity to absorb frustrating realities was overwhelmed and s/he would become overly inhibited (anxious, depressed, insecure).

Depending upon the psychosexual stage at which overgratification or overfrustration supposedly occurred, the child remained fixated on the issues of that stage and developed a corresponding mental disorder—depression, obsessive-compulsion, hysteria, and so on. In short, character pathologies were seen as expressing the long-term effects of particular fixations at specific stages. Causation was more-or-less wholly external and operated in a linear, deterministic manner.

All of this presupposes that the infant is a *tabula rasa*—a blank slate waiting to be written on by the vicissitudes of random experience. From an astrological perspective, such a presupposition is unsupported. Horoscopes reveal that children have innate, complex, and highly individualistic personalities from birth. These personalities, or character types, clearly originate in conditions independent of external experience.[56] Accordingly, we cannot accept the presupposition that pathologies of character are wholly a product of random childhood events. Such a presumption gives far too much weight to externally originating conditions, such as parental failures, and not enough to innate characterological predispositions.

As discussed previously, the inability to recognize innate modes and styles of functioning is largely responsible for the lack of a psychoanalytic psychology of character types. Astrology suggests that so-called mental disorders may simply be pathological extensions or exaggerations of innate modes of functioning that operate from birth. In this continuum view, the etiology of character pathology is a special case of character development in general, and is far more complicated than the conception of any particular and direct cause.

It is becoming increasingly evident that there is insufficient evidence to presume that any particular developmental conflict, trauma, or other "cause" is the source of adult psychopathology (Hillman, 1996; McWilliams, 1994; Shapiro, 2000; Tyson & Tyson, 1990). Thus, it may be a mistake to identify adult pathology with one or another stage of infant or child development. Certainly, this is consistent with astrology. For astrology implies that specific defenses and types of pathology derive not merely from instinctual conflict (Freud) or faulty parenting (object relations) at specific stages, but from an innate, pre-existent psychic structure that generates lived experience and then responds to that experience in a manner consistent with its own nature. Recognition of this fact would enable us to specify character types as embodiments of innate psychic forms (archetypes), the hypertrophy of

---

[56] Astrology implies that an entity's inborn character is not the product of experiences in *this* life, for this life is yet to be lived. However, inborn character may well be the summary product of habits developed in prior incarnations. This view holds that character is a product of non-randomly generated internal experiences and their subsequent effects (karma). Whether one is talking about experiences from a prior life or a yet-to-be-lived life, a karmic perspective suggests that all such experiences are derivatives of consciousness and thus purposeful (non-random).

which can cause problems. This is precisely what astrology provides with its detailed descriptions of sign-planet systems.

Such a perspective constitutes a formal view of neurosis as opposed to a psychogenetic view that emphasizes childhood antecedents as presumed causes. According to Shapiro (2000),

> At present we can say very little about the etiology of psychopathology, either with regard to particular types or in general. Indeed, the search for causes—some would say the preoccupation with causes—has had its problems. The field historically has been prone to the discovery of oversimplified causes and sources, psychological as well as biological, of the various sorts of psychopathology. (p. 15)

One of the strongest reasons for rejecting the identification of adult psychopathology with presumed prototypes in early childhood is the consistency of its symptoms with the adult character and its attitudes and modes. While a childhood precursor of this or that adult trait, pathological or otherwise, can easily be found, the distance between the childhood stage and the adult pathology is huge. In short, precursors are not causes. Evidence suggests that all adult symptomatology is in character; that is, the child's innate endowments, biological, neurological, and psychological, are operating from birth and predispose that child to develop along particular characterological lines. It is precisely this pattern of development that is prefigured in the horoscope.

By the time adulthood is reached, the individual has had innumerable opportunities to develop and refine his/her particular worldview. Countless experiences have been processed and assimilated into a pre-existing character template—a character type—just as food is metabolized to sustain and develop a pre-existent biological template or body type. To presume that experience is the ultimate cause of character is no more logical that to suppose that food is the ultimate determinant of body type. If one is predisposed genetically to be small boned, thin, and weak, a mere change of diet is not going to make one large boned, hefty, and strong. A proper diet can certainly help, but it cannot replace what one inherently is.

Of course, this is not an argument for psychogenetic or neurophysiological causation, for psychopathology is too complex psychologically to have direct and simple neurophysiological causes. As suggested in Chapter Seven, one's genetic inheritance and physiology may be shaped by a pre-existent soul that has reincarnated. Suffice to say that innate personality endowments contribute to the formation of psychopathology.

THE FORCE OF CHARACTER

Although an exacerbation of internal conflict and subsequent anxiety requires pathogenic circumstances, how the individual responds to such circumstances is determined by the existing personality. A person's attitudes, intelligence, sensitivities, values, aptitudes, and so on, all come to bear on *how* s/he reacts to pathogenic circumstances. Different patterns of response, as symbolized by horoscopes, will predispose the individual to develop particular restrictions and distortions of character in an attempt to forestall anxiety. One person may minimize the significance of pathogenic circumstances, another will deny their existence, another will detach from them, another will become compliant, another rageful, another controlling and vindictive, and another may learn from the experience and develop a compassionate resolve to do better than the perpetrator.

This latter type of adaptive response is actually quite common, as evidenced by longitudinal studies of individuals who were raised in highly dysfunctional families. Despite disadvantages of growing up with parents who were alcoholic, abusive, severely neglectful, abandoning, and/or who suffered from serious mental illness, these children still grew up to be successful and happy adults with good marriages and high standing in the community. Developmental psychologists variously refer to such kids as "optimizers," "survivors," "thrivers," and "resilient children." The very conditions that one might assume would predispose a child to psychological problems seem not to have affected these children—or, at least not in a way that involves significant pathology. Resilient children appear to have been born with a strong and adaptive character that was not overwhelmed by circumstances that would be pathogenic to less gifted children.

We should not assume that resilient children necessarily have "better" horoscopes than those that go on to develop mental disorders. There are thousands of case examples of people born with difficult hard aspects and corresponding difficulties in childhood who rise to the challenge and succeed magnificently in adult life. Again, how a person responds to pathogenic circumstances may be of greater significance than the circumstance itself. Adaptive responses are in character, so to speak, and are not determined by anything outside.

All of this is consistent with Whitmont's destiny concept and Hillman's acorn theory, both of which propose that each life is formed by a particular pattern—a destiny image—that represents the soul's code of fate. Likewise, Shapiro argues that whatever psychopathological tendencies exist in a person were probably there from the beginning. Such tendencies would be particularly evident in the way the child responded to and made meaning out of difficult early experiences. There is an underlying continuity in pathological development that derives from innate imbalances and conflicts within the character that were present from birth. Again, this directly contradicts the fixation-regression hypothesis that psychopathology is a consequence of fixation and regression to an earlier developmental level.

Shapiro's formal view of neurosis is based on a general principle of structural continuity, or a continuity of general regulatory structure (of general ways and attitudes), which allows for the development of psychopathology as an inherent feature of the character organization. This view, which is entirely consistent with astrology, implies that pathological character development, like particular symptoms, must also be in character. In other words, development must proceed, so to speak, from the inside, through transformations and elaborations of what already exists. The presence of internal conflict and anxiety presses individual development toward hypertrophy of those anxiety-dispelling propensities (defenses), generally inhibitory, already in existence.

An individual with Venus square Saturn, for example, may experience a conflict between her need for control (Saturn) and her need for pleasure (Venus). Initially, this may be experienced as a father's excessively rigid and punitive measures toward the child's toilet training. Her need to "hold it" (Taurus/Venus) is under pressure from an overly demanding Saturnian authority. Gradually her tendency to over-control her Venusian impulses for pleasure and intimacy takes more and more extreme forms—stinginess, depriving herself of food, not allowing herself to initiate social relationships, and so on. This inhibition of behaviors and attitudes vis-à-vis her Venus serves as a defense against loss of control of her Venusian impulses and, thus, anticipation of subsequent punishment (Saturn).

It would be a mistake, however, to presume that her adult symptoms derive from the earlier developmental conflict involving harsh toilet training. For her experience with her father was merely the prototype of later experiences and attitudes that follow the same general pattern. That the pattern is symbolized astrologically underscores that her early experiences with her father, and subsequent anxiety-dispelling attitudes, are innately characterological and not merely the consequence of faulty parenting. Moreover, this same character structure may result in different outcomes with different people.

One girl suffers social isolation and severe depression, while another goes on to sterling success as a highly disciplined ballerina.[57]

POST-CHILDHOOD EXPERIENCES

After childhood, subsequent stages have their own impact on the developing personality. While in some instances the rudiments of psychopathology are evident early on, the full flowering of such pathology may require additional, post-childhood experiences to flush out the inherent propensity and bring it to full bloom.

As stated, developmental derivatives of earlier modes of action remain within every adult's repertoire. These modes of action, being less volitional, entail a diminished self-awareness and, particularly, a diminished sense of agency. Likewise in psychopathology, defense styles develop that forestall anxiety by limiting and distorting self-awareness and the experience of agency. These defensive styles are characterized by the hypertrophy of developmentally early modes, or derivatives of such modes. Impulsive modes are Arian, rigid modes are Taurean, obsessive modes are Geminian, and reactive modes are Cancerian.

The impetuous person (Aries) avoids deliberate, planful action and is comfortable only when large areas of activity are left to the spur of the moment; the retentive person (Taurus) allows himself little spontaneity, and then only in very limited circumstances; the obsessive person (Gemini) is comfortable only when engaged with thinking, but avoids feeling, whereas the reactive person (Cancer) exaggerates and indulges her feelings (however superficially) but avoids thinking. In short, each of the personal signs avoids a sense of agency by exaggerating early modes of behavior that precede conscious, planful action.[58]

While some adult modes of psychopathology (psychopathic, borderline, obsessive, hysteria,) can be seen as derivatives of developmentally early modes/archetypes, this does not imply a regression. One cannot order adult pathologies on a linear, developmental scale. That is, one cannot say that

---

[57] I know of one case involving a woman with Venus square Saturn that, in fact, did become a ballerina. The hard work, strenuous conditioning, and self-discipline characteristic of Saturn was combined with a grace and beauty of movement that is Venus' province.

[58] It is noteworthy that all such behaviors are related to signs that can be described as pre-Leo and thus pre-Solar. Since Leo motivates and underlies the solar function of decision making, which, entails conscious self-awareness and a sense of agency, it logically follows that signs which precede Leo would operate in a manner that are relatively absent Leo/Solar qualities. In this regard, they are considered prevolitional.

psychopathy derives from trauma at the Aries stage, or hysteria derives from frustration at the Cancer stage. One needs to assume that these modes, being already available, may hypertrophy in the course of development over a much longer period.

Shapiro (2000) points out, for example, that psychopathic personality achieves its adult form when it has been integrated with cynical, opportunistic attitudes that can only be acquired later. Although essential traits of psychopathy are analogous to the infant's immediate reactiveness to what is before him, we cannot really say that the infant resembles the adult psychopath. Unlike the infant, psychopathic impulsivity and aggressiveness tends to be combined with cunning and a scornful, manipulative attitude that seems rooted in a deep distrust and hostility toward one's fellow humans, such as might be symbolized by a hard aspect from Pluto to Mars. Pluto, in other words, makes its own contribution to the antisocial personality symbolized predominantly by the Aries-Mars archetype. Conditions that foster cynicism may turn the developing character decisively toward a defensive reliance on this prevolitional (Aries) mode, but the disorder itself cannot be reduced to that mode. Psychopathy is far more complicated than a single archetype (Aries) even if that archetype resides at its heart. Recall the inevitability of comorbidity in any pathological development.

In short, adult pathology cannot readily be fitted into childhood prototypes. "Altogether, rather than regression to stages of early development, we must look toward the adaptation or defensive employment of what has been retained from early development" says Shapiro (p. 55). In other words, the psyche appropriates prevolitional modes in the service of whatever pathology to which it is predisposed.

PATHOGENIC CHARACTER

We have seen that psychopathy (antisocial behavior) is not simply regression to a childhood Aries prototype; rather, it entails the appropriation of an Aries/Mars prevolitional mode to avoid a sense of agency. Such appropriation serves a defensive purpose. The person "acts out" his impulses rather than reflect upon the feelings that motivate them. He does not consider the likely consequences of his actions nor anticipate how distant interests could be impacted. He is too much in the moment. While consideration of future consequences is necessary for conscious, planful action, reflections of this nature are apt to arouse anxiety and conflict in the psychopath. Accordingly, he simply avoids the matter by acting without forethought. Psychopathic behavior is, indeed, reckless, but it also serves to dispel the anxiety that would otherwise accompany feeling and thinking about the situation at hand. The point is that psychopathic behavior is a consequence not simply of regression to an Aries/Mars mode of being; rather, it is a product (compromise formation) of a poorly resolved, intrapsychic conflict that, for defensive reasons, entails an over reliance upon (hypertrophy) of Aries/Mars traits.

Of course, early developmental trauma can be a factor in adult psychopathology. It simply is not the only factor, nor even the main factor. The psychogenetic point of view has validity only when it is not applied in an oversimplified and reductionistic way. A behavioral trait originating at one point in development may serve an entirely different function later and thus become independent of the circumstances that determined its origin.

For example, a three-year old may initially develop Taurean self-control (the ability to retain) as a reaction formation against the urge to soil. However, self-restraint in the adult serves a variety of different purposes—to save money, conserve resources, preserve intimacy, and so on. Such behaviors do not constitute a defense against a wish to soil unless a trauma occurred during toilet training that prevented a clear resolution of that developmental conflict. In such instances, the urge to retain is apt to be excessive due to the underlying fear involved. However, even if an earlier trauma did occur, this does not preclude the occurrence of difficulties in subsequent stages that may have their own effects on over-retentiveness. In other words, later contributions to the development of psychopathology can occur that have nothing to do with earlier, unresolved developmental conflicts. In fact, astrology would suggest that a stressful astrological configuration will not only manifest in a prototypical childhood event, but will continue to generate analogous events until it becomes integrated.

Consider, for example, the following case. A man with Pluto in the 2nd opposed Saturn in the 8th reports that when he was three years old, and unable to adequately control his urge to soil, his mother flew into cold rages. She would glower, shake him roughly, impugn his masculinity, and castigate him for his disgusting failure. The abuse and subsequent shame he suffered, not to mention the frequent ruptures in his attachment to his mother, predisposed him to borderline personality disorder (2nd house pathology).

His Pluto-Saturn opposition also involved a square to a Sun-Jupiter conjunction in the 5th, thus forming a powerful and difficult T-Square. When he was an adolescent (5th house stage), his father went bankrupt as a consequence of a gambling addiction. Their home, car, and various belongings were repossessed and the family descended into humiliating poverty. This was particularly mortifying in light of the primary developmental thrust of adolescence—the attainment of self-esteem.

Note that the traumatic loss of security during this 5th house period further contributed to the early injury that occurred during the 2nd house/Taurus stage of development, thus exacerbating an incipient, borderline pathology. Subsequent difficulties with social relationships, break-ups with girlfriends, loss of friends and early job terminations—none of which were inherently unusual in themselves—all fed into a deep, underlying belief that nothing in his life could be trusted to endure.

This case illustrates how the links between early developmental phenomena and psychopathology are not that simple. My client's borderline disorder cannot be explained merely on the basis of traumatic toilet training, for there were many additional experiences that reinforced and exacerbated the initial trauma of that period. Certainly, his adult behavior echoes the psychology of the toddler—an inordinate need for security and stability. However, intervening events played a crucial part in the eventual outcome. That he displays Taurean/borderline traits to an excessive degree derives not merely from trauma during the Taurus stage of development, but from a host of other contributing factors that occurred during later stages. Failure to recognize these factors leads to the psychogenetic fallacy; that is, the tendency to attribute to later behavior the presence of elements deriving from an earlier period that are presumed to be determinant. In fact, any form of disturbed behavior is likely to be overdetermined—a consequence of multiple, intersecting contributors at different stages of life—in addition to innate character.

One of the primary values of an astrological chart is that it shows how a single pattern will continue to manifest over the course of a lifetime. The childhood prototype is merely one manifestation of an ongoing pattern of experience. Later manifestations of the pattern will tend to reinforce, color in and flesh out the outlines of the original prototype.

The danger of a purely psychogenetic point of view is the reductionistic and deterministic assumption that adult forms of pathology necessarily are caused by early developmental failures. Astrology provides a corrective in showing that psychopathology derives from an innate, inborn character structure. Psychological conflicts and deficiencies are mirrored by environmental conflicts and deficiencies, which manifest most acutely during those developmental periods that correspond to the nature of the archetypal issue. Outer manifestations of the conflict continue to occur and, in so doing, provide a vehicle for resolution of the inner conflict. Such configurations evolve toward more integrated states through a repetition of the pattern and through ongoing efforts to bring it into harmony.

Ideally speaking, my client's T-square will evolve into more integrated and finely balanced versions that increasingly allow for greater fulfillment of the relevant, underlying needs. From this perspective, childhood traumas and subsequent pathology may simply be progenitors of what ultimately become powers of soul, as was illustrated in the example of Carl Jung in the previous chapter.

TELEOLOGICAL CAUSATION

An alternative to the causal-reductive analyses of traditional psychoanalytic theory is teleological or "final" causation. Teleology, or goal directed behavior, is based on the notion that the psyche is pulled toward higher, future states in addition to being driven by lower, earlier ones. In an effort to actualize itself, the psyche naturally evolves toward states of increasing differentiation and integration of parts. Humanistic psychology and Jung's theory of analytical psychology are teleological models. In Jung's view, the Self, or unity archetype, is both the cause of psychodynamics while also being the ultimate end or purpose of psychic activity. Self-realization is the final summary product of a spontaneous and purposive striving toward psychological wholeness and self-healing.[59]

Jung claimed that the process by which this occurs was evident in the symbolism of dreams during periods of tumult and confusion. He observed that certain dream symbols represented attempts of the future personality to break through. These symbols had teleological significance in that they functioned as lures to pull the dreamer forward toward new character formations—new, more integrated ways of being. Jung concluded that unconscious mental contents sometimes had a prospective (forward-looking) function. They symbolized and thus pointed the way toward higher states of consciousness.

I believe that critical, formative events of childhood can be interpreted in a similar light. The most difficult challenges of childhood are often symbolized by outer planet configurations that (1) tenant personal houses, and/or (2) form hard aspects to the personal planets. Saturn and Jupiter seem to represent a middle ground in that they can go either way; that is, they can

---

[59] This has an interesting parallel in Hindu concepts of *Brahman*, which is simultaneously the dynamic behind manifestation and the common denominator of all that is manifested. From this (Hindu) perspective, realization of oneness with Brahman is the final purpose behind the strivings of matter and consciousness at all levels.

operate as challenges to the personal planets, or themselves be challenged by the transpersonal planets. Because Uranus, Neptune, and Pluto represent higher states of consciousness, they correlate to events that require an elevated perspective: non-attachment and resilience (Uranus); sacrifice, compassion, and surrender (Neptune); and a willingness to endure pain, wounding, and mortification in order to bring about healing and renewal (Pluto). However, when these planets are bound up in a conflictual way with personal houses and planets, there is an impingement of collective energies upon personal needs, especially as these needs are felt during childhood. Thus the child is initiated into a dimension of consciousness that s/he is not yet able to master, but which provides a glimpse of a destiny—a calling or *daimon*—that beckons from the future.

One of the advantages of a zodiacal development model is that it becomes possible to understand how intrapsychic conflicts are, in part, an inevitable and inherent consequence of different time-space orientations. For example, if Uranus and Venus are in hard aspect, this constellates a conflict between the Aquarian and Taurean parts of the psyche. Whereas Taurus is oriented toward holding on to that which provides security in the immediate present, Aquarius is aware that in the fullness of time all attachments must be relinquished. Recall that Taurus correlates to the stage of 2 through 4 years, whereas Aquarius signifies 65 to 77. Attachment needs (Taurus) conflict with non-attachment needs (Aquarius) because they derive from different time-space orientations. Taurus thinks: "what is important is what I have right now." But Aquarius thinks: "what is important is what I am evolving toward; that is, my future self, and thus I should not be attached to present circumstances."

In effect, this is an internal conflict of Taurean and Aquarian values. If unintegrated, this conflict might crystallize as a compromise formation that manifests as repeated involvements with lovers whose affections are erratic or unstable in some way. Such a lover embodies a Uranian message: "Expect the unexpected and don't get too attached; everything changes—including my affections!" Of course, the individual may embody this attitude him or herself, in which case others may be seen as clinging and possessive. The point is that such experiences provide a vehicle for working out the conflict and integrating the respective functions.

Almost invariably such a pattern of experience has a prototypical manifestation that occurs early in life. A person's ultimate accomplishments are prefigured in the challenges and hardships of childhood. Again, this is Hillman's (1996) "acorn theory," which proposes that childhood sufferings and traumas are necessary to the fulfillment of one's ultimate calling; they are, in effect, preparations for it. Such experiences seem to be symbolized by outer planet configurations that impinge on personal planets and houses. In this regard, it would be just as fair to say that a mental disorder is caused by the future as by the past. For the outer planet is the representative of a later stage of consciousness, which intrudes from the future into an earlier developmental period and pulls the child forward—however unwillingly—toward a wider and deeper perspective.

More often than not, this is initially experienced as a shocking change of circumstances (♅), a devastating loss (♆), or a traumatic violation (♇). Such events set the mold, as it were, for that issue which becomes the child's cross to bear and wound to be healed in later life. It may be that the specific struggle in which every soul engages is precisely designed to facilitate a movement toward greater wholeness and, ultimately, reunion with the whole. Admittedly, this is a matter of some speculation. It is tempting to suppose that pathological outcomes may merely reflect the magnitude of the challenge.

If, for example, Neptune in the 8th is opposing Venus in the 2nd, this again symbolizes a clash of time-space orientations. As ruler of Pisces, which signifies the last stage of life (77 and beyond), Neptune symbolizes experiences that require a renunciation of attachments and a willingness to accept the inevitable losses of old age. Venus, however, as ruler of the Taurus stage (2 through 4), signifies our capacity to form attachments and acquire possessions that provide for a sense of security. One might assume that an 80-year old is more-or-less prepared for the deterioration, dissolution, and degeneration that is a nearly unavoidable component of this decade of life. However, for a three year-old to experience such a process in the context of the primary developmental thrust of the Taurean stage—stability, solidity, and constancy—is another matter entirely.

If a three-year has to suffer a loss of security due to some kind of Neptunian dissolution—a parent dies; a flood destroys her home and washes away the family assets; mother gets sick and is hospitalized; a sibling drowns in a boating accident and the family is plunged into prolonged grief and guilt—she is likely to be overwhelmed. Yet, such experiences presage a pattern of experience that requires the child to integrate a Neptunian attitude and perspective into her Venusian sensibilities, a daunting task at any age.

In the above example we can see how the developmentally appropriate task of Venus and the 2nd house—achievement of self and object constancy—is impinged upon by the energies of Neptune. Again, this transpersonal planet is related to the developmental task of old age, which is surrender and letting go. While it would be adaptive for a 4-year old to surrender willingly the loss of her mother to cancer, it is not realistic to expect her to do so. The intrusion of such a Neptunian process into the life of a child would swamp her capacity to adapt. Accordingly, her response would likely be a maladaptive utilization of Neptunian defenses against Venus, such as denial accompanied by a compensatory fantasy of magical reunion; or, perhaps a Venusian defense against Neptune, such as inordinate resistance to any subsequent ending or loss that might occur.

Jung theorized that conflict, compensation, and unification are basic to the future growth and realization of a healthy personality. In response to trauma, the psyche tends to compensate in the opposite direction—a reaction formation—such that the dreaded experience is kept at bay. In the case of our four-year-old, her Neptune can be utilized as a defense against Venus: deny the personal loss and substitute a fantasy of transcendent future love. Thus, as an adult, she may continually abandon her lovers (beating fate to the punch) in a hyper-search for the ideal lost love with whom she yearns to reunite. Simultaneously, her Venus can be utilized as a defense against Neptune by overfunctioning in anticipation of further dreaded, Neptunian experiences; hence, she becomes inordinately clinging, insecure, and possessive in an attempt to ward off anticipated dissolution of attachments. By applying such maladaptive strategies, she is attempting to repress the painful feelings, memories, and meanings associated with this planetary aspect.

Jung would say that growth and repair are possible only through regression of the ego to the very deepest levels of the unconscious psyche. Here powerful integrative forces urge compulsive repetition of previously experienced conflicts for the sake of future self-actualization. Again, this is teleological or final causation—that for the sake of which a thing occurs. In order to come into balance—achieve wholeness, or psychic unity—the girl will eventually have to re-experience and integrate the split-off, Neptunian trauma to which her conscious personality has defensively compensated. To the extent that this can be achieved, a gift is realized, which is symbolized by the integrated version of Venus opposed Neptune: transcendent capacity for love and artistic inspiration, or perhaps a sense of unlimited physical resources and boundless prosperity that can be shared with the less fortunate. This will not be achieved, however, without a struggle.

THE CASE OF MADONNA

Something like this occurred with Madonna, the American singer and actress who has achieved superstardom (Figure 26, page 383). During Madonna's fourth year, she watched her mother slowly waste away with breast cancer, certainly a Neptunian tragedy. Despite little Madonna's desperate pleas for her mother to get well and play, she died the following year when Madonna was five. Note that Madonna's Neptune, which squares Venus, is just inside the cusp of the 3rd house (the period of five through 9). Madonna says that the death of her mother was one of the defining days of her life.

For two years following her mother's demise she was fearful of her own mortality and vomited whenever she had to leave the house. According to her biographer, Andrew Morton (2001), she is still haunted by a recurrent nightmare of dying before her time.

One could surmise that Neptune's square to Venus is a signature of the lost love-object, especially considering that Neptune's location (3rd house cusp) corresponds exactly to Madonna's age (5 years) when the tragedy occurred. As ruler of Taurus, Venus symbolizes our attachment needs on a physical level. Neptune square Venus often means that sacrifice and loss preempt the attainment of a secure attachment. It is also significant that Madonna's Neptune is conjunct her Jupiter, which as ruler of her 4th and dispositor of Saturn in the 4th is a significator of mother. Her Neptunian experience of losing her mom at ages four-five would seem to be symbolized by Neptune's conjunction with Jupiter in the 2nd and their mutual square to Venus.

I suspect that this three-planet aspect also prefigures an issue with Jupiterian religion and the God-concept, for no amount of prayers could save her mother from the ever expanding, creeping, degenerative disease of cancer—itself a Jupiter/Neptunian image. "If God is good," little Madonna once asked, "Why did He take my mother?" (Morton, 2001, p. 52).

Madonna's father, a strict Catholic, was left to bring up Madonna and her five sisters and brothers. He banned TV, was sternly moralistic, and required his children to attend daily catholic services. This certainly fits Saturn in Sagittarius in the 4th. Father energy dominated the household. That is, father (Saturn) assumed the role of nurturing parent (4th house). However, the fact that Saturn is in Sagittarius suggests a strict religious upbringing. In order to belong and to be loved, conformity to traditional religious values was required.

Note also that Saturn is quincunx Mars in the 9th, suggesting a problem between Saturnian control and the Martian impulse for freedom—in this case, Madonna's freedom to defy Catholic doctrine (♂ ♉ 9th ⚻ ♄ ♐ 4th).

Madonna loved her Dad, but she continually fought with him about religion, considering her Catholic upbringing a farce. "So often I would be confused about who I was worshipping, God or my father," she says (Bego, 1992, p. 19).

Again, the fact that Mars is in the 9th, which is ruled by Sagittarius, and Saturn is in the sign of Sagittarius, underscores that the conflict between these two planets could revolve around religious themes. Mars' placement in Taurus suggests the conflict may involve discordance between bold sensuality (♂ ♉) and traditional Catholic doctrine (♄ ♐).

While the problem with authority/religion may originate with Saturn in Sagittarius in the 4th, it transfers the conflict to Jupiter via dispositorship. Jupiter's conjunction to Neptune and square to Venus tells the next phase of her story, namely that her religious upbringing underscored and led directly to her conviction that God took her mother (Neptunian loss), and the subsequent impossibility of satisfying her need for a constant object (Venus). Not surprisingly, Madonna became disillusioned with religion after her mother's tragic passing.

Looking at Madonna's case from the perspective of developmental stages is especially interesting. Jupiter-Neptune straddling the cusp of the 3rd house clearly corresponds to Madonna's experience of losing her mother at age 4-5. And Saturn's position in her 4th at age 11 appears to signify the peak of her harsh, religious training at the hands of her father. That Saturn is disposed by Jupiter, which leads back to an earlier age when her mother became sick, suggests that memory of that experience was reactivated and appraised anew at age 11. One might surmise that Madonna's remembrance of God's failure to save her mother only underscored and further entrenched her bitter disillusionment with religion during that 4th house stage.

For most of her childhood prior to her mother's death, Madonna did her best to be good. However, prayer and obedience did not keep her mother from dying; nor did it keep her father from remarrying. For the three years before her father remarried, Madonna clung to him emotionally and physically. She did everything she could to please him. With the loss of her mother, it was critically important for Madonna to know that her father was a secure and constant object. She even slept with him to relieve her nighttime terrors and dreams of death.

Recall that the Sun, as father, symbolizes the child's chief admirer and greatest fan. As Madonna put it, "Like all young girls, I was in love with my father and I didn't want to lose him" (Bego, 1992, p. 23). In fact, she was her father's favorite. However, when Madonna's progressed Sun went over Pluto in the 12th just as she turned nine, her father remarried, which was a rebirth for him, but which Madonna took as a betrayal and abandonment. She was furious with her father and hated her stepmother.

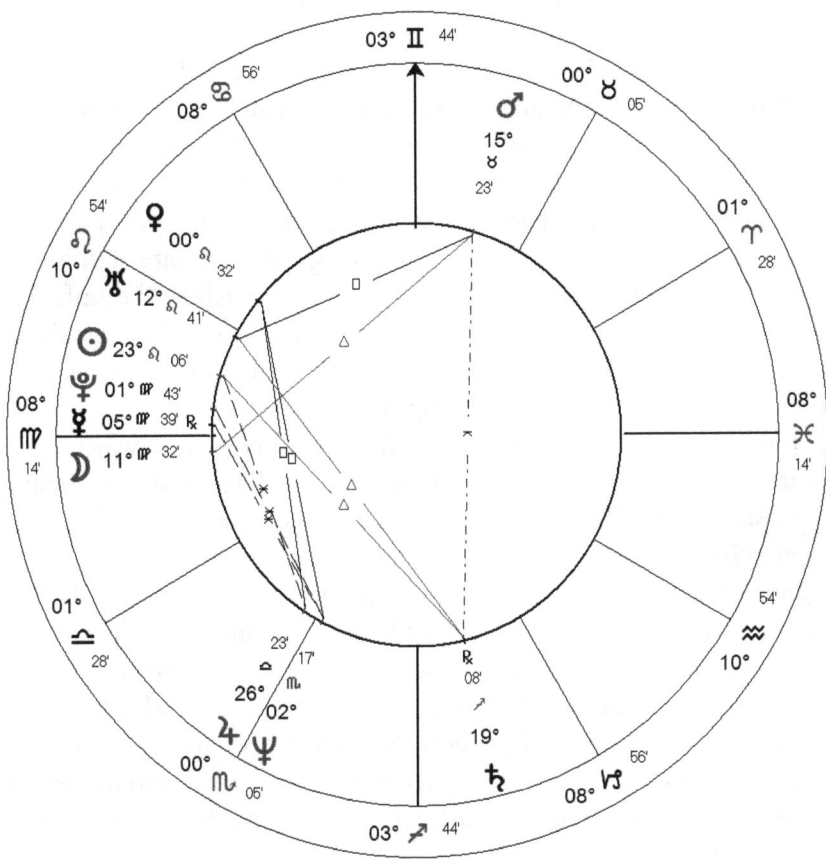

Figure 26: Birthchart Madonna. 8/16/58, 7:05am, Bay City, MI.

Feeling replaced by the other woman and deeply hurt by her father's shift of affections, Madonna decided she could get by without anyone. One of her biographers, Mark Bego, writes: "Unwilling to open herself to more heartbreak, at a young age she learned to stand confidently on her own" (p. 23). However, I suspect that Madonna was anything but confident at this point in her life. More likely she repressed her pain and compensated with a tough-girl persona that entailed a denial of any need for personal love. "Once you get hurt really bad when you're young, nothing can hurt you again," Madonna later said (p. 20). And as if to show that she no longer needed her father's love or approval, she began to openly defy him. Her act of rebellion against moral authority persisted for decades.

That same year that her father remarried (age 9), Madonna began dancing and performing. "She [my mother] taught me my love of dancing," says Madonna (Bego, 1992, p. 16). Madonna's intense need to dance at this time could be construed as an attempt to escape her pain and merge with her dancer-mother in the bliss of transcendent, Neptunian movement. Bego recalls a song from the Broadway show, *A Chorus Line*, titled "At the Ballet." In the song, the three girls sing about escaping painful childhood experiences by taking dance classes. The moral of the song is that in spite of unhappy home lives and traumatic realities, everything was somehow "beautiful" at the ballet. "For Madonna, it was like this," says Bego. "She could forget about her stepmother, the nuns at school, her sibling rivalries, even the death of her mother, for hours at a time during her dance lessons" (p. 24).

Interviews with Madonna suggest that her dance lessons, which inaugurated her artistic career, were compensatory to the grief she was feeling over losing her mother to cancer, and her father to another woman. Dance inspired in Madonna the dream of an artistic career in which she could become famous—infinitely loved by multitudes. At nine years old she had already made herself into a star, at least in her own mind. And she has held onto her stardom with a ferocious tenacity ever since. I believe that Madonna's loss of her mother and subsequent feelings of betrayal by her father are symbolized, in part, by the Neptune/Jupiter square to Venus. In losing both parents (albeit in different ways), there was a feeling of abandonment and profound loneliness that is a hallmark of Neptune. In Madonna's own words:

> We are all wounded in one way or another by something in our lives, and then we spend the rest of our lives reacting to it or dealing with it or trying to turn it into something else. The anguish of losing my mother left me with a certain kind of loneliness and an incredible longing for something...If I hadn't had that emptiness, I wouldn't have been so driven. Her death had a lot to do with me saying—after I got over my heartache—I'm going to be really strong if I can't have my mother. I'm going to take care of myself. (Taraborrelli, 2001, p. 13).

In the above quote, we catch a glimpse of her need to achieve stardom to assuage the emptiness and loneliness she felt from childhood. "The incredible longing for something" was for love and attachment—a longing so deep and so painful that only something extraordinary could fill it. Terrified of her need for personal love, which she associated with pain and loss, she has attempted to obliterate her loneliness with the mass adulation that comes from celebrity. In other words, if Venus is personal love, Neptune is universal love—love on a transpersonal, collective level. When personal love is repudiated, it merely goes underground and resurfaces later in gigantic proportion. Madonna's childhood cry, "I don't need anyone," eventually returned as a need for everyone. But everyone can never be someone, and while it may soften the blow and seem on the surface to be more than a fair exchange, in the end it does not satisfy. Like a drug, Madonna needed more and more of the thing that substituted for what she really wanted: personal love. Morton (2001) captures it thusly:

> A look through her file shows clearly that since childhood Madonna dreamed single-mindedly of becoming a celebrity...It started with the small stuff: a show of exhibitionism at family gatherings, hogging the spotlight at school concerts....By the time she moved to New York, she was on the slippery slope, rapidly moving from recreational self-absorption to flirting with the hard stuff, avidly sniffing success. Pretty soon she had pawned her dance career for a hit of fame, never really coming down from the high of seeing her first single go to number one in the charts. From then on she was hooked, utterly addicted to fame, mainlining on mass adulation...(p. 17).

It would be a mistake to reduce Madonna's drive for success to merely a neurotic displacement of her Venusian needs for love and attachment. Surely other factors come into play when considering the enormity of her talent and achievements. Having her Sun and two planets in Leo certainly adds to her charisma. Still, a psychological approach to chart interpretation strives to understand the underlying sequence of motivations that contributes to the over or underfunctioning of any particular part of the chart. In Madonna's case, it is instructive to trace the flow of her dispositorships, starting with Saturn in Sagittarius.

A planet's dispositor always shows the consequence of its expression; that is, what happens as a result of the disposed planet. Jupiter disposes Saturn. Thus a consequence of Madonna's strict Catholic upbringing and deprivation of maternal love (♄ ♐ 4th) was her disillusionment with conventional religion when her mother died (♃ ☌ ♆ 3rd). When Neptune aspects a planet, that planet often becomes associated with illusion, fantasy, unreality, and subsequent disillusionment. Recall her statement: "If God is good, why did he take my mother?" With Jupiter disposed of by Venus (and also squaring it), religion's failure became associated with the loss of (and subsequent repudiation of any need for) a personal love or secure attachment (♃ ♆ □ ♀ ☊). Finally, a consequence of Venus is Sun in Leo in the 12th house.

As the final dispositor, the Sun has added authority and significance, like a deep lake into which psychic energy pools. Whatever we may say about Madonna's Sun, however, needs to be understood in the context of that which precedes it—namely, Venus and its aspects. The Sun is always motivated to satisfy the need of Leo; however, in this case, that need is indissolubly associated with everything that Venus signifies in the chart. There is a clear line of descent, in other words, from Saturn to Jupiter to Venus to the Sun.

Of particular importance are Venus' aspects, for these show the degree of difficulty that Venus has in striving to satisfy its own needs. If there is trauma here, as indicated by the square to Neptune/Jupiter and confirmed by the loss of her first love object (mother), this will have a direct bearing on what Venus ultimately communicates to the Sun. If Venus could speak, it might sound very much like Madonna when she says: "The anguish of losing my mother left me with a certain kind of loneliness and an incredible longing for something. If I hadn't had that emptiness, I wouldn't have been so driven..."

In effect, Madonna was driven to overcompensate on a solar level to make up for her Venusian anguish, which can be defined as an intense longing for attachment and relationship at a personal level. Morton (2001) muses about Madonna's loss of her mother:

> The loss of the one person who gave her patient, unconditional love changed forever her relationship with the outside world, making her stronger and self-reliant, yet with an insatiable need for love matched by fear of commitment. She had given her love once to someone she had completely trusted, and that person had gone from her life. [Subsequently] her quest for love without strings would define her behavior, in public and in private, and provide the momentum behind the relentless ambition and craving for attention that has propelled her to universal fame. (p. 48).

Morton's analysis makes clear that Madonna both wanted personal love and feared it at the same time. This is consistent with the Jupiter-Neptune-Venus conflict. Jupiter expands the need for Venusian love, while also creating an ethical problem—how much is too much? That is, are certain kinds of love and pleasure morally wrong? Neptune, in turn, can create an idealization of the Venusian object, while also involving it with a fear of loss and disillusionment. A compromise formation is to reject church teachings regarding sex and marriage, and substitute instead a Dionysian ethic of unbridled sensual pleasure. Combine this with a lack of commitment in order to avoid anticipated loss, and beat fate to the punch by dumping your paramours before they dump you, and we have a pretty good description of Madonna during the 80's and 90's.

All of this was evident in Madonna's early notoriety as a promiscuous vamp with an ever-expanding stable of lovers, both male and female—Sean Penn, Warren Beatty, Dennis Rodman, Jose Canseco, Vanilla Ice, Sandra Bernhard, Jenny Shimizu, Prince, and J.F.K. Jr. being the more famous among them. One gets the impression that Madonna was on a search for her lost love while also running from it. With regard to her mother's death, Morton (2001) asks:

> Has this resulted in lasting emotional damage? Madonna seems to have spent a lifetime searching for love, yet continually rejecting or discarding those who loved her, always afraid of being hurt once more. Although she is in control of her artistic and business life, she has all too often lost control of her love life. In contrast to her supremely self-confident public image, the private Madonna is often uncertain and unsettled in her relationships. 'She can stand before 80,000 people in a stadium and hold them in the palm of her hand. Yet off the stage she is the most insecure woman I have ever met,' says her ex-lover Jim Albright. (p. 29).

In the above quote we see how Madonna's wounded Venus both underlies and provides the motivation for her "supremely confident public image." In other words, behind the Sun in Leo is Venus with its difficult square to Neptune and Jupiter; thus, behind the relentless craving for mass adulation (Sun) is a desperate longing for a secure relationship—a relationship that Madonna feared may never be fulfilled. Again, it was precisely her "intense longing to fill a sort of emptiness" that fueled her insatiable solar drive. "Had her childhood taken a different path," writes Bego, "she might never have blossomed into the high-priestess of rebellious self-expression that we have come to know as Madonna" (1992 p. 27).

To appreciate how difficulties with Venus ultimately affect the Sun, we need to understand the nature of the conflict that Venus is experiencing with Jupiter and Neptune. Whereas the Venus square to Neptune symbolizes an association between attachment needs and renunciation of attachment, the square to Jupiter complicates things by adding an ethical dimension, as if to say, "It's right and proper that you should sacrifice your need for relationship, pleasure, and sensuality." If Jupiter conjunct Neptune had its way, it would make a religious virtue out of such a sacrifice. In fact, this is precisely what Pope John Paul II did, for he had the identical aspect (Jupiter conjunct Neptune square Venus). Pope John Paul II would ultimately become a figure with whom Madonna was indissolubly linked. Bego notes, "Even as a child, Madonna's perception of the world had always been a tug of war between the profane and the sacred" (1992, p. 29).

As always with hard aspects, there tends to be a compromise formation in which the needs of one planet are compromised for the sake of the other. The functionality of the compromise is a measure of the degree of integration between the planets. Clearly, Madonna has exaggerated her Venus at the expense of her Jupiter/Neptune; yet, the influence of Jupiter and Neptune is readily apparent. As an artist, she incorporates religious symbolism into her videos, music, and lyrics. Almost invariably, however, she does so with an irreverent, mocking attitude—such as masturbating with a crucifix on stage during one of her live performances.

The Jupiter/Neptune square to Venus, which symbolizes a conflict between sensual pleasure and morality/spirituality, is clearly evident in various titles of her songs and albums—*Like a Virgin, Immaculate Conception, Material Girl* (versus Spiritual Girl), *Papa Don't Preach* (to the Pope about an out-of-wedlock pregnancy), *Justify My Love, Forbidden Love, You Must Love Me, Bad Girl, What It Feels Like For A Girl*, and numerous other titles that reflect this configuration. In 1989, the video for her hit song *Like A Prayer*, with its links between religion and eroticism, was condemned by the Vatican and caused Pepsi-Cola to cancel a sponsorship deal with the star. Pope John Paul II famously banned Madonna from performing in Italy.

Again, it is noteworthy that Pope John Paul II has the identical aspect: Neptune conjunct Jupiter square Venus. As stated, a hard aspect can oscillate between two extremes. Either Venus or Jupiter/Neptune is expressed excessively and in a way that resists the other planet's right of expression.

If there is a moralistic denial and condemnation of bodily pleasures, then Jupiter/Neptune predominates. If there is a rejection of church edicts that forbid bodily pleasures and, instead, an orgiastic celebration of unbridled sensuality, then Venus predominates over Jupiter/Neptune. In effect, Madonna embodies one side of the conflict, the Pope the other.

Reportedly, the birth of her out-of-wedlock daughter, Lourdes (named after a place of miracles and the sighting of the Holy Mother), has been healing for Madonna. And her marriage to Guy Ritchie and the birth of her second child was, for a while at least, a steadying influence (they divorced in 2008). Perhaps the experience of being a wife and mother helped to heal her mother-wound and may augur a more serious and mature phase in her career. This seems to be the case. Following the birth of Lourdes, she produced the sublime *Ray of Light*, which is considered one of her finest albums to date.

It is also reported that Madonna's discovery of the Kabala and Eastern religion has inspired her music. So perhaps her religious disillusionment is being repaired as well. While space does not permit a fuller exploration of Madonna's chart, suffice to say that her art as well as her personal life reflects a continuous striving to integrate her Neptune/Jupiter-Venus square. In effect, this aspect not only symbolizes the early, tragic loss of her mother, it also presages what Madonna was to become—a brilliant songwriter and performer whose work reflects a continuous obsession with the theme of love versus morality/spirituality. One could say that she has successfully sublimated her religion-versus-pleasure conflict into her art.

With regard to Venus' rulership of Taurus and thus its association with material security, it is important to note that Madonna has achieved near boundless prosperity as one of the most commercially successful artists the world has ever known.[60] Jupiter and Neptune, of course, both have to do with boundlessness in different ways; Jupiter because it is oriented toward expanding boundaries to the realm of the possible, and Neptune because it symbolizes infinity—that is, the final expansion of boundaries to include the All and the One. Despite (or perhaps because of) the aspect to Venus being a square, this merely seems to have provided the drive for Madonna to realize the ultimate potential of this tripartite archetypal combination.

---

[60] According to the Guinness Book of British Hit Singles, Madonna is the third most successful chart act of all-time, beaten only by Elvis Presley and Cliff Richard. From *Like A Virgin* in November 1984 to *Secret* in October 1994, she amassed an amazing run of 32 consecutive top ten hits. No other female singer in the pop arena has been as prominent or as successful over such a long period (to date, twenty years).

To the extent that Jupiter and Neptune are integrated with Venus, we might expect that Madonna will feel compelled to share some of her wealth in philanthropic (Jupiter) and charitable (Neptune) activities. In fact, her generosity in this regard is well documented. She has quietly paid for drug rehabilitation therapy for numerous friends and family members, is a well-known supporter of AIDS charities, is a 'quiet donor' for breast cancer (the disease that killer her mother), and every Friday after Thanksgiving she makes an annual pilgrimage to children's wards of hospitals in Manhattan and Harlem where she distributes gifts and spends time with the children in an attempt to relieve their suffering.

THE SIGNIFICANCE OF TRANSITS & PROGRESSIONS

The manner in which developmental unfoldment contributes to the personality is highly variable. Not only do people have different planetary configurations in various house-stages, they also experience a variety of transits and progressions during the periods that correspond to those house-stages. Momentous transits and progressions can presage major organizational shifts in development. The developmental stage at which such transits and progressions occur must be considered in order to fully glean their meaning and significance. Of course, the transit/progression may not directly involve the house that corresponds to the stage during which it occurs.

For example, Madonna has natal Saturn in Sagittarius in the 4th house, which would correlate to being raised by a conservatively religious father who ruled the family with a rigid Catholic mentality. Her general attitude toward that mentality involves her natal Mars' quincunx to Saturn, which was earlier noted. The point is that during her 4th house developmental stage (age 9-14), her progressed Sun conjuncted natal Pluto in the 12th. Although this progression did not directly involve the 4th house, it did occur as an overlay to the primary developmental thrust of the 4th house period.

During her 9th year when progressed Sun went over Pluto, her father remarried. This was traumatic for Madonna in that he was her sole remaining parent and a source of unwavering security. Madonna recalls her rage and defiance of the world around her. "I certainly wanted really badly either to find out my parents weren't my real parents—so I could be an orphan and feel sorry for myself—or wanted everyone to die in a car accident so I wouldn't have parents" (Bego, 1992, p. 26-27). Note the Plutonic intensity and extremism of this statement. She wanted to eliminate her father and stepmother.

Madonna was subsequently saddled with responsibilities, like baby-sitting and diaper-changing the baby that was a product of her father and stepmother's new marriage. "In fact," says Bego (1992), "she viewed herself as Cinderella, burdened by a stepmother and lots of work" (p. 22). In one sense, this scenario reflects her Saturn in the 4th—burdensome duties, a strict father, loneliness, maternal deprivation, and an onerous stepmother, all of which peaked during the 4th house stage (9-14). On the other hand, it also reflects her Sun's progression over Pluto in the 12th—a deep sense of betrayal and the murderous rage she felt toward both parents. This conjunction corresponds to Madonna's sense of violation, as if she had been eliminated and replaced by her stepmother. It was during this period that the full implications of her mother's death hit her. As she put it, "I didn't resent having to raise my brothers and sisters so much as I resented that I didn't have my mother" (p. 23).

Recall that Neptune is singularly related to her mother's passing in that the loss occurred exactly during that period that correlates to Neptune's 3rd house position (age 4-5). And since Neptune in Scorpio is disposed by Pluto, her loss at 5 years old was transferred to her 12th house Sun, which conjuncts Pluto. Madonna's very sense of self—her identity—was powerfully impacted at 9 years old when her progressed Sun conjuncted Pluto. Her father remarried and she had to fully face the consequences of her mother's death: Daddy was sleeping with another woman and Madonna was completely alone and would remain motherless forever! In other words, the full implications of her natal Sun-Pluto conjunction would be most acutely realized at precisely the year she turned nine years old.

One consequence of this was her realization that life was short and that death could come at any time. "She realized how short life really was," writes Bego, "too short to settle for anything less than everything you desire" (p. 27). Accordingly, it was during this period that she resolved to pursue her own 12th house dreams with a ferocious intensity. Bego (1992) notes that Madonna still has endless nightmares about death. Despite regular health checks, particularly for breast cancer, she sees herself in a race against time, desperate to achieve as much as she can before death comes again, this time for her.

SUN LEO CONJUNCT PLUTO IN THE 12TH

A hallmark of Madonna's career is her ability to reinvent herself. One year she's a blond, the next a brunette, a lesbian this year, then abruptly a mother and a wife. Pluto, of course, rules processes of death and renewal.

Madonna's propensity for regenerating her public image is consistent with her Sun-Pluto conjunction. One could almost say that rather than resist death, she is compelled to embrace and assimilate it; thus, she dies and is reborn, over and over.

I suspect that Madonna's penchant for drawing attention to herself by transforming her public image is a defense against a fear of not existing. To fully understand this, one must appreciate the blend of archetypal energies that make-up her solar position: the Sun is in Leo, conjunct Pluto, and tenanting the 12th. Like everything in astrology, the devil is in the details. The 12th house is a spiritual environment that requires surrender to a higher power. Planets here must be consecrated to the collective; that is, they must sacrifice their personal goals for the greater good of the whole. There is a pull toward giving up, letting go, and dissolving into anonymity—that is, into God. Sun in Leo, however, is not disposed to such an end. Its intention is to stand out and be noticed!

Sun in Leo in the 12th is thus an anomaly, like an actress strutting on a stage encased in fog at the edge of a precipice with no audience in sight. Adding Pluto to the mix further complicates the picture, for now our actress is aware that climbing up the precipice toward the stage is a beast that threatens to devour her. For Madonna that beast is death, and her 12th house stage is the collective unconscious against which she struggles to remain differentiated. Madonna's greatest fear is precisely what Sun in Leo conjunct Pluto in the 12th symbolizes: an early death that destroys all opportunity to express and distinguish herself. In this context, to be distinguished (famous) is compensatory to being extinguished.

Evidence for this is apparent in Madonna's near pathological desire to stand out from the crowd and be noticed. In her biography, she bitterly complained that her stepmother would buy all the kids the same outfit. Madonna also had to wear uniforms to Catholic school. "I was dying for some individuality," she proclaims, not realizing, of course, the astrological significance of her remark (Bego, 1992, p. 27).

Madonna tried everything to look different than her brothers and sister, from odd-colored socks to bows in her hair. This was always the pattern: Madonna would do anything to avoid blending in with the collective and drowning in an undifferentiated soup of anonymous others. She is so intent on being noticed that her one-time lover, Warren Beatty, once quipped: 'She doesn't want to live off camera, much less talk.'

Since her mother did disappear, it could be argued that Madonna's intention thereafter was to not disappear. Thus she compensates her fear of disappearance by exaggerating her appearance, whether through constant hairstyle and color changes, dramatic clothing (cone breasts on stage), or outright nudity.[61]

One wonders, who is the real Madonna? Morton writes, "A consummate mistress of disguise, she has always cleverly hidden herself in the mystery of her mythology" (2002, p. 19). This in itself is testimony to paradoxical quality of Sun Leo in the 12th. On the one hand, she commands attention with striking changes of appearance; while on the other she seems not to exist at all, for she is disguised in the archetypal garb of her persona-of-the-moment. Thus with Sun Leo in the 12th Madonna tends not only to shock and titillate by continually altering her image, she does so by identifying with glamorous movie stars of past eras—archetypal goddesses of the silver screen, such as Monroe, Harlow, and Dietrich, all with dramatic effect.

Again, this fear of disappearing, of not having an authentic identity, is consistent with the symbolism of her 12th house Sun. On one side, the Sun is dispositor of Venus, with all its memories of a tragic loss of her earliest attachment (mother). On the other side is the conjunction with Pluto, which disposits Neptune and brings with it, again, memories of maternal death. Sandwiched between these two planets, the Sun compensates a fear of invisibility by striving for maximum visibility, as if desperately trying to not *not* be noticed. While it is easy to attribute such antics to an exaggerated need for attention, we must consider what underlies this compulsion. Simply put, it is a fear of not being noticed; that is, of disappearing, or not existing.

Recall that the ultimate impact of her mother's death was a huge, perpetual emptiness and longing for love. It triggered in Madonna the realization that life is fleeting and that one can die at any moment. This fear of melting away, of dissolving, of being rendered invisible, has been a dark and constant companion ever since Madonna's mother passed away. When her progressed Sun conjuncted natal Pluto at nine years old, this fear was brought to a head. "It made me grow up fast," she said. "I want to do everything *now*...I've got to push myself so hard because I have demons. I won't live forever and when I die I don't want people to forget I existed" (Bego, 1992, p. 28). This statement precisely captures the meaning of Sun in Leo conjunct Pluto in the 12th.

By exaggerated self-expression and attention seeking—a hypertrophy of the solar principle—Madonna's Sun in the 12th compensates a fear of

---

[61] Madonna created a scandal in 1992 with the highly publicized release of her book, *Sex*, which depicted a nude Madonna in various S&M scenarios. 1,500,000 copies of the $50 book were sold in a matter of days.

dissolving into oneness. Desperate to resist the black hole of chaos that threatens to absorb her, she is compelled to stand out so as to not blend in.

If the 12th house is the house of addictions, then what one is addicted to is suggested by the nature of the planets and signs that tenant this house. It is fascinating to recall Morton's (2002) depiction of Madonna's addiction to celebrity. "She was hooked, utterly addicted to fame, mainlining on mass adulation" (p. 17). In short, the expression of her Sun in Leo, which is the final dispositor of her chart, is compensatory to the demands of the environment in which it is placed—the 12th house of surrender, of renunciation of ego, of loss and grief and endings. The extremes to which she will go to avoid self-dissolution—continual dramatic transformations of her self-image, masturbating on stage with a crucifix, S&M scenarios on film, and a book, *Sex*, that celebrates her own nudity—is testimony to Sun conjunct Pluto.

Madonna's life story dramatically illustrates that while many disorders do correlate to early developmental stages, a disorder is not merely the consequence of a failure to master a specific developmental task of childhood. Rather, the difficulty may also be a consequence of a later stage intruding into an earlier stage. I call this *future shock*. The archetypal process of a later stage initially overwhelms the child's capacity to adapt, thus impairing her ability to satisfy the requirements of the earlier period. Madonna's childhood illness following her mother's death—vomiting, fears of dying, and anxious attachment to her father—must certainly have compromised her early schooling, as it occurred during the 3rd house stage. Yet Neptune, the muse of poetry and music, being in the 3rd, also prefigured what Madonna would later come to master in her adult life—song writing.

Intrusion of collective energies into childhood can eventually motivate transcendent accomplishments via sublimation of the conflict into culturally valued ends. Madonna's early experience of loss seems to have provided the fertile soil out of which a successful song writing and performing career grew. It is significant that Neptune, which rules music, tenants the 3rd house of writing and communications. Few realize that Madonna is not only a talented performer, she writes most of her own music as well. Note that Neptune is in Mercury's house (the 3rd), whereas Mercury, which rules her 10th house of career, is in the house of Neptune (the 12th). In addition, the two planets are in sextile. These connections underscore how songwriting is a key component of Madonna's professional life. And Neptune's sign placement in Scorpio is especially relevant to the fact that her songwriting and accompanying videos often entail explicitly sexual (Scorpio) themes.

SUMMARY

A zodiacal developmental model not only looks backward in terms of fixation-regression, but also forward in terms of telos-progression. Certain kinds of character types are a consequence not merely of fixation at early developmental stages, but of intrusion of developmental demands from later, not-yet-experienced stages. Whereas the developmental bias of the fixation-regression model is toward the past (even though there is limited agreement among exponents as to which stages and experiences correlate to which disorders), a telos-progression model is based on the forward-moving, self-actualizing tendencies of the psyche.

The sequence of zodiacal signs symbolizes an arrow of time in which later sign-stages are more complex, unified, and evolved than earlier ones. In natal charts, outer planet impingements on personal planets and houses symbolize new character formations struggling to break through. The future personality, as it were, through the medium of shocks, losses, and betrayals, is attempting to pull the child forward toward that which s/he is ultimately destined to become—more resilient, integrous, and God-centered. Without such painful experiences one may never find the incentive, nor develop the compassion, to realize higher states of being. This is precisely what we mean by teleology—a final goal for the sake of which an event occurs.

In effect, the real story always parallels the archetypal story. For the archetypal story is a kind of meta-story, a narrative of soul that takes place at a higher level of abstraction than the concrete events that make up our daily lives. We presume that early experience determines personality and fate because we have been taught to think in linear, deterministic terms. It is the world-view in which we are immersed and entranced. Yet, astrology suggests just the opposite: that early experience is but a catalyst for the working out of some fundamental malady of soul, the healing of which fosters Self-realization.

Early experience, in the final analysis, may simply be the first and thus prototypical manifestation of an innate, inborn story with intrinsic power to use the mundane world as a vehicle for its manifestation. Just as a play must have actors and a stage to come alive, so we, too, must cast our inner drama with the people and circumstances of our daily existence. And just as a playwright must appropriate actors for his play's purpose, so likewise we appropriate people and events for the sake of an inner script, authored by the soul, and performed for its own redemption.

* * * * *

References

Abrams, J. (1991). Epilogue. In C. Zweig and J. Abrams (Eds.), *Meeting the shadow.* Los Angeles, Jeremy Tarcher.

Atwood, G, & Stolorow, R. (1993). *Faces in the cloud.* Northvale, NJ: Jason Aronson, Inc.

Averill, J.R. (1980). The emotions. In E. Staub (Ed.) *Personality: Basic aspects and current research* (pp. 133-199). Englewood Cliffs, NJ: Prentice Hall

Bache, C.M. (1994). *Lifecycles: Reincarnation and the web of life.* New York: Paragon House

Barrow, J., & Tipler, F. (1986). *The anthropic cosmological principle.* New York: Oxford University Press.

Battista, J.R. (1978). The science of consciousness. In K. Pope & J. Singer (Eds.), *The stream of consciousness* (pp. 55-87). New York: Plenum Press.

Beck, J. (1995). *Cognitive therapy: Basics and Beyond.* New York: Guildford Press.

Bego, M. (1992). *Madonna: Blond ambition.* New York: Cooper Square Press.

Bowlby, J. (1969). *Attachment and loss: Vol 1. Attachment.* New York: Basic Books.

Cerminera, G. (1950). *Many Mansions.* New York: Penguin Books.

Chambon, P. (1981). Split genes. *Scientific American, 244*(5), 48-61.

Chapple, C. (1986). *Karma and creativity.* Albany, NY: State University of New York Press.

Chess, S., & Thomas, T. (1986). *Temperament in clinical practice.* New York: Guilford Press.

Cunningham, A.J. (1986). Information and health in the many levels of man. *Advances, 3*(1), 32-45.

Deci, E.L. (1980). Intrinsic motivation and personality. In E. Staub (Ed.) *Personality: Basic aspects and current research* (pp. 35-80). Englewood Cliffs, NJ: Prentice-Hall, Inc.

Engel, L., Ferguson, T. (1990). *Imaginary crimes.* Boston: Houghton Mifflin Co.

Epstein, S. (1980). The self-concept: A review and the proposal of an integrated theory of personality. In E. Staub (Ed.) *Personality: Basic aspects and current research* (pp. 81-128).

Erikson, E.H. (1959). Identity and the life cycle. *Psychological Issues,* Monograph 1. New York: International Universities Press.

Erikson, E.H. (1968). *Identity, youth and crisis.* New York: W.W. Norton & Company.

Fraser, J.T. (1975). *Of time, passion, and knowledge.* New York: Braziller.

Freedman, J. & Combs, G. (1996). *Narrative therapy.* New York: W.W. Norton & Company.

Freud, S. (1937). Analysis terminable and interminable. *Standard Edition, p. 238.* London: Hogarth Press.

Friedman, M. (1985). Toward a reconceptualization of guilt. *Contemporary Psychoanalysis,* October, 21(4), 501-547.

Genes that move to fight disease. (1980, September). *Newsweek,* p. 58.

Geringer, Joseph (2001). "Night Stalker: Richard Ramirez: From the Bowels of Hell," in Courtroom Television Network LLC. Serial killer/Mass murderer Archive - Crime Library. Section: Richard Ramirez. www.crimelibrary.com/ramirez/index.

Gibson, M. (1998). *Signs of mental illness.* St. Paul, MN: Llewellyn Pub.

Goleman, D. (1995). *Emotional intelligence.* New York: Bantam.

Gopnik, A., Meltzoff, A., & Kuhl, P. (1999). *The scientist in the crib.* New York: William Morrow & Company.

Gootnik, I. (1997). *Why you behave in ways you hate.* Granite Bay, CA: Penmarin Books.

Greenacre, P. (1952). Pregenital patterning. *Int. J. Psychoanalysis,* 33:410-415.

Greene, L. (1997). *The horoscope in manifestation.* London: Center for Psychological Astrology Press. (p. 1-2, 6-7)

Griffin, D.R. (1988). Introduction: The reenchantment of science. In D.R. Griffin (Ed.), *The reenchantment of science* (pp. 1-46). Albany, NY: State University of New York Press.

Guggenbuhl-Craig, A. (1971). *Power in the helping professions.* Dallas, TX: Spring Publications.

Guggenbuhl-Craig, A. (1991). Quacks, charlatans, and false prophets. In C. Zweig and J. Abrams (Eds.), *Meeting the shadow.* Los Angeles, Jeremy Tarcher.

Hall, M.P. (1954). *The essential nature of consciousness.* Los Angeles: Philosophical Research Society.

Hall, M.P. (1936). *Astrology and reincarnation.* Los Angeles: Philosophical Research Society.

Harvey, J. & Katz, C. (1984). *If I'm so successful, why do I feel like a fake? The imposter phenomenon.* New York: Saint Martins Press.

Hill, J. (1993). *The astrological body types.* San Francisco: Stellium Press.

Hillman, J. (1996). *The soul's code:* New York: Random House.

Horowitz, M.J. (1987). *States of mind: Configurational analysis of individual psychology.* New York: Plenum Medical Book Company.

Horowitz, M.J. (1988). *Introduction to psychodynamics.* New York: Basic Books.

Huxley, A. (1944). *The perennial philosophy.* New York: Harper & Row.

Jantsch, E. (1980). *The self-organizing universe.* Oxford, England: Pergammon Press.

Jones, J. (1995). *Affects as process.* Hillsdale, NJ: The Analytic Press.

Jung, C.G. (1933). *Modern man in search of a soul.* New York: Harcourt & Brace.

Jung, C.G. (1945). The relations between the ego and the unconscious. In *Collected Works.* Vol. 7. Princeton: Princeton Univ. Press, 1953. (First German edition, 1945.)

Jung, C.G. (1952). *Answer to Job.* Collected Works, Vol. 7, Bollingen Series 20. New York: Pantheon.

Jung, C.G., (1953). *Two essays on analytical psychology.* Collected Works, Vol. 7, Bollingen Series 20. New York: Pantheon. p. 238.

Jung, C.G., (1953). *Psychology and Alchemy.* Collected Works, Vol. 12, Bollingen Series 20. New York: Pantheon.

Jung, C.G., (1953). *Alchemical Studies* Collected Works, Vol. 13, Bollingen Series 20. New York: Pantheon.

Jung, C.G., (1955). Synchronicity: An acausal connecting principle. In C. Jung & W. Pauli, *The interpretation of nature and psyche* (pp. 1-146). New York: Pantheon.

Jung, C. G.(1958). *Psychology and religion: West and East. CW 11.*

Jung, C.G., (1960). *The structure and dynamics of the psyche.* Collected Works, Vol. 8, Bollingen Series 20. New York: Pantheon. p. 96, 441

Jung, C.G. (1961). *Memories, dreams, reflections.* New York: Vintage Books.

Jung, C.G. (1964). *Man and his symbols.* Doubleday: New York.

Jung, C.G., (1971). The transcendent function. In J. Campbell (Ed.), *The portable Jung* (p. 274-5). New York: The Viking Press.

Kaiser, H. (1965). *Effective Psychotherapy.* Louis B. Fierman (Ed.). New York: The Free Press.

Kandel, E.r. (1983). From metapsychology to molecular biology: Explorations into the nature of anxiety. *American Journal of Psychiatr, 140*, 1277-1293.

Kegan, R. *The evolving self.* Cambridge, MA: Harvard University Press

Keeney, B. (1983). *Aesthetics of change.* New York: Guilford Press, p. 72, 123

Kelly, G.A. (1955). *The psychology of personal constructs: A theory of personality (2 vols.).* New York: W.W. Norton.

Koestler, A. (1978). *Janus: A summing up.* New York: Vintage Books.

Kohlberg, L. (1976). *Collected papers on moral development and moral education.* Cambridge, MA: Center for Moral Education.

Krippner, S. (1988). Parapsychology and postmodern science. In D.R. Griffin (Ed.), *The reenchantment of science* (pp. 129-140). Albany, NY: State University of New York Press.

Lawlor, R. (1982). *Sacred geometry.* New York: Crossroad.

Linedecker, C.L. (1991) *Night Stalker.* New York: St. Martin's Press.

Lichtenberg, J. *Psychoanalysis and motivation.* Hillsdale, NJ: The Analytic Press.

Maxmen, J. & Wards, N. (1995). *Essential psychopathology and its treatment.* New York: W.W. Norton & Company.

Mahler, M. (1975). On human symbiosis and the vicissitudes of individuation. *J. Amer. Psychoanal. Assn.*, 23: 740-763.

May, R. (1967). *The art of counseling.* New York: Abingdon Press.

McMullin, R. (1986). *Handbook of cognitive therapy techniques.* New York: W.W. Norton & Company.

Maturana, H., & Varela, F. (1980). *Autopoiesis and cognition.* Dordrecht, Holland: Reidel.

Maslow, A. (1968). *Toward a psychology of being.* Princeton, NJ: Van Nostrand.

McAdams, D. (1993) *Stories we live by.* New York: William Morrow & Company. p. 179-186.

McWilliams, N. (1994). *Psychoanalytic diagnosis.* New York: The Guilford Press.

Miller, G.A., Galanter, E., & Pribram, K.A. (1960). *Plans and the structure of behavior.* NY: Holt.

Miller, P. (1983. *Theories of developmental psychology.* San Francisco, CA: W.H. Freeman & Company.

Moody, R. (1975). *Life after life.* Atlanta: Mockingbird Books.

Morton, A. (2001). *Madonna.* New York: Saint Martin's Press.

Naumen, E. (1995). *Medical Astrology.* Cottonwood, AZ: Blue Turtle Publishing.

Obama, B. (1995). *Dreams from my father.* New York: Three Rivers Press.

Piaget, J. (1926). *The language and thought of the child.* New York: Harcourt Brace.
Piaget, J. (1937). *The construction of reality in the child.* New York: Basic Books.
Perry, G. (1998). *Essays in psychological astrology.* San Rafael, CA: AAP Press. p. 39-49.
Perry, G. (1998b). *Introduction to AstroΔPsychology* (p. 155-156). San Rafael, CA: AAP Press.
Perry, G. (2000). From royalty to revolution. Part II. *The Mountain Astrologer.* (90), April/May, p. 105-115.
Perry, G. (2021). *Mapping the landscape of the soul.* San Rafael, CA: AAP Press.
Pert, C. (1987). Neuropeptides: The emotions and bodymind. *Noetic Sciences Review,* (2), 12-17.
Playfair, G., Hill, S. (1978). *The cycles of heaven.* New York: Avon Books.
Pribram, K. (1978). What the fuss is all about. *Revision, 1*(3/4), 14-18.
Rieff, P. (1959). *Freud: The Mind of the Moralist,* New York: Viking.
Ring, K, (1998). *Lessons from the light: What we can learn from the near death experience.* New York: Insight Books.
Sabom, M. (1981). *Recollections of death: A medical investigation.* New York: Harper & Row.
Sampson, J., & Weiss, H. (1986). *The psychoanalytic process.* New York: The Guildford Press.
Schafer, R. (1976). *A new language for psychoanalysis.* New Haven, CT: Yale University Press.
Schuon, F. (1984). *The transcendent unity of religions.* Wheaton, IL: Theosophical Publishing.
Seymour, P. (1988). *Astrology: The evidence of science.* London: Penguin Books.
Shapiro, D. (1965). *Neurotic Styles.* New York: Basic Books.
Shapiro, D. (2000). *Dynamics of Character.* New York: Basic Books.
Sheehy, G. (1974). *Passages: Predictable crises of adult life.* New York: E.P. Dutton & Co., Inc.
Smith, H. (1976). *Forgotten truth: The primordial tradition.* New York: Harper & Row.
Smith, H. (1982). *Beyond the post-modern mind.* New York: Crossroad. p. 153
Sperry, R. (1981). Changing priorities. *Annual Review of Neuroscience, 4,* 1-10.
Spitzer, R.L. More on psuedoscience in science and the case for psychiatric diagnosis: A critique of Rosenhan's "On being sane in insane places" and "The contextual nature of psychiatric diagnosis." *Archives of General Psychiatry, 33,* 4359-470.

Stevenson, I. (1980). *Twenty cases suggestive of Reincarnation*. Charlottsville, VA: University of Virgina Press.
Stevenson, I. (1998). *Where reincarnation and biology intersect.* Westport, CT: Praeger Pub.
Taraborrelli, J.R. (2001). *Madonna: An intimate biography*. New York: Berkeley Books.
Tart, C.T. (1981). Transpersonal realities or neurophysiological illusions? Toward an empirically testable dualism. In R. Valle & R. von Eckartsberg (Eds.), *The metaphors of consciousness* (pp. 199-222). New York: Plenum Press.
Tyl, N. (1988). *Astrological timing of critical illness. Early warning patterns in the horoscope.* St. Paul, MN: Llewellyn Pub.
Teilhard de Chardin, P. (1959). *The phenomenon of man*. New York: Harper & Row.
Tobyn, Graeme. 1997. *Culpeper's Medicine*. Element: Shaftsbury, Rockport, and Queensland.
Watzlawick, P. 1976). *How real is real?* New York: Random House.
Tyson, P., & Tyson, R. (1990). *Psychoanalytic theories of development.* New Haven, CT: Yale University Proess.
Watson, L. (1973). *Supernature.* Garden City, NY: Doubleday.
Weiss, B. (1992). *Through time into healing.* New York: Simon & Schuster.
Welsh, Alexander. 1987. From Copyright to Copperfield: The Identity of Dickens. Cambridge: Harvard UP.
White, M., & Epston, D. (1990). *Narrative means to therapeutic ends.* New York: W.W. Norton & Co.
Whitmont, E. (2007). "The Destiny Concept in Psychotherapy," *Journal of Jungian theory and practice*. Vol. 9, No.1, 2007, p. 25-26, 28
Wiener, N. (1954). *The human use of human beings: Cybernetics and society* (2nd ed.). New York: Avon. p. 84
Woolger, R. (1988). *Other lives, other selves.* New York: Bantam Books.
Woolger, R. (2000). *Soul dramas. Past lives and the body.* Manuscript from Woolger Training International.
Wilber, K. (1979). Physics, mysticism, and the new holographic paradigm. *Revision*, *2*(2), 43-55.
Young, J., & Klosko, J. (1993). *Reinventing your life.* New York: Plume.
Zweig, C., & Abrams, J. (1991). *Meeting the shadow.* Los Angeles: Jeremy Tarcher.

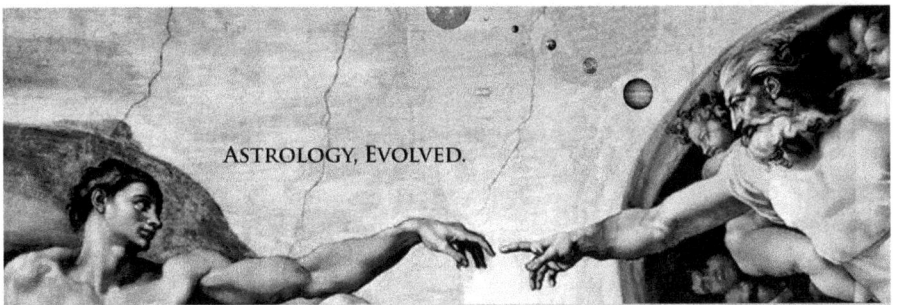

ASTROLOGY, EVOLVED.

Live, online classes leading to DIPLOMA IN ASTROPSYCHOLOGY

Explore... Planets in Signs & Houses • Aspects as Personal Myths • Chart Synthesis
Psychopathology and Healing in the Birthchart • Transit Analysis & Conscious Evolution
The Horoscope as Evolving Story • Counseling Skills • Synastry & more

Glenn Perry, PhD
Program Coordinator

SIGN-UP FOR OUR
FREE NEWSLETTER

INTERACTIVE & TRANSFORMATIVE

Learn a single, integrated system in a methodical, step-by step manner that includes structured assignments, practice exercises, quizzes, and live online classes.

INTEGRATED PROGRAM

Course materials are coordinated so you're not learning a mishmash of techniques from different teachers. Reading assignments are supplemented by over 100 audio files.

COMPREHENSIVE & CROSS-DISCIPLINARY

We honor astrological tradition while also integrating relevant concepts from depth psychology. The resulting synthesis is maximally relevant to 21st century human beings.

CLASSES FORMING NOW
Complete details online

DEPTH & SOPHISTICATION

Moving from inner to outer, AstroPsychology goes beyond predictive, event-oriented astrology by revealing the circular feedback relations between subjective and objective reality.

THE ACADEMY OF ASTRO▲PSYCHOLOGY
Complete program details at astropsychology.org | 321-610-3670

www.ingramcontent.com/pod-product-compliance
Lightning Source LLC
Chambersburg PA
CBHW051857160426
43209CB00006B/1332